Constituent Interests and U.S. Trade Policies

SIE *Studies in International Economics* includes works dealing with the theory; empirical analysis; political, economic, and legal aspects; and evaluation of international policies and institutions.

Keith E. Maskus, Peter M. Hooper, Edward E. Leamer, and J. David Richardson, Editors
Quiet Pioneering: Robert M. Stern and His International Economic Legacy

Bjarne S. Jensen and Kar-yiu Wong, Editors
Dynamics, Economic Growth, and International Trade

Kala Marathe Krishna and Ling Hui Tan
Rags and Riches: Implementing Apparel Quotas under the Multi-Fibre Arrangement

Alan V. Deardorff and Robert M. Stern
Measurement of Nontariff Barriers

Thomas Cottier and Petros C. Mavroidis, Editors
The World Trade Forum, Volume I: State Trading in the Twenty-First Century

Rajesh Chadha, Sanjib Pohit, Alan V. Deardorff, and Robert M. Stern
The Impact of Trade and Domestic Policy Reforms in India: A CGE Modeling Approach

Alan V. Deardorff and Robert M. Stern, Editors
Constituent Interests and U.S. Trade Policies

Gary R. Saxonhouse and T. N. Srinivasan, Editors
Development, Duality, and the International Economic Regime: Essays in Honor of Gustav Ranis

Constituent Interests and U.S. Trade Policies

Alan V. Deardorff and Robert M. Stern, Editors

Ann Arbor

THE UNIVERSITY OF MICHIGAN PRESS

Published in the United States of America by
The University of Michigan Press
Manufactured in the United States of America
♾ Printed on acid-free paper

2001 2000 1999 1998 4 3 2 1

A CIP catalog record for this book is available from the British Library.

Cataloging-in-Publication Data applied for
ISBN 0-472-10932-4

Preface and Acknowledgments

This book contains the papers and discussants' comments prepared for a conference, "Representation of Constituent Interests in the Design and Implementation of U.S. Trade Policies: The Sweetland Conference," which was held at the University of Michigan on November 8-9, 1996. Each of the papers was revised subsequent to the conference to take into account the comments of discussants, conference participants, and the editors. The discussants' comments are based on the conference versions of the papers and thus have not been altered to reflect the changes that authors made in their papers.

The impetus for the conference was provided by a grant received from the Ford Foundation to study the role of constituent interest groups in U.S. trade policies. We had planned originally to hold a workshop at the beginning of the grant period in order to help us define the focus of our research and policy outreach efforts. But in the course of our planning, it happened that a University of Michigan alumnus, John Sweetland, and his wife, Gayle, had made some generous gift commitments to the University of Michigan's Department of Economics to establish endowed chairs in international economics, industrial organization, macroeconomics, and one other to be determined together with scholarships for graduate students to support each chair. The Sweetlands also made commitments to support undergraduate and graduate students to advance the study of the social sciences and business administration.

When the Sweetland gift commitments were received, the Department of Economics and Dean Edie Goldenberg of the College of Literature, Science, and the Arts were searching for a way to thank the Sweetlands for their extraordinary generosity. It so happened that John Sweetland had been engaged for many years in the importing of cement and had a keen interest in U.S. trade policies, particularly the antidumping law that he had had occasion to challenge. It was in this light that we decided to expand our workshop plan into a two-day conference and to use it as an occasion to express our thanks to John and Gayle Sweetland. Hence, we named it "The Sweetland Conference."

We were honored that John Sweetland was able to attend the conference. Unfortunately, Gayle Morris Sweetland was not in attendance. She had passed away a few weeks prior to the conference.

In the evening of the first day of the conference, John Sweetland presented a keynote address that is reproduced in this volume. The reader will note that he chided Alan Deardorff in his address for having remarked at one point that trade economists typically considered cement as the prototype example of a *nontraded* good!

The funding for the conference was provided in part by the aforementioned grant from the Ford Foundation and by grants from units of the University of Michigan, including the Department of Economics, International Institute, College of Literature, Science, and the Arts, Office of Vice-President for Research, and the Horace H. Rackham School of Graduate Studies.

The planning and implementation of a conference requires a great deal of effort and attention to detail, and we were fortunate in this regard to enlist the very able services of Tonia Graham and Judith Jackson of the School of Public Policy. They also shouldered the responsibility of preparing the camera-ready copy for publication. We are extremely grateful to them for their outstanding work.

Alan V. Deardorff
Robert M. Stern

Contents

Part III. Sectoral Producing Interests: Industry/Labor

Part IV. Other Constituent Interests

John W. Sweetland

Keynote Address, Foster Library, November 8, 1996

John W. Sweetland

In addressing this group—as distinguished and as talented as it is—I am reminded of President Kennedy's remark before a group of Nobel prize laureates in the East Room of the White House, "There has not been so much talent in this room since Thomas Jefferson dined alone." I have been most impressed with the clarity of the papers presented and the vigor of the discussion at the conference. Bob Stern and Alan Deardorff are to be complimented on the organization of this outstanding conference.

However, much to your disappointment, I'm sure, I'm not going to talk about U.S. trade policy. As one deeply committed to the public university and particularly the University of Michigan, I'd like to talk with you tonight about what underlies that commitment.

First, I want to talk about Michigan. When my wife Gayle and I were asked to make a major gift to the $1 billion Campaign for Michigan, there was no question about our response. We just had to figure out the best way to make that gift so that it would create the greatest good for the University.

My college years were interrupted by the Korean War. Uncertainty about the direction my life should take was reflected in my transcript, which looked like the College of LS&A catalogue. I dropped out mid-way through my junior year, was quickly drafted, and after basic training went to officers candidate school and returned to Michigan four years later as a different person. More mature, married and a father of two.

While I was stationed on Guam with the Corps of Engineers, I took a two-semester sequence in the principles of economics at what is now the University of Guam. I was intrigued—really enjoyed what I was learning. When I returned to Michigan, economics became my undergraduate major and the field in which I completed my Master's degree.

My memories of Michigan, and especially the Department of Economics, are, to this day, compelling and rewarding. We had a great faculty and interested students and I know I received an outstanding education.

Our first gift to Michigan was designed to build up the Department of Economics that taught me the importance of understanding and has contributed to a life-long process of learning. My partner and I had some success in parlaying a modest investment in an all but bankrupt Florida importer of cement into the two largest cement import operations in the United States—in Florida and then California. It was a fascinating time—from 1975 to 1990—with circumstances of ample supply abroad, demand exceeding domestic capacity in the United States, favorable exchange rates, excess bulk shipping capacity and new technologies for material handling. We were able to optimize these factors for our two companies. Our gift has endowed a chair in International Economics—even though I learned afterward from Alan Deardorff that we had violated economic dogma—cement was used as *the* example of a commodity that did not lend itself to international trade. My interest in the world economy continues through our family company, The Winsford Corporation, which this year will export its products to over 50 countries from Azerbaijan to Zimbabwe.

But beyond this, we have shaped our bequests so that Michigan will be a major benefactor with the Department of Economics receiving the larger part. In doing so, we honor three people who were an important part of my life here in Ann Arbor at both the graduate and undergraduate levels. We have made provision for three additional chairs to be endowed, with graduate scholarships for each chair.

Most in academia underestimate the impact you have on your students. Many of them are difficult and seemingly disinterested. Others take up too much of your time—often on trivia. But in recognizing these individuals who made a significant impact on my life, we are also recognizing what is important in the relationship between faculty and student. And it is this relationship, more often than course content, that can shape and change lives.

The first chair will be the Shorey A. Peterson Chair in Industrial Organization. Shorey was a shepherd. He shaped the lives of many of his students and guided them through their graduate work. That is not to say he was easy. He had a look of disdain that made you wish you could disappear when he detected any degree of inanity. He did not suffer fools gladly. But he and Eleanor invited his students into their home for dinners and evenings of stimulating discussion. I remember one evening, Mike Scherer, who went on to serve the Federal Trade Commission, Northwestern, Swarthmore, and now Harvard with great distinction, an economist from General Motors and myself discussing with Shorey the policy implications of GM exceeding 2% of GNP. The management of General Motors subsequently made that a moot point. We maintained a close relationship after graduate school with many visits to his home when my travels took me this way. He had a genuine interest in my career as it developed and was a warm supporter. We celebrate Shorey's contribution to this special place by remembering how important it is to be a shepherd.

When I had completed my undergraduate work, I was just getting started in understanding the richness of the discipline of economics. I wanted to go on to graduate school but my first two and a half years did not bode well for my acceptance. Shorey and I discussed this and he suggested that we should go down to see Gardner Ackley, who was then Chairman of the department. Shorey explained to Gardner my situation—overall, my transcript was not pretty but my work in the last year and a half suggested I would do well at the graduate level. Gardner said "okay" and that was that! No exams, no tests—just acceptance.

However, it is not for this reason that the second endowed chair will be the Gardner M. Ackley Chair in Macroeconomics. Gardner was a model of the dedicated public servant this country most desperately needs. When John F. Kennedy was elected in 1960, his platform consisted largely of two points—the missile gap (later proven to be non-existent) and, "We have to get this country moving again." He promised a more vigorous government role in stimulating growth. Two names appeared on most lists for the Chairman of the President's Council of Economic Advisers; Walter Heller from Minnesota and Gardner Ackley from Michigan. Heller got the nod and did a good job with some help from Michigan and Harvey Brazer, who was deeply involved in creating the Investment Tax Credit Act.

In Lyndon Johnson's administration, Gardner was Chairman of the CEA. While he never publicly expressed an opinion on the Vietnam War, he was adamantly opposed to financing it by printing more money. He pressed for a tax increase. Now, to argue for a tax increase for an unpopular war with a President like Lyndon Johnson, who dominated the Washington scene, was an act of immense courage. And to have succeeded, attests to the soundness of his policy and the persuasiveness of his arguments. I think we always underestimated what a giant task Gardner undertook to bring that about. He stands as a role model for the public servant who seeks the best, regardless of the consequences. We could use a hearty dose of that in Washington today.

The third chair in my bequest will be the Warren Smith Chair in a field to be determined by the Department and the Dean of the College. While Warren was a great teacher and also served on the Council for Economic Advisers, it is not for that he is being celebrated—he was a friend.

I related a few moments ago the process by which I was to be admitted to graduate school—took about three minutes. But shortly thereafter, I came to the realization that I was in deep trouble—I was facing an "F" or at best a "D" in Warren Smith's class in Money and Credit. I was working my way through school and that, together with the demands of family life, meant that something had to slip—and in this case it was Money and Credit. I explained all of this to Warren and tried to get him to understand that the miserable results of my two mid term exams did not reflect my true understanding of the subject matter. He listened to my sad story and responded by making me a deal—my grade would be the grade on my final but he would not give me an "A." I wrote an "A" final and the "B" was adequate for graduate school. Warren Smith's humanness in this story is something that is required of all of us. Shakespeare recognized this in his foray into economics—the Merchant of Venice: "The quality of mercy is not strained, it droppeth as the gentle rain from heaven upon the place beneath: it is twice blessed; it blesseth him that gives and him that takes." (IV., i., 184) Warren Smith knew what Shakespeare meant.

It is our hope that the added resources our gifts have brought, and will bring in the future, will increase the standing of economics at Michigan. But in achieving academic excellence, it is also our hope that the qualities embodied in the Peterson, Ackley and Smith chairs—being a shepherd, giving one's self to public service and being a friend—will continue to be a part of the very fabric of the Department. My education at Michigan was much the richer because this was true when I was here. The need today, whether it's in international trade policy or coming to grips with domestic entitlements, is for people who can bring judgment, a sense of responsibility and compassion to the solutions of the problems that surround and, sometimes, seem to overwhelm us. And despite the trend in economics today, these attributes are, to me, of greater value than the latest mathematical models.

Now I want to turn your attention to a major threat to our public universities and indeed our society as we have known them over these past decades. I was on campus three weeks ago when the names of the candidates recommended to the Regents by the Presidential Search Advisory Committee were made public. At that time, Regent Phil Power made the comment that excellent public universities "may be the signature creation of American society in the 20th century." He probably should have included the 19th century, for one of President Abraham Lincoln's achievements was the signing of the Morrill Act in 1862. This act, which had been debated in Congress for years, created our system of land grant colleges. Within a year of its passage, nine states started land grant colleges—Iowa State, Kansas State, Michigan State, Rutgers (New Jersey), Penn State and what are now the Universities of Vermont, Minnesota, Missouri and Wisconsin. Think of the major impact these great institutions and many, many others created by this legislation have had on their regional economies and how they have contributed to the national good.

But our public universities are at risk! Last March, Anthony Lewis wrote a column in *The New York Times* entitled "Sunlight and Shadow." He started by writing "California, land of the possible. So it used to be: the state where optimism was policy and the policy worked. Not today." He compared the policies of two Republican governors—50 years apart. Earl Warren devoted his energies toward the expansion of the University of California system—he himself had risen from poverty by way of Berkeley—and making education available for all Californians. Pete Wilson, on the other hand, has focused on the politics of division, appealing to the dark side of human nature on issues such as affirmative action and immigration. His "three-strikes" law is making, in Lewis' words, "California the world capital of incarceration."

The University of California and the California State University systems were models for much of the nation and were virtually free. But that all has changed. In the last five years, fees have quadrupled. Prisons have become the growth industry in California. As recently as 15 years ago, California spent six times more on higher education than on prisons. In 1994, the prison budget was larger than that for higher education. And the cost of prison care is estimated to be 18% of the state budget early in the next century leaving, under current budgetary formulas, only 1% for higher education.

Seventeen prisons have been built in the past 15 years—15 more will be needed in the next 5 years. Prison guards have the same salary—about $45,000—as an assistant professor in the University of California system.

This craziness is not confined to California. Michigan's budget for corrections is very close to its support for higher education. A state-by-state survey, especially in the industrial states, I am confident would see this trend across the country.

Lewis closed his column by writing, "What happens in California, it used to be said, is a preview of what will happen to all of America. We have to hope that that is no longer true."

But it seems to me that hope alone is not adequate to the task. What amazes me is that no one of national stature is speaking out against this distortion of values. The ethicists, the political scientists, and the economists are all silent. What economic analysis would suggest that this model represents the best allocation of resources? How would one argue a brief for this position in the court of human values that would be plausible to a jury of our peers?

The public universities that are at risk from this perversion of priorities must take the lead in focusing our nation's attention on what has been happening. They need to make the case anew for the richness that the universities have brought—and will bring—to their regions and the nation. But we all must join in this campaign. We have been the beneficiaries of this gift to our country—we need to insure that it is available to future generations.

One of the facets of World War II that mystifies me to this day, is that none of the institutions in Germany stood up to the madness that was Hitler. Germany had a great university system, indeed the model for Michigan and, subsequently, other U.S. universities. But that great university system was silent. Germany had a well developed Christian community with strong Roman Catholic, Lutheran and Reform churches and seminaries. But only a relatively unknown Lutheran pastor, Dietrich Bonhoffer, is recognized today as being publicly vocal against the crimes of Nazism. He stood virtually alone and became a martyr.

America today has great universities and a diversified and active religious community. But we need voices that will say that our values, as reflected by our public expenditures at the federal and state level, are wrong. Education—from head start to graduate school—has made our nation great. We cannot afford to lose that because of spending policies that appeal to the dark side of human nature and do not represent what is best about this great country.

Part I

Introduction and Overview

CHAPTER 1

Introduction

Alan V. Deardorff and Robert M. Stern

This volume contains the papers and comments that were commissioned for "Representation of Constituent Interests in the Design and Implementation of U.S. Trade Policies: The Sweetland Conference," a conference held in Ann Arbor on November 8-9, 1996. This conference served a dual purpose. First, it helped us to sharpen the focus of an ongoing project of research and policy outreach on issues of the political economy of U.S. international trade policies, in connection with a grant from the Ford Foundation. At the same time and more important, it allowed us to honor John Sweetland and his late wife, Gayle, for the generous gift commitments that they have made to the Michigan Department of Economics. These include an endowed chair in international economics and three additional endowed chairs and related financial assistance for graduate and undergraduate students.

The conference authors and discussants were drawn from academic institutions, the private sector, and the Ways and Means Committee of the U.S. House of Representatives. In setting forth the aims of the conference, those involved were asked in particular to address: (1) the objectives of trade policy sought by the various interest groups who were the subject of their paper or comments; (2) how each group's interests are identified and promoted and what means are used for these purposes; (3) the extent to which the objectives and behavior of each group conform to how the political economy of trade policy is treated in the economics and political science literatures; and (4) how effective each group has been in achieving its objectives. To assist participants who were not conversant with the literature on the political economy of trade policy, we provided them with the introductory and concluding chapters of the 1996 book edited by Anne O. Krueger, *The Political Economy of American Trade Policy*, as well as a chapter on the "Political Economy of Trade Policy," by Dani Rodrik that was published in 1995 in Volume III of the *Handbook of International Economics*. While these chapters were aimed especially at an academic audience, they nonetheless provided an indication to the nonacademic participants of many of the important aspects and limitations of the manner in which the political economy of trade policy has been modeled theoretically and empirically. These chapters also contained many useful bibliographic references.

The individual conference papers were revised following the conference to take into account the comments of the discussants as well as points raised during the floor discussion. It was decided to include the discussants' comments as they were originally prepared based on the conference versions of the papers, in order to capture the concerns and criticisms raised by discussants in the conference sessions. We trust that readers will find the comments interesting and informative in their own right and useful supplements to the individual papers.

To assist the reader in determining which chapters may be of greatest interest, we provide brief summaries in Section I that follows. Then, in Section II, we reflect on what we have learned from the papers and commentaries about how constituent groups may influence the design and implementation of U.S. trade policies.

I. Structure and Overview of the Volume

The keynote speech delivered by John W. Sweetland in the evening of the first day of the conference has been reproduced above. In this speech, Mr. Sweetland talked about his undergraduate and graduate experiences at the University of Michigan and the personal considerations that he had in mind in designating the endowed chairs to be established in international economics, industrial organization, macroeconomics, and one additional field to be determined. He also spoke at length about the importance of the public university in U.S. society.

Following this introductory chapter, Chapter 2 by Alan V. Deardorff and Robert M. Stern provides an overview of the modeling of the choices and consequences of U.S. trade policies. Deardorff and Stern review the normative and political economy approaches to the modeling of trade policies and identify the major limitations of these approaches. They then discuss the *transaction-cost approach* developed by Avinash Dixit in his 1996 book, which may provide a middle ground between the other approaches and enable some hitherto imperfectly understood issues of trade policy to be addressed. After discussing briefly the empirical literature relating to the normative and political economy approaches, they provide a sketch of the main features of the U.S. trade-policy process, focusing in particular on the roles played by the agencies of government together with the important constituent interest groups in the U.S. economy. They then consider how each of the modeling approaches can be interpreted in its representation of the behavior and interaction of these constituencies. Setting modeling issues aside, they also ask what can be learned from the past half-century of U.S. trade-policy experiences and conclude that there has been a distinctive movement towards more liberal and open trade in the United States and elsewhere. In their concluding remarks, they discuss the implications of the interplay of the different modeling approaches for research and policy in light of their observation about the ways in which trade liberalization and increased openness have evolved.

In his commentary on the Deardorff and Stern paper, Gene Grossman expresses his agreement on the limitations of the political economy literature, especially since there are many trade-policy phenomena that remain unexplained and there is not much guidance offered on the choice of policies. He notes that there is a need to pay greater attention to identifying the important agents and constituent interest groups involved in the trade policy process and the factors shaping their behavior as well as the existing institutional and informational constraints. Grossman suggests that more attention should be devoted to determining why trade policies rather than other policies tend to be used, how the patterns of trade policy and sectoral protection change over time, and how different constituent interest groups use the policy process to attain their objectives. He takes issue with Deardorff and Stern's characterization of the transaction-cost model as occupying a middle ground between the normative and political economy approaches. In his view, what is needed are better political economy models that pay greater attention especially to the political environment and that point the way toward more effective design of the institutions and rules of trade policy.

Part II of the volume deals with the context of U.S. trade policies. In Chapter 3, Robert E. Baldwin discusses U.S. trade policies and the role of the executive branch. Baldwin first surveys the models that economists and political scientists have used to analyze the making of trade policy, noting that these models typically do not distinguish between the roles and interactions of the President and the Congress. On the basis of the observation that Congress has delegated much of its traditional authority over trade issues to the President since the 1930s, he then proceeds to develop a game-theoretic model in which the President favors increased trade liberalization and has certain foreign policy objectives in mind, while Congress is more inclined towards granting import protection or seeking greater access to foreign markets. In this model, the President is assumed to have a "first-mover" advantage, in which case his actions can result in a more favorable outcome for both the Congress and the President than would otherwise be the case. Baldwin reviews the presidential roles in trade policy since the 1950s and notes that the success or failure realized depends importantly on whether or not the President has taken a leadership role in undertaking trade-policy initiatives. Thus, when presidential leadership is weak or absent, the Congress will play a stronger role with much less favorable outcomes because of its protectionist orientation. He also notes that most Presidents typically place great importance on achieving foreign policy objectives by means of trade policies.

In his commentary on Baldwin's paper, Geza Feketekuty notes that the bargaining process between the President and the Congress should be characterized in dynamic terms insofar as both participants can alter the process and shape the policy agenda. Furthermore, he points out that the process may be different before trade negotiations begin and at their conclusion, and that foreign interests may be especially important in the concluding phase. Feketekuty also notes that Baldwin may underplay the attention given by policymakers to consumer interests in the negotiating process and the importance attached to expanding U.S. exports. Finally, he takes issue with Baldwin, arguing that the availability of fast-track negotiating authority enhances presidential power rather than limiting it.

In Chapter 4, I. M. (Mac) Destler discusses Congress, constituencies, and U.S. trade policy. He focuses on the overall role that the Congress has played in trade policy and how this has affected constituent interests. His basic premise is that since the 1930s the Congress has in effect delegated primary responsibility for trade policy to the President and to administrative bodies such as the U.S. International Trade Commission. This is in contrast to Baldwin's views expressed in Chapter 3 that there is an interaction between the President and the Congress on trade matters, and that it is important that the President take the leadership initiative to ensure realization of the benefits from trade liberalization. While Destler does not deny that Congress can and does in fact at times influence the trade-policy agenda, he argues that there is more show than substance involved. Destler views members of Congress as not seeking power in making trade policy. Rather, it is more important for members of Congress to maintain and enhance their political standing at home and in Washington. What matters then is taking more general positions on trade issues and not necessarily catering to the narrow interests of particular constituencies in the districts and states. The outcome of this process is that, since the President is more inclined to favor trade liberalization, constituent interests seeking special treatment end up with much less than they would have obtained if Congress had not delegated much of its authority over trade issues. Destler identifies four conditions that will facilitate achievement of the benefits of trade liberalization: (1) presidential priority to trade expansion; (2) bipartisan support; (3) close executive-congressional working relations in support of open trade policy; and (4) broad support for free trade as the guiding principle for trade policy. In considering the outlook for trade policy, Destler believes that Clinton may well be able to break the 1997 stalemate and win some form of fast-track negotiating authority from Congress in 1998. He notes, however, that concerns over trade and the environment and the impact of trade on wage inequality could dampen the pace of liberalization.

In his commentary, Richard L. Hall notes that Destler has attempted to reconcile the protectionist impulses of Congressmen with the apparent disregard of constituent interests represented by Congressional approval of continuous movement towards freer trade in the past several decades. Hall characterizes the major assumptions made by Destler as follows: (1) members of Congress are self-interested, not ideological; (2) self-interest takes the simple form of electoral self-interest; (3) electorally self-regarding Congressional members will cater to their homogeneous "high-demand" constituencies; (4) the stronger the industry presence in a state or district, the more responsive will Congressional members be; and (5) the members will then respond to constituent interests by voting to support protectionist policies. However, according to Hall, the evidence suggests that high demand constituencies have not received the protection from Congress that they might want. He suggests that Destler has mischaracterized constituent interest groups by treating them as high demand constituencies rather than being heterogeneous in their preferences. Hall gives an example of how different constituencies in an electoral district may have different preferences as concerns protection or freer trade, and he argues that members of Congress will then have to take these differences into account in their legislative behavior. Looked at in this way, he maintains that it makes the supposed Congressional abdication of trade policy that Destler notes more understandable. It may not be surprising therefore to observe U.S. trade policies becoming more liberal over time in individual sectors when heterogeneous preferences are taken into consideration. Hall suggests further that there is a need to rethink the ways in which legislators respond to group interests. He points out that protectionist-minded groups tend to contribute more heavily to representatives who have the *strongest* predispositions toward protectionism. There is also a tendency to contribute most heavily to the electorally safest members. While this type of constituent-group behavior may appear to be irrational, it can be understood by taking into account that groups are primarily interested in mobilizing supportive legislators to work as agents on the group's behalf. That is, groups seek legislative participation from representatives on issues that affect the group interests, rather than seeking votes on measures as such. Of course, as Hall notes, legislators are responsive to group interests and to the associated political benefits involved, but lobbying activity consists mainly of providing information and helping to reduce the transactions costs that legislators face. Lobbying then is by no means simply an effort to buy votes. Hall's emphasis on heterogeneous preferences of constituents and the practices of legislators in the ways in which they represent their constituents are considerations that need to be addressed in the future modeling of the political economy of trade policy.

Part III of the volume is devoted to a series of sectoral papers that consider the trade-policy interests of industry and labor. The sectors include: automobiles; steel; textiles and apparel; semiconductors; aircraft; and financial services. These are by no means the only sectors that play important roles in the trade-policy process, but they nevertheless are illustrative of how sectoral interests make their influence felt and what the results have been in recent decades.

In Chapter 5, G. Mustafa Mohatarem addresses trade policy and the U.S. auto industry: intended and unintended consequences. He provides a brief discussion of the basic economics of the auto industry, stressing the size of the firms, the number of workers employed directly and indirectly in the industry, the very large capital requirements and associated economies of scale, the importance of consumer expenditures on autos, and the high political visibility of the industry. Until the mid-1970s, the presumption was that the U.S. auto industry did not require trade protection. But pressures for government assistance from the Big Three and the United Auto Workers heightened dramatically in the face of the successive oil shocks of the 1970s and the recession in 1981-82. It is well known that a Voluntary Restraint Agreement (VRA) limiting auto imports from Japan was introduced in 1981, and it remained in place until 1994, even though it had become nonbinding several years earlier. Industry profitability increased significantly during the 1980s, but, what was not fully anticipated, the VRA led to sizable inflows of foreign direct investment and start-up of Japanese auto transplants. All of this tended to undermine the protective aspects of the VRA, as these transplants were able to operate on a highly cost-efficient basis in the United States. This in turn has provided the transplants with an important political voice in U.S. trade policy, making it unlikely that U.S. auto firms could hope to achieve the kind of trade protection in the future that they achieved during the 1980s. Mohatarem notes further that developing countries seeking to expand their domestic auto industries by means of protective measures are best advised to protect domestic production rather than specific companies. His view of the VRA is that it gave the Big Three breathing space and thus alleviated the otherwise serious adjustment costs that might have occurred if the industry had been left unprotected.

Chapter 6 by Douglas A. Brook deals with steel and trade policy in a changed environment. Brook focuses on the role that the large integrated steel companies have played in the U.S. trade-policy process. These companies have been concerned in particular with the use of subsidies by foreign steel producers and alleged dumping in the U.S. market and with the use of U.S. trade-law remedies to deal with what is regarded as "unfair" trade practices by foreign suppliers. He describes the highly pro-active role of the different industry groups and associations that have been formed to deal with trade-related issues. He also reviews the trade policy experiences of the steel industry in the light of the political economy models of trade policy and associated empirical studies cited in works by Rodrik (1995) and Krueger (1996). He concludes that there are some issues deserving of further study, including the extent to which the steel VRAs helped the integrated producers through difficult times, how the changing structure of the industry has affected the unanimity of the industry's positions on trade issues, and the reasons why the industry has been able to maintain a powerful voice in Washington. As was also seen in the case of the U.S. auto industry, the steel industry has entered an era in which it cannot look to the policy authorities for trade protection as in the past. But so long as it is perceived that there is still widespread use of subsidies abroad and world overcapacity, continuing efforts will be made to use the U.S. trade remedy laws to "level the playing field."

In Chapter 7, "U.S. Trade Policies for the Textile and Apparel Industries: The Political Economy of the Post-MFA Environment," Robert E. Scott points out that textiles and apparel have received more, and more persistent, trade protection over a long period of time than any other U.S. manufacturing sector. However, this protection has been increasingly porous, and there has been a decline in and divergence of interests between the two sectors as textile producers have become more efficient and have turned more and more to export markets. There has also been an increase in the power of apparel retailers that has made interests even more divergent. The declining influence of Southern Democrats and the importance of the industry in the South may account for the loss of influence of apparel producers especially. Scott argues that the market power of apparel retailers has grown significantly, making it possible for these firms to capture monopsony rents. As a consequence, he points out that the removal of protection would redound especially to the apparel retailers' benefit rather than to consumers. Scott is critical of the failure of the NAFTA to improve the positions of the textile and apparel industries because of how U.S.-Mexico bilateral trade has responded to the peso depreciation. Finally, he calls attention to issues of labor rights and labor standards in the United States and abroad. It is interesting that the decline of the U.S. textile/apparel industries and the increased divergence of interests parallels what has been observed in the ability of other major U.S. manufacturing sectors to mobilize support for continued trade protection.

Douglas Irwin points out in Chapter 8, "The Representation of Economic Interests in U.S. Semiconductor Trade Policy," that this industry does not conform to the behavior of import-competing industries such as those treated in the preceding chapters. The main concern rather has been in taking actions to open Japan's market to U.S. semiconductor producers. There have nonetheless been pressures as well to deal with alleged dumping of memory chips by Japanese firms in the U.S. market. The U.S. semiconductor industry is a high fixed-, low marginal-cost industry, is subject to volatile market conditions and profitability, and engages significantly in R&D. The Semiconductor Industry Association (SIA), which was formed in 1977, serves as the focal point for the trade-policy activities of the industry, although it hardly speaks with one voice since the interests of so-called merchant and captive firms may not coincide and there may be significant product specialization between firms. Labor in the industry is not particularly active since there is relatively high interfirm mobility of workers. The first Semiconductor trade arrangement was concluded in 1986, and it involved Japan's agreement to end dumping in the U.S. market and in third markets and to improve access of U.S. semiconductor producers to Japan's domestic market and to back this up with attainment of a set market-share target. The Semiconductor Agreement was extended in 1991 for an additional five years, although without dumping provisions but with continuation of the 20 percent Japanese domestic market-share target. By 1996, the U.S. market share reached 30 percent, so that when it came time to consider extending the Agreement once again, it was decided not to do so and instead to establish a more informal arrangement to deal with disputes and share information among producers. Irwin notes how important the pressures exerted by a small number of firms were and how the U.S. policy authorities accommodated these interests. But it turned out that downstream user industries were able to mobilize and to offset the more protectionist influences in the industry.

And again, we now see that this industry has evolved to the point where it exercises comparatively little influence on U.S. trade policies.

In Chapter 9, "U.S. Trade Policy vis-à-vis the Aircraft Industry," Raymond J. Waldmann and Jay Culbert note that government-supported foreign competitors, in particular Airbus, threaten U.S. industry's leadership of the aircraft industry. They discuss three examples in which Boeing has been involved in seeking to shape U.S. trade policies: (1) the 1979 GATT Aircraft Code; (2) the 1992 U.S.-EC Bilateral; and (3) the Uruguay Round Negotiations. The U.S. position on the GATT Aircraft Code during the Tokyo Round was formulated in large measure by the Aerospace Industries Association and the Aerospace Industry Sector Advisory Committee, and it was communicated to the Office of the U.S. Trade Representative. It resulted in multilateral removal of tariffs on aircraft and a variety of strictures on government support. Because of concern that the Aircraft Code was not working well, especially because of continuing subsidies provided for Airbus, bilateral discussions with the Airbus governments were initiated in the mid 1980s. There was also consideration of taking more direct action under Section 301 as well as in the GATT. This culminated in the 1992 bilateral agreement that was designed to reduce Airbus subsidies and other inducements. In the Uruguay Round, the industry position was that, in addition to the bilateral, the GATT Subsidies Code should apply to civil aircraft, and the European Union finally agreed to this with some qualifications. These actions thus demonstrate how, in Boeing's view, trade policies can help address the fundamental challenges posed by government-sponsored competition. In contrast to the other industry sectors considered in the preceding chapters, the U.S. aircraft industry's influence on U.S. trade policy appears to have been at its greatest in recent years.

Chapter 10, by Harry L. Freeman, deals with the role of constituents in U.S. policy development towards trade in financial services. Freeman describes in particular the initial impetus in the 1970s for including services in the Tokyo Round negotiations and subsequent efforts led by American Express, the American International Group, and other service providers to include services in the Uruguay Round negotiations that started in 1986. He notes that negotiations on financial services were not concluded in the Uruguay Round because the United States was dissatisfied with the liberalization commitments that other countries were prepared to make. Negotiations were resumed in 1995, but the United States remained disappointed especially in what some of the major developing countries were prepared to offer, with the result that the negotiations were suspended. The European Union and Japan were anxious to keep the financial sector negotiations going, and they worked out an agreement with the United States for a two-tier arrangement that would involve reciprocal liberalization for those countries that agreed to make commitments but would withhold liberalization and therefore most-favored-nation (MFN) treatment of financial services for those countries not prepared to make commitments. The deadline for negotiations was then extended until the end of calendar 1997. Freeman discusses the factors that are likely to come into play from the standpoint of the major countries involved and the role of private sector providers of financial services. He predicts that some type of tiered arrangement is the most likely outcome.

In his commentary on the sectoral papers, James A. Levinsohn notes how much we can learn about trade policy issues from industry specialists. He calls attention to Mohatarem's points that an unintended consequence of the auto VER was that it was undermined by Japanese investment in U.S. transplants, and that comparative advantage in today's setting may be company- rather than country-specific. While acknowledging many of the limitations of the political economy models discussed by Brook, Levinsohn stresses that the simplifications and rigor of modeling are nonetheless important to careful analysis. Levinsohn also questions Brook's characterization of the notions of fairly priced steel imports and excess capacity in the industry insofar as it downplays the relatively low prices that benefit users of steel. Levinsohn calls attention finally in Scott's paper to the split between the textile and apparel sector support on issues of trade liberalization and protection and how this sector has declined in importance. But Levinsohn questions Scott's negative interpretation of how NAFTA has affected the industry, and suggests that issues of foreign labor standards require more extensive discussion than was possible in Scott's brief paper.

In his commentary, Gary R. Saxonhouse remarks that too little attention appears to be given to U.S. trade policies designed to benefit export industries. Certainly, the experiences of Boeing and American Express are instructive in their ability to influence U.S. trade policies in ways that furthered their corporate objectives in foreign markets. Also, the fact that the Semiconductor Industry Association had effective veto power over the bilateral agreement with Japan is further testimony to the powerful role that U.S. export interests have played in designing trade policies. Saxonhouse suggests that these foreign market-access activities may, in part, have been intended strategically to forestall further foreign entry into the U.S market. In any case, the experiences of these three sectors suggests that export promotion may be as common as import protection. What remains to be explained in cases like these is how these sectors were able to exercise such influence on the trade-policy process.

Part IV of the volume deals with a variety of other constituencies and issues pertinent to U.S. trade policies. These include: trade policy and the environment; trade and human rights; trade law and trade policy; and trade policy and the media.

Daniel C. Esty discusses environmentalists and trade policymaking in Chapter 11. He notes the relatively recent role that environmental groups have come to play in trying to influence trade policy and the resistance that these groups have encountered. Two events, the NAFTA and the 1991 GATT tuna-dolphin decision, brought issues of trade and the environment to the fore. The environmental groups were split on NAFTA, and the pro-NAFTA groups were instrumental in shaping the negotiating process to include special environmental provisions in the Agreement and in reinforcing the NAFTA commitment through negotiation of the Environmental Side Agreement. It is thus evident that environmental groups want safeguards to serve environmentally-sound ends. Esty raises more generally the question of what role the environmental groups should play in the trading system, particularly with reference to the WTO. He discusses a number of objections to such involvement, especially that environmental groups may represent special interests and interfere with the pursuit of trade liberalization, and that they may possibly disrupt the intergovernmental process and procedures on which the WTO is based. But he points out that it is unlikely that environmental groups would be unduly influential since they would be part of a diverse set of lobbying interests in any case, and that many of these groups are acting in the public interest. He further notes that providing access for environmental groups to WTO investigation procedures would serve to enhance the availability of information and encourage fruitful international dialogue. Some concern has been expressed that the proliferation of environmental groups could be disruptive and that it could be difficult to determine which groups should be invited to participate in the trade policy process. But he suggests that this might not be so serious, since the quality of work that different groups do would become evident, and that environmental groups would have to contend with other constituencies especially from the business community. He cites here the way that the USTR opened the policy process to environmental groups in the NAFTA debate with generally positive results. The economic case for involving environmental groups in the trade policy process stems from the importance of transboundary and global externalities that reflect possible market failures. These groups can provide needed information and analysis designed to address these concerns. The political case rests on expanding the idea of a global society to encompass non-governmental voices, inform public opinion, and improve the quality of WTO deliberations and decisions by introducing greater transparency.

In his commentary, Richard C. Porter recognizes the importance of environmental concerns, but he questions whether environmental groups should play a role in the WTO because it is intended to be an intergovernmental organization. Porter argues that it is production or consumption that causes environmental externalities, not trade per se, and that domestic tax/subsidies represent the optimal government policies, not trade sanctions. Porter cites the Montreal Protocol that was designed to reduce the environmental damage caused by CFCs by focusing directly on activities using CFCs and providing assistance to developing countries to make the transition to reduce their use of CFCs. The focus was thus on getting national governments to take effective action. In his view, accordingly, there is no need to include the representation of environmental groups in the WTO. Their proper role is at the national level.

T. N. Srinivasan addresses issues of trade and human rights in Chapter 12. He points out that these issues have received a great deal of attention in political discourse and policy in the United States and elsewhere in recent years. Labor standards raise all of the important economic, moral, philosophical, and political problems involved in using trade policy as a means to enforce human rights, and they are accordingly the focus of Srinivasan's paper. He takes issue with the sweeping claims that have been made of the universality and eternity of certain *core* labor standards, often without regard to the diversity in the content and scope of labor standards for countries at different stages of development. Further, he points out that, while most nations have signed and ratified a set of covenants that go beyond the core labor standards, it appears that almost none of the rights involved are satisfied in reality. With regard to the concern in high income countries about labor standards in developing countries, Srinivasan suggests that, if the concern is really serious, the high income countries might consider relaxing their immigration restrictions or making income transfers to workers and to families in poor countries, especially when it is desired to reduce reliance on child labor. This would be far better than using trade sanctions to enforce higher labor standards. In considering the economic issues involved, Srinivasan shows formally that diversity in labor standards is legitimate and consistent with the case to be made for gainful trade based on comparative advantage. It is granted that there may be situations in which low labor standards can be considered as a market failure, and, if so, the optimal policy is some domestic tax/subsidy arrangement rather than trade policy. Srinivasan is especially critical of a proposal by Dani Rodrik and empirical work by Alan Krueger that seek to establish a rationale for using trade policy to enforce labor standards. He also cites the conclusions of other empirical research that suggests that labor standards play no significant role in shaping national trade performance or attracting foreign direct investment. Srinivasan considers whether issues of labor standards are best dealt with by the International Labor Organization (ILO) or the WTO. He favors using the ILO since it is the organization that was originally created to deal with these issues and not the WTO because this would involve the use of trade sanctions. Finally, he is critical of the inclusion of labor standards in bilateral, plurilateral, and regional trade agreements since they may not be in the interest of developing countries.

In his commentary, Robert Pahre notes that the acceptability of moral arguments for universal labor standards tends to change over time. He also points out that there are serious problems in using immigration policies and international transfers to deal with labor standards. A central point in Srinivasan's argument is that presumably altruistic motivations for achieving higher labor standards may be *hijacked* by protectionists. While there is no compelling empirical evidence that labor standards are in fact hijacked, there is nevertheless some scope for analyzing hijacking when policy makers are considering the use of coercive sanctions to enforce higher standards. The outcome of his analysis depends on the size of the human rights and protectionist lobbies and whether there is complete or incomplete information available.

Richard O. Cunningham, in Chapter 13, "Trade Law and Trade Policy: The Advocate's Perspective," takes issue with the central premise of the political economy view of trade policy that trade policy is politically determined. Rather, from the standpoint of the international trade law practitioner, the investigation for and the granting of import relief reflects responses to well established legal definitions and procedures that may justify such relief. He asserts that domestic political pressures rarely affect the outcome. The same applies to cases involving foreign market access. The trade lawyer is in effect then to be viewed as an advocate, not a policymaker. Based on this perspective, Cunningham explores three types of trade cases: (1) antidumping and countervailing duties; (2) discretionary import relief under the escape clause, market disruption, and the national security amendment; and (3) unfair foreign trading practices. With respect to antidumping and countervailing duties, he notes that these relate to the effort to redress unfair trading practices that have long been acknowledged to exist and require correction. While acknowledging that the administration of the unfair trade procedures is subject to interpretation by the Department of Commerce and the International Trade Commission (ITC) and that there are examples of powerful sectoral interests that have been granted protection, Cunningham maintains that most of the cases are brought by relatively small industries who typically lack any significant ability to exert political pressure. Moreover, the political makeup of the ITC Commissioners will prevent any predisposition in deciding the investigations, and Congressional oversight of the Department of Commerce will help to insure that the unfair trade laws are vigorously enforced. These remain matters of law and interpretation rather than trade policy as such. But he does discuss two exceptions that reflect the intrusion of policy: (1) how to assess countervailable subsidies for nationally owned industries that have been privatized as in the case of steel; and (2) imports of softwood lumber from Canada. Nonetheless, what strikes Cunningham is how difficult it was for the domestic interests to affect the outcome in these cases. He also notes that policy considerations may enter in the settlement of cases especially when there appears to be some overriding political or diplomatic imperative and the petitioning U.S. industry agrees to the outcome. The examples he cites include: (1) the 1986 and 1996 settlements of the Canadian softwood lumber cases; (2) the 1978 Trigger Price Mechanism for steel imports; and (3) antidumping investigations of uranium imports from Russia and other former Soviet republics. Discretionary import relief cases involve rarely used derogations from the principle of "free but fair" trade, and domestic political forces seldom enter into the deliberations and decisions. In connection with the escape clause, he reviews the Harley-Davidson case as an example of the way in which the escape clause is designed to work to bring about a successful adjustment assisted by temporary protection. On the other hand, neither the steel nor copper industries succeeded in obtaining escape relief in their 1984 petitions despite the political importance of these industries. He notes that the national security amendment and market disruption law are of little practical importance given the end of the "cold war." In recent years, there have been more actions designed to deal with alleged unfair trade practices in foreign markets. These actions differ from import relief petitions since the U.S. Government may not necessarily be in a position to resolve the situation unilaterally and there is no effective control over other actions that a foreign government might take to counteract any constraints imposed on its policies. It is also now the case that the WTO may come to play a more important role in these types of disputes. Cunningham argues nonetheless that some important successes have been achieved by industry interests that have promoted

Section 301 actions against alleged unfair foreign government practices. Cunningham's overall conclusion is that raw political power is seldom used to affect trade policy outcomes.

In his commentary, John D. Greenwald agrees with Cunningham that in most cases constituent political interests have no particular bearing on the outcome of a trade law case. In cases that do become politicized, what matters is the effectiveness of the means chosen to pursue the action rather than political muscle. Greenwald seeks to expand Cunningham's paper to emphasize: (1) the influence of foreign governments on U.S. trade policies; (2) the role and influence of bureaucratic and agency interest in decision making; (3) the process and forces that shape the provisions of U.S. trade law; and (4) the central role of trade law in U.S. trade policy. Greenwald notes that since the Japanese auto VRA in 1981 almost all industry-motivated trade initiatives have been under existing U.S. trade law or threats of petitions under this law. Resort to trade law thus now represents the only effective way in which industry interests can be pursued, and, with the advent of the WTO, dispute settlement procedures will strengthen the role of trade policy built on trade law. While this situation might appear not to be to the liking of the Congress, Greenwald notes that most members of Congress favor an open global trading system and look upon trade law remedies as a means of responding to constituent interests for assistance. In considering the process of shaping U.S. trade law, Greenwald acknowledges that it is overtly political, but there are nonetheless important constraints on what domestic interest groups can accomplish through lobbying if it means violating U.S. or WTO law and procedures. This, it turns out, is important for these interests to understand when they are bringing their influence to bear on the policy authorities. According to Greenwald, more attention needs to be given to the biases of bureaucrats and top level agency officials concerned with trade issues, citing the different views of ITC Commissioners, the roles and interests of individual Congressmen and Senators, the perceived pro- or anti-free-trade bias of particular U.S. Government agencies and whether agencies face political constraints in acceding to constituent pressures. Greenwald also calls attention to the role that foreign governments play in bringing pressure to bear in settling U.S. trade law cases, citing such examples as the steel VRAs, the semiconductor antidumping cases, Canadian softwood lumber, uranium imports from the former Soviet Union republics, and the pre-1996-election antidumping case involving Mexican tomatoes. In these cases, the leverage of the U.S. interests comes from their role as petitioner in accordance with U.S. trade law, and the foreign governments have responded by seeking settlements to safeguard their interests. Greenwald provides a brief case study of the use of an antidumping petition filed by Cray, which is the dominant U.S. producer of supercomputers, against a major Japanese producer, NEC. He points out Cray's vulnerability to increased competition from Japanese producers of supercomputers and the possibility that U.S. national security interests would be damaged if Cray were to experience prolonged difficulties. The only option then that Cray had strategically was to file an antidumping petition that sought to deal with allegedly predatory pricing by Japanese supercomputer producers.

In Part I of Chapter 14, Joe H. Stroud provides some reflections on trade policy and the media from the standpoint of his position as editor of *The Detroit Free Press*. He notes that journalists are inherently oversimplifiers of complex issues in an effort to make the issues understandable to their readers. Stroud characterizes himself as favoring a relatively open trading system, but this has not always been easy to defend in cities like Detroit where it has been widely believed that trade is a danger rather than a boon to its residents. He cites some particular issues that journalists must confront in their reporting on trade matters in the popular press: (1) how to evaluate supposed expert opinion and make sure it is reflected accurately in reporting, opinion writing, and op-ed pages; (2) given the increasing fragmentation of the means of communication, how to provide serious continuity of coverage of trade issues; and (3) how to draw especially on the academic community for help in informing the press and the public on trade issues. Stroud is especially concerned about how fragmentation of the means of communication may lead to a "dumbing down" of the discussion of trade issues and to less coverage of these issues. He is also worried about the possibility of becoming overly influenced by interest group propaganda or passions as reflected for example in the rise of the Buchanan anti-trade candidacy in the 1996 election campaign, although it did appear that these extreme views did not in the end carry the day with the American public. In any event, it is the responsibility of the press to continue to present the essential features of trade issues using informed and reliable debate and data.

In Part II of Chapter 14, Jutta Hennig reflects on issues of trade policy and the media from the standpoint of a journalist writing for a specialized newsletter, *Inside U.S. Trade*, which is a highly respected source of information on trade issues that is widely used by members of the trade policy community as well as by reporters from more general newspapers. Hennig is critical of the way in which daily newspapers tend to present trade issues as a battle between free trade and protectionism rather than as a mixed picture of tradeoffs. This can make it difficult to report accurately the facts of a story, and it may lead to overlooking other important considerations (e.g., foreign policy or national security) that shape trade policy decisions. It also tends to overlook the complexities of constituent interest groups who may have heterogeneous trade-policy preferences ranging somewhere between protectionism and freer trade. She also points out that the ways in which constituents influence the policy process can be indirect and complex. The most successful constituents are engaged in export and foreign investment activities and identify most closely with objectives of the Administration in office. By the same token, there are some constituencies who may have powerful support in the Congress (e.g., steel, lumber, agriculture, and textiles/apparel) and may at times be able to influence policies to their own benefit. She notes that large firms may not always be successful in getting an Administration to act on their behalf, and there are examples of smaller companies that are successful because they are situated in a politically sensitive location. The final point that Hennig makes is that reporters who fail to understand the details of an issue may not be able to tell the story "like it is." They can be misled by policy officials who are interested in representing their accomplishments in a favorable light. This is a problem especially for journalists in the general press.

Part V of the volume provides further overview and commentary. John H. Jackson addresses in Chapter 15, "Constituent Representation: Exploring the Context of the Key Policy Questions." In setting the context, he points out that some kinds of constituent representation may be beneficial in providing information and analysis since governments may lack the resources to do everything themselves. Of course, there may also be special interest advocacy that can have harmful effects on national welfare. Jackson identifies the different types of decision makers who are the target of constituent representation and the various techniques by which constituent representation is implemented domestically and internationally. He also points out that governmental institutions themselves have become constituent representatives in international organizations or tribunals and in domestic judicial systems. In passing, he brings up the issue that national governments may wish to regulate and control constituent representation and policy advocacy, with campaign contributions being a case in point in the United States. Jackson recommends that more attention be given to studying how specific forms of constituent representation may affect economic welfare and income distribution. He notes here that the antidumping and countervailing duty rules have been severely criticized while there have also been efforts by some groups to change these rules to serve special interests. Jackson cites a second example of intellectual property protection that merits further study to determine how it may affect development of new ideas and techniques. A third example concerns the need for evaluation of the advocacy and implementation of environmental legislation and administrative actions. Finally, Jackson calls attention to the important roles that institutions and constitutions play and how they can be utilized to attain welfare enhancing results.

In Chapter 16, Marina v.N. Whitman discusses U.S. trade, trade policy, and challenges for the new administration. She identifies three challenges. The first involves regional issues relating to Latin America and Asia. Both Presidents Bush and Clinton had earlier promised an expansion of NAFTA, and it was widely expected that Chile would be the first to qualify. However, the Clinton Administration experienced difficulty in getting the Congress to go along, so that Chile's entry has been put on hold. For this now to go forward in the second Clinton Administration, it will most likely require fast-track negotiating authority, which is something that the Congress may not be in the mood to grant, particularly if it includes such things as labor and environmental standards. The Asian issues concern the United States trying to expand its access to Japan's market and how to deal with China on such matters as support for human rights, insufficient intellectual property protection, and discriminatory barriers involving imports and foreign direct investment. There are also important issues of national security at stake in U.S.-Asian relations. The second challenge relates to U.S. leadership in the WTO on a number of sectoral negotiations, pursuing the implementation of the various Uruguay Round agreements especially in agriculture and textiles/apparel, supporting and strengthening the use of the dispute settlement procedures, and working out negotiating strategies for new issues such as competition policy, trade and environment, and labor standards. The third and perhaps most important challenge is to institute domestic policy measures that will reduce protectionist pressures and continue the momentum for trade liberalization. Such measures include: appropriate macroeconomic policies with more flexible use of fiscal policy and avoidance of currency misalignments; policies dealing with labor-market adjustments and problems of wage inequality; and effective implementation of growth policies.

Bruce Wilson provides an overview in Chapter 17 of trade and the 105th Congress. Trade was not high on the agenda of the 104th Congress in 1995-96 and not much was accomplished therefore. Wilson expects that there will be a reintroduction of many of the same legislative initiatives presented but not passed in the 104th Congress as well as Congressional oversight of U.S. global and regional trading arrangements. However, he notes that there has been a definite erosion in the political support for freer trade in both the newly elected House and Senate, and this does not portend well for controversial legislation such as the renewal of fast track authority. Wilson sees China as representing the most significant trade issue facing the United States in the next several years. There is the question on what terms China might be approved for WTO membership, and how to deal with issues of human rights and continuance of Most Favored Nation (MFN) treatment of U.S. imports from China.

II. What Have (or Haven't) We Learned?

When we organized this conference, our hope was to learn more about how international trade policy is really formulated in the United States. The papers written for the conference did provide an excellent overview both of what academic economists and political scientists have learned about this process, and of what goes on in the interactions between the many parts of government that are involved in trade policy and the many parts of the private sector that seek to influence them. The discussants' comments, and also the open discussion among conference participants, reinforced this impression that we were learning about the formation of trade policy from those who really make it happen. However, when the conference was over, we realized that it had provided us more questions than answers. It had become clear only that our understanding of the political process underlying trade policy is very limited and incomplete. Even those academic economists who are at the forefront of modeling this process acknowledge this, and we are very far from having a consistent theoretical framework that will make sense of all the fascinating bits of information that arose during the conference. In the end, perhaps, the greatest contribution that the conference may have made was to illuminate our ignorance rather than remove it.

In reflecting on the conference papers and discussion, therefore, what we have learned has not so much been answers to the questions we started out with, as that there are far more questions than we realized at the start. In particular, there are a number of issues of modeling and the role of different constituent interest groups that merit further exploration. These include the following:

1. Most political economy models are focused on the influence that industries have on trade policies, based upon their roles in the economy as competitors with imports or as exporters, and as employers of scarce versus abundant factors of production. Little, if any, attention has been given to the roles of the many other interest groups such as those identified in Chapter 2 below, and those represented in some of the later chapters in this volume. And yet we found that these other interest groups in many cases do believe themselves to have substantial stakes in trade policy, and some of them have begun in recent years to play increasingly prominent roles in the trade-policy process. Models of the political economy of trade policy will remain decidedly incomplete, and for some purposes misleading, until they take these other constituent interests into account.

2. There is the further question of whether the existing models accurately represent the role of the interest groups that they do involve. The lobbying process is realistically much more complicated than is allowed for in the existing political economy models, especially insofar as non-monetary interactions may be as important as monetary contributions. We recognize, and in fact learned from some of the early political economy models, that complication for its own sake will not help us much. But nonetheless it seems likely to be important that lobbying activities often require time and other resources as much as money, and that the motives of those involved may not be, as a first approximation, selfish. How much of this non-monetary lobbying activity goes on, and what is its form and avowed purpose?

3. Lobbyists apparently spend a great deal of their time and effort dealing with government bureaucrats rather than elected officials. Just what is it that both the lobbyists and the bureaucrats wish to achieve by virtue of these interactions?

4. Much of the political economy modeling has focused on the activities of import-competing industries that are seeking protection. This ignores the fact that export industries are quite active in seeking access to foreign markets through the lowering of foreign barriers and other means. Indeed, the role of export interests is widely believed within the trade policy community to have been an important force favoring the trade liberalization that we have observed during the past fifty years under the GATT, and yet these export interests are only imperfectly dealt with, if at all, in our models. In particular, the export interests seem not to have taken the most obvious route to their own aggran-

dizement: pursuit of export subsidies. As a part of the broader issue of why the system settles on some policies and not others, we need better understanding of why export interests seek and get the help that they do.

5. There is considerable evidence from the sectoral studies that sectoral influences on trade policies have become less important over time. That is, the industries that have been most prominent in seeking and obtaining protection in the postwar period, such as textiles, autos, and steel, have seen much of that protection being phased out, without any obvious other industries replacing them, at least on the import competing side. This suggests a need to consider what the appropriate time horizon is to use in modeling protection and to take into account those forces that tend to undermine special interests in the course of time.

6. Why are trade and not other policies used in particular circumstances? It is somewhat surprising that those who specialize in studying trade policy have so little to say about this important issue, beyond the second-best idea that trade policies are typically inferior to other policies for just about any purpose. The real world clearly does not share this view, and yet we still do not know why.

7. What are the future prospects for U.S. industries seeking protection? Have conditions changed so as to make import protection more difficult to obtain? What are the other forms of influence besides trade policies that may be used in the future by constituent interest groups?

8. How do existing trade laws and institutions shape or constrain the behavior of interest groups? Without including most interest groups in our models, there is no way we can address this question, and yet it is arguably of paramount importance. Interest groups have tremendous potential to do both good and ill to society at large, and which of these they do depends not only on their motives but also on the constraints and incentives that they face. Trade policies, especially, seem to offer unusual potential for unintended adverse consequences, and the institutional framework for trade policy can be designed to avoid those consequences or not. And yet, without understanding the motives and means of the interest groups affected, we cannot hope to design those institutions to foster positive outcomes.

9. How does the public form its views on trade issues? This may be at the heart of many of the issues raised above, since it often seems that it is public misunderstanding of the effects of trade and trade policy that encourages what economists almost uniformly view as mistakes in policy. Why is it so hard to educate the public to the realities of international economics? Are there ways in which the media can provide more effective information to the public on trade issues? Are there reasons why various interest groups themselves may be successfully thwarting such efforts? We do not know the answer, but in the end it may be necessary for political economy models of trade policy to include within them the activities of those who build them.

The foregoing list by no means exhausts all of the issues that deserve more attention. It includes only some of the most interesting, and sometimes troubling, issues that arose in our own minds during the conference and during our reading of the conference proceedings. Hopefully, readers of the chapters that follow will find a trove of additional issues that will pique their interest and lead to further study and elucidation.

CHAPTER 2

An Overview of the Modeling of the Choices and Consequences of U.S. Trade Policies

Alan V. Deardorff and Robert M. Stern

I. Introduction

Our paper is designed to provide the context for the theme of the conference, which is "The Representation of Constituent Interests in the Design and Implementation of U.S. Trade Policies." In Section II, we first review the normative and political economy approaches to the modeling of trade policies. The normative approach is the basis for the traditional analysis of the welfare effects of trade and the choice of policies designed to correct distortions in the economy and to achieve first-best optima. The political economy approach provides an analytical framework for understanding of the choices made by policy makers in a political setting in response to the lobbying and related activities of producing interests. We identify the major limitations of these approaches and then discuss what Dixit (1996) has referred to in his recent work as the "transaction-cost approach," which may provide a middle ground between the other approaches and enable us to address some hitherto imperfectly understood issues of trade policy. We also include in Section II a brief discussion of the empirical literature pertinent to the normative and political economy approaches.

In Section III, we provide a sketch of the main features of the U.S. trade-policy process, focusing in particular on the roles played by the agencies of government together with the important constituent interest groups in the U.S. economy. We then consider how each of the modeling approaches can be interpreted in its representation of the behavior and interactions of the different constituencies. Setting the modeling issues aside, we also ask what can be learned from the past half-century of U.S. trade policy experiences, and we observe that there has been a distinctive movement towards more liberal and open trade in the United States and elsewhere.

In Section IV, we conclude with some summary remarks and discuss the implications of the interplay of the different modeling approaches for research and policy in light of our observation about the ways in which trade liberalization and increased openness have evolved.

II. Issues of Policy Design and Choice

Economic theories have traditionally been divided into two categories, positive and normative, the former attempting to describe what is, the latter what ought to be. Analyses of economic policies, such as international trade policies, have similarly been of these two types. Normative analysis of trade policies has included, for example, theories of the optimal tariff, while positive analysis, since it must describe the behavior of policy makers, has typically been labeled the political economy of trade policy. In this section we will briefly review these two strands of literature. Then we will discuss a new approach to policy analysis, dubbed by Dixit (1996) the "transaction-cost" approach, and examine what it may say for the design of international economic policy.

The Normative Approach to Policy Making

The normative approach to policy making has a very long history in the field of trade policy, extending back to the earliest writings of Smith and Ricardo on the desirability of free trade. Normative analysis starts with a conception (often implicit) of a social welfare function of the Bergson-Samuelson variety, which is built up from the utility functions of individuals. In other cases, normative conclusions are motivated only by a Pareto efficiency criterion, that is, that no opportunities remain unexploited that would improve the welfare of one individual without harming another. On these bases, trade theorists have established some now classic results:

- That free trade is Pareto optimal for the world as a whole if domestic markets are not distorted.
- That free trade is Pareto optimal for a country whose domestic markets are not distorted, provided that the country is too small to influence its terms of trade.
- That a large country can optimally exploit its power over the terms of trade, and therefore over its trading partners, by levying a positive tariff, provided however that other countries do not respond in kind.
- That while trade intervention may be welfare improving even for a small country if distortions exist within it, a better policy will always deal more directly with those distortions.

Distortions here refer to all manner of departures from the norm of perfect competition that has provided the benchmark for optimality in a closed economy since the work of Arrow and Debreu. A short list of such distortions would include: externalities, positive or negative, across consumers and/or producers; market power on the part of buyers and/or sellers that enables them to influence prices; policies that intervene in markets causing differences in the prices faced by different consumers and/or producers; and noneconomic objectives that enter the social welfare function with or without appearing in utility functions of individuals. Any of these will give rise to the potential for benefit from some sort of policy that itself introduces another distortion. Ideally such a policy should be designed either to correct or offset the distortion by making the policy-induced distortion equal and opposite to the distortion being corrected. Trade policies, because they distort prices faced by both producers and consumers, are almost always suboptimal and often welfare worsening. As we suggested some years ago in Deardorff and Stern (1987), use of trade policy is like "doing acupuncture with a fork" since no matter how well you aim the first prong (distortion), the other will cause unwanted damage. The one exception is the terms of trade argument for a large country, where the failure of individual producers and consumers to internalize their country's effect on the terms of trade distorts both of their decisions equally.

A critical issue in any normative policy analysis, however, trade or otherwise, is the distribution of income. If the income distribution matters to society, as it surely must, then one could include it in the above list of distortions, with the implication that the first-best policy for dealing with it would be one that directly redistributes income without itself introducing other unwanted distortions. Such a policy would be a system of lump-sum taxes and transfers, defined as payments that do not depend on any behavior that is in the control of those affected. In the static world of Arrow-Debreu general equilibrium, where either time does not exist or where all transactions to the end of time are contracted in advance, such a policy is easy to define. In the real world, however, it is impossible both to base such payments on observables that are truly outside the control of the individuals whose income is to be altered, and to have the resulting payments do any good in improving the income distribution. Most obviously, basing payments on observed income will induce both payers and recipients to deliberately earn less income, so as to alter the payments in their favor. Therefore the prescription of using a first best policy for redistributing income is not helpful.

In the field of public finance, there is a large literature dealing accordingly with "optimal taxation," attempting to identify how best to use the necessarily distorting tax policy tools that are available. In the field of international trade, the issue of income distribution has been dealt with primarily by arguing that, in this case, trade policies are not even second best. Dixit and Norman (1980, 1984) have shown that removal of trade policies can be accompanied by changes in commodity (consumer) taxes and subsidies in such a way as to leave all consumers at least as well off as before. A corollary is that any desired change in income distribution can be achieved better by using commodity taxes and subsidies than by using trade policies, even though the former are themselves only second best since they too provide incentives to alter behavior.

These strong implications of normative analysis of trade policies are viewed by some as rather troubling, since they prescribe policies that are so at variance with what we see being used in the world. The only first-best use of trade policy that the normative analysis allows is to improve the terms of trade. This motivation would suggest at best, however, that trade would be restricted only by large countries, whereas we typically observe the largest trade barriers used in developing countries, many of which are economically quite small. At the same time, normative analysis provides hardly any rationale at all for policies that promote trade, rather than restricting it, although the new trade theory has identified certain special cases where subsidies to trade may be welfare improving for strategic reasons. Therefore the normative analysis identifies as optimal a world that is so far from what we actually observe that one may wonder about its relevance, and even its accuracy.

The Political Economy Approach to Policy Making

In part because of dissatisfaction with normative theory as a means of understanding actual international trade policies, the political economy approach has been developed by a variety of authors over the last two decades especially. This literature has taken the positive approach of trying to *explain what is, not necessarily what ought to be*, and that has meant modeling the political process in some fashion along with the economics of trade. Since this literature has been ably surveyed several times, most recently by Rodrik (1995) and by Helpman (1995), rather than duplicate their efforts, we will simply provide a short overview, based largely on their contributions.[1]

The unified treatment that characterized the normative approach has not been possible for the political economy models, largely because there is no consensus model of the political process. Instead, various authors have identified different features of the political environment and political processes to stress in their modeling, and they have consequently obtained a corresponding variety of conclusions. The five principal types of model are listed in table 2.1, which has been adapted mainly from Rodrik (1995) and Helpman (1995). The first two of these model types attempt explicitly to model the political electoral process, along with the economics. The last three, on the other hand, deal more abstractly with political forces, assuming that lobbyists and/or policy makers set political contributions and/or levels of protection to maximize their own welfare given the action of the other group. In effect, they model protection as the result of an equilibrium between supply and demand for protection along the lines outlined by Baldwin (1982).

The most straightforward modeling of the political determinants of protection was done by Mayer (1984), who explicitly modeled a simple political environment in which tariffs are selected by direct democracy, that is, by majority vote. Letting the level of protection be voted on directly means that it will be set to favor the median voter. By combining this assumption with a standard model of international trade (Mayer considered both a Heckscher-Ohlin (H-O) model and a specific factors (SF) model), Mayer was able to predict tariffs based on the distribution of ownership of factors of production. Un-

TABLE 2.1. Types of Political Economy Models of Trade Policy

Modeling approach	Author(s)	Who sets tariffs?	How it works	Protection depends on
Median-voter approach (Direct democracy)	Mayer (1984)	Median voter: by selecting tariff that maximizes that voter's welfare	Population derives income from industries, possibly protected. They vote on level of tariff, which therefore maximizes the income of the median voter.	+ median voter's share of ownership + number of people in industry + size of sector – elasticity of import demand
Campaign contributions approach (Electoral competition)	Magee-Brock-Young (1989)	Politicians and lobbyists jointly: Parties select tariffs to benefit their associated factor, while lobbyists contribute to their probability of election.	Elections depend on contributions. Factor owners contribute to precommitted political parties to maximize their earnings.	outcome of Nash game
Tariff-formation function approach	Findlay-Wellisz (1982)	Industries: by spending resources on lobbying and optimizing on the given tariff-formation function.	Tariff assumed to depend directly on resources spent on lobbying. All individuals maximize their incomes.	+ relative effectiveness of pro- vs. anti- protection dollars. – number of people in industry + size of sector – elasticity of import demand
Political support function approach	Hillman (1989)	Policy makers: by selecting tariffs to maximize given political support function.	"Political support" depends on industry profits and efficiency. Policy makers maximize political support.	– weight of efficiency in political support + size of sector – elasticity of import demand
Political contributions approach	Grossman-Helpman (1994)	Politicians: to maximize objective function defined on contributions and welfare.	Single incumbent chooses policy to maximize contributions and economic welfare. Industry (specific factor) lobbyists offer optimal contributions contingent on policies.	– number of people in industry – weight attached to welfare + size of sector – elasticity of import demand

Source: Adapted from Rodrik (1995) and Helpman (1995).

fortunately, if factors are narrowly owned while consumer interests are broad, this approach predicts counter-factually that tariffs will be nonexistent, or even negative. In the H-O model, if labor ownership is broad while capital ownership is concentrated, the model delivers protection on the labor intensive good, which seems more plausible. And if a small cost of voting is added to the SF model, decision can be taken away from the median voter and a broad pattern of protection favoring specific factors can emerge. However, the approach suffers in all cases from the unreality of the assumption that individual tariffs are determined by majority vote, which is virtually never the case in practice.

Magee, Brock, and Young (1989) (MBY) sought greater realism in modeling the electoral process by assuming representative democracy. To the 2×2×2 H-O trade model they added two political parties, one favoring free trade and the other protection, plus two lobbying groups, representing the interests of the two factors of production. Parties announce their intended levels of protection in their political platforms, adjusting these levels to maximize their probabilities of election given the contributions they expect from lobbyists responding to those platforms. Lobbyists then set their optimal contributions in response. This model has much greater realism than the direct democracy model, but it is much weaker in its ability to yield clear implications. It is, for example, the only approach from which Helpman was unable to derive a clean expression for the level of protection, as reported in the final column of table 2.1, where it is noted only that protection depends on the Nash equilibrium of a game.[2] Furthermore, the attempt at greater realism is perhaps inevitably unsuccessful, since it can never capture the full richness of what actual political parties and lobbying groups are able to do, or how their interaction results in an electoral outcome.

An alternative approach, therefore, has been to focus not on the actual mechanics of the political process and it methods of making decisions, but rather to model the larger forces that interact in producing policy outcomes and the ways that participants in the process deal with these forces. The first such example actually predated Mayer's (1984) direct democracy model, and was provided by Findlay and Wellisz (1982). They subsumed the entire policy-making process into a black box, so to speak, that translated lobbying expenditure into tariffs. This "tariff formation function" was then the basis for optimization by owners of sector-specific factors, who would choose their levels of lobbying to maximize the net benefits to them of securing protection.

A second such approach was, in a sense, the mirror image of the tariff formation function approach. Hillman (1989) started instead from a "political support function," which in effect translated the tariff provided by a policy maker into the level of political support that he or she would receive in return. This, then, was another black box, this time on the industry side, although Hillman did assume that the support arising due to the profits generated by the tariff would be tempered by a loss of political support in other dimensions due to the tariff's induced economic inefficiency. Thus here it is the policy maker, not the industry, who optimizes, balancing the political gains from providing protection against the political losses from inefficiency, both of which were embodied in the political support function.

Just as the tariff formation function approach focused on the decision to demand protection, leaving the supply of protection unexplained, the political support function approach focuses on the supply of protection, leaving the demand for it unexplained. These two approaches were therefore complementary, and it was natural that the next step would combine them. This was the contribution of Grossman and Helpman (1994).[3]

In this "political contributions approach," the lobbying expenditures of Findlay-Wellisz become direct payments, but instead of contributing to the campaigns of political parties as in MBY, the Grossman-Helpman industries make payments directly to policy makers already in office. Also, the contributors stipulate that their payments are in return for protection—in fact they offer an entire schedule of payments to the policy makers, stating the amounts that they will contribute as functions of the protection provided. The policy makers, in turn, make optimal choices from these schedules, which were themselves determined optimally by the industries. In effect, then, the political contributions approach combines the tariff formation function and the political support function, each however now being derived as the optimal response to the other.

At the present time, the political contributions approach of Grossman and Helpman is the state of the art in the political economy of trade policy, and it has indeed proven to be a useful and versatile analytical framework. Its authors have succeeded in applying the approach not only to the original problem of explaining tariffs, but also to explaining competition and cooperation in tariff setting, the politics of free trade areas, and other issues.

These political economy models have moved us well beyond the limited understanding of international trade policies that we had before they were developed. We now can see a variety of reasons why the political process yields outcomes that economists view as suboptimal. Furthermore, that understanding has been embodied in an analytical framework where we can observe the tradeoffs of competing interests and even predict, to an extent, how the political and economic systems will respond to changes in the conditions that they face.

As for explaining the level of protection itself, most of these approaches yield predictions of what considerations will lead to more or less protection. Helpman (1995) expressed each of the above approaches to political economy in a unified modeling framework and was able to derive the explicit tariff formulas that were predicted by four of the five approaches. The implications of these tariff formulas in terms of what motivates protection are listed in the final column of table 2.1. It is interesting that the approaches all agreed on the (positive) importance of both industry size as well as inelasticity of demand in giving rise to protection for a sector. Each approach also has its own distinctive parameters that influence protection, while the approaches disagree on the role of the number of people in an industry in determining its protection.

On the other hand, there still exist a number of issues that are unexplained by any of these political economy models. This, in fact, was the theme of Rodrik (1995), who noted several such gaps in the theory. These were:

Why is international trade not free? The models explain why governments intervene in the economy, which is in order to alter the distribution of income in favor of certain interests. But they do not explain why intervention in trade is the tool used for this purpose, except by assuming that it is the only tool available. We know from the normative approach to trade policy that trade intervention is not first best for this purpose, and optimizing governments and/or industry interests could therefore gain more of whatever they are seeking by using other policies. Thus if those other policies were included in the political economy models, they would imply that trade of small countries would be free. Rodrik reviews several papers that have provided partial but rather specialized answers to this question. He concludes (p. 1476) that "a sufficiently general and convincing explanation for this phenomenon has yet to be formulated."

Why are trade policies universally biased against trade? Even with only trade policies admitted into the models as tools, many of them have the unfortunate implication that trade should be subsidized as often as it is taxed. That is, the same considerations that lead a government to favor an import-competing industry with a tariff should lead it to favor export industries with export subsidies. Yet this is clearly not the case in the real world, where explicit export subsidies are confined primarily to agriculture, while tariffs and other trade restrictions have been applied pretty much across the board for industrial products. One answer to this is to point to the GATT prohibition against export subsidies, but this seems only to beg the question, since the GATT prohibition (against export subsidies but not against tariffs) remains unexplained. Rodrik finds only a handful of explanations for the bias against trade in the literature, the most successful in his view being a combination of history (that tariffs were the best or only way that early governments had to generate revenues) and some model of persistence, or bias in favor of the status quo.

What are the determinants of the variation in protection levels across industries, countries and time? Here there has been more work done, both empirical and theoretical, and indeed part of the motivation for the political economy literature on trade policy has been to explain or illuminate some of the empirical work that preceded it. But while reviewing with approval some efforts to explain what has been observed empirically, Rodrik's assessment (p. 1482) is that "these empirical regularities overlap only imperfectly with the results of the theoretical literature." We shall have more to say on this below.

The Transaction-Cost Approach to Policy Making

While it seems clear that the normative approach to policy making suffers from its failure to incorporate political considerations that in fact prevent optimal policies from being undertaken, the political economy approach perhaps goes too far in the other direction. With all policies being determined endogenously, there is no scope for policy analysis itself to make any contribution. That is, the same model that tells us that the policy makers will use tariffs to protect special interests also tells us that it is useless to ask them to do otherwise. They are, at least in the models that address their behavior explicitly, already behaving optimally given their incentives and constraints. They are already taking into account, to the extent they are willing, any effects on the broader social welfare that we might tell them about. Indeed, if there really were a role for scholars to play in formulating policy, a proper political economy model should already have incorporated those scholars into the model. There seems accordingly to be no scope for analysts of policy to contribute to the improvement of the world economy, except perhaps by diligently carrying out their assigned role as information providers.

A possible escape from this conundrum is provided by the literature on public choice, of which the political economy approach to policy making is really a part. Buchanan and Tulloch (1962), and later writings by Buchanan and others, distinguished between the individual policies made by policy makers and the framework, or constitution, within which those policy makers operate. As Dixit (1996) puts it, there is a distinction between *policy acts* and *policy rules*. Policy acts are determined endogenously by policy makers interacting with other interests and within the framework of constraints and incentives that the policy rules provide, and it is therefore useless to try to change those acts at that level. But the policy rules are set less frequently and from behind a "veil of uncertainty" as to how the rules will affect those who set the rules. The proper role for policy analysis is therefore to inform the setting of the rules. Thus, for example in the context of the Grossman-Helpman political economy model of trade policy, it is pointless to tell the policy makers that tariffs benefit industries at the expense of consumers. They already know that, and they are taking it into account when they balance the contributions they receive against the general interest. However, one could still press for a revision of the rules that would, say, make contributions more difficult, or that would enhance the incentive for policy makers to respond to social welfare. Unfortunately, constitutions are seldom rewritten, and therefore if the only hope for improving public policy is through that channel, an idealistic advocate of improved public policy might be forgiven for being discouraged.

Dixit (1966), however, has argued for a middle ground between the normative analysis and the more positive political economy approach. He argues first that the distinction between policy acts and policy rules is too extreme. On the one hand, policy rules are never really formulated behind a complete veil of uncertainty. Framers of a constitution always have clear ideas of where their own interests lie, at least in the short run, and they cannot be expected to ignore those interests in formulating the rules that they themselves will live by. At the same time, many individual policy acts have implications for future policy rules, as they may influence precedents or expectations of future policies. At both levels, then, makers of both policy rules and policy acts will typically have both some degrees of freedom for working in the public interest, but also some stake in the outcome themselves that limits their degrees of freedom in other dimensions. Policy making is in fact, Dixit argues, an ongoing process that occurs in real time and that blends both the private incentives of the policy makers to respond to special and general interests, together with an evolution of the rules of policy that gradually may change those incentives.

While this may seem very confusing and imprecise, Dixit suggests a fruitful way to sort out how policy is constrained, but that may nonetheless guide that evolution. This is to focus on "transaction costs." He defines these as any distortions in the political and/or economic environments that interfere with the direct pursuit of the optima that a normative analysis might identify. These include things like uncertainty and asymmetric information, incomplete contracts, agency problems,[4] bounded rationality, and no doubt many others. The proper role for policy analysts, then, is not to tell policy makers what to do (the policy acts) on an ongoing basis, or to wait for infrequent opportunities to revise the entire constitution of policy. Rather policy analysts should be watching for opportunities that arise more frequently to make changes in the rules of policy, and their recommendations should be formulated against the backdrop of the transaction costs that may already be evident in the kinds of policy rules that are currently in place. That is, they should be looking for changes in rules and procedures that allow the economic and political systems to deal more effectively with transaction costs. These changes may be only small and incremental, but on occasion they may involve or lead to regime changes that are sizable in scope.

Dixit gives only one formal example of how this might work. He builds a model of common agency, in which multiple principals are served by a single agent whom they attempt to influence for their own benefit. With the acts of the agent only imperfectly observable by the principals, they will in general be unable to motivate a first-best outcome for all concerned, even if they were to act together. The reason is the problem of moral hazard that routinely arises in such cases, reflecting a tradeoff between efficiency and risk sharing, and this is one example of a transactions cost. An additional transaction cost is also present here, however, if the principals cannot act together. Acting independently, and even if each cares only about a separate dimension of the agent's behavior, they nonetheless will provide incentives to the agent to skimp on its service of other principals, in order to get more for themselves. The result is even worse than the second-best outcome that could have been achieved had they acted together. Dixit shows, however, that if principals can be prevented from penalizing the service to other principals, perhaps by removing their access to information about that service, then the principals acting separately will do better than even the second-best outcome they could have achieved together. That is, in this context in which an agent provides separate services for multiple principals, the principals will be better served if each is *not* told what the agent has done for others, as compared to all having full information. This is an example, albeit rather abstract, in which it would serve no purpose to instruct the agent simply to implement a first-best policy, since the agent cannot be expected to ignore the incentives coming from the principals. But a change in the framework of policy, in this case changing the information that is available to the principals, is both possible and may be agreed upon, since it permits a more efficient outcome that can benefit all and that none will have the means or incentive to undermine.

In this view, institutional arrangements that condition policy choices should be viewed as "coping mechanisms" for dealing with transaction costs, and they should be judged not on whether they yield first-best outcomes but rather on whether they do better than alternative arrangements that are available for the same purpose. Thus in Dixit's example above, the underlying transaction costs, which arise first from moral hazard and second from the presence of multiple principals, make a first-best outcome impossible. Allowing each of the multiple principals independently to lobby the agent may be far from optimal, but as a means of coping with these transaction costs it may nonetheless be better than alternatives that, say, might neglect the interests of many of these principals altogether. On the other hand, once it has been discovered by means of economic analysis that this particular coping mechanism can be improved upon by restricting the information available to the principals, it becomes possible to improve the coping mechanism. And note that such an improvement may not need to wait for a complete overhaul of the policy regime such as might accompany a new constitution.[5] Rather, coping mechanisms can be modified in both small and large ways, and in real time, as either the system or our understanding of it evolve.

What does all of this have to do with trade policy? Here, alas, we are on our own, since Dixit's book does not address the questions that we would most like his approach to answer for our purpose here. The closest he comes to applying his transaction-cost approach to trade policy is a thoughtful discussion of the international trading system in the second half of the twentieth century, from the GATT to the WTO. He uses transaction costs, for example, to explain the presence of exceptions in the GATT and WTO rules on tariff bindings. Without the safeguards clause, which permits countries to raise tariffs when a surge of imports causes major damage to a domestic competing industry, the GATT would be unable to sustain its cooperation in the face of its Prisoners' Dilemma incentives to defect. Dixit also discusses other features of the GATT and WTO rules, such as the treatments of textiles, agriculture, and nontariff barriers, all of which he sees as coping mechanisms but not especially good ones.

Dixit does not address the questions that Rodrik identified as being unanswered by the political economy approaches to trade policy, and we may ask whether the transaction-cost approach offers any better hope of resolving them. We will focus only on the first two of Rodrik's three questions: Why is international trade not free? And why are trade policies universally biased against trade? Interpretations of these questions, in light of the political economy literature, might be: Why do policy makers redistribute income by taxing imports instead of (more efficiently) subsidizing production? And why do they also seem to favor import-competing industries over export industries, taxing imports but not subsidizing exports?

A simple, and hardly new, answer to both of these questions is that tariffs on imports are much less well understood by the public (and perhaps also by the policy makers and their constituents) than are subsidies. A subsidy to production is clearly a hand-out, and the public understands that. Even when a subsidy is provided not by direct payment but by a tax break, the public understands that as well. But the benefits from a tariff (or quota) on imports may not be understood as accruing directly to the industry that benefits, even though as economists we understand that the effect is the same as if they did. On the contrary, a tariff on imports may be viewed primarily as taxing foreign producers, and even its effect on domestic consumers is not always fully appreciated by the lay public. Furthermore, the beneficiary from a tariff appears to be the government, which collects the revenue, a fact that even adversely affected consumers might perceive as offsetting some of their loss (as indeed it does). Thus, the fact that a tariff has all of the effects (and more) of a subsidy to domestic producers is something that the producers may figure out, but that the rest of the citizenry may find difficult to comprehend. Similarly, regarding the bias against trade, while a government may protect its import-competing industries without complete public understanding, a similar attempt to assist export industries with a subsidy will be understood at once. Therefore both of Rodrik's questions can possibly be answered by noting the difficulty of the public's understanding the true effects of tariffs in contrast to the ease of understanding the effects of subsidies.

As far as we can see, this explanation of patterns of policy assistance does not fit well into any political economy approach to policy. But it may well fit within the transaction-cost approach. Problems of incomplete and asymmetric information have already been mentioned as sources of transaction costs, as well as the need for policy institutions to find ways of coping with them. Those problems had to do with knowing what a particular economic agent was doing. Here we are stressing a different kind of incomplete information: the incomplete understanding of economic cause and effect that characterizes a potentially important part of the public. This is a transaction cost as much as the others, and like the others it has led to coping mechanisms.[6]

One such coping mechanism is simply education. Over the last half century, the message of economists about the effects of trade policy has been repeated in schools, in the press, and even occasionally (though not recently) in presidential debates. It may be argued that this has been in part responsible for the remarkable reduction in tariffs that has been achieved over this period. Of course, the reduction occurred in conjunction with another coping mechanism, the GATT and the rounds of multilateral trade negotiation that it sponsored. As already noted, Dixit sees the history of the GATT as a good example of coping with transaction costs, which he identified as Prisoners' Dilemma incentives that would otherwise characterize trade policy in the absence of GATT-sponsored cooperation. But we would argue that the GATT, and now the WTO, has also been a mechanism also of coping with public ignorance about trade policy. And it truly has been an exercise of coping with the cost, not removing it, for the rule of the GATT has not so much been to educate the public about the true effects of trade as to instill instead a sense of international obligation that may have some of the same effect. We return to this point at the end of Section III.

Of course, no coping mechanism is perfect, and this has been true in spades of the GATT success in bringing down tariffs. To some extent, at the same time as the public has come to recognize some of the adverse effects of tariffs, use has merely shifted to trade policy tools that are even less comprehensible, such as quotas, voluntary export restraints, and government-to-government political pressures. The increasing resort to NTBs, as tariffs have fallen, is well documented, although their overall quantitative significance has not been definitively measured.[7] Our own view is that the decline in tariffs has done far more good than the harm caused by the NTBs that have replaced them. But the rise of NTBs has meant that the informational transaction costs in trade policy that remain will be more difficult to cope with than those we have faced previously.

Empirical Evidence

Our discussion thus far has focused on the conceptual aspects of the different approaches to the modeling of trade policy. In this connection, it may be useful to supplement this discussion with reference to some of the pertinent empirical literature and methodology used.

The Normative Approach

A variety of empirical methods have been used to study the cost of protection or subsidies and its counterpart, the reduction/removal of these policies. These methods include: (1) partial equilibrium estimates by commodity group/sector, based primarily on assumed values of demand and supply elasticities; (2) partial equilibrium industry studies using econometric analysis; and (3) computable general equilibrium (CGE) model simulations. These studies typically yield estimates of the welfare effects of tariffs and NTBs of various kinds, with varying degrees of precision depending on the assumptions used especially in choosing or estimating the critical elasticity parameters and different market structures.

Illustrative studies include: (1) Hufbauer and Elliot's (1994) partial equilibrium estimates of the cost of U.S. protection by sector; (2) review of measurement of NTBs by Deardorff and Stern (1996); (3) econometric analysis of the U.S. auto sector by Berry, Levinsohn, and Pakes (1995); and Martin and Winters (1996), which contains several CGE analyses of the effects of the Uruguay Round agreements. While these different types of studies each have certain methodological limitations, they are nonetheless useful in calling attention to the orders of magnitude of the welfare effects of existing trade policies and changes in these policies. They can serve accordingly as a kind of benchmark in determining how significant the departures from first-best optima may be. Of course, there will still remain a need to understand why these trade policies are used in the political context and what their impact will be through time as coping mechanisms may or may not come into play.

The Political Economy Approach

There is a very substantial empirical literature that has sought to explain the determinants of trade policy. These include both regression-type studies and case studies of the experiences of individual countries and sectors. Many of these studies have related to U.S. trade policy, although some cross-country studies have been done as well. Rodrik (1995) surveys many of the pertinent regression studies, while Krueger (1996) contains case studies of a number of important U.S. sectors that have been the object of U.S. trade-policy actions. Some of the key findings and hypotheses that emerge from the various studies are summarized in tables 2.2 and 2.3.

As already mentioned, Rodrik notes (p. 1480) that there has not been a very close link between the theoretical and empirical research, and that the empirical research has thus often been designed in an intuitive rather than rigorous manner. From the final column in table 2.1, industry size and employment would appear to be important theoretically, although the expected sign of employment is not the same for all the models. However, the actual evidence summarized in table 2.2 appears to emphasize many other factors that are not represented directly in the different modeling approaches. Much the same can be said about many of the key hypotheses derived from the U.S. case studies summarized in table 2.3. This is not to deny the accomplishments of the formal political economy models described in table 2.1. But it suggests nevertheless that these models provide only a limited understanding of what in fact are the main determinants and consequences of trade policy in the United States and other countries.

III. Representation of Constituent Interests

In this section, we first discuss the main features of the U.S. trade-policy process and then interpret this process in the light of the modeling approaches just discussed. We consider thereafter what can be learned about the design and consequences of U.S. trade-policy experiences in the past half century since the end of World War II.

Structure of the U.S. Trade-Policy Process

In figure 2.1, we present a schematic overview of how the U.S. trade-policy process is structured and its various functions. This will of course be very fa-

TABLE 2.2. Summary of Key Results of Empirical Studies of the Determinants of Protection

1. Protection across industries

Protection received by an industry is higher when:

- it is a labor-intensive, low-skill, low-wage industry;
- it has high import penetration, has experienced an increase in import penetration, or has been in decline;
- it produces consumer goods rather than intermediate goods;
- it engages in little intra-industry trade;
- its customers are not highly concentrated.

There is mixed evidence on whether high levels of industry concentration result in greater protection.

Tariffs and NTBs may be complements.

2. Protection across countries or institutional contexts

- Average tariff rates tend to decrease as capital-labor ratios increase.
- Poor countries tend to tax agriculture while rich countries subsidize it.
- NTBs are higher in countries that are economically large, have higher unemployment rates, have larger average size and smaller average number of parliamentary constituencies, and use proportional representation as their electoral system (subject to the degree of autonomy of party leaders).
- In U.S. antidumping proceedings, the determination of dumping depends on technical factors while the determination of injury is more political and is affected by industry concentration, size, and employment.

3. Protection over time in the United States

- The average tariff level tends to rise in recessions.
- Historically Republicans have tended to raise tariffs and Democrats to reduce them.
- The delegation of tariff setting to the Executive Branch has resulted in the lowering of tariffs and reduced susceptibility to narrow pressure groups.
- There may be higher levels of protection when the political parties are divided between the Executive Branch and the Congress.

4. Protection over time in developing countries

- In a deep economic crisis, when economy-wide macroeconomic reforms are introduced, it may be easier to introduce trade-policy reforms as well.

Source: Adapted from Rodrik (1995, pp. 1480-87).

TABLE 2.3. Summary of Key Political Economy Hypotheses Based on Case Studies of U.S. Sectoral Trade Policies

1. **U.S. economic and political interests are not effectively served by protectionism.** The interests of final consumers are not taken into account. No consideration is given to the effects of protection on the costs to other industries. Protection introduced in periods of recession tends to remain in place.
2. **Simple rather than complex arguments are most effective in obtaining industry protection.** Considerations of "fairness," "equity," job loss, the "need" for an industry, and maintenance of incomes are often invoked in seeking protection.
3. **Political clout is crucial in obtaining protection.**
4. **Institutions may be designed to constrain protection**, as for example, in NAFTA and the Uruguay Round agreement in which protection is to be phased out over time.
5. **Protection may not actually help protected sectors because of offsetting market-induced responses and technological change.**
6. **Protection is more likely when there is unanimity among the firms involved.** User industries appear generally unwilling to oppose protection that raises their input costs.
7. **Effective lobbying and organization of interest groups are important determinants of protection.**
8. **Past protection can be expected to lead to future protection.** History matters.

Source: Adapted from Krueger (1996, pp. 431-41).

miliar to trade specialists. Nonetheless, it will be helpful in clarifying the subsequent discussion of the advantages and limitations of the different modeling approaches. The top part of the figure depicts the Executive Branch, Congress, and the main administrative agency, the International Trade Commission (ITC), which investigates especially alleged violations of U.S. trade laws. We also show membership in the World Trade Organization (WTO), which is the bridge between U.S. domestic trade laws and their international counterparts as embodied in the WTO charter. The locus of U.S. trade policies is centered in the Executive Branch, in particular in the Office of the U.S. Trade Repre sentative (USTR), which was established in the 1960s in an effort to concentrate in a single agency the responsibilities for decision making on trade matters and international trade negotiations that previously had been carried out on an interagency basis at the cabinet level. The National Economic Council was established by the Clinton Administration in 1993 and presumably provides recommendations on the overall directions of U.S. trade policies. The

Council of Economic Advisors (CEA) dates from the period immediately following World War II, and it provides information and analytical evaluations of all aspects of U.S. economic policies, both domestic and international. One of the three CEA members typically is an academic specialist in international trade and finance. The USTR maintains close working relations with firms and labor organizations by means of the so-called Industry Sector Advisory Committees (ISACs) that are especially active in periods of international trade negotiations. The USTR also works closely with the pertinent Congressional committees that deal with issues of trade policy.

In the U.S. Congress, the two most important committees involved in the trade-policy process are the House Ways and Means Committee and the Senate Finance Committee. Other congressional committees also deal often with trade issues when these issues bear upon their policy domains. But traditionally the Ways and Means and Finance Committees play the major roles in the trade-policy process because of their authority over tax and expenditure decisions. The division of authority on trade issues between the Executive Branch and the Congress has of course been discussed extensively over the years. In this connection, it seems fair to say that, during the period since World War II, the Executive Branch played the decisive role until the early 1970s. Since then, the Congress has become much more active in defining the trade-policy agenda and the design of trade policies.

In the bottom part of figure 2.1, we depict the array of constituent interests who are affected by trade policies and who in turn may influence the choice and design of trade policies by a variety of means. These include political contributions to candidates and parties, facilitating legal actions on behalf of trade clients, advocacy of the public interest, and providing information on trade and related issues to the branches and agencies of government and to the other constituent interests noted.

Economists typically associate efforts to influence trade policies with the activities of private-sector producing interests. These interests embrace both firms and workers across the economic spectrum, including agriculture, manufacturing, and services. This is not to say, however, that these sectoral activities share common objectives, since the producing interests may differ depending upon their position in the economy, that is, whether they are import-competing, export, or nontradable sectors, and the degree of foreign ownership and operation. Furthermore, the ways in which sectoral influences are expressed may stem directly from the firms and workers themselves or through a variety of organizations, including sectoral associations, organized labor, political action committees (PACs), and specialized lobbying, consulting, and legal firms. We also designate a separate category of law firms that specialize in the provision of legal services in connection with the administration of the trade laws on behalf of their clients. While we have not had the opportunity to gather evidence on the lobbying and related expenditures and other activities of private-sector producing interests, it is our impression that these interests

Figure 2.1. Structure of the U.S. Trade Policy Process

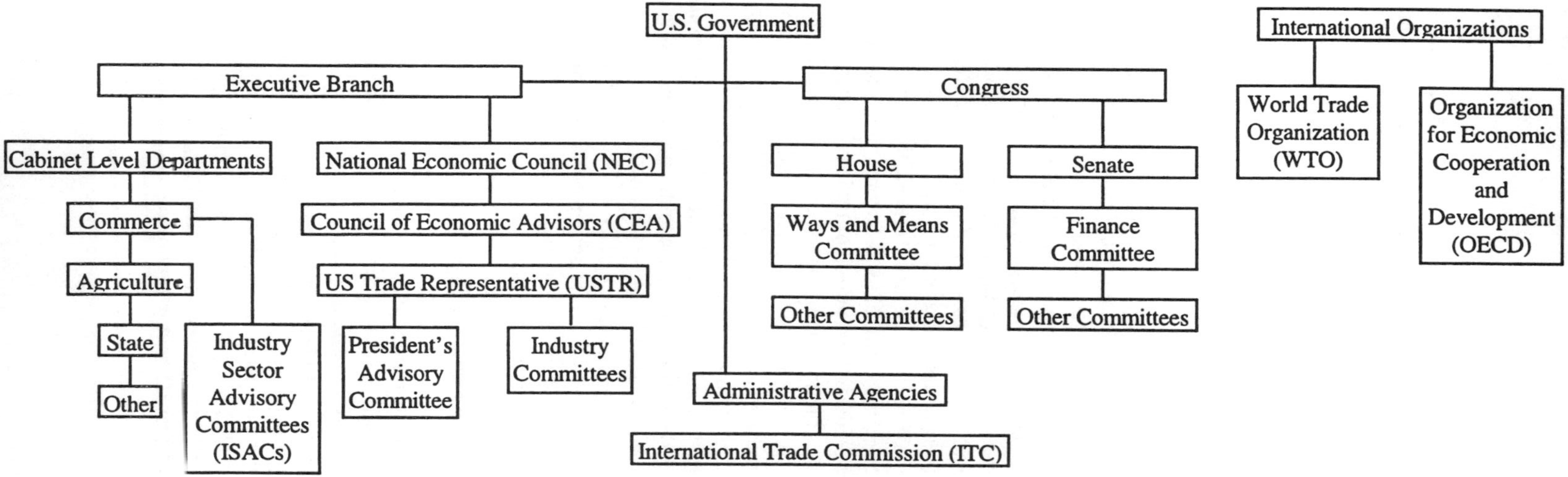

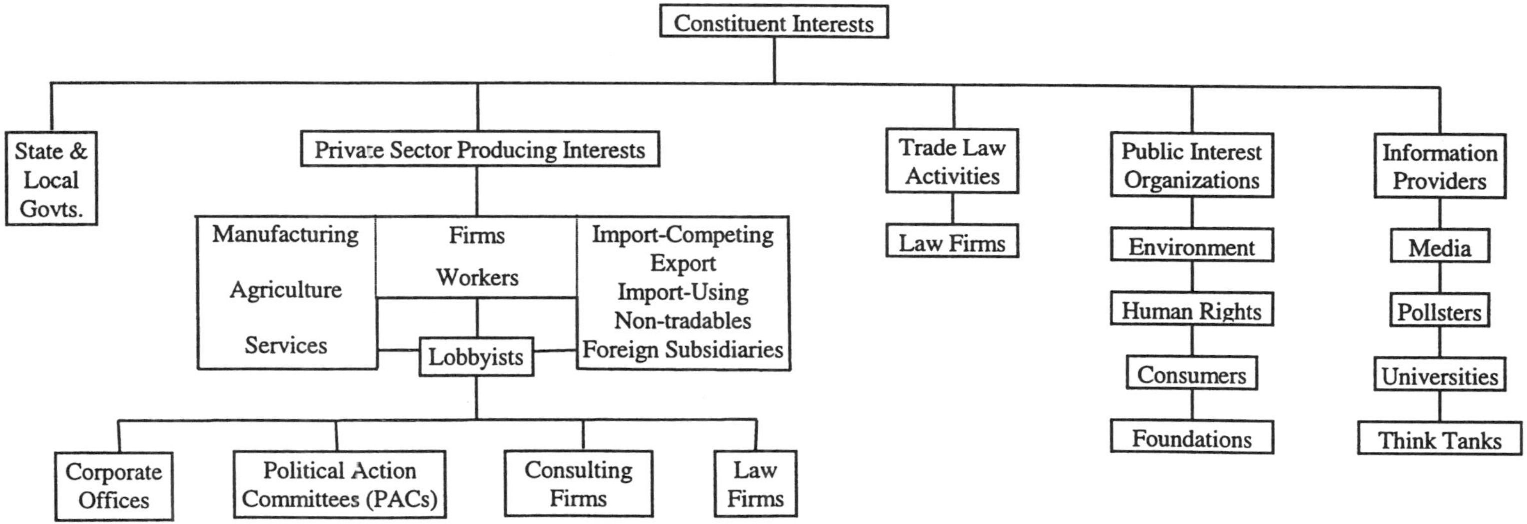
Constituent Interests
State & Local Govts.
Private Sector Producing Interests
Manufacturing
Agriculture
Services
Firms
Workers
Import-Competing
Export
Import-Using
Non-tradables
Foreign Subsidiaries
Lobbyists
Corporate Offices
Political Action Committees (PACs)
Consulting Firms
Law Firms
Trade Law Activities
Law Firms
Public Interest Organizations
Environment
Human Rights
Consumers
Foundations
Information Providers
Media
Pollsters
Universities
Think Tanks

account for the major share of the resources designed to influence trade policy. But there are other constituent interests to consider as well.

Thus we indicate a category that represents the public interest, including organizations that specialize in providing information and that seek to influence government policies relating especially to the environment, human rights, and consumer choice and welfare. These public-interest organizations have grown increasingly in number and size especially since the 1970s and have given voice to concern about the ways in which U.S. trade and other economic policies impact on the environment and on economic, social, and political conditions both in the United States and in other nations. Many of these groups were especially active in the NAFTA debate in 1992-93, and they have continued to be involved in many current trade policy issues. These public-interest organizations are by no means uni-dimensional, in the sense that some may promote a policy agenda favoring economic efficiency and growth while others may take more absolutist positions that place much less emphasis on economic efficiency and growth as ends in themselves and greater emphasis on social and political objectives. We also include foundations in the public-interest category. They provide financial support to some of the advocacy organizations and especially to academic institutions and "think tanks" that we depict as information providers. Foundation support can serve both the general public interest as well as special interests.

The final category shown in figure 2.1 refers to information providers. These include print, broadcast, and electronic media that gather and disseminate economic and other information to government and to the various constituencies noted and that may pursue particular economic policy objectives depending on their target audiences. Academic institutions also serve as providers of information on trade and other economic policies, both through classroom teaching and through the dissemination of theoretical and applied economic research. We include here as well think tanks that specialize in economic research, some of which parallels what goes on in academic institutions, but which commonly involves some particular policy orientation dependent in large measure on the sources of funding.

It is difficult to determine without further study how important and effective the different constituent interests may be in influencing trade policy. Nonetheless, it is evident from figure 2.1 that the trade-policy process has a complex structure involving a host of agents and principals. The branches and agencies of government provide the impetus for trade-policy initiatives that are intended to serve the public interest as well as to cater to special interests by implementing protectionist measures that restrict import trade and by furnishing subsidies that are designed to expand exports. While our discussion has been focused on trade policy, we should also mention that the agencies of government and constituent interests are involved in policy activities that affect inward and outward foreign direct investment (FDI), banking, and portfolio investment, all of which may have a direct or indirect bearing on trade and trade policies. It is important to emphasize in any case that there is a continuous interaction between the agents of government and the multitude of principals who comprise the constituent interest groups noted. It is interesting in this light now to consider how the trade-policy process is represented in the different modeling approaches that were discussed in the preceding section.

Modeling U.S. Trade Policies

We have distinguished three modeling approaches to U.S. trade policies: (1) the normative approach based on a social welfare function; (2) the positive approach based on political economy; and (3) the transaction-cost approach that is a middle ground between the foregoing two approaches. We shall discuss each of these in turn using the framework in figure 2.1.

Normative Approach

As already discussed, the normative approach to trade policy assumes that the government has an objective function whose arguments include welfare maximization and optimal resource allocation under conditions of perfect competition. For a system like this to operate successfully, there would be a need for a government that in itself works perfectly and that is capable of implementing policies that will achieve its welfare maximization and efficiency goals. Whether and how governments can in actuality be organized and operated to attain the conditions of this first-best world is not dealt with in this normative modeling approach. On the theoretical level at least, it is required that the government be omniscient and behave, so to speak, as a beneficent dictator. But what remains unclear in these circumstances is why governments will be created to begin with and, if they are created, what the rules may be that will guide their policy choices. The normative approach thus seems to take the existence of perfect government for granted and interprets government's role in policy making as implementing the prescriptions of the normative approach for the general benefit of society.

In terms of our figure 2.1, it is as if the Executive Branch can play an omniscient and beneficent role. But given the structure of the U.S. Government noted in the figure, together with the variety and complexity of the constituent interests, it might appear that a leap of imagination is required to make the normative approach viable. This is all the more true once account is taken of the possible violations of one or more of the modeling assumptions noted above. It might be argued nonetheless that it may not be necessary to model the structure of the trade-policy process in detail. This will be the case especially if policy makers are somehow guided by welfare and efficiency objectives in formulating and executing trade policies. If so, the normative approach can provide the framework for evaluation of alternative policies based on the conventional welfare analysis that is familiar to trade economists.

Clearly, however, this may be stretching things, because the normative approach does not explain why governments choose the trade policies that they do, especially when these policy choices are so frequently at variance with first-best optimal criteria. It is for this reason that so much attention has been devoted to the political economy approach to which we now turn.

Political Economy Approach

As noted above, the political economy approach is especially valuable insofar as it enhances the understanding of the forces that shape the choice and design of trade policies. What the different political economy models have in common is that they give greater weight to some individuals and interest groups than to others in determining policy choices overall. Welfare considerations thus either do not enter at all in the policy process or enter only alongside distributional considerations. In terms of our figure 2.1, trade policy choices will be influenced both in the Executive Branch and in the Congress especially, whereas the investigatory power of the ITC is based mainly on the facts and legal interpretations embodied in U.S. trade laws as they were formulated in those other branches. According to the political economy approach, the private-sector producing interests, together with the trade law actions of legal firms acting in their behalf, are the driving forces determining the trade policy choices of government. There is also scope for international actions since policy choices may be interdependent particularly in the cases of large countries and trading blocs.

Because the political economy approach focuses primarily on the influence of producer interests in determining policy choices and electoral politics, figure 2.1 suggests that there are some potentially important interests that this approach does not take sufficiently into account. These include the variety of public interest and advocacy organizations, especially those that are concerned with issues of trade and the environment, human rights, and other noneconomic, trade-related objectives such as the fostering of democratic political and social institutions. This applies also to the role played by information providers. In essence, then, the political economy approach is incomplete and needs to be adapted to make allowance for those other constituent group activities. But what is perhaps the main limitation of the political economy approach is that, because it is not concerned with the pros and cons of alternative trade policies, it offers no guidance to policy makers in choosing among the available policy alternatives. As already stressed, this is what the normative approach seeks to accomplish. The question then is whether or not Dixit's transaction-cost approach provides a useful middle ground between the other two approaches.

The Transaction-Cost Approach

To understand issues of trade and other economic policies, the transaction-cost approach emphasizes that society is comprised of numerous agents acting on behalf of numerous principals and carrying out numerous policies in real time.

Our figure 2.1 is thus helpful in calling attention to the multiplicity of constituent groups who care about what government does and who seek to influence its policy choices. Unless we take this broad view, it appears to us difficult to comprehend the choice and outcome of trade policies. An amalgam of the normative and political economy approaches is therefore essential. To help accomplish this end, we need especially to study how the different constituencies are organized and how they intersect with each problem in the trade-policy process. One way to do this is to consider particular trade policy changes and their economic effects over time. It would be essential in this regard to identify the transaction costs at issue that stand in the way of achieving first-best results and at the same time to consider the coping mechanisms that are operative. These coping mechanisms will be indicative of the success or failure of the government in reducing transaction costs by its policy actions and associated efforts on the part of both the government and different constituent groups to mitigate the consequences of both market and political failures. We shall return to these matters in our concluding section, but, before doing so, it might be worthwhile to put our modeling discussion aside and to consider what can be learned from observation of the overall experiences of U.S. trade policies in the past half century.

What Can Be Learned from the U.S. Trade-Policy Experiences of the Past Fifty Years?

In reflecting on the U.S. trade-policy experiences in the half century since the end of World War II, it is useful to consider these experiences within the transaction-cost framework as involving the interplay between the forces of trade liberalization and protectionism/export subsidies as a dynamic process occurring in real time. It is beyond the scope of our paper to review the quantitative dimensions of the post-World War II effects of U.S. trade policies. Nonetheless, our reading of the literature and assessment of the actual outcomes of the trade-policy process strongly suggest on balance that the U.S. economy has been subject to a distinctive liberalizing orientation and resultant overall improvement in economic welfare, even when changes in income distribution are taken into account. If our interpretation is correct, it appears that the coping mechanisms involved in U.S. trade policies have been sufficiently powerful so as to reduce transaction costs over time. We realize of course that not everyone would accept this conclusion, citing especially the frequent resort to nontariff protectionism in the past two decades or more and the long-standing restrictions applied especially to trade in agricultural products and apparel.

But granting this, the general orientation of U.S. domestic and trade policies in favor of market-based outcomes and the lowering of U.S. and foreign trade barriers has in our judgment ruled the day. As noted in our earlier discussion, this has been reinforced by the existence and influence of the General Agreement on Tariffs and Trade (GATT), which provided the context and authority for trade liberalization and nondiscrimination for GATT members by means of the GATT articles of agreement and the periodic multilateral trade negotiations that have taken place, most recently with conclusion of the Uruguay Round negotiations and creation of the WTO in 1994. U.S. leadership has without question been the driving force in helping to reduce tariff barriers as well as trying to address the problems created by NTBs. This process has of course been far from perfect, but, in our view, the outcome has nevertheless been highly beneficial to the major industrialized and developing countries involved in the global trading system. The increasing tendency in recent years in many newly industrializing countries and in the former socialist economies to reduce and remove barriers to domestic production and trade and to move towards market-based resource allocation has thus far served to reinforce the liberalizing orientation of the global economic system.

We cannot say with certainty of course whether the movement towards increased liberalization will be continued in the future. But it appears to us to be a reasonable working assumption that this will be the case. Our view here is colored by the prospect of a stronger international body represented by the newly created WTO that has put in place what promises to be a more effective dispute settlement mechanism. It will clearly require time and experience to determine whether the WTO can fulfill its expectations. Much will depend on how the major actors in the global system respond and whether they will use the WTO to fend off special interests domestically that may seek to influence national policies that contravene WTO rules and obligations. There is also the issue of whether the spread of regional trading arrangements will help or hinder the liberalizing process. In our view, regionalism is likely to turn out to be a liberalizing force, especially insofar as it leads smaller countries to lock in the reduction of domestic and external barriers in exchange for market access. The key here will be whether this can be done in a welfare enhancing manner.

A final consideration that deserves mention is the important role played by international investment in the global economy. It has been the case that restrictions on international capital flows among the major industrialized countries especially have been markedly reduced in the past half century. This is evidenced by the significant narrowing of interest differentials, which can be taken as a sign of increased efficiency in the functioning of international financial markets. These markets have also witnessed many innovations by international financial institutions that have been reflected in changes in their organizational structure and increases in the kinds of international financial instruments available to market participants. The tendency of international financial markets to move closer to conditions of perfect international capital mobility is really quite remarkable, even given the downside of possibly excessive exchange-rate volatility in today's floating rate system and problems of domestic monetary management that some countries have encountered.

Equally important have been the substantial increases in foreign direct investment and the associated trade accounted for by multinational corporations (MNCs). While most FDI is carried out by MNCs operating among the group of major industrialized countries, there have been sizable movements of FDI to the newly industrializing countries, especially in East and Southeast Asia and also in Latin America. What is so important about FDI is that it serves to foster more efficient international allocation of resources and the transfer of technology. Again, FDI may have its downside, but this pales in comparison to the truly significant benefits that MNCs have brought about.

We conclude this section by emphasizing how powerful the forces of liberalization of international trade and international investment have been in the past half century for the United States and other countries in the global economic system. The question at hand then is how we can relate this experience to the modeling of trade policy that has been the subject of our preceding discussion.

IV. Conclusions and Implications for Research and Policy

In broad terms what our discussion reveals is a history of far more intervention in international trade than can be explained by the normative approach to analysis of trade policy, yet also a reasonably steady and quite substantial movement towards more open markets and more liberal trade in the past half century. The political economy approach to trade policy has provided important insights into why it is that the prescriptions of normative analysis often fail to be observed. But it has so far neglected to incorporate various constituent interests other than producing interests who appear to have played important roles in the U.S. trade policy process. Furthermore, the political economy approach alone seems ill-equipped to explain the steady movement toward freer trade that has occurred.

Staiger (1995) provides an interesting model of gradual trade liberalization that results when producer interests are gradually eroded over time. What happens is that early partial liberalization causes the specific factors in protected sectors to depreciate and migrate elsewhere, and this makes further future liberalization politically feasible. Here political economy helps to explain the pace of liberalization, but it does not explain why it occurs at all, which depends in Staiger's model on an assumed "political will" to liberalize.

Our conjecture, following these various lines of research but especially Dixit's discussion of transaction costs, is that this "political will" may be found in the ongoing efforts of the many interested actors in the economy to cope with the transactions costs that have led to protection in the first place. Focusing only on producer interests, and especially those who compete with imports, has enabled the political economy approach to explain protection. But that approach will have to incorporate additional interests, including not only other producers but also many of the other interests that we identified in figure 2.1, if it is to explain more fully why these political forces result in protection rather than other more direct policies of income redistribution and, especially, if it is to explain the overall movement toward more liberal trade that we have witnessed in the post-World War II period.

We speculated earlier that one of the transaction costs that may explain protection is the difficulty that the public has in understanding the true effects of trade and other policies. If that is true, then the movement towards more liberal trade may be the result of increasingly successful efforts on the part of many of the interests in figure 2.1 to cope with this lack of understanding. In the long run, one of the most important constituent interests in U.S. trade policy may be our very selves!

NOTES

[1] Both surveys provide ample references to the literature that can be consulted for more detailed analysis and discussion.

[2] That is, equilibrium is defined as levels of protection for each party that are optimal given the level of protection provided by other party. However, it is apparently not possible to solve for this equilibrium in an explicit form comparable to the formulas obtained from the other models.

[3] Feenstra and Bhagwati (1982) also modeled supply and demand for protection interactively, as a game between labor and government.

[4] This refers to the problems that arise when one individual, the agent, acts on behalf of another, the principal. The problem is for the principal to devise a system of incentives that will induce the agent to act in the principal's interest.

[5] That of course depends on what the existing constitution says. In the example, if the existing constitution mandates freedom of information, then the needed change to restrict the principals' knowledge of each others' benefits might require a constitutional change. For while it is in their collective interests to restrict information, each individually would have an incentive to seek information given the freedom to do so.

[6] As noted in Table 3 below, Krueger (1996) suggests a number of examples of simple arguments favoring protection that achieve public acceptance even though the protection may be detrimental to consumer welfare.

[7] See Deardorff and Stern (1996) for an analysis of methods of measuring NTBs.

REFERENCES

Baldwin, Robert E. 1982. "The Political Economy of Protection," in Jagdish Bhagwati (ed.), *Import Competition and Response*. Chicago: University of Chicago Press.

Berry, Steven, James Levinsohn, and Ariel Pakes. 1995. "Voluntary Export Restraints on Automobiles: Evaluating a Strategic Trade Policy," in process, January 30.

Buchanan, James M. and Gordon Tulloch. 1962. *The Calculus of Consent*. Ann Arbor, MI: University of Michigan Press.

Deardorff, Alan V. and Robert M. Stern. 1987. "Current Issues in U.S. Trade Policy: An Overview," in Robert M. Stern (ed.), *U.S. Trade Policies in a Changing World Economy*. Cambridge, MA: MIT Press, Chapter 2, pp. 15-68.

Deardorff, Alan V. and Robert M. Stern. 1996. *Measurement of Nontariff Barriers*, report prepared for the Organization of Economic Cooperation and Development.

Dixit, Avinash K. 1996. *The Making of Economic Policy: A Transaction-Cost Politics Perspective*. Cambridge, MA: M.I.T. Press.

Dixit, Avinash K. and Victor Norman. 1980. *Theory of International Trade*. London: Cambridge University Press.

Dixit, Avinash K. and Victor Norman. 1984. "Gains from Trade without Lump-Sum Compensation," *Journal of International Economics* 21: 111-122.

Feenstra, Robert C. and Jagdish N. Bagwhati. 1982. "Tariff Seeking and the Efficient Tariff," in Jagdish Bhagwati (ed.), *Import Competition and Response*. Chicago: University of Chicago Press.

Findlay, R. and S. Wellisz. 1982. "Endogenous Tariffs, the Political Economy of Trade Restrictions, and Welfare," in Jagdish Bhagwati (ed.), *Import Competition and Response*. Chicago: University of Chicago Press.

Grossman, Gene M. and Elhanan Helpman. 1994. "Protection for Sale," *American Economic Review* 84: 833-850; reprinted in Alan V. Deardorff, James Levinsohn, and Robert M. Stern (eds.), *New Directions in Trade Theory*. Ann Arbor, MI: University of Michigan Press.

Helpman, Elhanan. 1995. "Politics and Trade Policy," Discussion Paper No. 1269, Centre for Economic Policy Research, London (November).

Hillman, Arye L. 1989. *The Political Economy of Protection*. London: Harwood.

Hufbauer, Gary C. and Kimberly A. Elliott. 1994. *Measuring the Costs of Protection in the United States*. Washington, D.C.: Institute for International Economics.

Krueger, Anne O. 1996. *The Political Economy of American Trade Policy*. Chicago: University of Chicago Press.

Magee, Stephen P., William A. Brock, and Leslie Young. 1989. *Black Hole Tariffs and Endogenous Policy Formation*. Cambridge, MA: M.I.T. Press.

Martin, Will and L. Alan Winters. 1996. *The Uruguay Round: Widening and Deepening the World Trading System*. New York: Cambridge University Press.

Mayer, Wolfgang. 1984. "Endogenous Tariff Formation," *American Economic Review* 74: 970-985.

Rodrik, Dani. 1995. "Political Economy of Trade Policy," in G. Grossman and K. Rogoff (eds.), *Handbook of International Economics, Vol. III*. Amsterdam: North-Holland.

Staiger, Robert W. 1995 "A Theory of Gradual Trade Liberalization," in Alan V. Deardorff, James Levinsohn, and Robert M. Stern (eds.), *New Directions in Trade Theory*. Ann Arbor, MI: University of Michigan Press.

Comments on Conference Version of Paper

Gene Grossman

Deardorff and Stern question how much we understand about the formation of trade policy and about the role that economists can play in promoting better policies. I suppose I was asked to serve as discussant in order to allow me to defend the accomplishments of the political economy literature. But no such defense is warranted. The literature on trade policy formation falls short in many important ways: its assumptions are unrealistic; its predictions fail to explain many observed phenomena; and, most importantly, it fails to give much guidance on what we as trade economists can and should be doing to promote better policy outcomes. Indeed, some would read the literature as suggesting that nothing can be done. In my comments I shall mostly agree with Deardorff-Stern, except perhaps in their assessment of where the literature should go from here.

Let me begin by restating some of the Deardorff-Stern criticisms of the political economy literature as seen from my own perspective. I will do this by listing the "ingredients" I would hope to find in a model (or empirical analysis) of the choice of trade policy and the "pudding" I would expect it to deliver.

My basic criticism has to do with the mode of modeling that has become commonplace in the trade policy literature. It seems to me that the discipline we have chosen to impose upon ourselves when engaging in economic modeling has not been applied consistently when it comes to political economy. In traditional economics, when we model the interaction between agents that takes place in a market environment, we do so by first specifying our assumptions about how people behave, what informational and other constraints they face, and what rules guide their interactions. Then we derive some predictions about equilibrium outcomes. Finally, perhaps, we evaluate the normative properties of those outcomes.

In principle, "political economy" modeling ought to proceed in exactly the same manner. Politics, like economics, is about interactions between self-interested citizens, although it focuses on interactions that take place in a different (non-market) realm and subject to different sets of rules. The constitution and political system define the rules of interaction, and agents act to further their objectives given the constraints they face. Yet, most authors of political economy models of trade policy have felt at liberty to take shortcuts. All too often, the players, their objectives, and the constraints under which they operate are never made explicit.

Consider first the players. In all countries, trade policies are set and administered by career politicians and bureaucrats. The first thing that a model of political economy ought to tell us is who are these individuals, and what are their motivations. For example, do lawmakers seek only re-election when setting the nation's laws? Do they seek popularity so that they might run for higher office? Do they seek personal income and leisure? Do they pursue an ideological agenda? Simply enjoy doing good? We cannot hope to be able to predict what trade policies will be set by the elected representatives unless we have some notion of what they are trying to achieve when contemplating their choices.

Yet many political economy models paint the lawmakers with only the broadest brush. No one would tolerate an economic model in which a firm was treated as maximizing an "economic power function" or as applying a "price formation function." Why should we be willing to accept less when it comes to the modeling of legislators and parties than we do in our modeling of consumers and firms?

Moreover, the bureaucrats who administer trade policies have yet to make even a cameo appearance in the political economy literature. Who are these individuals and what do they seek to accomplish when they interpret the laws? Do they seek to ingratiate themselves with the legislators? Avoid conflict with their superiors? Further the public interest? Without knowing which of these is the case, we cannot hope to give good advice about what reforms of the antidumping statutes would be beneficial, or what changes in the rules for government procurement.

We also need to know who are the players that interact with the politicians to shape trade policy. Of course members of the "general public" play a role as voters, but most of us believe that other actors are important in the choice of trade policies besides the multitude of atomistic voters. In particular, trade policy seems to be influenced by the actions of "special" interests. But what are these interests?

Deardorff-Stern do a good job of listing the constituent interests in trade policy, and in pointing out that few of these have been introduced into political economy models of policy formation. In my view, we have made almost no progress since Mancur Olson's seminal book in understanding which groups will be organized and represented in the policy process, and which will be mobilized on particular issues. To take just one example, how could we have hoped to predict the outcome of the NAFTA negotiation without knowing that the environmental movement would become a key player in this policy debate? Which trade issues of the future will environmental interests focus upon? When will consumer groups or the media play a role? And when will producer interests be divided for representation along industry lines as opposed to factoral lines? These are critical questions for understanding trade policy that have received far too little attention up to now.

Next, we need to identify the instruments of political interaction. How do the interest groups interact with the politicians? It is not enough to say that they engage in "lobbying" or that they "exert pressure" on the government. Do they pay tributes or bribes? If so, to whom, and with what constraints? Do they provide information to politicians? Provide services to the politicians? Get out the vote? Traditional economic models are very clear about the tools of interaction: prices, quantities, capital investment, R&D, advertising, etc. In contrast, political economy modelers have been all-too vague about what the interest groups can do.

Finally, informational constraints seem especially important in political settings. Of course, information is important in traditional economics, but at least there we can argue that consumers and producers have some incentive to collect the information they need to make judicious decision. Since each voter knows that her own single vote hardly ever will be decisive in an election, she has virtually no reason to become informed about the issues.

The lack of perfect information is all too apparent in American trade politics. A majority of Americans do not know the name of their Congressperson. More than 90% are unaware that the United States restricts its imports of cheese by means of a quota. And even fewer are aware, I would suspect, that a voluntary restraint agreement tends to raise the price of import-competing goods. In view of these circumstances it seems important to model what information the voters do have, who has incentive to provide them with information, and how the informational asymmetries may vary in different policy settings. Yet the political economy literature on trade policy has paid almost no attention to informational issues to date.

What should we expect of the work on political economy? Deardorff-Stern covered much of this ground, but let me review.

First, political economy models should tell us which policy instruments will politicians use to achieve their objectives, and why would they use (inefficient) trade policy tools at all.

Second, they should be able to explain the time path of protection: why do protectionist pressures rise at some times and fall in others? Why has there been such a strong trend toward liberalization in the post-war years? Why have so many less developed countries undertaken "reforms" of late, after several decades of import substitution and pervasive distortions?

Third, the theory should be able to explain the pattern of protection. That is, why are certain special interests successful where others are not? And why are some more successful than others? This is one of the questions that Elhanan Helpman and I have tried to address in our work. But I am not sure that we have the right answers. Or, at least, I am reasonably sure that our model omits important considerations, because some of our answers seem to be at odds with the evidence. The question of which special interests will succeed and which fail has been asked too few times in the literature.

A related point is that political economy models should be able to explain why it is that import-competing interests have been, on the whole, more successful in the trade policy game than export interests. And they should be able to explain why declining industries are generally more successful, at least for a while, than expanding ones.

On the whole, the theoretical literature falls short on most of these dimensions. What the literature offers so far mostly is stories about why we may see departures from laissez faire (i.e., partial triumphs of the special over the general interest). There is very little on what form these departures will take, in which industries and time periods they will occur, and—most importantly—under which institutional rules of the game.

I should say, parenthetically, that the empirical literature has, in my opinion, delivered even less. Most of the empirical studies pay far too little attention to endogeneity (what is the cause and what is the effect), to spurious correlation (what is the structural variable and what is merely correlated with it) and to distinguishing cleanly between competing hypothesis. What we have instead is lists of partial correlates with industry protection, many of which are almost impossible to interpret because they are measured holding constant an arbitrary list of covariates.

So where should we go from here? Deardorff-Stern counsel a "middle ground" between normative theory and political economy. They see the "transactions cost" approach as offering just such a middle ground. But I am not really sure I understand what they mean. How could an analyst interested in the choices and consequences of trade policy take an approach that is different from the political economy approach? What disciplines does the transactions cost approach place on the modeler? How does one go about building a transaction cost model of trade policy? Would it look any different from a political economy model?

In my mind (and I believe Avinash Dixit would agree with me on this) what we need is simply better political economy models. These models should include the policy makers as explicit actors. They should emphasize informational asymmetries. They should make clear the instruments of political interaction. They should endogenize who are the active players in the political game, which presumably would vary with the type of policy and with the institutional setting.

And what should be the objective of all this? I believe the goal of this type of policy analysis is exactly what Deardorff-Stern mention, but then reject. With a better understanding of the political pressures that give rise to policy in particular instances and settings, we as economists can help to develop better institutions and better rules of the trade-policy game. Deardorff-Stern are pessimistic about the prospects for institutional reform; after all, they say, "constitutions are seldom rewritten". But rules of the game do change: we might see campaign finance reform in the coming years, as well as term limits, campaign spending limits, publicly funded political information etc. We might also hope to see changes in the organization of the bureaucracy, in the procedures for appointment of ITC Commissioners that change their incentives, and so on. At the international level, we might have rules that restrict unilateral actions by governments, rules that impede the progress of regional trade agreements, rules that punish environmental offenses, etc. Only if we understand the political economy of policy setting can we advise on which of these rules will be beneficial to the general interests and which not.

Part II

The Context of U.S. Trade Policies

CHAPTER 3

U.S. Trade Policies: The Role of the Executive Branch

Robert E. Baldwin

Prior to the Reciprocal Trade Agreements Act of 1934, tariff levels were set by Congress under its constitutional power "to regulate commerce with foreign nations." In granting the president authority under this Act to decrease (or increase) import duties up to 50 percent from their 1930 levels as part of foreign trade agreements with other countries, Congress undertook an institutional change that marked a fundamental shift in the trade policymaking process of the United States. Since that date, there has been an uneasy sharing of the responsibility for trade policy between the executive and legislative branches of the federal government.

This paper focuses on the manner in which the differing motivations of the President and the Congress work themselves out in the trade-policy formulation process. Special emphasis is given to the role of the president. The paper begins (Section I) with a brief survey of models of the trade policymaking process that have been formulated by economists and political scientists, with particular attention being given to the behavior of the President versus Congress. Section II then outlines a game-theoretic framework for analyzing the process by which the different actions of these two actors yield a particular trade-policy outcome. Section III describes particular historical incidents that illustrate two key features of the analytical framework, namely, the importance of the President taking a leadership role in proposing trade legislation to Congress and using his various powers to secure acceptance of his key objectives and, secondly, the importance of foreign policy considerations in motivating the trade-policy actions of the President. The last section summarizes some of the conclusions.

I. Trade Policymaking Models of Economists and Political Scientists

Economic Models

In modeling the political economy of trade policy, economists generally do not distinguish between the executive and congressional branches of the federal government. Both branches perform the role of supplying various forms of trade policies to the citizenry, who economists divide into producers and consumers. It is usually assumed that consumers are individually too small and are too numerous to be able to overcome the free-rider problem and thus do not actively lobby the government with regard to trade policy. In contrast, some or all of the producers are assumed to be able to organize into common interest groups and, through the lobbying process, to become demanders of various trade policies. It is also often assumed that production takes place within a specific-factors framework, with capital in each sector being the specific factor. The owners of specific-capital organize and seek to maximize their rents by lobbying the government for favorable trade measures.

In the simplest economic models, elected public officials, the suppliers of particular trade policies, are motivated by a desire to be returned to office (or gain public office, if not already elected) and, consequently, are responsive to the lobbying demands of the various pressure groups. In one of the earliest formal models (termed the tariff-formation function approach by Rodrik (1995) in his recent survey article), Findlay and Wellisz (1982) utilize this framework to depict trade policy being determined endogenously in a two-good, specific-factors economy as the outcome of a lobbying game between an import-competing industry that favors protection and an exporting industry that opposes import protection. With a given level of lobbying activity (labor is the only resource used in lobbying) by one of the sectors, the more resources that are devoted to lobbying by the other sector, the higher the tariff obtained by the protectionist industry or lower the tariff obtained by the free trade industry. However, there are diminishing returns to lobbying in both sectors. For any given level of lobbying by the other industry, there is an optimum amount of lobbying for the other sector. The intersection between the two reaction functions depicting this relationship determines the Cournot-Nash equilibrium tariff level, where each group is devoting the optimum amount of resources to lobbying, given the labor resources used for lobbying by the other group.

A more explicit modeling of the government's motivations is provided in models based on the notion of a political-support function that were developed by Stigler (1971) and Pelzman (1976) to analyze domestic regulatory processes and then adapted to international trade-policy situations by Hillman (1982). Under this approach the government is responsive to lobbying pressures from rent-seeking common interest groups but, in maximizing its political support, is also aware of the antagonism of voters to tariff increases because of the resulting decline in their welfare as consumers. Hence, the government chooses the level of tariffs (and thus domestic prices) that just balances the additional support from industry-specific interests who favor increased tariffs against the additional political disfavor on the part of consumers caused by increased tariffs.

The most elegant economic modeling of the motivations of the government and special interest groups and of the manner in which these two sets of political actors interact has been done by Grossman and Helpman (1994). The government maximizes a function that is a weighted sum of the contributions from lobbying groups who are the owners of the sector-specific capital (contributions are valued because they can be used to finance campaign spending) and the aggregate welfare of the country's citizens, which equals aggregate income plus trade tax revenue plus total consumer surplus (this figure is valued because the government cares about aggregate well-being). Lobbying groups offer a schedule of contributions to elected officials that is contingent upon the trade policies (tariffs or export taxes and subsidies) implemented by the government. The objective of each lobbying group is to maximize its welfare net of political contributions.

In the game between the government and lobbyists, the latter move first by offering a schedule of contributions related to trade-policy actions of the government, and the government then selects those contributions and associated trade policies that maximize its objective function. The equilibrium set of contributions is one which maximizes the joint welfare of each lobby's members, given the contributions of the other lobbies and the anticipated decision rule of the government, and also the government's welfare function. One implication of the first-mover role of lobbyists is that, if there is only one lobbyist or if the lobbyists are so concentrated that they account for a negligible fraction of the total voting population, the single lobbyist or group of lobbyists capture all of the surplus from their own political contributions. In other words, the lobbyist for an industry provides the government with just enough funds so that the government is indifferent between providing the trade policy sought by the sector and instituting free trade for the sector.

Models of Political Scientists

Many political scientists also do not make a distinction between the role of the executive and congressional branches of government in analyzing international economic behavior. The state is treated as a rational unitary actor primarily interested in increasing the political and economic power of the nation-state relative to other countries (see, for example, Krasner,1976).

One well-known model that illustrates this approach is the so-called theory of hegemonic stability. First proposed by an economist (Kindleberger, 1981) and popularized by political scientists, e.g., Gilpin (1987), this theory maintains that the existence of a hegemonic power is a necessary condition for a liberal international trading and financial system. The hegemon is so large that it gains from providing the collective benefits associated with free trade and stable exchange rates even with free-riding in the form of protection and undervalued exchange rates by smaller states. The model predicts that in the absence of a dominant power such as Great Britain in the nineteenth century or the United States in the twentieth century protectionism and beggar-thy-neighbor exchange-rate policies will prevail in the world economy.

Various criticisms have been made by a number of political scientists of this simple version of the theory. For example, it has been pointed out that repeated game theory and the theory of collective action both indicate that cooperation among countries is quite possible in the absence of a hegemon and that the international institutions created during hegemonic periods can serve as facilitators of cooperation in post-hegemonic periods. The criticism most relevant to the contents of this paper is that the theory of hegemonic stability and other models that view the state as a single actor treat domestic political processes involving political parties, industry interest groups and the two branches of the federal government as a black box. This deficiency can lead to incomplete and misleading explanations of international economic policies.

Although political scientists who are concerned with understanding broad international political and economic behavior by governments often do not distinguish between the executive and congressional branches of government, those who attempt to explain how trade policies are determined do generally distinguish between these two institutions. Two distinct theories have emerged from these trade policy studies of political scientists: one emphasizes the dominance of the President in the policymaking process, while the other stresses the importance of Congress in setting trade policy.

The classic work on documenting the role of Congress in setting trade policy is Schattschneider's (1935) analysis of logrolling during the legislative process that produced the Tariff Act of 1930. In contrast, the study of U.S. trade politics after the Reciprocal Trade Agreements Act of 1934 by Destler (1986) emphasizes the role of the President in shaping trade policies. According to Destler, Congress realized that setting tariffs on individual products invariably resulted in levels of protectionism that were economically harmful to the country and therefore deliberately delegated part of its constitutional authority to regulate foreign commerce to the Executive branch in order to insulate its members from protectionist pressures (also see Pastor, 1980). David Lake (1988) also stresses the importance of the President's role in the formulation of trade policy. In Lake's framework, foreign policy-oriented presidents are mainly concerned with promoting the power and wealth of the state. However, they cannot act unilaterally but must bargain with politically mobilized interest groups within society both directly and through the legislature.

Lohmann and O'Halloran (1994) [also see O'Halloran (1994)] propose a framework with elements of both the presidential and congressional dominance hypotheses. They argue that Congress delegates trade policymaking to the President in order to implement more efficient trade policy outcomes. "However, under divided government, the majority party in Congress may be better off constraining the President's use of delegated authority, thereby forcing the President partially to accommodate congressional demands for more protection." (p. 627).

II. The Trade Policymaking Roles of the President and the Congress: A Framework for Analysis

It is clear that in recent years the President and Congress have each played important roles in shaping U.S. trade policy and, thus, that any model of the policymaking process must take account of the influence of both the executive and legislative branches of the federal government. Three different aspects of the trade policymaking process in which the President participates are: (1) enacting new trade legislation, such as legislation authorizing a new round of trade negotiations or approving the results of such a negotiation; (2) negotiating with other governments or international institutions with regard to the extent of liberalization in a multilateral or regional trade agreement and the settling of current bilateral trade disputes; and (3) administering the various trade laws passed by Congress, e.g., Section 301 of the 1974 Trade Act and the safeguards, antidumping, countervailing-duty provisions of U. S. trade laws.

As noted by many observers, modern Presidents tend to favor increased trade liberalization, especially once the reductions in import barriers involved in previous protection-reducing negotiations have been completed.[1] Representing a much broader constituency than individual members of Congress, Presidents give greater weight in their trade policy decisions to the general standard-of-living benefits of trade liberalization than Representatives or Senators and less weight to the concerns of particular industry groups. Furthermore, as stressed by Lake (1988) and discussed in further detail in Section III, because of their special foreign policy responsibilities under the Constitution, Presidents are more concerned with the foreign policy implications of trade-policy actions than members of Congress.

In contrast, Congress tends to favor legislative changes that make it easier for domestic industries to obtain import protection or to gain greater access to foreign markets. Individual members are less influenced than the President by the national welfare or foreign policy implications of trade policies, since their constituents do not generally associate these broad concerns with any particular member of Congress. However, they are sensitive to particular industry groups who are affected economically in a favorable or unfavorable manner by changes in international trading conditions and who can significantly influence the election prospects of a member of Congress by bloc-voting and the funding of political ads.

Congress no longer, as in the pre-1934 period, seeks protection through legislative initiatives aimed at raising import duties on broad groups of products.[2] The strong economic position of the United States that emerged after World War II undermined the traditional economic ideology that high import barriers were needed to protect the U.S. standard of living, and members of Congress are now not under significant political pressure to press for general protectionism. As authors such as Lohmann and O'Halloran (1994) point out, this does not mean that Congress now has little more than veto power over presidential legislative initiatives. Congress has long provided producers who are injured by increased imports with the means of gaining import relief through the safeguards, antidumping (AD), countervailing-duty (CVD) and other "fair trade" laws. In recent years, it has asserted its protectionist predilections by increasing significantly the degree of contingent protection, especially through the AD and CVD laws. In addition, with Section 301 of the

1974 Trade Act and Super 301 under the 1988 Trade and Competitiveness Act, Congress established a mechanism administered by the Executive branch by which industries can seek greater access to foreign markets. Members of Congress have also attempted to influence trade policy in a more protectionist manner by exercising oversight authority more extensively through the confirmation and monitoring processes related to agencies of the Executive Branch dealing with trade policy.

Just as Congress no longer tries to set duties over a broad set of commodities, the President generally does not seek to liberalize trade by reducing the degree of administered protection or modifying such administered market-opening provisions as Section 301 of the 1974 Trade Act. Congress seems to have successfully made the point to Presidents that changes in these policies should be left to the legislative branch.

Given these roles of the President and Congress, the determination of the extent of trade liberalizing power granted the President under legislation authorizing a new round of multilateral trade negotiations or a new regional agreement and the changes in administered protection and administered market-opening laws embodied in this legislation can usefully be modeled as a bargaining game between the President and Congress. Not only does this framework provide insights into the process by which the two branches of government reconcile their conflicting goals, but it can be used to demonstrate the significance of whether the President or Congress takes the lead in shaping trade policy legislation.

In the following analysis, it is assumed that the President requests authority from Congress to negotiate a free trade agreement that can vary in its degree of trade liberalization by its product coverage and speed of implementation. The proposals by Congress involve such actions as easing the requirements for obtaining import relief under the safeguard, AD and CVD provisions of U.S. law and modifying the labor-standard and rules-of-origin provisions of existing free trade agreements.

The economic model developed by Grossman and Helpman (1994, 1995) to study endogenous protection and the politics of free trade areas is utilized in analyzing the behavior of the President and Congress. Thus, the United States and the countries being considered for the free trade agreement are assumed to face exogenously given world prices. Individuals in the United States have identical preferences, with each individual maximizing utility given by $u(c) = c_0 + E_{i=1..n} u_i(c_i)$, where c_i denotes the consumption of good i and $u_i(A)$ is an increasing and concave function. The world and domestic prices for good 0, which serves as a numeraire, equal 1. It is produced only with labor under constant returns to scale and with an input-output coefficient equal to 1. Thus, the wage equals 1 in a competitive equilibrium. Every other good is produced under constant returns to scale using labor and a sector-specific factor. Consequently, the rewards to the specific factor in sector i are $A_i(p_i)$, where p_i is the domestic producer price. Each individual receives a surplus of $S_i(q_i)$ / $u_i[D_i(q_i)]-q_iD_i(q_i)$ from consuming good i, i = 1, ...n, where q_i is the domestic consumer price for good i. The difference between the domestic consumer price and the producer price for an imported good is the import duty.

Both the President and Congress each maximize their respective social welfare functions, which include the income of labor, the rents earned by the specific factors, tariff revenues (which are redistributed to individuals), and total consumer surplus. However, Congress gives greater weight to the income received by the sector-specific factors than the President, especially those in import-competing sectors, whereas the President gives greater weight to consumer surplus and the income of labor than Congress. Furthermore, the President's welfare function includes the rents earned by the owners of sector-specific capital in the export sectors of the free trade partner. The President reasons that the gains to specific factors in the partner country's export sectors due to increased interregional trade in response to elimination of tariffs between the two countries act, in conjunction with the gains to U.S. exporters, to improve political and security relations between the United States and the partner country.

The welfare functions of the President and Congress are also assumed to reflect a short-run concern for preserving the status quo distribution of incomes. This means that increases in real income are given relatively less welfare weight than decreases in income.[3] Thus, the reductions in rents to the owners of the sector-specific capital in import-competing sectors as a consequence of trade liberalization are given greater weight than increases in rents obtained by capital-owners in export sectors.[4]

As Grossman and Helpman (1995) explain, the welfare effects of the free trade proposal can be indicated by considering a product that is imported by both the United States and its prospective free trade partner and on which the foreign country levies a higher import duty than the United States. (In cases where the U.S. import tariff is higher, the impact on the United States will be the same as the impact on the foreign country in the case to be considered.) Because of the small country assumption, the two countries can purchase unlimited amounts of the good from the rest of the world at the fixed world price plus their respective import duties. The formation of the free trade area causes the import duties to fall to zero for the two partners but remain the same for the rest of the world.

Consider the case where the endowment of the specific factor employed in the U.S. industry is relatively small so that the *total* U.S. supply curve for the product does not suffice to satisfy the foreign country's import demand at its pre-free trade, higher import price. Consequently, the foreign country must continue to import the good from the rest of the world after the free trade area is formed. However, producers in the United States will export all of their supply to the foreign country to take advantage of the higher price, and U.S. consumers will satisfy all of their demands by importing the good from the rest of the world. The U.S. specific factor used in producing the good gains due to the higher price it receives, while the rents earned by the foreign specific remain unchanged. Consumers in both countries continue to pay the same price as initially but tariff revenue falls in the foreign country and increases in the United States. Grossman and Helpman (1995) term this case one of *enhanced protection*, since the U.S. specific factor gains from the trade diversion.

The other extreme case is where the total U.S. supply curve of the good is sufficiently large to satisfy the foreign country's import demand at the lower U.S. domestic price. Producers in the foreign country lose due to the lower price but consumers in the foreign country gain. Tariff revenues also decline in the foreign country. Producers in the United States continue to receive the same price and U.S. consumers pay the same price. Grossman and Helpman (1995) describe this situation as one of *reduced protection*, since rents to foreign producers decrease.

In the intermediate case, the total supply curve of the United States is sufficient to reduce the price in the foreign country below its initial level but not large enough to reduce it to the initial U.S. price. Producers in the United States gain and those in the partner country lose. Aggregate welfare rises for the United States and may either increase or decrease in the foreign country when the changes in tariff revenue and consumer surplus are taken into account.

Assuming that, on balance, a free trade agreement with the foreign country increases social welfare as calculated by the President, figure 3.1 depicts changes in the various components of the President's social welfare as the extent of liberalization within the free trade agreement increases due to wider product coverage and a shorter time schedule for full implementation, holding U.S. contingent protection measures at their initial level. The curve Op indicates the losses in social welfare due to the reductions in rents to the sector-specific factors employed in domestic import-competing sectors, while the curve Oc shows the net gains to U.S. consumers combined with the gains in rents to specific factors in U.S. export sectors. The curve Of depicts the combined consumer and exporter gains plus the foreign policy benefits of the reciprocal duty cuts that are associated with gains to specific factors in the foreign country's export sectors. The maximum increase in net social welfare for the President, given the initial level of contingent protection, is achieved with the degree of liberalization indicated by OL.

An increase in U.S. contingent protection reduces the returns earned by specific factors employed in the partner-country's export sectors by withdrawing zero-duty treatment for some U.S. imports and also increases the degree of uncertainty of export earnings in general. This has the effect of reducing the benefits from the foreign policy component in the President's social welfare function and is shown in figure 3.1 by drawing Of′ below Of as contingent protection increases. Moreover, it is assumed that the increment in the foreign policy component of social welfare that is associated with a given increase in trade liberalization decreases as the level of contingent protection rises, thus tending to reduce the welfare-maximizing level of liberalization. The welfare of domestic consumers also declines as the level of contingent

Figure 3.1
President's Social Welfare Function

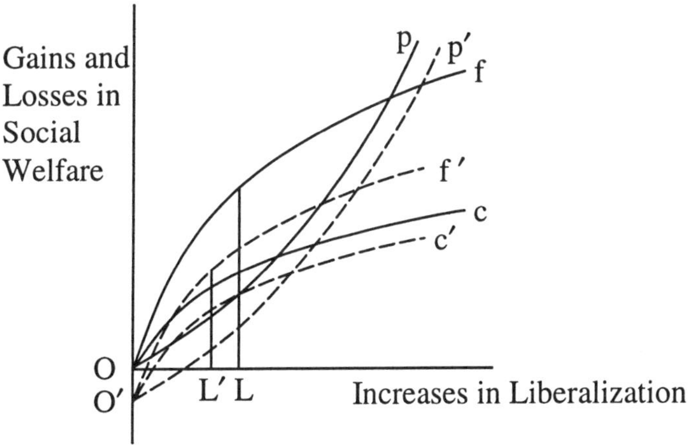

Figure 3.2
Congress's Social Welfare Function

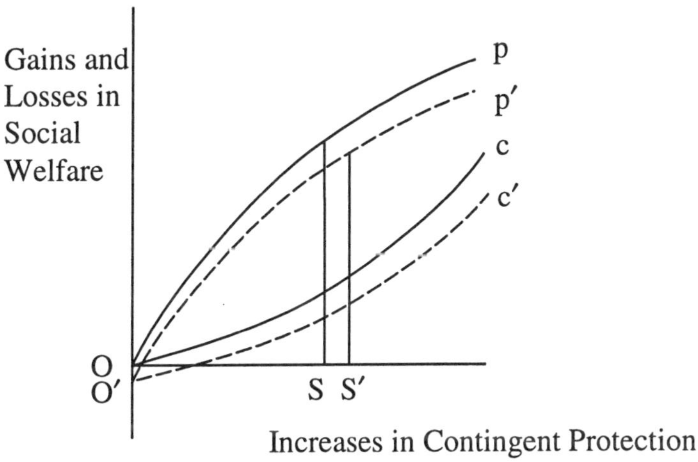

protection rises. In contrast, the welfare losses to domestic capital owners in import-competing sectors from liberalization decrease as the level of contingent protection rises, thereby shifting the curve Op in figure 3.1 down to Op′. While various plausible net effects on the President's social welfare can be postulated, it is assumed here that negative foreign policy and consumer effects outweigh the positive domestic producer effects so that social welfare for the President declines as contingent protection increases, given any degree trade liberalization. In addition, the optimum degree of liberalization by the President decreases as contingent protection rises.

Members of Congress are assumed to weigh losses to import-competing producers from trade liberalization more heavily than gains to exporters and consumers because they are more vulnerable politically to the lobbying pressures of producer groups than the President. Figure 3.2 depicts how the two components of Congress's social welfare function change as the degree of contingent protection increases, given a particular level of trade liberalization under a free trade agreement. The curve Op indicates the increase in social welfare for members of Congress as the degree of contingent protection rises and actual and expected rents accruing to import-competing U.S. specific factors rise, while the curve Oc reflects the reductions in Congress's social welfare due to the decrease in consumer surplus associated with increased contingent protection as well as the losses to exporters as the likelihood of retaliatory actions by the foreign country rises. The distance OS indicates the increase in contingent protection that maximizes Congress's social welfare function, given a particular level of trade liberalization under the free trade agreement.

Increases in the degree of trade liberalization under the free trade agreement reduce the component of Congress's social welfare based on the rents earned by U.S. import-competing specific factors and increase the component associated with welfare of consumers and exporters' component, given a particular level of contingent protection. The curves Op′ and Oc′ in figure 3.2 indicate these changes. It is assumed that the losses to import-competing producers more than offset the gains to consumers and exporters so that social welfare for Congress falls as trade liberalization increases, holding contingent protection constant. Since it seems plausible that a given increase in contingent protection is valued more highly by import-competing producers the greater the extent of trade liberalization, the optimum increase in contingent protection for Congress is assumed to increase as the extent of trade liberalization rises. This is shown in figure 3.2 by making the new optimum contingent protection level, OS′, greater than OS.

With these relationships, the reaction curve of the President, PP, which indicates the President's optimal level of trade liberalization within the free trade agreement for different levels of increases in contingent protection, can be drawn as shown in figure 3.3. Similarly, the Congress's reaction curve, depicting its optimal increase in contingent protection for different levels of trade liberalization, is drawn as CC in figure 3.3. The point ov on the horizontal axis indicates the maximum level of increase in contingent protection that the President will accept without vetoing the implementing legislation. In contrast, any trade liberalization proposed by the President that exceeds oj will be rejected out-of-hand by Congress. The Nash equilibrium, N, indicates the combination of trade liberalization and increase in contingent protection at which the President and Congress are each choosing the optimal level of trade liberalization and rise in contingent protection, given the policy variable selected by the other.[5]

Equal social welfare contours for the President and Congress are represented by curves such as pp and cc, respectively. Moving to the southeast along the PP line represents less social welfare for the President, while moving to the northeast along the CC line indicate less social welfare for Congress. As is obvious from the shapes of the various curves, the President and Congress can each raise their social welfare compared to the Nash equilibrium if they have the first-mover advantage. The optimum tariff-cutting proposal for the President if he can move first in the bargaining game is to offer the degree of reciprocal tariff liberalization indicated by the point P_s. Congress will respond by accepting the proposed liberalization but adding the increase in contingent protection indicated at P_s. In contrast, C_s is the equilibrium point if Congress has the first-mover advantage. As the reaction lines are drawn, with a first-mover advantage Congress achieves both less liberalization and greater contingent protection than under the Nash equilibrium, whereas the President settles for less contingent protection but also less liberalization.

At the President's optimum first-mover point, P_s, not only is the President's level of welfare greater than at the Nash equilibrium, but Congress's welfare is also higher than at the Nash equilibrium. Furthermore, although not a necessary outcome, the welfare level attained by Congress in figure 3.3 at the President's optimum first-mover point is even higher than its own optimum first-mover point, C_s. These relationships add further support to the position of those who emphasize the self-interest motivation of Congress in allowing the President to move first in proposing the degree of trade liberalization.[6] There are also tangent points between the two sets of equal social welfare contours that are southwest of P_s and to the left of the line CC at which both the President and the Congress would reach higher social welfare levels than at P_s. Given the repeated nature of the bargaining process between the President and Congress, a cooperative equilibrium that is enforced with appropriate threat strategies is possible in this area.

III. The Leadership and Foreign Policy Roles of the President in Trade Policymaking: Selected Historical Examples

Presidential Leadership

The role of the President in the trade policymaking process prior to the enactment of the Reciprocal Trade Agreements Act of 1934 is well illustrated by President Harding's response to the sharp fall in agricultural prices in 1921.

Figure 3.3

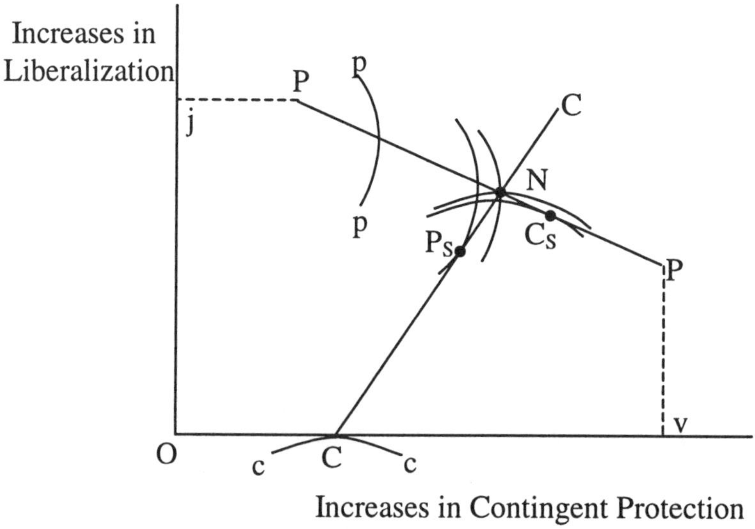

He sent a message to Congress urging a prompt increase in tariffs on agricultural products. In contrast, since the passage of the Reciprocal Trade Agreements Act, it has been the President who has taken the lead in setting tariff rates or asking Congress for more authority to alter these rates. From 1934 to 1962, Congress restrained the tariff-cutting powers of the President by extending this authority for only short periods at a time, usually three years. However, it was the President who would initiate the proposal for extending the time period or for new duty-cutting authority and thus set the terms of the debate in Congress. Moreover, having a proposal come from the President rather than originate in the Congress makes it more difficult for congressional members in the President's own party to vote against the proposal.

The Eisenhower years provide a good example of the extent to which trade policy can be influenced by a President who can initiate trade legislation.[7] With the election of a Republican President and Republican Congress in 1952, it was the expectation of many Republicans in Congress that the reciprocal trade agreements program would be eliminated or significantly curtailed, especially with Representative Reed, a longtime protectionist, becoming the Chair of the House Ways and Means Committee. Initially, neither President Eisenhower nor Secretary of State Dulles took a firm stand on trade policy and did not immediately propose renewal of the expiring trade agreements program. As a consequence, a protectionist bill was taken under consideration by the Ways and Means Committee, which, among other provisions, considerably eased the requirements for gaining escape-clause relief and eliminated presidential discretion in escape-clause cases and in peril point determinations. President Eisenhower responded by requesting a one-year extension without any modifications so that a commission could undertake a complete review of U.S. foreign economic policy. Despite widespread sentiment among Republicans for a protectionist bill, Republican members of Congress apparently were unwilling to reject this seemingly modest and reasonable request of their new popular President, and a one year extension with only mildly protectionist features was passed.

The Randall Commission Report essentially supported the existing trade agreements program and recommended extension for 3 years with the President being given an addition 15 percent tariff-cutting authority. It was also recommended that the existing escape clause and peril point procedures be retained. President Eisenhower accepted these recommendations and proposed them to Congress in 1954. However, Representative Reed and his protectionist colleagues rejected a three-year renewal and refused to hold hearings on the bill. The result was again a stalemate and another one-year renewal of the existing legislation. The President proposed the same three-year extension with an additional 15 percent duty-cutting authority in 1955. However, as a result of the 1954 congressional elections, the Republicans lost control of both the House and Senate. Consequently, the hard-core protectionist Republicans in the House did not have the same power as in the previous two years and President Eisenhower was able to obtain a three-year renewal from the Democrat Congress, but with an easing of the requirements for obtaining escape-clause relief and a provision permitting protection of industries essential for national defense purposes, essentially the oil industry.

Another renewal was obtained in 1958, this time for 5 years with an additional 25 percent duty-cutting authority. The 1958 renewal effort was more successful than earlier ones, in part because the Administration took a more activist position in lining up bipartisan congressional and public support for the extension. The Cold War argument was also pushed more vigorously. However, a provision was included enabling Congress to override by a two-thirds vote presidential rejections of favorable escape-clause decisions. Thus, what we seem to learn in the Eisenhower years is that a President who is prepared to exert political pressures on Congress can obtain legislation that provides at least modest trade liberalization, although at a cost of permitting Congress to tighten the laws dealing with contingent protection.

Arguably the most successful post-World War II President in achieving his trade-policy objectives was President Kennedy.[8] Rather than simply asking for an extension of the Reciprocal Trade Agreements Act, President Kennedy proposed a new tariff-cutting approach in which tariffs would be uniformly reduced by 50 percent, with a bare minimum of exceptions. The main argument for this tariff-cutting authority was that the formation of the European Community (EC) was causing European members to increase imports from each other at the expense of imports from the United States as tariffs within the EC were being reduced to zero and, therefore, that it was necessary to seek a general reduction in European and U.S. tariffs in order to reduce the margin of preference held by EC members. The merits of linking Europe and the United States more closely economically also had great appeal to President Kennedy and his close advisers for foreign policy reasons. To gain acceptance of this proposal by Congress, the Kennedy Administration conducted an unparalleled campaign to sell its ideas. President Kennedy made the trade bill a key part of his legislative agenda and led the fight for it. In his message to Congress on the proposed bill, he concluded with the following statement: "At rare moments in the life of this nation an opportunity comes along to fashion out of the confusion of current events, a clear bold action to show the world what it is we stand for. Such an opportunity is before us now. This bill, by enabling us to strike a bargain with the Common Market will 'strike a blow' for freedom."[9]

Not only did President Kennedy use the powers of his office to rally support for the bill, but he made key concessions to protectionist interests in order to reduce opposition to the proposal. In particular, a voluntary quota system was established for cotton textile imports in 1961 and a formal international marketing agreement for cotton textiles was negotiated in 1962. This agreement permitted the use of quotas to prevent "market disruption." President Kennedy also assured the oil industry that oil quotas would be continued and included a national security provision in the new trade bill. Other steps taken to reduce opposition to the proposal were the inclusion in the bill of a provision establishing a special trade adjustment assistance program for workers injured by increased import competition that extended the period workers would receive unemployment compensation, the announcement of a special program to assist the Northwest lumber industry, and the acceptance of the Tariff Commission's recommendation to raise tariffs on carpets and glass under the escape clause provision. With this combination of presidential lobbying and concessions to potential opponents plus a Democrat House and Senate, the Trade Expansion Act passed with surprising ease and led to significant multilateral tariff reductions in the Kennedy Round of GATT negotiations.

In contrast to President Kennedy, President Nixon was not very successful in using his leadership position to further his trade policy goals. President Nixon failed to take full advantage of his first-mover role, perhaps because of his increasing preoccupation with the Watergate affair, and Congress essentially "took charge" of writing the Trade Act of 1974.[10] The consequence was a weakening in the President's power in formulating trade policies. This shift in trade policymaking power back to Congress persists to the present time. Perhaps the most important restraint imposed on the President under the 1974 Act is the so-called "fast track" requirement for trade agreements covering nontariff trade barriers and distortions. The 1974 Act as well as subsequent laws authorizing negotiations on nontariff trade matters require that the negotiated agreements be approved by both branches of Congress before becoming legal obligations of the United States. The agreements must, however, be voted on an up or down basis by Congress without the possibility of amendments and within a given time period. The Act also established an elaborate consultative procedure between the trade negotiators and both Congress and various private interest groups during the negotiations and further stipulated that members of Congress (ten) be official advisers to the U.S. delegation conducting the negotiations.

Prior to the 1974 Trade Act, the multilateral trade agreements negotiated under GATT (which dealt with tariff reductions) did not require congressional approval before becoming legally binding. However, Congress specified that certain products be excluded from duty cuts, limited the extent to which duty levels could be reduced on others products, and required that significant cuts be introduced gradually. In authorizing negotiations not just on tariffs but also on nontariff trade barriers in the 1974 Trade Act, Congress decided to continue the traditional implementing procedures with respect to tariffs but to require congressional approval of any agreements reached on nontariff matters. The Nixon Administration asked for negotiating powers on nontariff issues broadly similar to those on tariffs, but the request was rejected.

One consequence of the new implementing procedures is that members of Congress and various special interest groups have become involved in the negotiations at a micro-management level. Under the threat of the rejection of the agreement by Congress, administration officials have sometimes been pressured into negotiating detailed provisions that favor a particular interest groups at the welfare cost of the general public. This has occurred, for example, in negotiations on antidumping and other unfair trade issues. The implementing legislation also often includes numerous details that are not needed to implement the negotiated agreement but that are aimed at favoring a few special interest groups. Of course, the requirement that negotiated agreements submitted to Congress be voted up or down with no amendments is preferable to a procedure whereby the many details of the agreement could be modified through the usual amendment process of Congress. But Congress could have put in place a procedure for nontariff trade negotiations that more closely followed the procedure for tariff negotiations. For example, to satisfy congressional concerns about granting the President too much power on trade matters, the law authorizing such negotiations could have contained provisions limiting the type or extent of permissible U.S. nontariff concessions or even requiring congressional approval for certain major changes. Multilateral negotiations would still be feasible under such provisions, while political pressures from rent-seeking special interest groups would be less than under the current implementing procedures.

The approval of the North America Free Trade Agreement (NAFTA) in the fall of 1993 illustrates both the difficulties a President faces by failing to intervene early in the legislative process and the great influence that a President has when he finally does become closely involved in the legislative process. In the election campaign of 1992, President Clinton initially did not pay much attention to NAFTA, which had been negotiated and signed under the

Bush's Administration, but still required congressional "fast track" approval. Although he had supported the agreement prior to becoming a serious presidential candidate, he apparently was concerned about losing the support of organized labor and environmental groups (Grayson, 1995, chapter 5). However, he eventually came out in favor of the agreement, but with the proviso that side agreements on environmental and labor-standard issues should be negotiated.

President Clinton also did not devote much attention to NAFTA in the early months of his Administration and, in particular, did not indicate his strong support for the agreement or intervene personally to line up congressional support. Such issues as health care and an economic stimulus package were considered more important, and it was the view of some in the Administration that pushing NAFTA too vigorously would jeopardize the legislation proposed on these other issues. Republicans in Congress supported the measure but did not believe it was politically appropriate to take the lead on NAFTA. It was not until late August of 1993, when William Daley was appointed special counselor to the President for NAFTA, that a concerted effort was organized by the White House to attempt to obtain the necessary congressional support for passage of legislation approving the agreement. However, by this time, opponents of the accord, mainly organized labor and various environmental groups, were well-organized and had been conducting an extensive campaign against its approval. In the early fall of 1993, polls of members of Congress concerning their likely voting patterns on the legislation indicated that the agreement would be rejected.

In an effort to reverse this likely outcome, the Clinton Administration—with the President's active participation – initiated a very active lobbying effort that included a special White House event in which ex-Presidents Bush, Ford, and Carter spoke in favor of the agreement and in which President Clinton made a very strong supporting statement, a television debate on NAFTA by Vice-President Gore and Ross Perot, visits to members of Congress and various private organizations by cabinet and sub-cabinet members of the Administration, and personal discussions by the President with undecided members of Congress. The President even criticized organized labor for its threats to members of Congress who supported the legislation. However, while these actions were undoubtedly helpful in increasing congressional support for the agreement, a major reason the President obtained enough congressional support to enact the legislation appears to be his willingness to strike political deals with individual members of Congress. Some involved promises to prevent NAFTA from causing injury to particular industries, e.g., the citrus and tomato industries in Florida and the flat glass, wine, and peanut industries in various states, but a number were unrelated to the agreement. These included construction of two C-17 military cargo planes, awarding American Airlines two international air routes to London, abandonment of plans to raise grazing fees on federal lands, and the reversal of an earlier decision to cut helium subsidies.[11]

As Grayson (1995) concludes, the failure of President Clinton to signal clearly in the early part of his Administration his strong support for NAFTA and his willingness to go all out to obtain congressional approval very likely enabled those who disapproved of the agreement to build a strong base of opposition that required extensive lobbying and deal-making by the President to overcome. But, the NAFTA episode also demonstrates the considerable power of a President to influence policy even when he does not become deeply involved in the decisionmaking process until its later stages.

Foreign Policy and Trade Policy

All Presidents since Franklin Roosevelt have supported trade liberalization, although they have varied considerably in their degree of commitment to this goal. Just why Presidents of both parties have adopted this position has not received much attention by economists. In particular, why have most Presidents taken the lead in proposing new trade-liberalizing negotiations with other countries? One might conclude that the broad base from which they are elected enables Presidents to gain political support by stressing the real income gains to the typical voter that are associated with the more efficient allocation of resources produced by reciprocal reductions in import protection. However, this argument is seldom used in presidential statements supporting trade liberalization, probably because of the very small effect of the typical trade agreement on the real income of the typical consumer. The economic arguments used by Presidents mainly stress the new jobs and more rapid growth associated with expanding export markets, coupled with assurances that jobs in import-competing sectors will still be protected. However, it is difficult to see that Presidents gain net additional political support from these argument. There do not appear to be any significant political constituencies lobbying for new export jobs, whereas there are well-organized political groups very much concerned about the loss of domestic jobs due to the increased imports resulting from reductions in tariffs and other nontariff barriers. Presidential claims that there will be a net increase in jobs seem to be directed more at deflecting the arguments of those concerned about job losses rather than aimed at actually gaining additional political support. Economists have also long pointed out that there is no reason for believing that trade liberalization will increase the net number of jobs.

While undoubtedly motivated by the standard-of-living gains to the nation from trade liberalization, it also appears that Presidents seek new trade liberalizing negotiations for broad foreign policy reasons. Although few presidential elections are determined on foreign policy grounds, Presidents seem aware that being perceived to be ineffectual as a foreign policy leader can be costly in terms of campaign contributions and votes. They also realize that their performance in the foreign policy area plays an important role in determining their place in history. Given their special foreign policy responsibilities under the Constitution, modern Presidents are expected by the electorate to maintain or enhance the position of the United States as the world's dominant political, military and economic power. Leaders of other nations also expect U.S. Presidents to continue the postwar tradition of taking the lead in trying to maintain harmonious political and economic relations in the politically sensitive parts of the world.

Modern U.S. Presidents have determined that promoting closer economic cooperation among nations by reducing trade barriers on a reciprocal basis is a useful means of meeting these responsibilities and expectations, and they seem willing to risk some net loss in short-run political support in promoting trade liberalization. In the early postwar period the connection between trade policy and foreign policy was drawn quite directly. For example, in his message to Congress in 1945 urging renewal of the trade program with an additional 50% cutting authority, President Roosevelt included the following statement: "If the economic foundations of peace are to be as secure as the political foundations, it is clear this effort must be continued vigorously and effective."[12] Secretary of State Cordell Hull also strongly emphasized this theme. As relations with the Soviet Union deteriorated and the Cold War began, foreign policy considerations became even more important. It was argued that the tariff liberalization helped to strengthen the so-called free nations of the world economically so that they could better resist Communist expansion. Secretary of State John Foster Dulles comments before the Committee on Finance illustrate this theme: "However, the menace is as much from subversion as from open armed attack, and in any event military arrangements are never dependable unless they rest on a foundation of economic health and mutual respect. Our concern for the good health and respect of other free peoples is most of all represented by our trade policies. . . . Thus, our Trade Agreement Act is not a mere piece of technical domestic legislation. It is a symbol of worldwide importance."[13]

Recent Presidents have continued to take the initiative in proposing trade policies designed to further their foreign policy agenda. However, with the end of both the Cold War and U.S. hegemony and the increasing import competition faced by domestic producers, the foreign policy purposes of U.S. trade policy have changed somewhat. An important objective of U.S. trade policy is still to promote worldwide economic stability, but Presidents are more willing to use trade policy to strengthen political and economic ties with particular groups of nations with which the United States has special national security concerns. The negotiation of free trade agreements, first, with Canada and then with Canada and Mexico (NAFTA) illustrate this shift. The Enterprise for Americas Initiative announced by President Bush in 1990, the Free Trade Area of the Americas (FTAA) proposed by President Clinton in 1994, and the more recent discussions on a New Transatlantic Agenda (NTA) are further indications of the change.

The proposals of Presidents Bush and Clinton for a free trade agreement among the countries of North and South American do not seem explainable in terms of the typical pressure-group political economy model utilized by economists to account for import protecting policies. While certain export-oriented industries would clearly benefit from such an agreement, there is little evidence that lobbying pressure from these sectors played a significant role in influencing the two Presidents. President Bush's proposal for a free trade zone from Anchorage to Tierra del Fuego seems to have been developed by a relatively small number of the President's close advisers within the Executive Branch and apparently came as a complete surprise to all outside this small group (Yopo,1993). Similarly, President Clinton's free trade proposal that he announced at the Summit for the Americas conference in December 1994 was the outcome of a broad review of U.S. policy in Latin America within the Executive Branch (speeches by Vice-President Gore, 12/1/93 and Under Secretary of Commerce Jeffrey Garten, 2/1/94).

In both cases, the promotion of U.S. foreign policy goals seemed to be a major purpose of the proposals. For example, in announcing plans for the Summit of the Americas, President Clinton stated that not only would reducing trade barriers create many new jobs but: "At the same time, the rising tide of democracy in this hemisphere helps make us more secure. Democracies tend not to fight one another; they make better partners in trade and diplomacy." (Remarks by President Clinton announcing the Summit of the Americas, March 11, 1994) In other words, both Presidents believed that expanded trade with the Americas would help to strengthen the new democracies in this region, together with the free market policies they were pursuing, and thereby promote the national security and economic interests of the United States. An indication that President Clinton realized that his free trade proposal was likely to lose him short-run political support on balance was his failure to stress it merits during the 1996 presidential campaign.

The formulation in 1995 of the New Transatlantic Agenda (NTA), which included the possibility of a free trade agreement between the European Union (EU) and the United States, also was motivated primarily by foreign policy rather than economic considerations. According to Stuart Eizenstadt, the Undersecretary of Commerce and former U.S. Ambassador to the European Union, various officials in Europe became concerned with what they perceived to be a shift in U.S. diplomatic energies toward the Far East and away from Europe as well as a preoccupation by the Administration with internal issues. The inability of the European countries to stop the fighting in Bosnia had also demonstrated the need for continued U.S. involvement in Europe's security (see Eizenstadt's opinion piece in the *International Herald Tribune*, December 8, 1995). In early informal talks between U.S. and EU diplomatic and trade officials, some Europeans, in particular Sir Leon Brittan, the EU's trade minister, and various British and German officials, proposed a free trade agreement, but this was eventually vetoed by the French who were concerned about what would happen to the Common Agricultural Policy. U.S. officials apparently also were not enthusiastic about this proposal. Consequently, the commercial parts of the final document signed in December 1995 by President Clinton, European Commission President Jacques Santer, and Felipe Gonzalez, the Prime Minister of Spain and then rotating president of the EU merely established a joint study group to explore ways of reducing tariff and nontariff barriers between the two blocs. It was not until after the document was signed that the first official congressional hearing was held on the NTA.

IV. Conclusions

Both the President and Congress currently exert considerable influence on U.S. trade policy. However, the political economy models of economists generally do not distinguish between the roles of these two branches of the federal government. In contrast, political scientists have more frequently focused on the distinctive roles of these two actors in the trade policy-determining process. As these political scientists point out, since 1934 the President has been given the primary role of initiating trade legislation to extend existing trade negotiating authority or provide for authority to undertake new multilateral or regional trade negotiations. This first-mover leadership role benefits the President in that he can significantly affect the nature of policy debate. When a President does not take advantage of this role, as Presidents Eisenhower and Clinton did not in the trade-policy debates that developed soon after their elections, protectionist forces are able to mobilize more effectively and it becomes much more difficult for the President to achieve his trade-policy goals. At the same time, these incidents also demonstrate the enormous power of a President when he finally does fully commit to a particular trade-policy objective.

A key part of the explanation why Presidents, in contrast to Congress, tend to favor trade liberalization is the foreign policy responsibilities associated with the office. Most Presidents believe that increased trade between the United States and other countries improve political, economic and security relations among the countries. Therefore, their proposals for trade agreements are motivated to an important extent by national security considerations. One consequence of the decline in U.S. hegemony since the late 1960s is a greater focus on regional security by a President, a change that helps explain the greater emphasis by Presidents in recent years on promoting regional economic agreements. Rather than attempting to reject such proposals, Congress, whose actions are influenced more than a President's by sector-specific lobbying pressures, typically seeks to include various measures in the enabling legislation that provide for increased administered protection or more extensive administered market-opening opportunities.

The interactions between the President and Congress as they pursue their different goals can be modeled in game-theoretic terms, as explained in Section II of the paper. The leadership role in proposing trade legislation that Congress has given a President is analogous to permitting the President to act as a Stackelberg leader. In explaining the model, it is shown that this grant of authority to the President can actually result in a more favorable outcome for the Congress as well as the President. However, other possible forms of interactions between the President and Congress are also examined in discussing the model.

NOTES

Research support from the World Affairs and the Global Economy program at the University of Wisconsin-Madison is gratefully acknowledge.

[1] Prior to the Reciprocal Trade Agreement Act of 1934, the attitude of presidents toward changes in trade barriers tended to be a function of whether they were Republicans (protectionists) or Democrats (trade liberalizers).

[2] Some industries, e.g., textiles and apparel, are powerful enough politically to gain sector-specific protection through the legislative process, but this has been unusual in recent years. There has also been an occasional serious effort, such as the Burke-Hartke Bill in 1970, to increase protection on a fairly broad list of products.

[3] This form of the President's and Congress's social welfare functions can be interpreted as the consequence of a set of equity-oriented ethical values that prevail in political life or simply self-interest motivations by politicians. Supporting the latter interpretation is the empirical finding by Kahneman and Tversky (1984) that individuals place greater welfare weight on the loss of a given amount of income than a gain of the same amount and, therefore, exert greater lobbying pressures to prevent or recoup declines than to obtain increases above historically normal levels.

[4] The decreases in the President's and Congress's welfare due to losses to import-competing capitalists are assumed to rise at an increasing rate and the gains to exporters to rise at a decreasing rate. Similarly, the consumer gains resulting from multilateral duty cuts are assumed to raise social welfare at a decreasing rate as the extent of the cuts increases. Furthermore, in the President's social welfare function, the gains resulting from the benefits to foreign exporters from reciprocal liberalization are assumed to increase at a decreasing rate.

[5] This will be a stable equilibrium if the CC line is steeper than the PP line.

[6] I am grateful to Simon Evenett for this point.

[7] For a detailed account of the relations between Congress and President Eisenhower, see Wilkinson (1960).

[8] See Preeg (1970, Ch. 4) for a discussion of the efforts by the Kennedy Administration to secure passage of the Trade Expansion Act of 1962.

[9] See "Legislative History of H.R. 11970, 87th Congress"; *Trade Expansion Act of 1962: Public Law 87-794*; Committee on Ways and Means; U.S. House of Representatives; Ninetieth Congress; First Session: Part I, p. 91. The date of the message from the White House was January 25, 1962.

[10] See Baldwin (1985) for a discussion of the formulation of the Trade Act of 1974.

[11] See Grayson (1995, Ch. 9) and various issues of the *Congressional Quarterly* from September to November 1993 for a more detailed list of the political deals made by the

Administration to secure the votes of particular members of Congress.

[12] See United States Government Publications, Series Set 10969, House Miscellaneous Documents, Document 124, House of Representatives, 79th Congress, 1st Session, U.S. Government Printing Office, 1945. The date of the message was March 26, 1945.

[13] *Hearings before Committee on Finance on Trade Agreements Extension*, U.S. Senate, 84th Congress, 1st Session, H.R. 1, Part II, Government Printing Office, 1955.

REFERENCES

Baldwin, Robert E. 1985. *The Political Economy of U.S. Import Policy*. Cambridge, MA: The MIT Press.

Destler, I. M. 1986. *American Trade Politics: System Under Stress*. Washington, DC: Institute for International Economics.

Findlay, Ronald and Stanislaw Wellisz. 1982. "Endogenous Tariffs, the Political Economy of Trade Restrictions, and Welfare," in J. Bhagwati (ed.), *Import Competition and Response*. Chicago: University of Chicago Press.

Gilpin, Robert. 1987. *The Political Economy of International Relations*. Princeton: Princeton University Press.

Grayson, George W. 1995. *The North American Free Trade Agreement: Regional Community and the New World Order*. New York: University Press of America.

Grossman, Gene M. and Elhanan Helpman. 1994. "Protection for Sale," *American Economic Review* 84: 833-850. Reprinted in Alan V. Deardorff, James A. Levinsohn, and Robert M. Stern (eds.), *New Directions in Trade Theory*. Ann Arbor: University of Michigan Press, 1995.

Grossman, Gene M. and Elhanan Helpman. 1995. "The Politics of Free-Trade Agreements," *American Economic Review* 85: 667-690.

Hillman, Arye. L. 1982. "Declining Industries and Political-Support Protectionist Motives," *American Economic Review* 72: 1180-1187.

Kahneman, Daniel and Amos Tversky. 1984. "Choices, Values, and Frames," *American Psychologist* 4: 3341-350.

Kindleberger, Charles P. 1981. "Dominance and Leadership in the International Economy: Exploitation, Public Goods, and Free Rides," *International Studies Quarterly* 27: 5-10.

Krasner, Stephen D. 1982. "State Power and the Structure of International Trade," *World Politics* 28: 317-347.

Lake, David A. 1988. *Power, Protection, and Free Trade: International Sources of U.S. Commercial Strategy, 1887-1939*. Ithaca, NY: Cornell University Press.

Lohmann, Susanne and Sharyn O'Halloran. 1994. "Divided Government and U.S. Trade Policy: Theory and Evidence," *International Organization* 48: 595-632.

O'Halloran, Sharyn. 1994. *Politics, Process, and American Trade Policy*. Ann Arbor: University of Michigan Press.

Pastor, Robert A. 1980. *Congress and the Politics of U.S. Foreign Economic Policy, 1929-1976*. Berkeley: University of Califoria Press.

Peltzman, Sam. 1976. "Towards A more General Theory of Regulation," *Journal of Law and Economics* 19: 211-240.

Preeg, Ernest H. 1970. *Traders and Diplomats*, Washington, DC: The Brookings Institution.

Rodrik, Dani 1995. "The Political Economy of Trade Policy," in G. Grossman and K. Rogoff (eds.), *Handbook of International Economics*, Vol. 3, Amsterdam: North-Holland.

Schattsneider, E. E. 1935. *Politics, Pressure, and the Tariff.* New York: Prentice Hall.

Stigler, George J. 1971. "The Theory of Economic Regulation," *Bell Journal of Economics and Managerial Science* 3: 114-141.

Wilkinson, Joe R. 1960. *Politics and Trade Policy*. Washington, DC: Public Affairs Press.

Yopo, Mladen 1993. "The Chilean Perception of the Americas Initiative," in R.E. Green (ed.), *The Enterprise for the Americas Initiative: Issues and Prospects for a Free Trade Agreement in the Western Hemisphere.* Westport, CT: Praeger.

Comments on Conference Version of Paper

Geza Feketekuty

Baldwin provides an interesting effort to model the bargaining process between Congress and the President on trade policy. His initial summary provides a good overview of the increasing sophistication of models of this type, and places his model at the frontier of such efforts.

At its current stage of development, Baldwin's model is a useful tool for analyzing historical events and gaining insights into the domestic politics underlying the trade negotiating process. Care needs to be taken, however, to draw policy conclusions from the model in its current form. The bargaining process between Congress and the President is far more dynamic than is reflected in the model. Moreover, the bargaining process between Congress and the President is quite different before negotiations begin than at the conclusion of the negotiating process.

I. Static vs. Dynamic Modeling

A shortcoming of the model is that it is a static model, in as much as it assumes that the economic interests affected by trade negotiations and the resulting political constellation of forces are predetermined, and all that remains is for Congress and the President to internalize those forces in their bargaining process. The model also assumes that the various interest groups have perfect information regarding the impact of possible negotiating outcomes on their economic interests.

In actuality, both the President and Congress can alter the political bargaining process by shaping the negotiating agenda, and by educating various interest groups on their economic interests. It should be possible, nevertheless, to build these dynamic elements into the model as shifts in the Presidential or Congressional welfare functions. It would be interesting to examine how the incorporation of such dynamic shifts in the model would affect Baldwin's conclusions, and how it might improve the utility of the model as a predictive tool.

How the President can change the underlying political constellation of forces was illustrated in the planning leading up to the Uruguay Round. Bill Brock, the U.S. Trade Representative in the early 1980s was very much aware that the constellation of political forces would be heavily weighted against further trade liberalization if a new Round of multilateral trade negotiations were to encompass the range of issues addressed in previous Rounds. He deliberately set out to change the political equation by extending the agenda to cover nontraditional issues such as services, intellectual property and investment. While some of the business interests involved were aware of the potential benefits from the inclusion of these topics in negotiations, it was not until Bill Brock embraced these issues that a sufficiently wide coalition of interests coalesced on any one of them.

More generally, one could make the observation that the President enjoys a first mover advantage by being able to define the agenda, and being able to mobilize supportive political forces at the outset.

II. Prenegotiation and Postnegotiation Bargaining

The bargaining processes between Congress and the President before the start of negotiations and at the conclusion of negotiations are quite distinct, both in terms of their dynamics and the players that are involved. More specifically, foreign interests and foreigners play a much more prominent role in the latter phase than in the former phase. By lumping these two phases of the process together, Baldwin both misses some important insights, and reaches some misleading conclusions regarding the tradeoffs between negotiated changes in the rules for administrative protection and negotiated reductions in traditional barriers at the border. In effect, foreign economic interests become an integral part of the President's social welfare function in the postnegotiation bargaining that occurs in connection with Congressional approval of a trade agreement under the fast track provision.

III. Producer Interests versus Consumer Interests

As a general matter it is true that producer interests are far more organized than consumer interests, and that the politics of trade is largely dominated by the political interplay among producer interests, (and highly focused special interests groups such as environmental groups.) This does not mean, however, that consumer interests, and the consumer welfare analysis that is carried out to demonstrate consumer welfare benefits, do not play a role in the political bargaining process. Particularly in the postnegotiation phase of the bargaining process between Congress and the President the consumer welfare gains play a role, albeit not the dominant role, in the process. Baldwin in his analysis overstates the exclusion of consumer interests in both the evolution and the evaluation of negotiating outcomes, as demonstrated by Congressional testimony presented by USTR before Congressional Committees in support of various negotiations.

Baldwin is even more off base when he suggests that "There does not appear to be any significant political constituencies lobbying for new export jobs." Ultimately, what enables U.S. trade negotiators to make the case for trade liberalization is that the negotiations will result in the reduction of foreign barriers to U.S. exports, thus creating new export jobs. Indeed, USTR is most successful in carrying out its negotiating mission to liberalize trade when it succeeds in balancing well organized import-competing interests with equally well organized export interests.

IV. Fast Track Legislation and the Balance of Powers

Baldwin argues that the "Fast Track" provision of the 1974 Trade Act constituted a major weakening of the President in formulating trade policies. This is rather curious, in as much as the whole rationale for the fast track provision was that it was necessary to strengthen the President's hand in negotiations with other countries. With the fast track provision, Congress in effect has agreed to bind its hands in the legislative implementation of trade agreements by assuring an up or down vote, within a strict time table, and with no amendments, on all trade agreements covered by the provision. With the fast track provision the President, in effect, gains the power to initiate changes in U.S. domestic laws that impact on trade and to get Congress to vote on them on an up and down vote.

V. Conclusion

Baldwin has developed a sophisticated model for analyzing the political bargaining process between Congress and the President. A number of further improvements in the model could make it more robust and more dynamic. One of the great strengths of the model is that it lends itself to further improvements. With such a tool, both scholars and policy makers could gain new insights into the political bargaining process, and develop better policy recommendations.

CHAPTER 4

Congress, Constituencies, and U.S. Trade Policy

I. M. (Mac) Destler

Much of the literature on Congress and trade has established, beyond reasonable doubt, the responsiveness of individual members to constituent interests concentrated within their districts, and to the national extensions of such interests. Connections to organized labor, for example, were reliable predictors of votes on domestic content legislation for automobiles in 1983, or NAFTA in 1993. The routine trade business in Congressional offices, moreover, is typified by dealings with economic interests seeking to get help, or avoid hurt.

This essay will neither add to nor subtract from that literature. Nor will it challenge the argument advanced by Rodrik (1995): that trade protection can be a rational policy course for political actors, even though it is suboptimal in comparison to other policy tools theoretically available. Indeed, this analysis assumes its rationality in terms of constituent politics.

The political logic of progressive special-interest domination has been set forth by many scholars, perhaps most grandly by Mancur Olson in *The Rise and Decline of Nations* (1982). Its applicability to trade was demonstrated empirically by how Congress handled the tariff in its first 142 years, and its politics chronicled and analyzed by E.E. Schattschneider (1935) in his classic work, *Politics, Pressures, and the Tariff.*

Certainly micropolitics of this sort continues to drive Congressional behavior on many issues—water projects and pricing, and grazing and mineral rights on public lands are just a couple of examples that spring to mind. And it continues to make its regular mark on trade policy: witness steel in the seventies, autos in the eighties, antidumping policy since 1979, and textiles from time immemorial. But it does not dominate. It explains many of our specific departures from the liberal trade ideal, but it does not explain the broader movement toward that ideal.[1] The micropolitics of trade protection does not explain the macropolitics of trade liberalization. And Congress has played a key role in both.

Like much of my previous work, this essay will focus on the macropolitics of trade policy, and hence on the overall role that Congress has played, and how this has affected representation of constituent interests. Regarding experience to date, the central question is how and why Congress has sustained, politically, *its post-Smoot-Hawley bargain with successive Presidents*: its delegation of product-specific trade policy authority to the executive branch and to quasi-judicial institutions like the U.S. International Trade Commission (USITC). Regarding the future, the question is whether Congress will continue to delegate authority in this manner.

To shed some light on these matters, and hopefully provoke reaction, the discussion here will be organized around four propositions:

1) For over 60 years, Congress has been an active co-conspirator in measures that weaken the hold of micropolitics on trade, and (as a predictable consequence) also reduce Congressional power over trade.

2) This behavior contradicts widely shared academic assumptions about Congressional behavior, but is consistent with an alternative set of assumptions.

3) This behavior has been reinforced by four trade-political conditions: executive branch priority to trade expansion; bipartisanship; effective executive branch dealings with the Congressional trade committees, and the intellectual dominance of free-trade arguments.

4) Erosion of any of these four weakens, marginally, the rather robust power-sharing system, and makes trade-liberalizing legislation substantially more difficult to obtain.

What follows aims to put flesh on those bones.

I. Post Smoot-Hawley: Congress as Liberalization Co-Conspirator

In the Smoot-Hawley Act, Congress passed comprehensive tariff legislation for the last time. Four years later, it began to delegate this authority to the President by enacting the Reciprocal Trade Agreements Act of 1934, which allowed his officials to negotiate reciprocal duty-reduction agreements with foreign nations. Reasonably regular renewals of this Act continued through the Eisenhower administration, and were followed by the grant of yet-broader negotiating authority in the Trade Expansion Act of 1962. After average tariffs had been reduced below 10 percent, Congress enacted "fast-track" legislation, which gave the executive branch the capacity to negotiate reductions in non-tariff barriers to trade that involved changes in other domestic law. Bills granting or extending this authority were enacted in 1974, 1979, 1984, 1988, 1991, and 1993.[2] The House of Representatives resisted renewal of this authority in 1997, but President Bill Clinton is committed to pressing his request again in early 1998.

Beginning before 1930, and continuing to the present, Congress delegated to regulatory authorities the power to impose countervailing duties against foreign subsidies, and antidumping duties for goods sold at "less than fair value." Shortly after World War II, Congress incorporated the GATT "escape clause" into our domestic law, establishing procedures by which firms or workers could seek relief from trade which caused them "injury." These laws were amended regularly: more often than not, the purpose was to make trade relief easier to obtain. But like the grants of trade negotiating authority, they were instances of Congress delegating its Constitution-given trade authority to persons not on Capitol Hill.

As a result of these acts of legislative commission, today's product-specific trade law is typically made by the executive branch and regulatory institutions. Tariff rates are now proclaimed by the President based on the results of international negotiations, and extended to all significant trading partners under the unfortunately-named "most-favored-nation" (MFN) principle. Industries facing particular trade pressures seek and obtain relief mainly through *quasi-judicial procedures* in which they must prove injury to the USITC and/or foreign unfairness to the Department of Commerce. During major trade negotiations, private sector interests are encouraged to lobby the executive branch directly through a statutorily-established, three-tiered system of advisory committees. And instructed to listen carefully is an executive branch agency created, expanded, and protected by Congress: the Office of the United States Trade Representative. (USTR)[3]

All this is well-known to trade policy scholars and practitioners. The reason for recapitulating this history here is that, taken together, these measures have had powerful impact on trade policy's *constituencies*—the subject of this book. Up to 1930, these constituencies went directly to Congress for specific trade action. Now, they must seek that action elsewhere. Legislation still matters to them, or course: it can establish rules, set priorities, make import relief (or export-market-opening action) easier or harder to obtain. And constituencies still matter to Congress: representing them is something members and their staffs take very seriously.

But Congress has tied members' hands regarding their ability to legislate constituency-specific trade measures. So if it is effective, product-specific trade policy action these constituents want, they are unlikely to get it on Capitol Hill. Non-binding resolutions backing semiconductor makers in their fight for Japanese markets? Certainly. Textile quota bills for the President to veto? Of course. Advice on who to talk to at USTR or Commerce? Sure. But something real? Not likely.

As argued at length elsewhere,[4] generations of executive and legislative leaders established this system of "protection for Congress," one that has curtailed the direct Congressional role in regulating trade. Delegation of authority did not, of course, involve abdication of all influence—far from it. Congress regularly sets limits on what USTR can negotiate: through legislation authorizing trade agreements, and through action on the results. It strengthens trade "hawks" within the executive branch through enactment and strengthening of provisions like Section 301. It tinkers regularly with the language of trade remedy statutes, usually to trade-impacted firms' advantage. And members continue to advocate constituents' interests within the larger policymaking system. But Congress has allowed the executive to lead on the big things. Even NAFTA, which Congress never *consciously* authorized in advance,[5] which triggered a firestorm of anxiety about the fate of U.S. workers in international competition, whose "symbolic politics"[6] created a broad new protectionist coalition, was in the end approved by solid Congressional majorities. And the Uruguay Round won overwhelming majorities, notwithstanding the furor over the new World Trade Organization (WTO).

Trade-liberalizing momentum has ground to a halt since then. But to date there has been little of the protectionist backsliding of the sort that followed the Kennedy and Tokyo Rounds. Congress did not enact the new fast-track authority the Clinton administration claimed to want in order to pursue further trade liberalization in the Western Hemisphere and with member states of the Asia-Pacific Economic Cooperation (APEC) forum. And the rank-in-file responded with open rebellion when President Clinton, backed by Majority Leader Dole and Speaker Gingrich, sought legislative action on debt relief for Mexico. Yet if the militant freshmen in the 104th Congress were in fact protectionist, they hid the fact well on the one major trade vote they faced—renewal of MFN status for China. For they backed the President here in somewhat higher proportion than did their more tenured brethren.[7]

Hence for sixty-plus years, Congress has simultaneously been yielding power on trade *and* approving major liberalization initiatives. It has done so while regularly sounding protectionist–enabling liberal traders to warn regularly of the wolf at their door.[8] But somehow the wolf never gets in. Or if he does, he spares most of the sheep.

II. The Logic of Congressional [In]action[9]

Three times within five years, Congress passes statutory textile quotas, but the House of Representatives falls eight, then eleven, then ten votes short of the two-thirds required to override the Presidential veto everyone expected. NAFTA is declared "dead" in the first half of 1993, but it passes in the second half. The Uruguay Round is put aside as too controversial to enact in September 1994, but it sails through in November and December. Congress regularly declares its authority over trade policy, and just as regularly gives it away.

Is there a pattern here? It does not seem to be the pattern set forth in much of the "new institutionalist" literature on Congress. This literature assumes that members determinedly pursue impact on policy. They need backing from constituents, which they purchase by providing policy payoffs. Legislators are thus, in practice, conduits of pressure from interest groups. Within Congress, the committees and subcommittees most responsive to the dominant constituencies come to play the pivotal role, and they use their power to control policy.[10]

This approach fits trade policy very well—for the years up to 1930! It is what E.E. Schattschneider described in 1935, in his classic book published just after the Reciprocal Agreements Act of 1934 rendered it obsolete. Were this mode operative today, we would expect Congress to *enact* textile quotas, adjusting the substance of the legislation to attract the additional ten or so votes needed. And we would expect Congress to *deny* fast-track legislation, since it curtails members' abilities to grant policy favors. Yet the opposite is what has been happening.

It is not as if the last twenty-odd years have not offered Congress ample reason or opportunity to re-seize direct power over trade. First came the general, Vietnam-induced Congressional reassertion of international powers beginning in 1973. Then came House procedural reforms of 1975 which weakened the Ways and Means Committee that had co-conspired in the delegation. The late 1970s brought growing pressure from trade-impacted business and labor as important sectors faced declining international competitiveness. The early 1980s brought an administration whose macroeconomic policies produced hitherto-unimagined trade deficits and even greater rises in the volume of imports, and whose trade policies met bipartisan disdain on Capitol Hill. Any or all of these factors ought to have pushed Congress to reclaim direct power, were that its wont. But Congress did not do so. Action was marginal, not fundamental.

How can we explain this? One way is to consider the possibility that *policy power* is *not* the predominant goal of members of Congress.

1. On the surface, both Congress and the executive appear locked in struggle over policy outcomes, but the stakes are asymmetric: executive branch players give greater priority to controlling trade policy outcomes than do Congressional players.

Legislators may specialize in their committee work, but they are—at bottom—generalist politicians. They cannot give trade issues anywhere near full-time attention. Even for members of the key trade committees, Senate Finance and House Ways and Means, trade competes with several other major matters within their jurisdictions: taxes, social security, and medicare, for example. Their counterparts at USTR, however, do spend virtually all their time on trade, and judge their professional success in office by their trade policy accomplishments.

2. For the generalist politicians who populate Congress, direct control over trade policy is not a necessary means to their broader goal: to maintain and enhance political standing at home and in Washington.

This formulation broadens David Mayhew's (1974) classic characterization of members as single-minded seekers of re-election to accommodate evidence that many legislators are also very much concerned about their roles in Washington and how these are viewed by public and press.[11]

2a. For the great majority of members to whom trade is but an occasional concern, it is sufficient to advocate the cause of constituent groups important in one's district—and the national extensions of these groups, and to strike general trade policy postures which appeal to one's support coalition.

For most members in most instances, it is simply not cost-effective to strive for direct, significant personal influence over trade policy outcomes. Nor is such influence necessary to the member. Mayhew points to three activities typical of re-election-seeking Representatives: advertising, position-taking, and credit-claiming. None of these requires actual impact on policy. The member with limited interest in trade need only take positions responsive to key trade-affected interests in her/his constituency, and/or to sentiment in broader ideological support groups. Interests not important to re-election can be diverted. And in cases where a member is obliged to support statutory trade protection (e.g., one who represents a textile district), she need give only her voice and her vote: an industry is unlikely to punish visible advocates of its legislation because other members of Congress prevent it from becoming law.

Of course, the individual member from a protectionist district may introduce an industry-specific bill and genuinely seek its enactment, only to be blocked by other members. Not all members must subscribe to the post-Smoot-Hawley bargain for it to remain effective.

2b. For legislators on the key trade committees (Senate Finance, House Ways and Means), and the (overlapping) minority which has singled out trade for special attention, controlling actual policy is neither the only, nor in most cases the best means, of enhancing political standing.

The interest of this group in *legislating* on trade is certainly greater than that of their non-specialist colleagues. They are *trade policy politicians* in the sense that they build their broader political standing, in part, on trade policy engagement. But even they need not give priority to actual impact on outcomes. They have, as alternatives, time-tested activities such as:

- issue entrepreneurship—speeches, press releases, hearings, travel to the capital cities of U.S. trading partners;
- marginal legislation for credit-claiming: the Gephardt amendment;
- major legislative proposals which no one expects will become law, but which are admirable for advertising and position-taking: the domestic content bill for automobiles, or the Gephardt amendment of 1986-87.

3. When individual legislators do seek influence over policy, legislation is often not the most effective means to that end.

They can lobby the executive, brandishing legislation as a "threat" that few fully believe but fewer can entirely dismiss—Senator John Danforth (R-MO) did this effectively on automobile imports in early 1981. They can pressure foreign governments, as Danforth also did with the Japanese on that occasion. Indeed, the intertwined executive branch and international bargaining games, on which officials "downtown" take the issue-specific heat, can offer well-connected members of Congress greater opportunity for impact than the procedurally cumbersome legislative game.

In a variety of ways, therefore, Senate and House trade specialists can be visible policy players, bashing the Japanese, responding to their constituents, claiming credit for diplomatic or administrative actions taken in these constituents' behalf, while retaining their ability to duck blame for outcomes unfavorable to them.

4. Hence, members of Congress find their interests well served by a system of power-sharing which gives them ample visibility and room for initiative but allows the buck to stop elsewhere. Administration leaders, who give greater priority to policy impact, also find their interests better served than they would be in a system where specific trade barriers were legislatively determined. They can exploit the leeway that the system of delegated authority gives them.

For legislators, this system is ideal for "blame avoidance."[12] For executive branch officials, it offers flexibility in terms of which interests to respond to, a capacity to build coalitions centered on positive policy purposes (like reciprocal agreements to reduce trade barriers). These coalitions do not tend to emerge autonomously. As John Odell and I wrote nine years ago, "There never was a free trade lobby," in the sense of a coherent, organized force that *initiated* pressure for trade policy liberalization. Rather, "People were invited in and organized by successive administrations."[13] But the system gives executive branch officials the leeway to mobilize internationalist business in support of trade expansion. And as their reward for "taking the heat," Congress grants these officials some leeway on product-specific trade policy.

5. Under this system, constituencies not favored by the executive get less than they would were Congress dispensing trade policy benefits directly. But the strong and persistent constituencies do tend to get <u>something</u>. This keeps them from going all-out to overturn the system.

In the years since 1934, executive branch leaders have typically tilted against (relatively active) protectionist interests and in favor of (relatively inactive) exporter interests. When the former amassed sufficient strength, however, they could win significant trade restraints. These were typically arranged with each industry separately, undercutting the prospects for Smoot-Hawley-style logrolling. But these trade restraints have been less than what industries desired, and more flexible than statutory protection: the textile-apparel coalition never got its global quotas, and the U.S. auto industry achieved only a limited Japanese-enforced VER. Moreover, contrary to the "slippery slope" metaphor favored by free-traders, such protection has typically receded as industry power (and economic need) diminished. Autos and steel are obvious examples, and now textile protection is following the same path.

Under this system, members of Congress still must respond to constituents. Their staffs frequently become expert at providing "technical assistance" to these constituents in navigating its complexities: who is doing what at USTR, or how to pursue trade remedies. But the members do not have to *deliver* for these constituents.

It is always theoretically possible, of course, for a constituent interest to break out from this system and win action from Congress directly. The Constitutional language on trade has not changed in 210 years. But the most potent protectionist interest, textiles, tried and failed in the 1980s. Since then, it has abandoned out-and-out protectionism in order to pursue special benefits within regional and global trade-liberalizing regimes. Less powerful interests get less from the system, but are even less likely to try to overturn it.

To describe and document this pattern of Congressional trade behavior, and its broad consistency with Congressional interests, is not to argue that its emergence was inevitable. Nor does the above analysis offer a serious explanation of why Congress behaves rather differently on, say, tax policy—where the same Congressional committees are much more prone to assert their power and distribute particularist benefits. Part of the explanation may be that our domestic trade policymaking system evolved under the international auspices of the GATT, now the WTO. This creates an international constraint on national policy and reinforces the role of the President in the U.S. policy process. More generally, this could be a story of "path dependent" behavior, one of institutions and processes launched for historically specific reasons which become self-reinforcing as participants find rewards for operating within the system.[14]

Whatever its underlying causes, the system persists. And if the above characterization of Congressional trade behavior is reasonably near the mark, the danger of Congress "going protectionist" is not very great. There are well-established norms that work against it. Still, the system works best when certain conditions are met.

III. Executive-Congressional System Maintenance: Four Conditions That Facilitate

In the management of U.S. trade policy, the executive and Congress are typically not adversaries but allies. USTR works hand-in-glove with the key trade committees: to cope with problem cases (like autos in the early eighties), to pressure foreign government to open markets, to draft legislation implementing the Tokyo and Uruguay Rounds. Their collaboration is most effective when four conditions are met.

First, the system works best when *the President* and USTR *give priority to trade expansion* and *tilt against import protection.* They need to use the leeway the system gives them to mobilize support for export expansion and limit new grants of protection. There is room for some tilting toward favored constituents—the Presidency is a political office too. But the primary emphasis must be on expanding trade, not curbing it. And in general it has been—from Robert Strauss's table pounding in the seventies to the aggressive use of Section 301 in Ronald Reagan's second term to the Clinton administration's framework talks with Japan. As these examples suggest, trade expansion initiatives are often not GATT-pure.[15] But the focus must be on opening other markets, not closing our own.

Second, support for trade liberalization needs to be *bipartisan.* This is important for two reasons. First, it provides for basic continuity when party control changes at the White House or Congress. Second, with the labor left and the Buchanan right generally opposed to trade expansion, it is hard to garner a Congressional majority from one party's members alone: a coalition of the center must be constructed when positive Congressional action is required.

Third, there needs to be *a close executive-congressional working relationship* in support of open trade policy. Specifically, this means close ties and mutual responsiveness between USTR and the two key trade committees, Senate Finance and House Ways and Means. And in practice, it is the U.S. Trade Representative who must take the initiative in building and maintaining this relationship.

Fourth and finally, post-war trade policymaking has benefited from the fact that *arguments for open trade have a normative advantage* in the broad policy community. Those who consciously divert protectionist pressures, or limit their responsiveness to them, find this job easier when they believe that this is right policy, and when their audiences are predisposed to believe this also. (This does not necessarily mean that they will relish making the argument in public.)

Compliance with these four conditions is helpful in countering the (modest) threat of Congressionally-imposed protectionism. It is truly important when further trade liberalization is at issue, and positive Congressional action is required. These four conditions were well-met in the first two years of the first Clinton administration. Since then, the record has been mixed.

Priority to Trade Expansion. In general, the Clinton administration has continued this emphasis. The President entered office determined to "elevate economics in foreign policy."[16] But he defined this as pressing harder for export expansion: when he spoke of "making change our friend," economic internationalization seemed prominent in his mind.

The specific record was exceptional—for the first two years. After time out for side agreements on labor and the environment, Clinton got Congress to approve George Bush's NAFTA. His USTR, Mickey Kantor, proved an adept "closer" on the Uruguay Round in December 1993, and won Congressional enactment of implementing legislation a year later. And Clinton signalled his determination to move further through his endorsement, in successive, fall 1994 summit meetings, of free trade among APEC nations by 2010 (2020 for the least developed), and negotiation of a Free Trade Area of the Americas (FTAA) by 2005. One press commentary—Brownstein (1994)—labeled it "a more ambitious record of trade liberalization than [that of] any President since at least Harry S Truman."

But in 1995, progress ceased. Perhaps chastened by Congressional reaction to the President's Mexican debt rescue plan, certainly concerned about how liberal trade played with important Democratic constituencies, USTR Mickey Kantor showed little readiness (as spelled out below) to compromise with the newly-Republican Congress on the specific legislative language of renewed "fast-track" authority. This effectively put the matter beyond the 1996 election. And on a range of trade issues, from Japan autos to Mexican trucking, consistent and forward-looking trade policy took a back seat to what was thought to play politically.

As his second term began, Clinton and USTR Charlene Barshefsky, Kantor's successor, asked Congress to renew fast-track authority so he could resume negotiations for trade liberalization. But the President delayed eight months in submitting a specific legislative proposal, and despite strong White House lobbying, Congress adjourned in November 1997 without taking action.

Bipartisanship. Here too, there was sharp contrast between 1993-94 and 1995-96, though the warning signs came earlier. Winning NAFTA approval required overwhelming Republican support; to build that support, the Clinton White House engaged former Representative Bill Frenzel, a respected Republican voice on trade during his twenty years' service, to act as counterpart to Chicago Democrat William Daley whom the administration had brought in to coordinate the legislative campaign. In the end, 102 Democrats and 132 Republicans voted yes. For the Uruguay Round, support was both stronger and more symmetrical between the parties: each backed the legislation by roughly 2-1 in the House, and almost precisely 3-1 in the Senate.

But partisanship pushed action on the Uruguay Round to a post-election "lame duck" session in 1994. Senate Minority Leader Robert Dole was uncooperative through the summer, and House Minority Whip Newt Gingrich forced postponement of his body's vote in September. The main reason, apparently, was the Republican strategy of denying the President *any* policy victories before the November election, even bipartisan ones. (They remembered the boost in public esteem he got from NAFTA the previous year.) But USTR Mickey Kantor made his contribution in June by proposing (for inclusion in the Uruguay Round implementing bill) fast-track language for future negotiations that gave priority to trade-related labor and environmental issues. This was read by Republicans (and by business interests) as a play to Democrat-oriented interest groups that had been turned off by NAFTA. It also would have extended fast-track to cover issues that (unlike mainstream trade policy) were marked by sharp partisan differences.

Kantor's proposal contributed importantly to the administration's failure to win any follow-on fast-track language in 1994, a significant loss within its broader Uruguay Round triumph. And it set the stage for partisan tensions over trade after the Republican capture of the House and Senate. The new Chairman at House Ways and Means, Bill Archer (R-TX), was interested in legislating extension of fast track, and began to move a bill through his committee. And Speaker Newt Gingrich was a staunch free-trader. But Kantor, fearing adverse electoral impact with labor and environmental advocates, was unwilling to meet the Republicans halfway. By 1996, trade bipartisanship was frayed as a result.

In September 1997, the White House did finally present a fast-track proposal responsive to Archer's concerns, and those of the business community. But now Clinton faced severe problems within his own party, as more than three-quarters of House Democrats declared themselves opposed. Despite strong support from the Republican majority, the administration was unable to round up the necessary 218 House votes, and Clinton asked Speaker Gingrich not to hold the scheduled November vote on the legislation. In the Senate, a bipartisan majority supported the legislation, but the House was sharply divided along party lines, with organized labor spearheading the opposition.

Executive-Congressional Relations. These went through the same cycle under Clinton and Kantor: effective (after a shaky start) in the uphill fight for NAFTA, and workable for the Uruguay Round implementing legislation, fast-track excepted, once the 1994 election was history. The number of legislators with strong interests in trade had declined from the 1980s, however. Bob Matsui (D-CA) rose to a prominent role on NAFTA, and he became Acting Chair of the Ways and Means Trade Subcommittee when criminal charges forced Dan Rostenkowski (D-IL) to abdicate his full committee chairmanship. But few of Matsui's junior colleagues seemed to share either his interest or his strong free-trade orientation. On the Senate side, Finance Chairman Daniel Patrick Moynihan's erudite readings of trade history were less relevant to the political management task than the political shrewdness and reputation of his predecessor, Lloyd Bentsen.

When party control shifted, the trade committees moved to the hands of legislators generally more clearly in the free-trade column, particularly in the House. But relations between Ways and Means chair Archer and the Clinton administration got off to a shaky start due to Kantor's ambivalence about fast-track as chronicled above. Personal relations were better when Barshefsky succeeded Kantor, but Archer went public in spring 1997 over his unhappiness with Clinton's delay in proposal new fast-track legislation. Cooperation improved when Clinton did submit his proposal in September, but neither Archer nor the President could move Ways and Means Democrats, who voted 4-12 against fast-track in committee. Matsui was steadfast but ranking Democrat Charles Rangel (D-NY), who had recently declared himself a convert to free trade, voted NO—reportedly because he wanted companion legislation to improve job opportunities for struggling Americans like many of his Harlem constituents.

Dealings with Senate Finance, by contrast, were more productive than expected. Under the leadership of Chairman William Roth (R-DE) and ranking Democrat Moynihan, committee leaders began to push fast-track energetically in June 197, and the committee responded to Clinton's September proposal by voting out a fast-track extension bill opposed by only one of its twenty members. Preliminary floor votes indicated that a bipartisan majority of more than two-thirds of the Senate was prepared to vote in favor.

Free Trade as Preeminent Idea. Judith Goldstein has highlighted the importance of free-trade ideas in postwar U.S. trade policymaking. Their intellectual dominance has robbed protectionism of its respectability, and continues to do so. In the 1980s, for example, labor Democrats who backed domestic content legislation for autos preferred to do so quietly. In 1993, when the NAFTA debate brought unvarnished protectionism back into prominence, Ross Perot's perverse version served to further discredit that cause, and made liberal traders (Vice President Gore included) look undeniably in the right, with history on their side. And Pat Buchanan's anti-trade stance in 1996 did not gain the resonance that many feared.

In 1997, however, critics of fast-track extension took a more sophisticated tack. Denying they were adversaries of trade per se, they put forth the argument that future trade agreements should include provisions, enforceable by trade sanctions, which addressed labor and environmental rules in the signatory nations. Such provisions were vehemently opposed by U.S. trading partners, as well as the U.S. business community. However, advocacy of labor and environmental negotiations allowed critics to deploy a powerful moral argument: that these human conditions were surely no less important than the intellectual property concerns that have been addressed in recent U.S. trade agreements and therefore should be addressed in U.S. trade policy.

Their success in blocking House approval of fast-track in 1997 assured that 1998 would be a decisive year for U.S. trade politics. What are the prospects?

IV. 1998 and Beyond: Further Liberalization, or Stalemate?

As discussed in the essay's opening pages, resurgent protectionism is not the current problem. Rather, the problem is gaining support for further trade liberalization initiatives.

The experience of 1997 underscores the difficulty. As the year began, trade advocates in the administration and Congress called for prompt Presidential submission of a fast-track proposal. Clinton delayed action, however, concerned about the response of labor and environmental constituencies and arguing the need to complete action on other matters first, especially the deficit reduction agreement reached with Republican Congressional leaders. It was not until mid-September that the President's proposal was submitted. In the meantime, critics mobilized—particularly organized labor and House Democratic Leader Richard Gephardt—while business interests waited to see just how Clinton would treat labor and environmental matters.

As discussed above, the critics developed an effective argument about the rightness of including labor and environmental provisions in trade agreements. The President, needing business and Republican support and recognizing that a statutory requirement for such provisions would achieve little for either workers or greens, submitted a bill limiting what they could cover. Senate Finance and House Ways and Means tightened the limits in the legislation they reported out of committee. In late October and early November, the White House lobbied legislators intensely, particularly House Democrats. But Clinton seemed to hit a brick wall. The restrictive treatment of labor and environmental issues, plus labor lobbying backed by the clout of campaign contributions, plus broad disaffection with the Clinton White House among House Democrats, all combined to limit their number supporting fast-track to a bit over forty, roughly one-fifth of the total. Even with two-thirds of Republicans in favor, the White House fell short of the number of commitments needed. So, as noted earlier in this essay, President Clinton asked Speaker Gingrich not to hold the scheduled November vote.

Clinton declared his determination to press the matter again in early 1998. The political prognosis was murky. Majority support appeared to exist for global sectoral and perhaps broader trade-liberalization negotiations conducted through the World Trade Organization. Regional agreements like the proposed Free Trade Area of the Americas were more controversial, lending themselves powerfully to the argument that ancillary issues (trade, environment, human rights) should be part of the negotiating package. In this analyst's judgment, it is still possible for Clinton to win new fast-track legislation in 1998, though perhaps with some limits on its substantive scope. But broad bipartisan support is lacking. To restore it over the long run, the administration and Congress need to find some way of addressing legitimate concerns about trade's impact on labor and the environment.

Moreover, as the 1997 experience suggests, these two issues show the greatest potential for undercutting, over time, the intellectual preeminence that free trade ideology has long enjoyed. Environmentalists, particularly the more radical groups, see the playing out of economic logic as a prime ravager of the natural world. Labor interests have long highlighted the impact of trade on wage stagnation and income inequality—the downside of internationalization.

Now trade economists are beginning to find something in this argument as well.[17] If their correlations look persuasive, we could find more "liberal" Democrats less apologetic about their protectionism, acting out of conviction as well as political circumstances. For the trade-income connection could give an intellectual respectability to trade-restrictive arguments that they have long lacked. It is unlikely to reverse the ongoing internationalization of the U.S. economy, or to turn Congress protectionist, but it could slow down governmental acts and inter-governmental agreements which reduce barriers further. And when the economy goes into recession, the audience for this argument will increase.

NOTES

[1] An interesting effort to reconcile these two is that of Douglas Nelson (1989), who sees the continuing triumph of micropolitics through the trade remedy laws, making them increasingly protectionist, even as the executive branch has gained control over "liberalization policy."

[2] See I. M. Destler, (1995, Ch. 4 and 9).

[3] The lead trade official was originally labeled the Special Representative for Trade Negotiations (STR), a position mandated by the Trade Expansion Act of 1962. The Trade Act of 1974 made STR a statutory *office* in the Executive Office of the President. The Trade Agreements Act of 1979 required the President to strengthen central coordination of trade policy: Jimmy Carter by expanding STR and renaming it "USTR."

[4] Destler (1995, Ch. 2).

[5] I know of no one in the executive branch or on Capitol Hill who thought a free-trade agreement with Mexico was conceivable during the four-year period for which Congress provided fast-track authority in 1988. And NAFTA talks had already begun when the Bush administration asked legislators to extend the fast-track time limit in 1991.

[6] For a superb treatment of this and the full range of NAFTA political issues, see Mayer (1997).

[7] The percentages were: *67.0%* (286-141) for the House overall, *75.3%* (64-21) for House freshmen; *72.0%* (167-65) for Republicans overall, *73.6%* (53-19) for Republican freshmen; and *61.3%* (119-75) for all Democrats, *84.6%* (11-2) for Democratic freshmen.

[8] See Robert Pastor (1983).

[9] This subtitle is a play on the title of Douglas Arnold's (1990) book, *The Logic of Congressional Action*, and that of Mancur Olson's *The Logic of Collective Action* (1965).

[10] For examples of the "new institutionalist" approach, see Shepsle and Weingast (1984, 1987), McCubbins and Schwartz (1984), and McCubbins, Noll, and Weingast

(1989). For a careful, interesting application of this approach to trade policy, see O'Halloran (1994).

[11] See Fenno (1973).

[12] See Weaver (1988, Ch. 2).

[13]Destler and Odell, (1987, p. 119). The quotes are from "two experienced Washington veterans" interviewed for the study.

[14]See North (1990, esp. Ch. 11).

[15]For an argument that departures from the multilateral ideal are both bad policy and dangerous politics, see Kreuger (1995). This author does not agree, at least with the political portion of Krueger's argument.

[16]Address to Los Angeles World Affairs Council, August 13, 1992.

[17] On the economics of trade and wages, see Collins (1998) and Cline (1997). For a more alarmist view of the substance and the politics, see Kapstein (1996). For a broad analysis of the impact of trade on "social cohesion" in the United States and elsewhere, see Rodrik (1997).

REFERENCES

Arnold, Douglas. 1990. *The Logic of Congressional Action*. New Haven: Yale University Press.

Brownstein, Ronald. 1994. "Clinton Drawing Blueprint of Global Economy," *Los Angeles Times*, December 5.

Cline William R. 1997. *Trade and Income Distribution*. Washington, D.C.: Institute for International Economics.

Collins, Susan (ed.). 1998. *Imports, Exports, and the American Worker*. Washington, D.C.: Brookings Institution.

Destler, I.M. 1995. *American Trade Politics*. 3rd Ed. Washington, D.C.: Institute for International Economics and the Twentieth Century Fund.

Destler, I.M. and John Odell. 1987. *Anti-Protection: Changing Forces in United States Policies. Policy Analysis No. 21*. Washington, DC: Institute for International Economics.

Fenno, Richard. 1973. *Congressmen in Committees*. Boston: Little Brown & Co.

Kapstein, Ethan B. 1996. "Workers and the World Economy," *Foreign Affairs*, May/June, 16-37.

Krueger, Anne O. 1995. *American Trade Policy: A Tragedy in the Making*. Washing ton, D.C.: American Enterprise Institute.

Mayer, Frederick W. 1997. *Interpreting NAFTA: The Science and Art of Political Analysis*. New York: Columbia University Press.

Mayhew, David. 1974. *Congress: The Electoral Connection*. New Haven: Yale University Press.

McCubbins, Matthew D. and Thomas Schwartz. 1984. "Congressional Oversight Overlooked: Policy Patrols versus Fire Alarms," *American Journal of Political Science*, 165-79.

McCubbins, Matthew D., Roger Noll, and Barry R.Weingast. 1989. "Structure and Process, Politics and Policy: Administrative Arrangements and the Political Control of Agencies," *Virginia Law Review*, 431-82.

Nelson, Douglas. 1989. "Domestic Political Preconditions of U.S. Trade Policy: Liberal Structure and Protectionist Dynamics," *Journal of Public Policy* 9: 83-108.

North, Douglas C. 1990. *Institutions, Institutional Change, and Economic Performance*. New York: Cambridge University Press.

O"Halloran, Sharyn. 1994. *Politics, Process, and American Trade Policy*. Ann Arbor: University of Michigan Press.

Olson, Mancur. 1965. *The Logic of Collective Action: Public Goods and the Theory of Groups*. Cambridge: Harvard University Press.

Olson, Mancur. 1982. *The Rise and Decline of Nations: Economic Growth and Stagnation, and Social Rigidities*. New Haven: Yale University Press.

Pastor, Robert. 1983. "The Cry and Sigh Syndrome: Congress and Trade Policy," in Allen Schick (ed.), *Making Economic Policy in Congress*. Washington, D.C.: American Enterprise Institute.

Rodrik, Dani. 1995. "Political Economy of Trade Policy," in Gene Grossman and Kenneth Rogoff (eds.), *Handbook of International Economics*, Vol. III. Amsterdam: Elsevier Science B.V.

Rodrik, Dani. 1997. *Has Globalization Gone Too Far?* Washington, D.C.: Institute for International Economics.

Schattschneider, Elmer E. 1935. *Politics, Pressures and the Tariff: A Study of Free Private Enterprise in Pressure Politics, as Shown in the 1919-1930 Revision of the Tariff*. New York: Prentice-Hall.

Shepsle, Kenneth A. and Barry R. Weingast. 1984. "Legislative Politics and Budget Outcomes," in G. Mills and J. Palmer (eds.), *Federal Budget Policy in the 1980s*. Washington, D.C.: Urban Institute.

Shepsle, Kenneth and Barry R.Weingast. 1987. "The Institutional Foundations of Committee Power," *American Political Science Review*, 85-104

Weaver, Kent. 1988. *Automatic Government: The Politics of Indexation*. Washington, D.C.: Brookings Institution.

Comments on Conference Version of Paper

Heterogeneous Preferences and the Practice of Group Representation in U.S. Trade Policy

Richard L. Hall

I. Introduction

The puzzle that motivates most studies in the political science of international trade policy is understandably different from most studies in the political economy of trade.[1] The political scientist, schooled in the electoral imperatives of distributive politics,[2] asks: "Why is trade so *free*?" The political economist, schooled in the welfare gains of unfettered markets, asks: "Why is trade so *closed*?" The political scientist looks at history and sees a dynamic of increasingly open markets. The economist looks at the present and sees an equilibrium of ubiquitous restriction.[3]

Destler represents the former point of view. He argues that the large scholarship in the political economy of trade policy does not take us far in explaining the historical trend towards a more open U.S. trade policy over the last half-century. He revisits several central assumptions in that literature and finds them wanting. His immediate goal is to reconcile the constituency-regarding and hence protectionist impulses of legislators with the apparently constituency-disregarding, increasingly free trade policies enacted or enabled by Congress. In so doing, Destler provides an interesting, potentially revisionist critique of the scholarship on Congress and foreign trade, a literature to which his contribution has already been immense.

In reflecting on Destler's revisionist essay, I will pursue two lines of discussion. First, I suggest that the theoretical worries that he identifies can be traced to a conceptual problem in empirical models of constituency. Second, I extend Destler's account of the "micropolitics" of constituency influence by reexamining the purposes and strategies of constituent groups. I suggest that our understanding of constituency representation in trade politics might suffer from a poorly stylized rendering of group objectives and hence group strategies, and I offer some revisionist suggestions of my own.

II. Heterogeneous Preferences in Trade Politics

The economic theory of legislative choice that Destler critiques rests on several, simple, more or less explicit, assumptions:

(1) Members of Congress are self-interested, not ideological, to the extent that these two impulses can be distinguished.[4]
(2) Self-interest takes the simple form of electoral self-interest. The expected effect of members' actions on their respective reelection probabilities is the only parameter that behaviorally matters. Members are "single-minded seekers of reelection," to use David Mayhew's phrase (1973), in trade policy as in all things.
(3) Electorally self-regarding members will act in ways likely to endear them to high demand constituencies, namely, industries and their workers who assert that they have suffered, or are likely to suffer, economic harm from foreign competition or foreign restrictions on U.S. imports.
(4) The stronger the industry presence in the member's state or district, the more responsive will the member be to protectionist interests. To the extent that an industry can provide election-relevant resources—say, campaign contributions—that are fungible across districts, industries can incite responsiveness by members from districts where industry employment may be thin.
(5) The member's responsiveness to constituency interests takes the form of voting support for relevant protectionist trade policies that come before her chamber.

In short, homogeneous high demand constituencies deploy their electoral connections and campaign funds to achieve protectionist ends. The consequences for collective choice by the chamber, in turn, are thought to be straightforward. Legislators with homogeneous, high demand constituencies have a high willingness to pay for protectionist policies; they enter into the market for votes, and purchase (or barter for) support from legislators with low demand constituencies. Various institutional arrangements serve to enforce the terms of legislative trade over long periods. Members representing strong protectionist constituencies relinquish formal authority over some other policy domain coveted by legislators with differently interested constituencies, in return for greater authority in trade policy. In the institutionalist literature that Destler cites, this distribution of jurisdictional property rights is achieved through the creation of standing committees and subcommittees; a panel assignment process that allows the self-selection of high demanders onto panels of their own choosing; and an allocation of procedural prerogatives and institutional resources that endows the preferences of panel members with greater legislative weight. Such is the "industrial organization of Congress," as Weingast and Marshall (1989) have termed it, and it remains the prevailing explanation for the persistence of inefficient distributive policies in various areas of congressionally made policy, trade being just one.[5]

Destler observes that distributive theory does not do so well in explaining policies that are not distributive. After all, high demanders of protection have not been getting all that they want—and seem to be getting less over time—from Congress. But is this a failure in the political economy of protectionist politics, requiring us to revisit and recast certain central assumptions that drive it? Destler says yes. I would cast the problem in a somewhat different way, namely, that the conditions of distributive theory have been variably, perhaps decreasingly, present in postwar congressional trade policy. Protectionist policies should follow *if* members represent homogeneous, high-demand constituencies, namely, protection-seeking domestic industries. But the same logic implies that such policies should be harder to find to when high demand constituents are heterogeneous in their preferences.[6] It is certainly true that distributive theorists seldom imagine a world that contains such constituencies. But that need not deter us from doing so.

Theoretical work in the study of legislative behavior (e.g., Arnold 1990; Fiorina 1974) and more recently in the political economy of trade policy (e.g., Grossman and Helpman 1994) suggests that we imagine a different world, one which builds on assumptions grounded in better empirics. Simply put, "homogeneous high-demander" may be a bad caricature on which to ground an understanding of constituency representation in trade policy, in the present if not in the past.[7]

Let me give the heterogeneity notion a bit more concreteness. A few years back I worked for a member of the Senate Finance Committee at a time when opening foreign markets to American agricultural products was prominent on the Committee's agenda. The member represented a highly rural, agriculture-dependent, Midwestern state. But even so, the state's agricultural sector included industries and firms that were of somewhat different minds about existing trade barriers. Many of the grain constituencies favored policies that would open foreign markets as a means of reducing nagging domestic surpluses. Many of the livestock interests feared greater competition from foreign beef and pork producers, especially Canada and Mexico. And, of course, some political organizations found themselves faced with representing the interests of both at once.

With no Pareto-optimal solutions in political sight, the Senator and his staff wrestled with ways to strike an electorally important but politically difficult balance between international market-minded and domestic market-minded agricultural interests. One event engineered by the Senator's staff came to symbolize in my mind how difficult such a balancing act could be. To appease livestock producers concerned about import competition, the Senator arranged the lease of an oversized passenger jet; had the seats stripped out of it; loaded it with several dozen head of the state's prime beef cattle; then flew them to South Korea as part of an unofficial trade mission that included a group of the state's prominent cattle ranchers. The well-publicized purpose of the trip was to help South Koreans develop a "taste" for U.S. beef. The strategy, of course, was to focus the attention of local producers on matters of export potential rather than import competition.[8]

This is but a single example, but insofar as it reveals the calculations of the constituency-minded legislator in trade politics, it may be something of a limiting case. Even a highly rural, homogeneous, agricultural state did not generate homogeneous high demand for agricultural protectionism in the mind of a single legislative agent. Nor does it now (see, e.g., Orden 1996). As several papers in this volume reveal, not all politics of trade policy is analogous to what has historically happened in, say, textiles; not all industries exhibit the unanimity of steel (Irwin, this volume). Rather, the political presence of constituency interests that favor free trade frequently matters within and across different industries and geographic locales (e.g., Freeman, this volume; Waldman, this volume). To the extent this is so, we need to investigate the extent to which and the conditions under which heterogeneous interests characterize election-relevant trade constituencies. The concept of constituency becomes not a single prototype but a variable profile.[9]

In particular, such a reconceptualization of trade constituencies makes more understandable the trend toward congressional abdication of its trade authority, which Destler and others rightly find puzzling. Members representing heterogeneous constituencies necessarily face political cross-pressures. Pleasing one subconstituency implies alienating another. As Fiorina (1974) has argued, moreover, unrequited constituents are more likely to punish than requited constituents are to reward. Hence when interested constituencies have compatible preferences, legislators should desire legislative responsibility so that they might credibly claim credit for responsive policies. To the extent that interested constituencies have conflicting preferences, legislators should relinquish legislative responsibility so that they might better avoid blame. Simply put, good political-economics should not assume that protectionist policies are a linear function of constituency demand. As homogeneous constituency demand goes up, representatives should legislate; as heterogeneous constituency demand goes up, representatives should abdicate.[10]

Arnold's masterful work on coalition-building in Congress elaborates this logic (1990). When otherwise desirable policies exhibit high, concentrated costs, members prefer (and hence leaders will propose) policy instruments for which the causal chain between the member's action and unhappy effects is long. The unpopular costs will ultimately appear, but they are less traceable to the deeds of any particular legislative doer. When the incidence of benefits is high while the costs are low, on the other hand, members seek policy instruments with a short causal chain. They want beneficiaries to believe that the happy policy effects flow from the legislator's deeds. Thus, members may abdicate general control over trade policy to the U.S. Trade Representative, thereby lengthening the causal chain. But they retain opportunities to intervene on behalf of ill-protected industries who seek compensation for subsequent harms. And as Destler observes, legislators frequently exploit these opportunities by lobbying the executive branch for anti-dumping remedies for ill-protected industries. Whatever benefits might follow from such efforts are far better than nothing, and the added advantage for the legislator is that these benefit-producing instruments exhibit a short causal chain.

In sum, there is good reason to think that constituency preferences in trade policy are considerably more heterogeneous than most work in the political economy of protection typically allows. The heterogeneity appears not only across industries; it often occurs within industries and, more importantly, within single states or district boundaries that structure the local geography of representation. As a result, the behavioral strategies of constituency-regarding legislators will exhibit, under specifiable conditions, protectionist impulses, blame avoidance, even free trade preferences. Recent theoretical work that weakens the homogeneity assumption thus strikes me as promising.[11] Among other reasons, it should help us understand why we often *don't* see protectionism, as well as understand why we too often do. In turn, it should help to explain why U.S. trade policy can, over time, at least in some industries, become more open.

III. Group Strategies and Their (Legislative) Behavioral Effects

My second line of discussion focuses on what Destler refers to as the micropolitics of constituency influence in trade policymaking. As I read it, a premise of his paper (and of this conference) is that constituency representation *is* group representation. Legislative agents respond to group principals.

It is not obvious that we should restrict our definition of representation in this way. Among other reasons, political economists (e.g., Denzau and Munger 1986) and political scientists (e.g., Arnold 1989; Jackson and King 1989) have modeled the processes by which unorganized interests get represented, why voters (and not simply organizations) sometimes matter in the calculations of policymakers. And democratic theorists from Schattschneider (1960) forward would bristle at this usage.

But as a starting point for understanding trade politics, responsiveness to group demands is a reasonable place to start. Destler suggests several ways in which we might modify our view of the (micropolitical) nature and logic of legislator responsiveness. I will extend and revise his argument by suggesting a move that I think might be important for the next generation of models of constituency representation.

My point of departure is the not-so-simple question: What do representatives do when they represent? What does the practice of responsiveness look like?

As I note above, most political economists and political scientists state or imply that legislative responsiveness takes the form of voting favorably on industry-supported measures. Insofar as legislative (as distinct from executive) action is concerned, the positions that legislators take are the principal phenomena to be explained. And groups figure prominently in the explanation.

Through campaign contributions, pressure-style lobbying, or threat of electoral retribution, organized groups bid for pro-protection votes from individual legislators, with an eye to buying the collective choice of a majority rule legislature.

In my view, this simplification captures only one and perhaps one of the least important things that legislators do in responding to groups. It is one of the least important things that groups care about. And it leads to some fundamental puzzles in theorizing about group strategy and influence in trade politics.[12]

Consider the alleged importance of industry campaign contributions in the creation of industry-protecting trade policies. One pattern is clear: protection-minded groups give most heavily to members with the *strongest* predispositions toward protectionism—members who, by dint of constituency or ideology, would be least likely to vote a free trade line regardless of their donors' views.

This is irrational behavior indeed. If groups want to "buy" votes, they ought to give most to legislators whose protection-relevant votes are most in doubt. That is the allocation strategy that should maximize the number of votes bought per dollars spent. Instead, they give most to members whose votes are least likely to be influenced by a few-thousand dollar contribution.

Neither is group rationality rehabilitated in models that assume groups contribute to campaigns in order to elect candidates of the sympathetic party, with an eye to predetermining the pattern of votes. For a second pattern is also clear: these same groups give most heavily to the electorally safest members—members most likely to win (re)election to congressional office regardless of the donor's decision to donate.

This too is irrational behavior. If groups contribute to campaigns with the purpose of electing sympathetic members, they ought to give most to sympathizers near the margin of winning or losing. That is the allocation strategy that should maximize the number of seats bought for dollars spent. Instead, they give contributions to candidates in campaigns where the outcome is least in doubt and thus least likely to be affected by a few-thousand dollar contribution.

Simply put, the most common models of constituency representation assume rationality on the part of legislators but imply *ir*rationality on the part of constituency groups. Anomalies such as this suggest theoretical rethinking and exposition, I believe, in the following way. The purpose of groups, in their various activities, is not to win support but to mobilize supportive legislators to work as agents on the group's behalf (Hall and Wayman 1990). Hence I think Destler is wrong when he argues that legislators can achieve a constituency-pleasing purpose by engaging in symbolic position taking, that is, without serious effort at affecting policy. Industry actors monitor legislative action closely; that is much of what lobbyists do. Hence they know the difference between empty symbolism and serious agency. And members know that they know. Members who wish to make subsequent claims of credit before these constituencies need to make claims that must be credible. Vigorous advocacy is what makes them so.

My premise, then, is that legislators make two important but qualitatively different kinds of choices with respect to every legislative issue that comes before them: what position to take, and how active to be (Hall 1996). Speeches, newsletters, advertisements and, most importantly, roll call votes capture the former. To understand the micropolitics of group representation, however, we need to investigate the latter. Groups know that right-minded voting is not enough; they want agency.

This, I think, is a distinction that implies a modeling difference. It recommends the form of behavior that we implicitly or explicitly investigate and thus clarifies the empirical hypotheses we derive. Do industry groups induce, through contributions or other resources, legislative responsiveness? Not insofar as votes are concerned. There is now a large empirical literature in political science and economics that investigates the effect of contributions on voting behavior. There is simply not much effect to be found, which suggests that if groups are rational, they do not learn.

But I think there is a logic and some evidence to suggest that groups do induce responsiveness in a different behavioral form. They do not seek to influence votes all that much (at least not directly). Rather they seek to incite legislative participation on the part of otherwise sympathetic members on issues that affect group interests. And the patterns of member participation in prefloor decisionmaking (as opposed to patterns of late-stage voting) are what matter most to the shape of the legislation that ultimately gets voted on (or whether legislation ever reaches the floor to get voted on.[13]

The logic rests on the simple premise that a member's legislative time, attention, and staff are valuable but scarce resources. Members must make rational resource allocation decisions in order to maximize their effect on policies. Groups want already sympathetic legislators to get in the games that the groups care most about. The more sympathetic members are position-wise, the more active should the group want them to be.

Of course, a member decision to actively participate on even a single issue is costly. The information and transaction costs of getting in the legislative mix are substantial for all but the most institutionally well-placed members (committee chair, party leader). How might groups induce costly participation? In two ways, I think. Through grass-roots campaigns, campaign contributions, and lobbying, groups not only reveal their position on an issue (no to NAFTA) but the intensity of their position (kill and maim NAFTA). They thus reveal to the member the level of political benefits (future contributions, vigorous electoral support) she might expect if she acts aggressively as their agent. The expected level of political benefits, then, increases the legislator's willingness to pay the substantial costs of participation.

But groups also act so as to affect the member's ability to pay. Lobbyists do sometimes use the access they buy to persuade a member to vote in a particular way. But as an empirical matter, lobbyists spend most of their time with members who would vote their way anyway. So what is lobbying mostly about? The most common response of lobbyists, typically thought to be disingenuous, is that they only "provide information." I do not think that is disingenuous at all. But neither is it a minor matter. Lobbying of this kind subsidizes the substantial information costs that the resource-constrained member would otherwise need to pay. Lobbyists enhance the ability of legislators that they would like in a given legislative game to get into the game. To the latter the former variously provide political monitoring, draft legislation, write amendments, distribute talking points, even write speeches that would require an active representative or her staff many hours of precious legislative time to produce. Lobbyists also subsidize member's legislative transaction costs. They identify the legislators with whom their legislative agent should deal (and those fence-sitters whose votes she might try to persuade); they negotiate with committee staff; they do labor intensive coordination and coalition-building work.

In sum, I disagree with the central premise of Destler's critique, namely, that that legislators need not, in the practice of representation, care about influencing policy. Groups most certainly care. And the considerable resources they invest in affecting policy are neither naive nor irrational. Those investments may not change votes, but they can induce legislative agency on the group's behalf. It is a substantively important matter in political modeling, then, to comprehend the conditions under which those investments, by both private and public groups, make a policy difference.

I have briefly sketched here two ways in which I think the micropolitical processes of trade policymaking might be better modeled. The first is to complicate the concept of trade constituency by allowing greater heterogeneity of preferences within industries and geographic districts. The second is to rethink the policy-relevant practices in which members engage when they represent the trade constituencies they do. Attention to these conceptual matters, I believe, will enhance our ability to unpack the puzzles that Destler rightly emphasizes.

NOTES

[1] I am referring here to the literature reviewed in Rodrik's essay (1995), which was circulated among participants in this conference.

[2] Political scientists sometimes use the word "distributive" differently than political economists. I am simply referring here to the distribution of private benefits by political actors and ignore the semantics of whether this is distributive or redistributive.

[3] See, for instance, Krueger (1996a; 1996b) and the opening paragraphs of Grossman and Helpman (1994). See Staiger (1995) for an economic theory of gradual trade liberalization. As I understand it, many works that examine intertemporal changes in trade

policies suggest that trade has not become that much more open, only that policies have shifted from tariff to non-tariff barriers.

[4] The debate over self-interest vs. ideology in legislative voting has been prominent in political economics and political science. (For a critique of both, see Jackson and Kingdon 1992.) A closely related tension appears evident in the political support calculation posited in Hillman's model of protection (1989).

[5] Again, I mean distributive in a political sense, namely, private benefits are concentrated and hence politically perceived while costs are dispersed and thus overlooked. Such policies may be efficient in a political (electoral) sense (Weingast and Marshall 1988), even if they are inefficient in an economic sense

[6] Or when members have countervailing incentives to represent competing but low demand constituencies. For an elaboration of how and why unorganized interests get represented in Congress, see Denzau and Munger (1986).

[7] Destler apparently explored this line of inquiry in an earlier paper. See citations to Destler and Odell (1987) in Destler, this volume.

[8] For an excellent account of the heterogeneity of agricultural interests expressed during the debate over NAFTA, see Orden (1996).

[9] Extra-geographic factors also contribute to the heterogeneity a member sees when she responds to constituencies. A substantial literature has now catalogued the dramatic rise in the number of interest groups and affiliated PACs over the last two decades. To win reelection in an era of high-priced media campaigns, legislators must please not only voters but donors. They engage in a never-ending "money chase" (Magleby and Nelson 1990), such that, in order to be competitive, candidates must respond to cash constituencies as well as constitutional constituencies. Representatives of agricultural states worry about the financial support of Archer-Daniels Midland as well as the voting support of district producers. And the interests of the two quite frequently diverge. The literature on moneyed interest groups as powerful constituencies is substantial and growing, both in political science (see below) and economics (see Rodrik 1995).

[10] Viewed in this light, abdication of policy authority is not an abdication of the agent's obligation to her district; rather, it is a consequence of it. For a test of this proposition in the area of interstate trade, see Hall and Wayman's analysis of the Natural Gas Market Policy Act (1990, esp. pp. 808-99; 812-813).

[11] See work reviewed in Rodrik (1995), esp. that by Grossman and Helpman (1994) and Magee, Brock, and Young (1989). Jackson and King (1989) provide another important move in the reconceptualization of constituency representation that may warrant greater attention in trade policy making. They argue that constituents have preferences for public goods (such as efficiency-enhancing and inflation-constraining free trade) as well as private benefits, such as higher income for textile workers and pork producers.

[12] This discussion draws on Hall (1994) and Hall and Wayman (1990) and refers to the literature critiqued therein.

[13] See Hall (1996, Chs. 1 and 9). This argument also applies to legislator interventions in agency decisions (after policymaking authority has been partly abdicated), such as

member lobbying in favor of anti-dumping remedies. I outline the general argument in Hall (1994).

REFERENCES

Arnold, R. Douglas. 1990. *The Logic of Congressional Action.* New Haven: Yale University Press.

Bauer, Raymond, Ithiel de Sola Pool, and Lewis A. Dexter. 1963. *American Business and Public Policy.* Chicago: Aldine and Atherton.

Dahl, Robert. 1956. *A Preface to Democratic Theory.* Chicago: University of Chicago Press.

Denzau, Arthur and Michael C. Munger. 1986. "Legislators and Interest Groups: How Unorganized Interests Get Represented" *American Political Science Review* 80:89-106.

Fiorina, Morris P. 1974. *Representatives, Roll Calls, and Constituencies.* Lexington, MA: D.C. Heath.

Grenzke, Janet M. 1989a. "Shopping in the Congressional Supermarket: The Currency is Complex," *American Journal of Political Science* 33:1-24.

Grenzke, Janet M. 1989b. "Candidate Attributes and PAC Contributions," *Western Political Quarterly* 42:245-64.

Grossman, Gene M. and Elhanan Helpman. 1994. "Protection For Sale." *American Economic Review* 84:833-50; reprinted in Alan V. Deardorff, James Levinsohn, and Robert M. Stern, eds., *New Directions in Trade Theory.* Ann Arbor, MI: University of Michigan Press, 1995.

Hall, Richard L. 1994. "Mobilizing Bias: Private Groups and Public Lobbies in Law Making and Rule Making." Department of Political Science, University of Michigan, Ann Arbor. Typescript.

Hall, Richard L. 1996. *Participation in Congress.* New Haven: Yale University Press.

Hall, Richard L. and Frank Wayman. 1990. "Buying Time: Moneyed Interests and the Mobilization of Bias in Congressional Committees.." *American Political Science Review* 84:797-820.

Hillman, Ayre L. 1989. *The Political Economy of Protection.* London: Harwood Academic Publishers.

Jackson, John E. and David C. King. 1989. "Private Interests, Public Goods, and Representation." *American Political Science Review* 36:805-23.

Jackson, John E. and John W. Kingdon. 1992. "Ideology, Interest Group Ratings, and Roll Call Votes." *American Journal of Political Science* 36:805-23.

Krueger, Anne O. 1996a. "Introduction." In Anne O. Krueger (ed.), *The Political Economy of American Trade Policy.* Chicago: University of Chicago Press.

Krueger, Anne O. 1996b. "Conclusions." In Anne O. Krueger (ed.), *The Political Economy of American Trade Policy.* Chicago: University of Chicago Press.

Magee, S.P., W.A. Brock, and L. Young. 1989. *Black Hole Tariffs and Endogenous Policy Theory.* New York: Cambridge University Press.

Magleby, David B. and Candace J. Nelson. 1990. *The Money Chase.* Washington, D.C.: Brookings Institution.

Mayhew, David R. 1974. *Congress: The Electoral Connection.* New Haven: Yale University Press.

Orden, David. 1996. "Agricultural Interest Groups and the North American Free Trade Agreement," in Anne O. Krueger (ed.), *The Political Economy of American Trade Policy.* Chicago: University of Chicago Press.

Schattschneider, E.E. 1960. *The Semisovereign People: A Realist's View of Democracy in America.* New York: Holt, Rinehart and Winston.

Staiger, Robert W. 1995. "A Theory of Gradual Trade Liberalization." In Alan V. Deardorff, James Levinsohn, and Robert M. Stern, eds., *New Directions in Trade Theory.* Ann Arbor, MI: University of Michigan Press.

Weingast, Barry R. and William Marshall. 1988. "The Industrial Organization of Congress." *Journal of Political Economy* 96:132-63.

Part III

Sectoral Producing Interests: Industry/Labor

CHAPTER 5

Trade Policy and the U.S. Auto Industry: Intended and Unintended Consequences

G. Mustafa Mohatarem

I. Introduction

The U.S. auto industry has been at the center of the domestic debate on whether to protect domestic manufacturing from foreign competition since at least the mid-1970s when imported automobiles first began to make significant inroads into the U.S. market. The key players in the debate have been: the "Big Three" U.S.-owned auto manufacturers; the United Auto Workers (UAW); the Japanese-owned auto manufacturers; public interest groups; the Washington-based policy think tanks; and the individual U.S. consumer. In addition, both the executive and the legislature in the U.S. played important and changing roles. Although the Japanese government appeared to be on the sideline, it too has played a significant role.

Historically, both the auto companies and the auto unions were strong supporters of free trade. Support from the UAW was instrumental in obtaining Congressional approval for both the Kennedy and the Tokyo Round of GATT agreements. The industry's support for free trade waivered in the late 1960s as imports began to make inroads into the U.S. market. By the mid-80s, all the major players in the industry had supported relief from imports at one time or another. Ford, Chrysler, and the UAW had became strong and consistent advocates of restraints on the Japanese auto manufacturers. General Motors (GM), on the other hand, waivered back and forth between support for free trade and specific protectionist measures against the Japanese.

Until the late 1970s, the industry was unable to obtain relief, in part, because the overall attitude of policy makers towards the industry was quite hostile and, in part, because GM remained committed to open trade. The industry was more successful at obtaining relief in the 1980s when all the firms in the industry ran into severe financial difficulties and joined forces to seek protection. The financial distress of the firms and the associated problems for the communities in which they were located also changed the policy makers' attitudes towards the industry. However, that success encouraged the Japanese auto manufacturers to establish U.S. production facilities, which by the end of the decade greatly diminished the value of protection obtained by the Big Three. These facilities also undermined some of the arguments the Big Three had used to obtain relief, provided the Japanese companies a stronger voice in the U.S. trade policy process, and limited the policy instruments available to provide protection for U.S.-owned manufacturers.

The success of the Japanese-owned auto manufacturing in the United States has changed both the policy debate and the policy process. The issues being debated no longer relate strictly to domestic versus import production. Instead, the arguments are now focused on whether foreign-owned manufacturers have sufficient local content so as to qualify as domestic. That means the policy instruments being debated are related to the "quality" of local manufacturing, i.e., whether foreign-owned U.S. manufacturers are sourcing sufficiently from the United States and from U.S.-owned parts suppliers. The policy process has also changed as Japanese-owned manufacturers have gained a significant voice in the U.S. political process.

The next section provides a brief account of the basic economics of the industry—you cannot understand the politics unless you "grasp" the underlying economics. In Section III, I provide an overview of the economic changes in the 1970s and early 1980s that led the industry to seek and for politicians to grant protection to the industry. Section IV describes the Japanese response to the U.S. trade restraints, in particular, their success in establishing significant U.S. manufacturing. Section V discusses how the Japanese success has changed both the policy debate and the policy process. Section VI discusses implications of these changes for future U.S. trade policy relating to the automotive industry. The paper concludes with thoughts on whether in hindsight, the U.S. auto manufacturers would have been better off without the protection they obtained in the 1980s.

II. Economics of the Auto Industry

Perhaps the most politically salient characteristic of the auto industry is its size. Auto firms are large in terms of both sales and employment. Other than for a short period immediately following the 1979 oil crisis, GM has been the largest firm in the United States and the world, and both Ford and Chrysler have been among the fifty largest. The industry employs large numbers of people. Total industry employment in 1995 was around 2 million. This figure only accounts for people employed in auto assembly and manufacturing of components. The number more than doubles if workers involved in sales and after-sales service are included. The industry is the largest consumer of industrial goods such as steel, aluminum, and copper. It also is the largest consumer of "high tech" products such as semiconductors, robots, and other electrical machinery. Finally, the industry has been at the forefront in the implementation of new manufacturing concepts as well as technology.

The size of the firms in the industry, in turn, is a function of the underlying production economics. The industry is characterized by significant economies of scale related to both production and vehicle development. It can cost as much as $2.5 billion to develop a new car line and to tool an assembly plant to produce it. The cost can be much higher if the new car line also requires new engines and transmissions. For example, Samsung, a Korean company planning to enter the auto industry next year, has announced that it will spend $5.0 billion to design and manufacture a single new car line. The conventional wisdom in the industry is that with fixed costs of this magnitude, a manufacturer needs to be able to produce 250,000 units of a car line to be profitable. Moreover, since variable costs are more or less constant, the higher the volume, the lower the average total costs.

With "big" companies you get "big" labor. Auto workers tend to work in very large and very capital intensive factories. In the past, it was not uncommon for a typical auto assembly plant to employ 5,000 or more workers. The number has now declined to around 3,000 or less per factory. Nonetheless, by any measure, auto factories tend to be large and to employ large numbers of people. The size and capital intensity make them easy to organize by unions. More importantly, once organized, workers can command significant wage premiums. For example, U.S. auto workers command a 100 percent premium over the U.S. all manufacturing average compensation. Significant premiums can be observed in many other nations, including Japan.

In a typical year, more than 15 million new vehicles are sold in the U.S. market Expenditure on a new vehicle tends to represent the second largest outlay after the purchase of a residence for most households. And, unlike a residence, these expenditures are made on a regular basis. Thus, consumers/voters tend to be better informed about auto-related issues than any other consumer good that they purchase. One of the real challenges the industry faces as it deals with the political process is that politicians tend to give much more consideration to the reaction of consumers/voters when it comes to auto-related policies than they do to policies related to other consumer goods.

The size of the industry and the impact of its products on consumer wallets gives it a political dimension that few other industries possess. Politicians recognize the positive impact of the industry on the local and the national economy. Therefore, they want to be seen as promoting its growth. But, at the same time, they recognize that voters are well informed about the price of an automobile and the factors that impact that price. U.S. trade policy as it relates to the auto industry is, therefore, the result of the complex interaction between the desire to have strong, domestic auto production that provides premium wages and, at the same time, affordable prices for consumers.

III. Changing Fortunes of the Domestic Auto Manufacturers

Until the mid-1970s, the operating assumption of the U.S. trade policy makers was that the U.S. auto producers did not need any trade protection. If anything, most U.S. policy makers held the view that competition from foreign manufacturers was required to provide market discipline. Thus, when VW began to make significant inroads into the U.S. market in the 1960s, its entry was widely welcomed.

The U.S. attitude was also reflected in the positions U.S. negotiators took in international trade forums. The U.S. agreed to lower its automotive tariffs without seeking reciprocal concessions in the sector. By the end of the implementation of the Tokyo Round GATT agreement in the late 1980s, the U.S. tariff on passenger cars had been reduced to only 2.5 percent, making the U.S. the most open auto market in the world.

Neither the U.S. auto makers nor the UAW played a significant role in these negotiations. This was not surprising given the worldwide success of the U.S. auto manufacturers. The established view remained that United States manufacturers and their workers were protected by their economies of scale and differences in product preferences between the United States and the rest of the world. Underlying this view was the belief that as long as energy prices remained low, Americans would prefer large cars that only American manufacturers could produce in sufficient volumes to be cost-competitive. Furthermore, both GM and Ford viewed an open U.S. market as protection against overzealous U.S. antitrust authorities.

The political landscape began to change following the first oil shock. The sharp increase in oil prices following the Arab oil embargo in 1973 increased the U.S. demand for small cars. American auto manufacturers began to import small cars from their foreign affiliates. The European and Japanese manufacturers also intensified their sales efforts in the United States. Within two years, the import share of the U.S. market had doubled, with imports exceeding 10 percent of the market for the first time.

It was at this point that the UAW changed its position and began demanding protection from imports. The change in the UAW's position was only, in part, related to the inroads by foreign-owned manufacturers. The union was much more concerned about the increasing imports by the American-owned manufacturers. The American auto manufacturers, especially GM, continued to support open trade. They believed that the inroads by the imports were temporary and would be reversed once oil prices stabilized. They were more concerned by threatened antitrust action than by the growing imports.

The second oil shock in 1979 had an even bigger impact. The jump in oil prices plunged the U.S. economy into the worst recession to hit the U.S. auto industry since the 1930s. U.S. motor vehicle production declined by almost 50 percent between 1978 and 1982. At the same time, the Japanese doubled their share of the U.S. market to over 20 percent. As a result, Ford and the UAW filed an escape clause petition for import relief with the U.S. International Trade Commission (ITC) in 1980. GM and Chrysler did not join the petitions. Chrysler had already earlier been granted substantial relief under the Chrysler Loan Guarantee Act. More importantly, during the debate over these subsidies, Chrysler had argued that its distress was related largely to overall economic conditions and correctable internal problems. Therefore, it could not very well turn around a year later and argue that imports were the cause of its troubles. GM's reasons for not joining were complex. The corporation's management was reluctant to abandon its support for open trade. Management also recognized that abandoning support for free trade would make it more difficult to oppose costly command and control regulations, which were viewed as a serious threat. Finally, the company remained concerned about potential antitrust action, which would be more likely in a closed market than in an open market.

The ITC concluded that while the industry was suffering serious injury, the cause of that injury was the severe recession and the shift in demand to small cars, and not the increase in imports. The absence of GM and Chrysler almost certainly doomed the relief petition. With two firms that accounted for more than half of industry's production not supporting the petition, it was impossible for Ford and the UAW to demonstrate injury to the industry. The ITC's decision to deny relief shifted the focus to the Congress and the Administration.

The eighties began with a political environment that was much more sympathetic. President Reagan had promised to help the industry during the election campaign. At the same time, legislators from the auto producing states assumed leadership positions in both houses of Congress. Congressman Dingell from Michigan became the leader of the effort in the House to obtain relief for the industry. Senators Riegle (D-MI) and Danforth (R-MO) led the effort in the Senate. They introduced a number of bills to impose restraints on vehicle imports from Japan. While none of these became law, they provided the leverage that the Administration needed to negotiate a Voluntary Restraint Agreement (VRA) with Japan. Starting in 1981, Japan agreed to restrict passenger car exports to the United States. These restraints were supposed to have been temporary. However, they stayed in place until 1994. The formal agreement with the United States ended in 1985, but the government of Japan chose to maintain the restraints at 2.3 million. The political symbolism of the restraint was such that they were maintained until well after they had become nonbinding.

The VRAs were strongly supported by the UAW, Ford, and Chrysler. GM initially supported the VRAs, but decided to oppose their renewal in 1985. GM's decision to support the VRAs was a reflection of the severe financial difficulties it and the rest of the industry faced in 1980 and 1981. In 1980, GM reported its first loss since the early 1920s. The increase in imports and the steep recession had threatened the very survival of the company. Thus, seeking temporary protection was a matter of survival.

By 1985, the financial condition of the company had changed. The VRA combined with the recovery in U.S. demand had helped to restore profitability. However, the company came under tremendous pressure from the UAW, Ford, Chrysler, and Congressional allies to continue supporting import restraints. There was also recognition within the company that with U.S. auto sales strengthening, continuation of the restraints could produce short-term profits.

Offsetting these benefits and pressures and carrying the day were a number of factors. First, GM executives increasingly recognized that the longer the VRAs remained in place, the more difficult it would be for the company to implement steps to improve its competitiveness. Second, by then it was obvious that the Japanese were successfully eroding the VRAs protection by building manufacturing capacity in the U.S. Third, there were important domestic regulatory benefits to opposing protection. Finally, GM's business strategy included high-volume imports of small cars from Asia. This strategy could not be executed as long as the VRAs were in place.

IV. Impact of the VRAs

There is an extensive literature on the market impact of the auto VRAs. Much, if not all of this literature deals with the impact of the VRAs on vehicle prices, profitability and employment in the U.S. auto industry. These are important issues and deserve the attention they have received. But, these studies have had a minimal impact on U.S. trade policy or on the trade policy of any other nation. This is because politicians seldom pay much attention to the "cost" of protection. They pay even less attention to the counterfactual—what would have happened in the absence of protection. That is, jobs not created in the auto sector or in other sectors of the economy as a result of protection provided the auto sector carry very little weight in the political debate. The only metric of interest to the politicians is whether a protectionist measure protected the firms and employees that originally sought protection.

By this metric, the VRAs can be considered a qualified success. They provided the domestic firms with temporary relief—relief long enough to implement changes necessary to become competitive. They also slowed, but did not stop the loss of UAW represented jobs in the industry. More important, they gave the U.S. manufacturers the breathing space necessary to improve the efficiency of their U.S. operations and the quality of their U.S. product. Today, the average U.S. assembly plant is almost as productive as the average Japanese assembly plant. American manufacturers have closed the quality gap. All three U.S. companies are now financially healthy and internationally competitive. Finally, U.S. consumers continue to enjoy lower auto prices than the rest of the word.

It would be wrong to believe that this favorable outcome was necessarily the result of protection alone or that it was predicted. In fact, this outcome came about largely because of a completely unanticipated development. The Japanese auto manufacturers responded to the VRAs by building assembly plants in the United States. Over time, these assembly plants eroded the protection provided by the VRAs. Neither the proponents nor the opponents of the VRA had expected this development.

Conventional wisdom in the early 1980s held that the Japanese auto companies were successful in the United States because of Japan-specific factors. It was widely believed that the Japanese were competitive in the United States because wages in Japan were lower, Japan's labor-management relations were superior, the Japanese worked harder and longer, the Japanese government provided more support to its industry, etc. Given the emphasis on Japan-specific factors, it is not surprising that the prevailing view was that the Japanese manufacturers would lose their competitive edge if forced to produce in the United States. This view led both the UAW and the U.S.-owned manufacturers to demand that the Japanese be forced to produce in the United States.

Much to the surprise of the American auto industry and, perhaps, even to the surprise of the Japanese auto manufacturers, the Japanese manufacturers were able to transfer their production system to the United States. While Japan-specific factors may have helped, the key to the Japanese success was their manufacturing system. This system, which is called lean production, resulted in both lower costs and higher quality than the mass production techniques of the American auto manufacturers. By building plants in the United States, the Japanese manufacturers demonstrated that lean production was transferable to the United States. In other words, they proved that competitive advantage in the auto industry was company-specific not country-specific.

V. Trade Policy Implications

The fact that competitiveness in the auto industry is determined by company-specific factors rather than country-specific factors has important trade policy implications, especially as it pertains to the instruments of protection. In the U.S. context, the success of the transplants has significantly changed both the trade policy making process as well as the instruments available to the policy makers. Japanese-owned auto companies now employ more than 40,000 workers in U.S. manufacturing plants. Consequently, they have gained an important voice in the political process. They have further enhanced their ability to influence the process by choosing to locate in different states. This gives them access to and support from almost as many senators as the Big Three can muster. In addition, since the Japanese have been expanding U.S. production while the Big Three had been retrenching until recently, the Japanese occasionally have better access to governors and other local officials. The net result is that the U.S. policy process will not permit explicit restraints on the expansion of transplant production. In fact, the opposite may be true because states now compete to attract even more Japanese investment.

The success of the transplants has also changed the terms of the policy debate. The debate is no longer over imports versus domestic production. In stead, it concerns transplants versus the traditional domestic manufacturers. Even though the transplants have been expanding production and adding employment, the Big Three retain a big edge in both production and employment. Because of this big edge, the political process still makes a distinction between the Big Three and the transplants. In particular, the Big Three are viewed as making a much more significant contribution to the U.S. economy than the transplants. The Big Three source more from the United States and, more importantly, source more from the traditional American-owned suppliers. This provides them with important political allies in the American supplier community. Most importantly, the UAW, which has failed to organize the transplants, remains closely aligned with the U.S. auto manufacturers.

In contrast, while the transplants are increasing sourcing in the U.S., they tend still to rely more on imported components. Moreover, a significant portion of their sourcing comes from the U.S. plants of their traditional Japanese suppliers. This has left them vulnerable to complaints by American-owned suppliers who claim that the Japanese-owned facilities deny them contracts even when they are competitive. The suppliers' complaints have registered strongly with U.S. policy makers. They have pressured the Japanese not only to increase sourcing in the United States, but also to do so with American-owned suppliers.

In many respects, the 1995 U.S.–Japan auto dispute was as much about pressuring the Japanese transplants to increase purchases in the United States as it was about opening the Japanese market to U.S. vehicles and parts manufacturers. Moreover, most of the measures that the Japanese agreed to undertake to resolve the dispute were related to transplants. The Japanese manufacturers committed to increase transplant production and to increase U.S. sourcing for their transplants. They also made a commitment to increase purchases from American-owned suppliers. The Japanese concessions related to opening their market were much less specific.

Now that the 1995 dispute has been resolved, the rhetoric has quieted down considerably. In part, this is a reflection of the currently stronger financial condition of the U.S.-owned auto manufacturers. But, in a larger part, it reflects the growing recognition that traditional trade protection measures will no longer work to protect the U.S. auto manufacturers. The Japanese have demonstrated that they can overcome any trade barriers by building vehicles in the United States. Furthermore, while there may be opportunities to increase costs for the transplants through political action, even these opportunities are limited by the growing political and economic influence of the transplants.

The U.S. auto industry's experience with protection has implications both for other industries seeking protection in the United States as well as for other countries that continue to protect or promote their domestic industries. Lesson one is to distinguish between protecting the production of a good in the United States versus protecting specific firms that produce that good. The experience of the U.S. auto industry suggests that trade protection is most valuable for firms in industries where the United States has become an uncompetitive production location. In industries where the United States remains a competitive location, trade protection can at best be viewed as providing a temporary, one-time reprieve—time to make the changes necessary to regain competitiveness. Trade protection will not help in the longer run because it will encourage more efficient foreign producers to locate production in the United States, perhaps, earlier than they otherwise would. In other words, in industries such as the auto industry, where the United States remains a competitive location, trade protection can encourage domestic production, but not necessarily by the uncompetitive firms that seek the protection.

Lesson two is that protection of uncompetitive, domestically-owned auto producers requires restrictions on both imports and investment in the country by more efficient foreign firms. While some countries, e.g., France and Italy, have adopted this policy, most find it politically difficult for obvious reasons. First, the costs of protection are too visible. Second, domestic manufacturers have a difficult time persuading policy makers that they are uncompetitive because of country-specific factors when other firms stand ready to produce in the country. And, most importantly, with most of the countries in the developed world suffering from high levels of unemployment, politicians find it difficult to turn away investors that are willing to create thousands of new jobs.

For countries that are trying to promote domestic auto production, the bottom line lesson is to protect production—not specific producers. This policy recommendation is especially applicable to countries with large or potentially large markets. Market size is important because of the economies of scale in the auto industry. Brazil provides a good example of a country following this type of policy. Over the last two years, it has raised its barriers to imports of vehicles, but lowered its barriers to investment in the auto industry. While it is too soon to judge whether this policy will succeed in promoting production of internationally competitive vehicles in Brazil, the early results point in that direction. Brazil has attracted investment by auto manufacturers from around the world. As these plants begin production in the next few years, competition in the Brazilian market will intensify. That competition should encourage Brazilian manufacturers to improve their competitiveness.

Brazil's policies stand in stark contrast to auto policies in Asia where some countries (e.g., Indonesia and Malaysia) are trying to encourage the development of "national" car companies. They have implemented both tight restraints on vehicle imports and on investment in the industry. They view Japan and South Korea as their models, both of which succeeded in developing strong, national auto industries even though they restricted both imports and investment by foreign-owned auto manufacturers. What is conveniently ignored by the proponents of the national car programs is that, in both Japan and South Korea, there was intense competition among domestic car manufacturers, which provided the market discipline. Absent this market discipline, it would be a surprise if either Indonesia or Malaysia succeeded in developing an internationally competitive auto industry.

VI. Conclusion

The VRAs were less successful in protecting the domestic manufacturers than their proponents had hoped for, but were also less costly than their opponents had feared. The VRAs did provide temporary relief to U.S. auto producers. They also slowed the erosion of UAW jobs. However, since the U.S. manufacturers recognized that this protection was being eroded over time by Japanese-owned production in the United States, they continued to improve their manufacturing efficiency and the quality of their cars. And, while U.S. consumers may have had to pay a somewhat higher price for their cars than they would have paid in the absence of the VRAs, they are still able to buy high quality cars at some of the lowest prices in the world.

Some observers have argued that the United States and the U.S. auto manufacturers would have been better off without the VRAs. These observers argue that without the protection of the VRAs, U.S. companies and their employees would have made an even more rapid adjustment to the Japanese competition. They further suggest that a quicker response would have prevented the Japanese from capturing more of the U.S. market.

It is possible that these observers are correct. However, neither the industry nor the country had the luxury of testing out their theory. It is quite likely that one or more of the U.S. auto companies could have gone under during the deep recession of 1980-1982 if Japanese car imports into the United States had not been restricted. From a trade policy perspective, the VRAs worked as well if not better than traditional escape clause relief would have worked. They provided the U.S. auto manufacturers with temporary protection, which the manufacturers utilized to restore their competitiveness. And, because they encouraged the Japanese manufacturers to expand U.S. production, they exerted competitive discipline on U.S. manufacturers. From the country's perspective, they avoided the very severe transition costs that would have resulted if one of the Big Three had failed. In this instance, one could argue that the ends justified the means. The United States today has a healthy automobile industry with both American and foreign-owned producers. Employment in the industry is nearing its all-time high. U.S. consumers enjoy some of the lowest prices in the world for cars and probably have more choice when it comes to purchasing a car than consumers in any other country.

CHAPTER 6

Steel: Trade Policy in a Changed Environment

Douglas A. Brook

I. Introduction

Today, the steel industry of the United States is in a trade policy environment unlike any it has experienced in the past three decades. Restructured, modernized, and price and quality competitive, U.S. steel no longer seeks or enjoys industry-specific protection. Anti-Dumping (AD) and Countervailing Duty (CVD) laws have become, for the steel industry, the quid pro quo for free trade. They set the limits on permissible behavior in the marketplace, akin to the concepts of regulated fair competition in the domestic economy.

This paper will identify the trade policy objectives currently sought by the integrated steel industry. It will examine how the industry's interests are determined and promoted and will assess the extent to which the industry conforms to the models of political economy of trade policy. Finally, it will address how effective the domestic integrated steel industry is today in achieving its public policy objectives.

A definitional note is in order at the outset. For most of its history, the steel industry in the United States was easily defined as a monolithic group of integrated manufacturers which made steel from iron ore and owned most of the factors of production—iron mines, railroads, coal mines, coke ovens, blast furnaces, etc. Steel firms were characterized by unionized workforces, large capital requirements and high barriers to entry or exit. However, over the past quarter century, the steel industry in the United States has been restructured and reformed. Now, in addition to the remaining integrated companies, the industry includes a significant minimill sector—smaller companies making steel from scrap in electric arc furnaces with mostly non-union workers and lower capital requirements. Restructuring has also resulted in a distinctly separate specialty steel sector and other smaller reconstituted companies in narrower product lines. These companies sometimes have either different or indifferent attitudes toward trade policy. For the purposes of this paper, therefore, the trade policy advocacy of the steel industry will mean that of the six remaining integrated companies – AK Steel, Bethlehem Steel, Inland Steel, LTV Steel, National Steel, and U.S. Steel (USX Corporation).

II. Trade Policy Objectives

Since the expiration of industry-specific protection in 1992, U.S. Trade Laws have been the only recourse available to counter dumped and subsidized steel imports. Curtis H. Barnette, Chairman and CEO of Bethlehem Steel refers to the 1990s as the era of Trade Law Remedies (TLRs). Barnette (1994, p. 4) says when the Voluntary Restraint Agreements expired in 1992 the Bush Administration "explicitly stated that the U.S. industry should thereafter rely on existing, GATT sanctioned, unfair trade remedies. Implicit . . . was an understanding that the Administration would allow the trade remedies to proceed objectively to their conclusion without political interference or compromise."

The overriding trade policy objective of the U. S. steel industry today is to ensure fair[1] competition free of the distortions that arise because of subsidies, dumping, and anticompetitive practices. In this era of Trade Law Remedies, the specific goals serving this objective are: (1) preservation and enforcement of U.S. Trade Laws and (2) conclusion of a Multilateral Steel Agreement (MSA) which eliminates the overcapacity, subsidies, dumping, and anticompetitive practices which distort much of the world's steel trade.

III. Trade Policy Determination and Promotion

Trade policy is a constant concern for the steel industry. Continued import penetration causes the industry to be ever-vigilant. Steel is a highly competitive business, sensitive to rapid and seemingly small changes in market conditions even at the peak of the business cycle. As long as world-wide overcapacity and extensive subsidization exist, along with the dumping which subsidies and closed markets facilitate, the possibility of unfairly priced steel in the U.S. market motivates the industry to stay engaged in trade policy debates.

The determination and promotion of trade policy objectives and strategies by the U.S. integrated steel industry are achieved through a combination of formal and informal means, some of which are described below.

- The American Iron and Steel Institute (AISI) is the industry's trade association. It plays a central role in the determination and communication of the industry's policy preferences. The staff, trade subcommittee, and U.S. members of the board of directors draft, debate, and articulate the industry's views. As such it is the "official" voice of the industry and its most formal policy-setting mechanism.
- The six integrated companies are the "petitioning companies" which filed massive AD/CVD cases in 1992. They generally share a common outlook on trade policy and, with varying commitment of resources, underwrite much of the industry's trade policy. They are the

largest members, most active participants, and biggest dues-payers to AISI. As a result, their views on trade tend to prevail in the Institute. The six also work outside of AISI on priority trade matters through two sub-groups.

(1) The law firms of Dewey-Ballantine and Skadden, Arps, Slate, Meagher and Flom are retained to: advise on trade matters; advocate Trade Law Remedy actions; monitor legal, administrative and legislative matters; and assist in trade lobbying efforts.

(2) The Task Force on Uruguay Round Legislation (TFURL) consists of the companies' Washington representatives, trade specialists and retained lawyers. TFURL began as a lobbying action group and clearinghouse during the final months of the Uruguay Round negotiations. It has continued to serve as a coordinating body for lobbying strategy and action.

- The Committee to Support U.S. Trade Laws (CSUSTL) is a diverse group of companies, steel and non-steel related, who have used or anticipate the future need to invoke AD/CVD laws. Formed during the Uruguay Round negotiations, CSUSTL has evolved into a permanent broad-based Trade Law lobbying group. CSUSTL provides a significant addition to the lobbying strength of the steel industry and represents one of the industry's most effective attempts at coalition-building.
- The House and Senate Steel Caucuses provide constituency-based support on issues important to steel. The Caucuses have proven to be an effective bloc for exerting influence with the Congressional leadership and with the Executive Branch. Members of the Steel Caucuses are the first points of contact on Capitol Hill for steel lobbyists.

Rodrik (1995) suggests that in an industry like steel there may be an element of persistence and status quo bias; that once successful, there is a tendency by a protected industry and its government toward continued protection. Today's experience of steel indicates that this does not exist in perpetuity. What does seem to continue is the industry's constant engagement in trade policy issues even in times when import penetration or unfairly priced imports seem less troublesome. This momentum can be explained by the start-up costs (in money, time, and political capital) which would be involved if the industry abandoned the trade policy arena, only to return in a time of crisis and attempt to rebuild its political influence.

IV. The Political Economy of Steel Trade

The prominence of the steel industry in trade policy has caused it to be the subject of considerable study. Analysts have endeavored to determine why certain public policies were implemented instead of others, how industry representatives and Government policymakers reached their strategic and policy decisions, and what the economic and social costs and benefits have been. Some models of the political economy of trade policy have been developed. How well does the actual behavior of the steel industry match these models?

From the viewpoint of the steel industry's experience, the models are instructive, but one-dimensional and incomplete. In addition, they also often tend to start from a hostile premise. Rodrik's (1995) survey work is perhaps most useful for comparison. He asks at the outset, "Why is international trade not free?" Then he ponders, "Why are trade policies universally biased against trade?" Perhaps an equally sound formulation might be: "Why does any nation allow foreign industries to compete - even unfairly - with its domestic producers?" Rodrik seems to think that in some international economic state of nature there would be totally unrestrained free trade among nations. Why is it not equally plausible that in such a state there would be no trade, except in goods not indigenously available? If this is the political economy, which is the more likely condition?

In describing some models of trade policy, Rodrik is quick to point out their shortcomings. He describes three models—the tariff-formulation function approach, the political support function approach, and the median voter approach. The first he critiques as lacking consideration for the preferences of politicians, the second he says lacks concern for the actions taken by influential groups, and of the third he opines, (p. 1466) "the downside, of course, is the lack of realism. . . ." Political situations cannot be fully explained, repeated, or predicted with such precision as these models imply. Even when considered together, these models tend to ignore the seemingly infinite and less quantifiable political considerations that impact public policy decisions. Rodrik admits that creating a comprehensive model is a tall order, and he points out that most models deal with the more political questions implicitly rather than explicitly. Unfortunately, this leaves much at the heart of trade policymaking woefully unaddressed.

The campaign contributions approach deserves a bit more scrutiny because of the pervasiveness of money in politics today. This model attempts to make a direct link between campaign contributions and the voting behavior of lawmakers. Rodrik (p. 1469) correctly explains, however, "... that only a small part of lobbying activity in real politics takes the form of financial contributions." In fact the world of campaign contributions is exceedingly complex. The notion that industry political action committees influence voting behavior by "pushing" contributions at lawmakers covers only one aspect of political money. It ignores the fact that most contributions are solicited ("pulled") rather than proffered; that political giving is also based on other relationships (constituency, past support, party or philosophical considerations, for instance); and that contributions from any one industry amount to only a small percentage of a lawmaker's total campaign treasury, engendering gratitude perhaps but not dependency. Finally, contributions come from both sides. A possible test of the political contributions model as an explanation of trade policy preferences would be to attempt to identify a bidding war or auction.

The models necessarily tend to reduce complex human political behavior to simple and direct cause-effect relationships, as in the study of rent seeking, protection, and innovation in the steel industry by Lenway, Morck and Yeung (1996). They argue that protection results in greater private returns for steel shareholders, higher wages for steelworkers, and bigger pay increases for steel CEOs, without any consideration of the vagaries of the stock market, the dynamics of union wage negotiations, or the determinants of CEO compensation. If these are important indicators of the reasons an industry seeks protection, the relative degree to which protection influences these outcomes remains to be determined. One suspects that other causes will rank as considerably more influential. Perhaps the survival of a company or an industry is a more certain predictor of common trade policy preferences among stockholders, managers and workers.

Rodrik (1995, p. 1481) catalogues the cross-industry determinants of levels of protection within a country as identified by a number of studies. They find that higher levels of protection exist when the following conditions are present. Only some of these characteristics apply to the steel industry.

- Labor intensive, low skill, low wage. (Steel is moderately labor intensive, though decreasingly so; the skill range is wide, and the wages are relatively high.)
- High import penetration, an increase in import penetration, and an industry in decline. (All of these conditions have existed for steel.)
- Regionally concentrated industry, with customers that are not highly concentrated. (This is somewhat true for steel. Production has been geographically concentrated, but that is starting to lessen; and the automobile and appliance sectors are highly concentrated and influential customers.)

For steel, high import penetration and an increase in imports would be the most reliable determinants of the industry's efforts to seek protection. At the time when steel sought the protection that led to the Trigger Price Mechanism and two rounds of Voluntary Restraint Agreements, imports had been steadily increasing and were approaching forty percent of the U.S. market.

In posing the question of why some policy options are chosen over others, Rodrik (1995, p. 1470) offers a choice for a hypothetical income transfer to garment workers. His five options are: (1) lump sum grants to present workers; (2) lump sum grants to present and future workers; (3) a permanent employment subsidy; (4) a permanent production subsidy; and (5) a permanent tariff. He views the options as progressively worse as one moves from (1) to (5) and wonders why (5) should be the policymakers' choice.

One assumes that he is talking about the United States only, since it is quite imaginable for any of the first four options to be employed in Europe or the Far East. Yet one cannot conceive of anything but option (5) being politically viable in the United States. There are procedural barriers, of course—finding revenue sources to offset the expenditures under Congressional Budget

Rules, for instance. But the reason is deeper than that. There are political and cultural values involved which constrain the range of policy options. Subsidization and lump sum payments, while perhaps more efficient to the theoretical economist, are simply not conceivable for the steel industry strategist. The ideas of lump sum payments or permanent subsidies are outside the limits of American political tolerance. Even putting aside today's political rhetoric about "corporate welfare," the notion of explicit direct payments or subsidies to steel workers or steel manufacturers violates our private sector political theology. These options are simply not viable for the political policymaker.

On the other hand, Rodrik may be giving too little credit to our political tolerance for export promotion, albeit indirect. There is considerable effort put forth by various elements of the state and federal governments to advance overseas sales and ventures by U.S. companies. Virtually the entire U.S. Foreign and Commercial Service of the Commerce Department is dedicated to this, as are numerous state and Federal trade missions and trade fairs, and the market-opening negotiations conducted by the U.S. Trade Representative. Direct subsidies to exporters, of course, would be as politically unacceptable as direct subsidies to industries impacted by imports.

Rodrik (1995 p. 1471) concludes there is "a serious gap in our understanding of what makes trade policy so politically efficient . . . when considerably more direct means of redistributing income certainly exist."

Krueger's (1995) work seems to start at this point. She has overseen sectoral studies to determine what can be learned about the political side of protection. The very thorough study of the steel industry by Moore (1995) in Krueger's project describes the sources of steel's strength in the past: the cohesive "steel triangle" coalition of carbon steel producers; strong Congressional representation and the steelworkers union; relative weakness of cohesive opposition groups; and the credible threat that Trade Law Remedies would produce judgments in favor of the industry. He also correctly concludes that today's restructured and downsized industry has a more shallow political reservoir on which to draw upon. However, he does not seem to address the fact that the political economic environment has changed as well.

Notwithstanding the rise of economic nationalist rhetoric by marginal political forces, there is little political appetite in the White House or Congress for quotas, subsidies or other such approaches to trade. On the contrary, policies are now aimed at market-opening objectives. Enforcement of domestic Trade Laws often serves as a point of leverage in international trade negotiations. Trading regimes today are characterized by objectives of openness and multilaterality, neither of which is conducive to sector-specific bilateral market limitations like the steel VRAs. Moreover, the Nation's foreign policy objectives are no longer tied to industrial development in other countries such that negotiated protection is preferable to Trade Law Remedies. (An exception would be the recent failed attempt by the Clinton Administration to achieve AD/CVD exemptions for products from "economies-in-transition.")

Krueger (1995, pp. 1431ff) concludes with seven themes gleaned from her project: (1) the question of the degree to which current trade policy is in the national interest; (2) the role of ideas in shaping the political process; (3) the economic determinants of political strength; (4) the role of institutions; (5) the extent to which individual actors are "rational;" (6) the importance of industry unanimity; and (7) the role of lobbying and organization. The experience of the steel industry suggests that some of these would be good areas for further study.

Krueger (1995) expresses her strongest objections to protection in dealing with the question of national interest. She chooses the short-term cost to the consumer as the measure of good and bad policy, and she laments that the interests of the final consumer are not considered in trade policy debates. For steel and others she says (p. 433), "protection was sought by industries experiencing difficulties because of a cyclical downturn." Surely in the case of steel, underpriced imports increasing over decades, forty percent import penetration, worldwide overcapacity, and protected or cartelized foreign markets amount to more than cyclical "difficulties" that would disappear with the turn of a calendar page. The issue of "national interest" is a slippery concept in studying protection. Were steel's import restraints economically inefficient? Perhaps. Would it have been in the national interest for the domestic steel industry to disappear? Perhaps not. In either case, would the decisions have been economic or political?

In discussing ideas, Krueger focuses on public opinion and the relative persuasiveness of ideas stated in terms such as free, fairness, need, and equity. In this context, these ideas are really the rhetoric of the political debate. The ideas which are most important, however, are the political philosophies and economic viewpoints that frame the policymakers' choices. One needs only to reflect upon the party breakdown in the votes of the ITC Commissioners on the steel petitions, as shown in table 6.1, to conclude that only basic philosophical differences could have led two groups of commissioners to come to such clearly different conclusions about enforcing the same Trade Laws with the same information.

TABLE 6.1. ITC Votes on Steel Petitions

Commissioner	Affirmative	Negative	Affirmative (%)
Nuzum (D)	30	14	68%
Newquist (D)	27	17	61%
Rohr (D)	24	20	55%
TOTAL	81	51	61%
Watson (R)	18	24	43%
Crawford (R)	13	31	30%
Brunsdale (R)	7	37	16%
TOTAL	38	92	30%

Source: Author's calculations, based on data provided by Dewey-Ballantine, LLP.

The votes closely track with these Commissioners' known political positions and economic philosophies. What would be the effect on public policy if one or two Commissioners were replaced by holders of different views. Or, what might have been the outcome of the Uruguay Round if the U.S. Trade Representative had been an economist rather than a lawyer-negotiator?

Krueger (p. 437) disdains the outcomes that derive from political strength. "For economists concerned with framing policy" she "questions the capacity of the political process to be constrained . . . to respond to broader interests." But economists do not alone frame policy, and it is this lack of appreciation for the role of political factors which marks the inadequacy of the current models of political economy of trade policy.

Political strength has many determinants. Understanding them can help us to understand policy choices. The size, visibility, concentration, vulnerability, and resources of an industry certainly can affect its political strength. But these require a transformer—something that turns the economic factors into strength. This could be a strong leader, a crisis of some kind, or some confluence of other political forces. The role of a forceful advocate can be defining. In the case of steel, Bethlehem's Curtis Barnette, a committed trade policy activist who takes a persistently strong position in favor of effective AD/CVD laws, is the dominant force in formulating AISI's trade policy position. Similarly, Geneva Steel's Robert Grow, the current Chairman of AISI, has forced anticompetitive practices to the forefront of the Multilateral Steel Agreement negotiations.

Krueger tends to view institutions as welcome constraints on the excesses that can result from pressures of specific industries and interest groups. Certainly public institutions can play the role of arbitrator or referee of the "public interest." But institutions can also be advocates and political actors. In the example of the steel industry, institutional factors may be quite important in explaining why the industry acts as it does and why the Government responds in the ways that it does. For instance, permanent advocacy institutions have developed. Prominent trade law firms and lobbying coalitions on both sides of the steel trade issue have become permanent players on the policy scene, forever scrimmaging even in the absence of major legislative policy battles. Similarly, some permanent staff members of key congressional committees have trade law agendas which they continually try to advance, even in times when industry advocates are not pressing for action. Also, organizational "personalities" are easy to identify. The positions and attitudes of the Department of Commerce, the U.S. Trade Representative, and the International Trade Commission are identifiably distinct, and in keeping with their functions and constituencies.

An area where considerable research could be done is to determine the extent to which protection helps the protected. The steel industry believes that its protective era, particularly the period of the last and most comprehensive VRAs, provided it with the opportunity to restructure and return to viability. Moore and Krueger (1995) opine that the rise of domestic competition from minimills was facilitated by the VRAs and was the real cause of the restructuring of the integrated sector. Thorough and independent analysis of this hypothesis remains to be done, however.

Industry unanimity has been an enduring characteristic of the steel industry in trade matters. Krueger (p. 439) is quite correct when she says that "there will be protection when the industry is unanimous." In the past, the companies in the industry allied with the United Steelworkers of America (USWA) in a unanimous position on trade and in a coordinated lobbying effort to achieve trade objectives. Today's industry is more diverse with minimills, specialty steel, and pipe and tube sectors threatening to disturb this unanimity. To date, they have all held together in a rather wary alliance but each clearly has a different foundation on which to base a trade policy position. The ability of the integrated sector to continue to dominate and control steel's trade policy agenda is an open question. Today, for instance, the specialty steel industry has proposed its own multilateral agreement in frustration over the stalemate in the MSA talks. With few past subsidies to be forgiven, the specialty industry is willing to concede on "grandfathering" past subsidies—a position which the integrated sector is reluctant to take in the face of nearly $50 billion in outstanding actionable subsides.

Finally, the role of lobbying and organizations is worth study. Why is steel successful in promoting its interests on Capitol Hill and in the White House? Some reasons seem apparent. First is persistence. The industry maintains a constant presence in the policy arena through the Washington offices of its companies and its retained lawyers. They are consistently first on Capitol Hill whenever a trade issue arises. Second is expertise. Its trade lawyers and lobbyists are among the most skilled at developing effective strategies and engaging in the arcana of Trade Law. They are experienced in trade legislative battles and know better than their opponents the intricacies of trade policymaking. Third, the industry still has powerful allies. The CSUSTL group, for instance, represents a strong lobbying coalition, going far beyond steel, in support of mutual objectives. The Steel Caucus and the industry's other Congressional supporters, while perhaps not so numerous as they once may have been, are often on the right committees and in the right leadership positions to affect policy on behalf of the industry.

V. Steel Industry Effectiveness

Compared to the days of industry-specific protections one might conclude, as Moore (1995) does, that the effectiveness of the steel industry has waned. But policy effectiveness is situational. It might be better to ask how effective the industry is in achieving its more limited policy objectives in today's policy environment.

In terms of winning by using Trade Law Remedies, the industry has had mixed success. The massive AD/CVD cases filed in 1992 resulted in a strong affirmation by the Commerce Department that dumped and subsidized steel was present in the U.S. market. However, the eventual judgments by the ITC gave a mixed result. Legal action has rendered only a partial success despite the cost to the petitioning companies, and the stock market was unimpressed with the outcome. On the day that the ITC decisions were announced, the industry lost $1 billion, or ten percent of its total stock-market valuation.

Administration policy has recently been a place of some success for the industry, after a marked lack of effectiveness with the two preceding Administrations. The Clinton White House pursued a policy of restoring strong AD/CVD provisions in the Uruguay Round, and the final negotiations went far towards achieving that result. However, concentrating solely on dumping, the industry was surprised by the Administration's decision to give the green light to foreign subsidies that the United States had previously opposed. Clearly the White House felt it had the political room to do this despite predictable dissatisfaction from steel and its allies.

On Capitol Hill, steel was effective in helping to build a coalition to support the Uruguay Round agreement, oppose attempts to weaken AD/CVD laws, and eventually to pass the implementing legislation. And most recently, the industry and its allies were successful in beating back attempts to weaken AD laws through so-called "short supply" legislation. The strength and persistence of the short supply advocates, however, indicate that Moore's (1995) observation that steel's opposition was weak and unorganized may no longer be the case.

And in ongoing negotiations on the Multilateral Steel Agreement, the USTR negotiators have remained faithful to the positions advocated by the industry. Although a separate agreement for the specialty steel segment may proceed independently, the integrated companies and USTR are aligned in their objectives for the MSA.

VI. Conclusion

The steel industry in the United States has changed dramatically over the past two decades and so have its trade policy preferences. Once seeking quantity protection from imports against which it could not effectively compete, the restructured industry today is unprotected by industry-specific trade restrictions. Its domestic trade policy preferences are now for fairly priced competition, governed by the U.S. Trade Laws. The steel industry remains effective in achieving its trade policy objectives. But the demands of the industry are more modest than in the recent past, and success is often related to its ability to find support among a broader industry coalition.

The models of political economy of trade policy have been found to be instructive but incomplete. The authors themselves admit that they have not yet completely explained why some policy preferences emerge over others. From the steel industry experience, it seems clear that the models have failed to understand the political side of policymaking. More work needs to be done on the role of advocates and institutions, the defining of political opportunities and constraints, and the determinants of political economic choices.

Looking toward the future, it is possible to foresee a steel industry whose trade policies address the conditions in other steel producing countries. As world-wide overcapacity continues to plague steel markets, efforts like the MSA to rationalize the industry through elimination of subsidies, break-up of cartels and the closing of excess overseas production facilities will increase. At the same time, the globally competitive U.S. steel industry can be expected to seek international business opportunities. In so doing, its trade policy goals may focus more on the competition and investment issues that inhibit the ability of U.S. companies to trade and invest abroad. Though this would seem to be a change from the traditional view of steel trade policy, it is merely another point in the continuing interaction of public policy and global steel trade.

NOTES

The author gratefully acknowledges the assistance of Evangeline Drossos, a graduate student at the University of Michigan School of Public Policy. The research, analysis, findings and opinions in this paper are the work of the author and do not directly or by implication represent the views of his employer or of the domestic steel industry.

[1] The terms "fair and "unfair" appear frequently in this paper. In most instances, as in this citation, the reference is to the provisions of U.S. trade laws which determine whether imports are actionable, such as being priced below cost or below the home market price. At other times, however, the terms "fair" and "unfair" are value-based and are used to persuade, founded on the idea that competition should occur on a level playing field. The present author notes that other normative terms, often referring to notions of good and bad public policy, frame much of the discussion by the authors whose models are discussed later in this paper. The question of the level playing field is an interesting concept in itself. Is this a peculiarly American idea that does not characterize the rules of competition for other nations?

REFERENCES

Barnette, Curtis, H. 1994. "Remarks at Paine-Webber Steel Trade Conference," unpublished.

Krueger, Anne O. (ed.). 1995. *The Political Economy of American Trade Policy*. Chicago: University of Chicago Press for the National Bureau of Economic Research.

Lenway, Stefanie, Randall Morck and Bernard Yeung. 1996. "Rent Seeking, Protectionism and Innovation in the American Steel Industry," *Economic Journal* 106: 410-21.

Moore, Michael, O. 1995. "Steel Protection in the 1980's: The Waning Influence of Big Steel?" in Anne O. Krueger (ed.), *The Political Economy of American*

Trade Policy. Chicago: University of Chicago Press for the National Bureau of Economic Research.

Rodrik, Dani. 1995. "Political Economy of Trade Policy," in Gene Grossman and Kenneth Rogoff (eds.), *Handbook of International Economics*, Vol. III. Amsterdam: Elsevier Science B.V.

CHAPTER 7

U.S. Trade Policies for the Textile and Apparel Industries: The Political Economy of the Post-MFA Environment

Robert E. Scott

I. Introduction

Textiles and apparel have received the highest levels of persistent, long-term protection afforded to any U.S. manufactured products in the post-World War-II era. The first cotton textile quotas were negotiated with Japan in 1937 (Finger and Harris 1996, p. 205) and the Multi-Fiber Arrangement (MFA), which ultimately replaced these quotas, will be in effect for another 10 years under the Uruguay Round trade agreements. Cline (1990, p. 191) estimated that the average equivalent level of protection in 1986 (tariffs plus the tariff equivalent of quotas) was 53% in apparel and 28% in textiles. In contrast, according to Hufbauer et al. (1986, p. 256) the Voluntary Restraint Agreements that limited Japanese auto exports to the United States beginning in 1981 resulted in an effective level of protection of approximately 11%.[1]

The political economy of the MFA, the preceding Long Term Arrangement (LTA) and its antecedents have been extensively studied. Finger and Harrison (1996) emphasize the role of administrative protection, including the escape clause and section 22 of the Agricultural Adjustment Act of 1935 as well as presidential politics, all of which led to the negotiation of a series of Voluntary Export Restraints (the LTA and the MFA). Examining product-level data, they found that both import competition measures and the statutory criteria for imposing a quota under the MFA are useful in explaining: (1) whether a quota exists; and (2) how the size of the quota changes over time. They conclude (p. 245) that products were more likely to be protected if they were made by sectors with "fewer employees, more plants, lower wages, lower profits, falling investment, higher import penetration and larger plant sizes," and if the imports originated in the richest developing countries (e.g., Hong Kong and Taiwan). Structural and geographic concentration helped limit free-rider problems and build key congressional support. In general, protection was found to be comprehensive but increasingly leaky, especially in the 1980s.

Destler (1996) has commented that Finger and Harrison's model did not adequately explain recent changes in trade policy in these sectors, nor shifts in the strategies of key participants. The interests of textile and apparel producers began to diverge in the 1960s, as the textile producers experienced rapid productivity growth, growing exports and a relatively stable trade deficit and employment levels. Apparel production was much more vulnerable to import growth, particularly during the 1980s, when import penetration nearly trebled (Finger and Harrison 1996, p. 224).

These differing experiences led to a divergence in the political positions of the textile and apparel industries according to Destler (1996, p. 257). This had two distinct consequences. First, the textile and apparel industries split on the North American Free Trade Agreement (NAFTA), with textile producers (as represented by the American Textile Manufacturers Institute, ATMI) supporting NAFTA in exchange for special provisions designed to encourage U.S. textile exports to Mexico (the "triple transformation" test regarding the origin of fibers in North American Apparel), while the apparel manufacturers and the unions were united in their opposition to NAFTA.

The second major consequence of the political split between textile and apparel producers was a change in strategy which contributed to the elimination of the MFA in the Uruguay Round. Prior to the mid-1980s, the two industries used their power in Congress to block approval of fast-track authority for multilateral trade negotiations until they were guaranteed that the MFA would be protected.[2] In the late 1980s the two industries changed strategies, and attempted to move formal quota legislation, which passed Congress and was vetoed on three separate occasions. However, they did not mount a significant effort to block fast-track authority for the Uruguay Round.

Destler (1996) suggests that these changes in textile/apparel strategy were the result of either: (1) the misguided influence of a few textile executives; or (2) the waning political influence of these industries. The next section of this paper proposes some alternative theories to explain the shifting trade strategies of textile and apparel industries in the last decade. The effects of NAFTA and its implications for textile and apparel interests are considered thereafter. The paper concludes with a discussion of issues for the future, including the role of organized labor and strategies for addressing new issues in trade such as international labor standards.

II. Sources of Variation in Textile and Apparel Strategies

The declining political power of textile and apparel producers, combined with the rising power and activism of apparel retailers are the most likely sources of the changing strategies of the textile/apparel complex. This section discusses three sources of evidence that illustrate these points.

Declining Democratic Power in the South

Finger and Harrison (p. 246) note that ability of the textile and apparel industries to obtain protection reflected the simultaneous concentration of political and economic power in the Southern states. In 1962, when the LTA was completed, Democrats from the South held more than half the chairs of standing committees in both the U.S. House and Senate. In addition, the textile and apparel industries provided a large proportion of the manufacturing jobs in many southern states. Thus the representatives from this region had both reason and ability to support these industries' requests for special protection, during the period when the LTA and the MFA were negotiated, 1962 to 1972.

Both of these measures of support declined sharply in the 1970s and 1980s. Figure 7.1 reports the Democratic Party strength in eight major regions of the country. In general, these graphs show declining Democratic strength in the south, the border states, and the Rocky Mountain Region, and level or rising support for Democrats in the rest of the country. Democratic shares rise sharply in New England and the Plains states in this period.

Early in this century, the Republican party was more isolationist than the Democrats, who generally favored free trade. The regional realignment of the Democratic Party's base in the 1970s and 1980s was also associated with a shift towards more concern about the loss of manufacturing jobs and the need to pursue fair trade policies. The NAFTA vote in the House is a particularly useful indicator of current party views on trade, because the vote was relatively close (*ex-ante*, at least). Table 7.1 shows that 60% of Democrats opposed NAFTA, while 75% of Republicans supported the Agreement. The President needed Republican support to obtain approval of the agreement. The historical positions of the parties on trade have reversed in the past few decades.

The sharp decline in the power and influence of Southern Democrats, combined with the strong support of the Republicans who replaced them for free trade policies, undermined the Congressional base of support for the MFA. It is interesting to note that the textile and apparel industries also pursued divergent approaches in the Uruguay Round negotiations. Some members of the textile industry sought textile market access concessions from develop-

TABLE 7.1. NAFTA Vote in the U.S. House of Representatives, November 1993

	Number of Representatives Voting			Shares of Each Party's Vote	
	Anti-Nafta	Pro-Nafta	Total	Anti-Nafta	Pro-Nafta
Democrat	156	102	258	60.5%	39.5%
Republican	43	132	175	24.6%	75.4%
Totals	199	234	433	46.0%	54.0%

Source: Mishel and Teixeira, (1993, table 1).

Figure 7.1. Democratic Party Strength in Congress, 1924-1994
(Percentage of Democratic Seats in Each Regional Delegation)

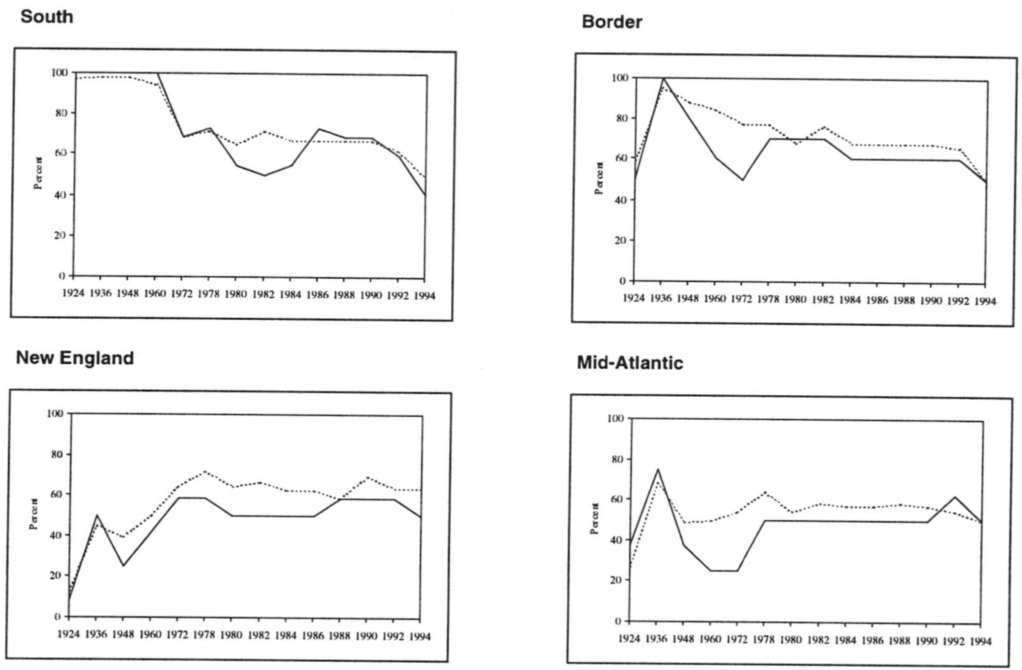

Midwest

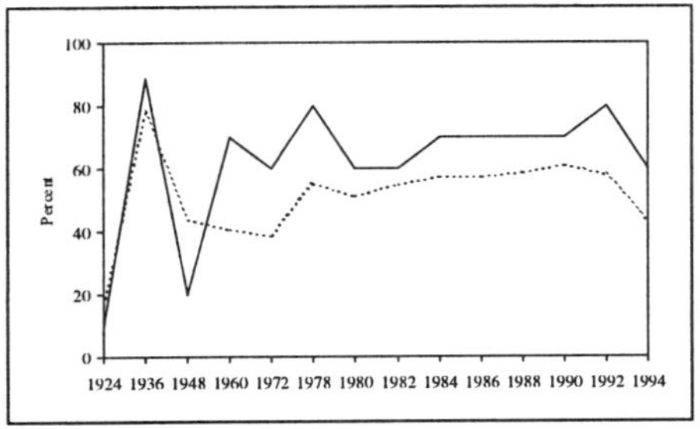

Plains

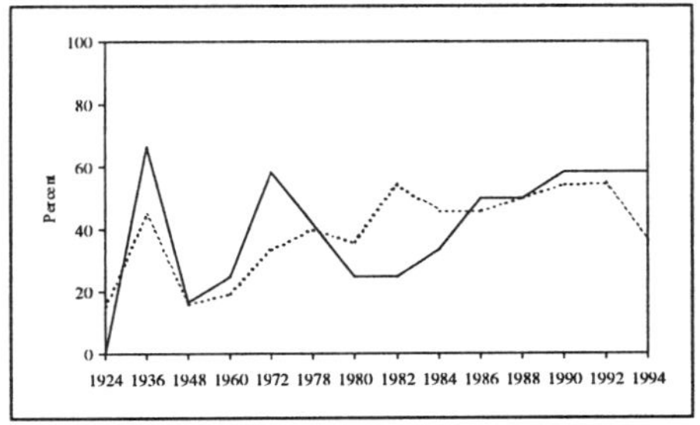

Rocky Mountain

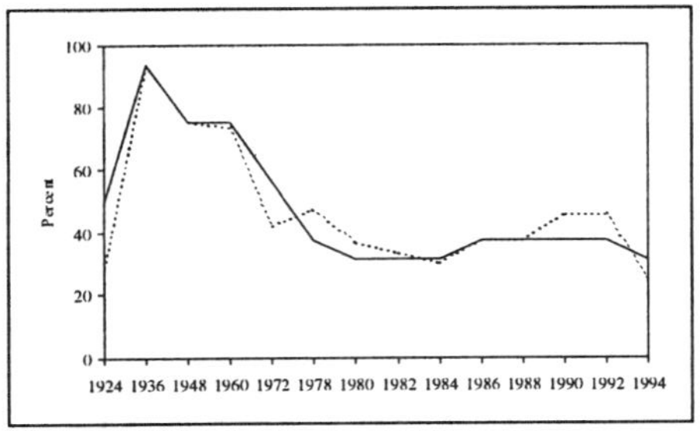

Pacific Coast

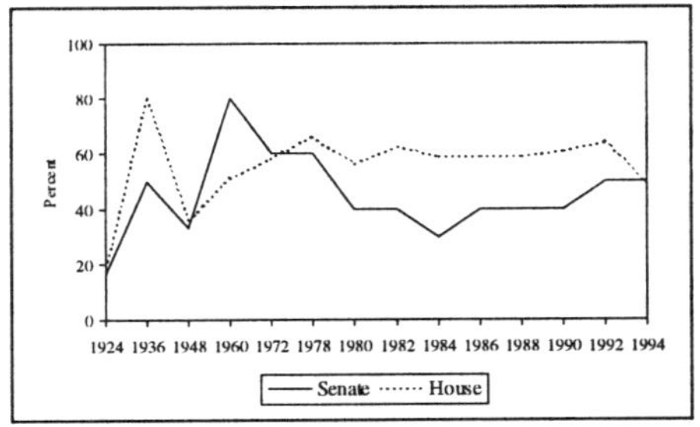

Source: Ornstein, et al. (1996, p. 16).

Figure 7.2. Regional Employment Shares for the Textile and Apparel Industries, 1947-1995*

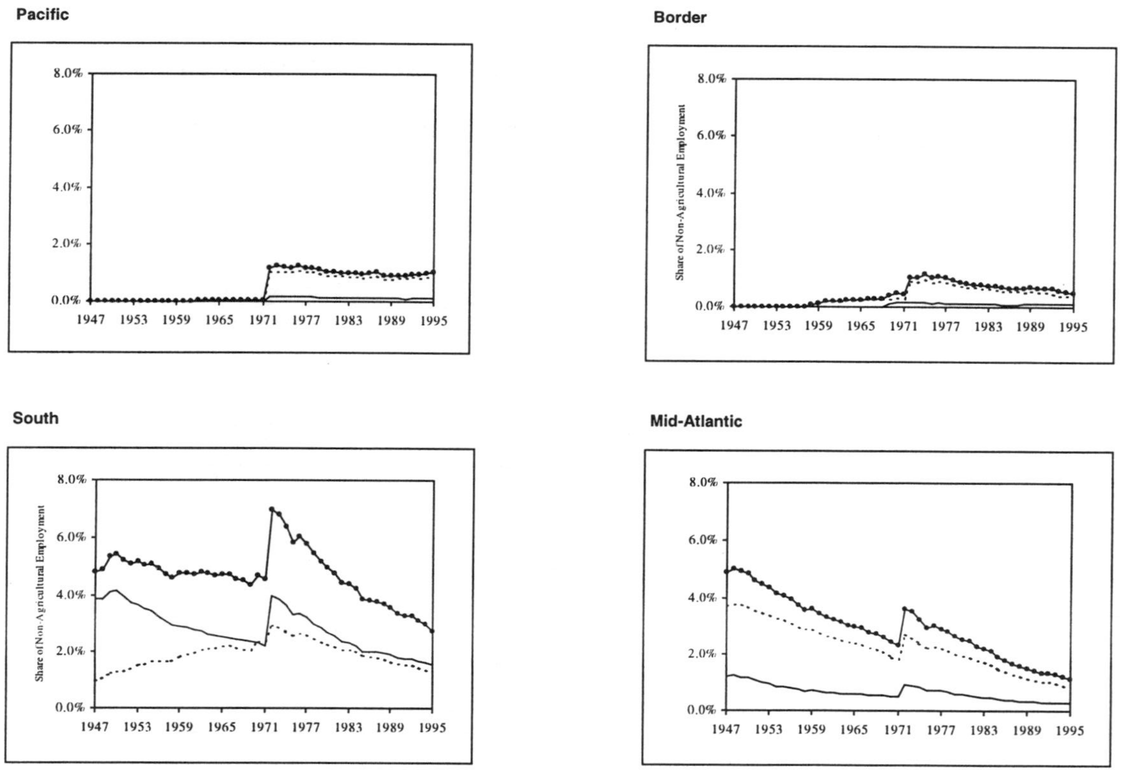

New England

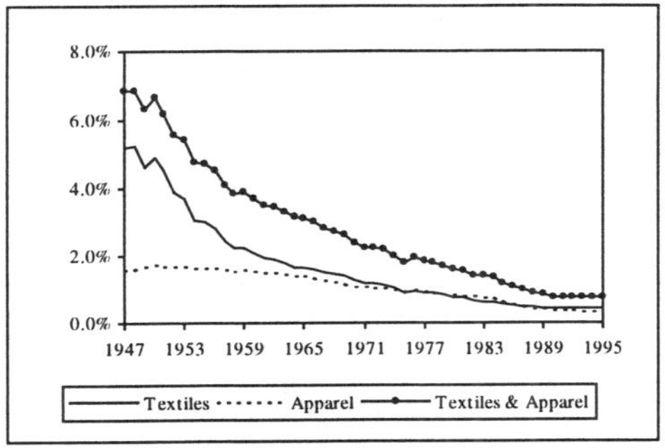

[*]Textile and Apparel Employment was less than one percent of total employment in the midwest and plains states throughout this period. No employment in these industries was reported in the Rocky Mountain Region.

Source: U.S. Bureau of Labor Statistics, "State and Area Employment, Hours and Earnings."

ing countries, in exchange for acquiescing in the phase-out of the MFA. Once again, the apparel industry and domestic unions fought an unsuccessful battle to keep these industries out of the GATT.

Falling Employment Shares

The changing industrial structure of the United States, and of the key apparel and textile producing regions in particular, also played a role in the decline in support for the MFA. Figure 7.2 reports the textile and apparel shares of total non-farm employment for these regions. Two trends in these data may help explain the intertemporal variation in support for the MFA.[3] First, the share of employment in the South rises in the 1950s and 1960s and then begins a secular decline in the early 1970s. The fall in employment shares reflects both rising imports and the general growth of employment in services and other non-traded goods during this period.

The second important trend is the sharp decline in the employment share of these two industries in New England. The sharpest decline occurs in the 1950s, as the industry moved to the South. This sharp decline probably generated support for the initial LTA with Japan in 1962 among legislators representing displaced textile and apparel employees in the Northeast. The rising employment share in the South in the 1960s and 1970s helps explain the support of the leadership of Southern delegations in applying pressure on the executive branch to negotiate and tighten the MFA. However, the sharp decline in the importance of employment in these industries through the 1970s and 1980s in the South undermined the natural base of support for protectionist policies.[4]

Increasing Concentration in the Retail Clothing Industries

At the same time that the base of support for textile and apparel protection was declining in the South and other producing regions, there was a concomitant increase in the market power of apparel retailers. One result of increasing retail concentration was the growth in the oligopsony power of apparel retailing firms. The most important implication of buyer-market power for our purposes is that it allows apparel retailers to price discriminate between imported and domestic suppliers, paying them different prices for very comparable products. For example, a shirt that costs a few dollars to make in China will often be sold in U.S. stores for $40 or more. This markup is not justified by quota rents and tariffs, which add at most 50 to 60% to the delivered cost of the product. Recent changes in information technologies, declining shipping costs and changes in consumer incomes and tastes appear to have resulted in substantial changes in the structure of retail apparel markets. Very high profit levels have been sustained in some segments of the industry, where price-cost margins have also been increasing.

Growing concentration in retailing has increased both the resources available to retailing interests, and also their direct financial interest in the elimination of the MFA system.[5] One study (Scott and Lee 1991, p. 27) predicts that imported apparel prices would fall by only 10%, much less than the 34.6% Cline (1990, p. 191) predicts in his study of the costs of protection in this industry.[6] Retail prices in Scott and Lee's model fall less than in Cline's model because apparel retailers capture most of the rents resulting from the elimination of quota rents and tariffs. As a result, Scott and Lee estimate that the consumer costs of apparel protection in 1986 were $3.7 billion, versus Cline's estimate of $17.6 billion.

From a political economy perspective, the estimated effects of quota elimination on apparel retailers is even more revealing. Scott and Lee estimate that domestic retailers and distributors of apparel would capture $1.9 billion in quota rents, and $6.8 billion in lost tariff revenues, amounts that would be transferred to consumers in the Cline model. These are substantial incentives for large retailers to lobby to eliminate protection.[7]

Concentration levels have increased since 1972 in most major channels, as shown in table 7.2, which reports the market shares of the 8 largest apparel retailing firms. The department store segments, where concentration is particularly high, sold large shares of all clothing in 1992.[8] Increasing retail market power created pressure to eliminate the MFA.

III. The Political Consequences of NAFTA

NAFTA has not provided the expected stimulus to U.S. textile exports, as shown in figure 7.3, which reports trends in U.S. imports, exports and the trade

TABLE 7.2. Industry Concentration Ratios by Store Type (8-firm)

Year	Department Stores	Men and Boys Wear Stores	Women's Clothing Stores	Family Clothing Stores	Shoe Stores
1992	71.2	27.4	35.4	52.3	47.3
1987	66.0	18.2	30.0	43.7	44.2
1982	57.8	13.4	28.2	32.3	37.6
1977	56.8	12.5	16.2	29.3	30.4
1972	51.4	13.6	15.7	24.6	27.6

[a]Addenda: Subcategories of Department Stores in 1992:
Conventional 78.3
Discount/mass merchandise 87.9
National Chain 100

Source: *U.S. Census of Retail Trade: Subject Series*, 1972, 1977, 1982, 1987, and 1992.

Figure 7.3. U.S. Textile and Apparel Trade with the NAFTA Countries, 1983-1995
(Industries in Standard Industrial Classification Sectors 22 and 23).

U.S.-Mexico Apparel Trade
(thousands of dollars)

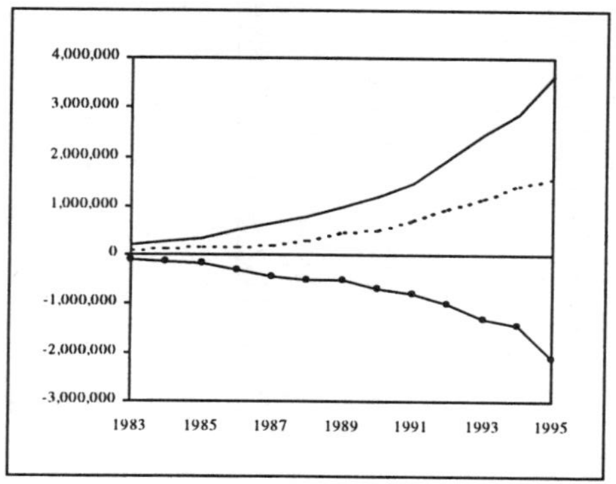

U.S.-Canada Apparel Trade
(thousands of dollars)

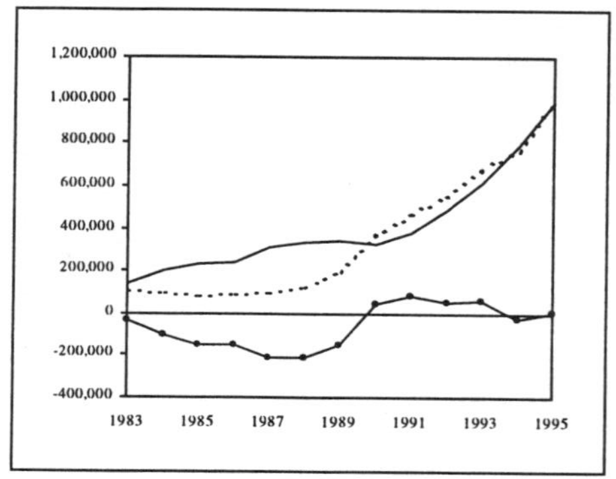

U.S.-Mexico Textile Trade
(thousands of dollars)

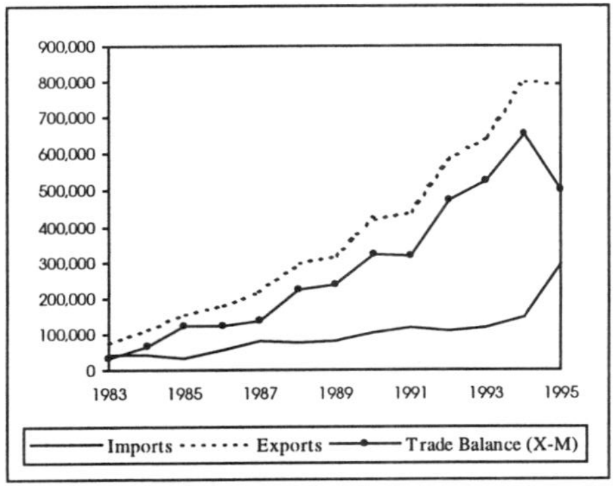

U.S.-Canada Textile Trade
(thousands of dollars)

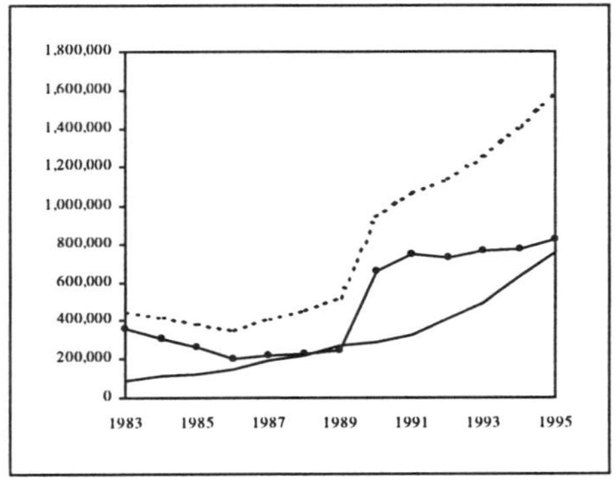

Source: U.S. Department of Commerce, International Trade Administration, special compilation.

balance for textiles and apparel, with Mexico and Canada.[9] After rising in 1994, U.S. textile exports did not increase in 1995, in the wake of the peso crisis, while imports nearly doubled. As a result, the bilateral trade surplus in this sector declined by about $150 million. Apparel imports, on the other hand, surged by 28%, after growing only 18% in 1995 (in nominal terms).

There was no significant change in textile or apparel trade balances with Canada in the post-NAFTA period. The United States has a substantial trade surplus in textile trade with Canada. Wages in the United States and Canada are much closer than those in the United States and Mexico. The United States lost approximately 12,000 jobs in the textile, apparel and related industries in 1995, alone, because of the declining trade balances with Mexico in these two sectors (Scott 1996, p. 3).

Thus, textile manufacturers have failed to realize the expected gains in exports to Mexico under the NAFTA. Despite these results, the industry is expected to support proposals to provide "NAFTA parity" to countries in the Caribbean Basin.[10] The results reported in figure 7.3 suggest that the split in the trade strategies of the textile and apparel industries may not be in the best interest of either sector.[11]

IV. Labor Rights at Home and Abroad: New Approaches

In the post-Uruguay Round era labor unions and others have accelerated their efforts to obtain the inclusion of enforceable labor rights in the GATT. The United States raised this issue unsuccessfully at the first WTO ministerial meeting in Singapore, in December 1996. In the United States, labor rights have been the subject of a new approach involving unions, consumers, government officials and apparel retailing firms. The issues involved include the conditions in "sweatshops" in the United States, especially in New York and California, and abusive labor practices in foreign garment factories, including child labor, physical abuse and forced labor.[12]

In the United States, campaigns have been organized by non-profit activists, such as Charles Kernaghan, Executive Director of the National Labor Committee and the Education Committee in Support of Worker and Human Rights in Central America. In a series of "actions," Kernaghan involved celebrity Kathie Lee Gifford because of her endorsement of a line of clothing made for Wal-Mart in New York and Honduras. Gifford met with Labor Secretary Reich and was ultimately recruited to support third party inspections and global corporate responsibility for worker rights.[13]

Sweatshop campaigns, involving firms such as The Gap and Kmart, represent a new approach to obtaining protection, along several dimensions. First, unions and non-profits are seeking to obtain trade relief for the industry by improving international labor rights, and making them enforceable through the WTO (and ultimately, through an increase in organizing and collective bargaining in developing countries). Second, the campaigns use celebrities and consumer pressure to influence government and corporate behavior. Finally, and most importantly, these campaigns are designed to motivate apparel retailers to support global, enforceable labor standards, so as to alleviate pressures from corporate campaigns. In the absence of national regulation and international labor standards, apparel retailers and design/import firms will confront serious free-rider problems. Firms that enforce higher labor standards (e.g., pay higher wages) may find it difficult to compete with firms that fully exploit unregulated labor markets, or labor standards that cannot be adequately enforced, as in the United States Thus these campaigns are explicitly designed to change the interests of participants in the political processes affecting the textile and apparel industries.

V. Conclusions

This section will summarize the findings pertaining to textiles and apparel. First, it is clear that the objectives of labor and the industries represented have shifted significantly in response to changes in the political environment over the past few decades. The split between the textile and apparel industries has weakened both in the trade policy arena. The textile industry may wish to reconsider its position, in view of the apparent failure of its NAFTA strategy. In the wake of the Uruguay Round and the planned elimination of the MFA, labor has shifted its emphasis to international workers rights, standards and enforcement. It remains to be seen if this strategy will be successful, in view of the opposition of many developing country governments. However, it should be noted that the European Union is also taking steps to support inclusion of labor rights in the WTO agenda.

Second, the objectives of these groups are identified and promoted through well organized unions and trade organizations. Each of these are under pressure to change. For example, the two leading unions in these sectors in the United States recently merged to form the Union of Needle Trade, Industrial and Textile Unions (UNITE).

Third, the objectives of the groups discussed here do appear to conform to the models of the political economy of trade policy. The decline of the textile and apparel industries, in relative and absolute terms, and changes in the regional political structure of the United States have greatly weakened the ability of these groups to maintain the old trade policy regime (the MFA).

Finally, the findings here suggest some questions about the *effectiveness* of strategies employed by the participants, as noted above. Textile producers have recently relied on reciprocal bargaining to obtain greater access to foreign markets in exchange for their consent to phasing out the MFA. It remains to be seen if this strategy will yield benefits in terms of domestic output, employment or firm profits. Recent success stories in the areas of labor rights are only a first step in the direction of reducing the differences in labor costs between developed and developing countries. The loss of jobs and output in U.S. textiles and apparel is likely to continue and accelerate over the next ten years, as the MFA is phased out and trade with Mexico and the Caribbean expands.

This paper also challenges the assumptions of the literature on the costs and benefits of textile and apparel protection (e.g., Cline). The usual story told is that consumers pay a huge bill to support the jobs of a few thousand workers in these sectors. A more accurate picture is that gains to consumers from eliminating the MFA will be smaller ($3 billion per year), and that apparel retailers and contract design/import firms will capture most of the resulting benefits ($8 to $9 billion per year), as suggested above. In addition, hundreds of thousands of textile and apparel workers will be displaced. Many of these workers will experience a reduction in earnings when they are reemployed, while others will drop out of the labor force altogether.[14] In this circumstance, it is likely that permanent losses to these workers will exceed efficiency gains to the economy from eliminating the MFA. From a distributional point of view, the elimination of the MFA may prove to be much more costly than most economists have predicted.

NOTES

[1] Hufbauer (1986, pp. 256-58) review other estimates of the effects of the VRAs which range from 2.4% to 15.3%. In an extensive review of more recent literature, Nelson (1996, p. 152) finds estimates of the consumer costs of protection which range from $1 billion to $14 billion. The latter figure includes the effects of quality upgrading. Hufbauer et al. estimate that protection cost consumers $2.4 billion in 1984.

[2] The industry also used other measures to block completion of the Kennedy and Tokyo Rounds, until it was assured that the industry's trade goals would be satisfied (Destler 1996, p. 258).

[3] The data in Figure 7.2 are from the Bureau of Labor Statistics Establishment data series for states and areas. There are problems with coverage at the industry level, which explain the discontinuities shown in the early 1970s in most of these charts. In particular, in the South, North Carolina (textiles and apparel) and Tennessee (textiles only) do not report employment data prior to 1972; in the Mid-Atlantic, Pennsylvania does not report any data prior to 1972; in the Border states, Maryland begins reporting some data only in 1970; in the Border States, Kentucky begins reporting in 1969 (textiles) and 1972 (apparel); and in the Pacific, California only begins reporting in 1972. In most of these cases employment is very substantial (often close to 100,000 workers).

[4] Charles McMillion of MBG Information Services in Washington, D.C. first pointed out the importance of changing industrial structure in conversations with the author.

[5] For example, Leslie Wexner, Chairman of the Limited (Women's Apparel Retailing Chain) became an active opponent of the MFA in the early 1990s, writing op ed pieces in major newspapers (e.g., *The Washington Post*).

[6] The oligopsony model in Scott and Lee also predicts even smaller estimates of the effects of eliminating the MFA on apparel of domestic origin than does Cline (2.6% vs. 18.9%).

[7] Although overall profit levels in some parts of the retailing industry are quite low (especially Department stores), many specially retailers, such as Liz Claiborne and The Limited have enjoyed exceptionally high profit and growth levels. Scott and Lee (1991, pp. 13-14) also note that leases and rent are an especially large share of costs for some retailers. This suggests that access to retail space may be a critical barrier to entry in retailing, and that owners of shopping malls may be capturing some of the rents available in this industry.

[8] Note that the data in Table 7.2 understate the effects of concentration because most apparel markets are regional and the data reported are national. Concentration in many regional markets is probably higher.

[9] NAFTA took effect on January 1, 1994.

[10] NAFTA parity proposals are expected to be put forward by the administration in early 1997. These measures would allow countries that have participated in the U.S. Caribbean Basin Initiatives (CBI) in the 1980s to obtain access to U.S. markets on the same terms as Mexico, under the NAFTA. Apparel producers would be the main beneficiaries of these CBI Parity proposals. Under the terms of the NAFTA, apparel tariffs and quotas are to be gradually removed, over a period of 10 years.

[11] Note, however, that some of the new textile imports from Mexico may be products from new plants owned by U.S. firms. Thus NAFTA could benefit some textile producers, through FDI, while reducing employment and output in the United States. Examination of textile production in U.S. owned plants in Mexico is an important area for future research.

[12] See, for example, Falk (1996, p. A31) and Sanchez (1996, p. A30).

[13] Bearak (1996).

[14] Many of the textile and apparel workers in the South are female and members of minority groups living in rural areas where alternative employment opportunities are severely limited (Scott and Lee, 1991, pp. 39-40).

REFERENCES

Bearak, Barry. 1996. "Kathie Lee and the Sweatshop Crusade," *Los Angeles Times*, June 14.

Cline, William R. 1990. *The Future of World Trade in Textiles and Apparel*, rev. ed. Washington, D.C.: Institute for International Economics.

Destler, I.M. 1996. "Comment," in Anne O. Krueger (ed.), *The Political Economy of American Trade Policy*. Chicago: University of Chicago Press.

Falk, William R. 1996. "Dirty Little Secrets: Half of Clothes Sold in U.S. Made for Substandard Pay," *Newsday*, June 16, A31.

Finger, Michael J. and Ann Harris. 1996. "The MFA Paradox: More Protection and More Trade?" in Anne O. Krueger, (ed.), *The Political Economy of American Trade Policy*. Chicago: University of Chicago Press.

Hufbauer, Gary Clyde, Diane T. Berliner and Kimberly Ann Elliot. 1986. *Trade Protection in the United States: 31 Case Studies.* Washington, D.C.: Institute for International Economics.

Mishel, Lawrence and Ruy A. Teixeira. 1993. "The Political Arithmetic of the NAFTA Vote," Briefing Paper. Washington, D.C.: Economic Policy Institute.

Nelson, Douglas R. 1996. "The Political Economy of U.S. Automobile Protection," in Anne O. Krueger, (*ed.*), *The Political Economy of American Trade Policy.* Chicago: University of Chicago Press.

Ornstein, Norman J., Thomas E. Mann and Michael J. Malbin. 1996. *Vital Statistics on Congress, 1996.* Washington, D.C.: Congressional Quarterly Inc.

Sanchez, Ray. 1996. "Misery for Haitian Workers," *Newsday*, June 16, A30.

Scott, Robert E. 1996. "North American Trade After NAFTA: Rising Deficits, Disappearing Jobs," Briefing Paper. Washington, D.C.: Economic Policy Institute.

Scott, Robert E. and Thea M. Lee. 1991. "Reconsidering the Benefits and Costs of Protection: The Case of Textiles and Apparel," Working Paper No. 105. Washington, D.C.: Economic Policy Institute.

CHAPTER 8

The Representation of Economic Interests in U.S. Semiconductor Trade Policy

Douglas Irwin

I. Introduction

The U.S. semiconductor industry does not neatly fit the standard model of an import-competing sector that presses the government for relief from foreign competition. The Semiconductor Industry Association (SIA), for example, led a successful push in the early 1980s to eliminate all tariffs on semiconductor products entering the United States and Japan.

Instead, the SIA's main trade-related complaint has concerned its allegation that Japan's market is unfairly closed to foreign products. The SIA formally requested government assistance in addressing this grievance when it filed a petition under Section 301 of the Trade Act of 1974 with the Office of the U.S. Trade Representative (USTR) in 1985. But because no overt governmental trade barriers were in place, the remedy sought and obtained to increase U.S. exports was an unusual one. Japan adopted a "voluntary import expansion" (or VIE) and committed itself to encourage greater domestic consumption of foreign-produced semiconductors through a market share target. Despite the controversy surrounding this measure, the market share target survived as a part of U.S. trade policy for a decade, having been perpetuated by three different U.S. Trade Representatives serving under three different presidential administrations.[1]

At the same time, certain producers in specific product areas (notably memory chips) have been beset by import competition. As a result, sporadic antidumping actions have also been a feature of U.S. trade policy toward the industry. These actions have not generally been supported by the industry overall (the SIA, for example, has taken no formal position on them) and were vociferously opposed by downstream users of semiconductors, most importantly computer manufacturers.

This paper analyzes how various groups (semiconductor producer and users and the government) interacted in the political realm in the determination of policy.[2] Section II discusses the organization of the semiconductor industry and its effect on trade policy lobbying efforts. Section III describes the economic and political factors shaping the industry's trade policy agenda in the 1980s. Section IV covers the negotiation of a trade agreement with Japan in 1986. Section V considers how semiconductor user industries influenced the agreement's 1991 renegotiation and its eventual expiration in 1996. Section VI concludes the paper.

II. Industry Organization and Trade Policy Interests

Semiconductor production is generally a high fixed cost, low marginal cost business. Rapid technological change and short product-life cycles also make it a risky one in which firms have a relatively short period in which to earn sufficient profits to recover their generation-specific R&D and capital investments. These distinctive aspects of the semiconductor industry give most firms an interest in obtaining government policies that will reduce the costs and risks of operating in the sector: more favorable tax treatment for R&D, relaxed antitrust restrictions on joint research ventures, greater patent protection for chip designs and innovations, and so forth.[3]

The Semiconductor Industry Association (SIA) was formed in 1977 to promote these common interests.[4] The SIA was initially composed of "merchant" firms, which tend to be small, less diversified firms that sell semiconductors to other users. The SIA broadened its membership in 1982 to include vertically-integrated "captive" semiconductor producers, such as IBM, Hewlett-Packard, Digital Equipment Corp., and AT&T. Captive producers added to the political standing of the SIA and moderated the SIA's stance on trade policy. Merchant firms, who potentially benefit from diminishing import competition and maintaining high prices for semiconductors, were forced to arrive at an industry consensus on policy positions with captive firms, who are likely to be net purchasers of semiconductors and benefit from low prices.

As an institution, the SIA is extremely small: in 1992, the entire SIA staff consisted of just 13 people, seven professionals and six office personnel. The members of the SIA deliberately created a small organization and located it in San Jose, California (not in Washington, D.C.) to ensure close contact with industry. While the SIA is the main forum for coordinating and implementing industry political efforts, the individual companies themselves are mainly engaged in carrying out these activities rather than the association as an independent entity.[5] The SIA has also subcontracted some of its policy activity to the law office of Dewey Ballantine to gain the counsel of politically astute Washington insiders.

Although current U.S. trade laws enable individual firms to seek import relief even in the absence of collective action by the industry, the factors influencing the latter remain important. The theory of political action often associates the cost and benefits of organizing collectively to the geographic and economic concentration of the industry. According to the 1987 Census of Manufactures, about a third of U.S. semiconductor employment was located in

California, with Arizona, Texas, and New York accounting for another third. Because of its concentration in "Silicon Valley," industry leaders know each other well and can easily capture the attention and services of California's powerful congressional representatives.

In terms of overall economic size, the industry is not negligible: In 1989, the value of U.S. semiconductor industry shipments was $25.7 billion and total U.S. employment was 184,000 (roughly 1.3 percent of total manufacturing employment). A handful of moderately sized firms, such as Intel, Motorola, Texas Instruments (TI), Advanced Micro Devices (AMD), have been the bulwarks behind the industry's political action. Other firms that have influenced trade policy include the then largest semiconductor producer in the world, IBM, and one of the smallest, Micron Technology, which specialized exclusively in DRAMs.

The theory of international trade points to the economic interests of various factors of production, such as labor and capital-owners, in shaping the configuration of trade-policy lobbying. The more specific and immobile are labor and capital in a given sector, the more their fate is tied to the fortunes of that sector and the more likely they are to seek protective government policies. In the many congressional hearings held on semiconductor industry policy in the 1980s, testimony was taken almost exclusively from corporate executives and industry officials, not labor representatives. The apparent lack of political activism among semiconductor workers can be explained by evidence that many of them have skills useful in various related industries, thereby ensuring that labor is mobile across the high technology sector; i.e., they do not have a particularly strong stake in the fate of semiconductor firms *per se* as long as other high technology sectors are performing well.[6]

Management, the principal capital-owners in the industry (merchant firms were not uncommonly still dominated by their founders), was mainly responsible for the industry's political action.[7] Yoffe (1988) argues that the high degree of personal involvement in lobbying by CEOs and upper management commanded respect among politicians and gave them access to policymakers at higher levels of government than the ordinary staff of an industry association could normally achieve.

The most important product designed and manufactured by the semiconductor industry is the integrated circuit, which includes logic chips (for arithmetic and decision-making functions), microprocessors (the central processing unit in computers), and various application-specific integrated circuits (configured for particular user needs). These products generally perform quite different functions and are imperfect substitutes for one another. Yet part of the trade dispute in the 1980s centered on a unique set of digital integrated circuits—memory chips—which are primarily used in computers to store and retrieve data in various forms. Dynamic random-access memories (DRAMs), for example, are a standardized product and almost perfectly interchangeable regardless of which firm produces them. Consequently, competition in this "commodity chip" market is particularly intense.[8]

III. The Semiconductor Industry's Trade Policy Agenda

In the 1980s, the U.S. semiconductor industry sought government assistance to deal with two problems it had with competition from Japan's industry. First, the SIA argued that Japan's market was unfairly closed to the sale of foreign semiconductors. Second, merchant firms (but not the SIA itself) periodically complained about the "dumping" of semiconductors by Japanese producers.

Market Access

Prior to 1975, imports of semiconductors into Japan were restricted by formal quotas and prior approval requirements, and foreign investment was so strictly regulated as to be essentially forbidden. Although these restrictions were liberalized in 1975, after which few formal governmental trade barriers remained in place, the U.S. share of Japan's market scarcely budged. Supported by evidence that was necessarily anecdotal, the SIA claimed that informal nontariff barriers lingered in Japan after 1975 and that MITI used active countermeasures to undermine the liberalization. (Other explanations for the failure of the formal liberalization to alter the U.S. share include the different structure of final demand in Japan and the importance of long-term relationships there.)

Section 301 of the Trade Act of 1974 gives U.S. exporters the ability to request that the government act on their behalf against foreign unfair trade practices. In the mid-1980s, it had been used to attack only government policies (unlike the antidumping laws which relate to the prices charged by private firms). Therefore, the SIA pinned the blame for the lack of market access squarely on the Japanese government, and only partly on the behavior of private firms or the structure of Japan's market. The SIA (1983, p. 6) described the remedy it felt was appropriate:

"U.S. firms must receive real, not 'cosmetic' market access, reflected in significantly greater participation by U.S. firms in the Japanese market. This will require an affirmative action program to normalize competition in Japan. The Japanese government should establish necessary programs to see that this result is achieved."

Dissuaded by the Reagan administration from filing a Section 301 petition in 1982, the SIA did so in 1985 under different circumstances (mainly the administration's view of market opening). The petition provided circumstantial evidence of market barriers in Japan: despite high shares in third markets, the U.S. share of the Japanese market remained fixed near 10 percent for a decade. The SIA suggested that Japan's government condoned anticompetitive practices and undertook active countermeasures to undermine the 1975 liberalization. These actions denied U.S. firms "fair and equitable market opportunities," and therefore were "unreasonable" under the meaning of Section 301. The SIA requested relief in the form of an "equivalence of market participation" in the Japanese market.

Dumping

The U.S. industry was buffeted by several shocks in the 1980s: greater capital investments by Japanese firms (partly, the SIA alleged, due to industrial policy), the large appreciation of the dollar on foreign exchange markets, and a 20 percent contraction of the semiconductor market in 1985. The latter was particularly concentrated on the DRAM market: sales slumped 60 percent because domestic shipments of microcomputers, which had increased by a factor of five between 1981 and 1984, fell 8 percent in 1985. As a result, DRAM prices plummeted, giving rise to the "dumping" charge.

The SIA never filed an antidumping complaint because captive producers opposed higher tariffs on semiconductors. But the issue was forced by a small semiconductor firm that (at the time) was not even a member of the SIA—Micron Technology of Boise, Idaho. In 1985, Micron filed an antidumping complaint against four principal Japanese exporters of 64K DRAMs—NEC, Hitachi, Mitsubishi, and Oki—alleging that these firms had been dumping DRAMs in the U.S. market. While the SIA remained formally neutral in the antidumping process, AMD, Mostek, Motorola, National Semiconductor, TI, and Intel all indicated their support for the petition during the investigation by the U.S. International Trade Commission (USITC).

Merchant members of the SIA soon followed suit: later that year Intel, AMD, and National Semiconductor filed for antidumping action against imports of erasable programmable read-only memories (EPROMs) from Japan, aimed primarily at Hitachi, Mitsubishi, and Fujitsu. In a highly unusual move, the Department of Commerce soon self-initiated an antidumping investigation into 256K and higher generations of DRAMs. This action demonstrated the government's support for the industry's efforts to prevent Japan from dominating the memory chip market.

IV. The Semiconductor Trade Arrangement of 1986

Trade relief is not just a function of an industry's demands, but also of the government's willingness to "supply" the demanded policies. In 1985-86, the U.S. government was willing to do so. Facing pressure from trade-sensitive industries and the Congress due to the gaping trade deficit, the Reagan administration used "market-opening" initiatives (such as self-initiated Section 301 actions) to divert protectionist pressure from efforts to close the U.S. market toward opening foreign (particularly Japan's) market.

Since no party (with the possible exception of Micron) had an interest in seeing the United States impose Section 301 sanctions or antidumping duties, U.S. and Japan government representatives sought to settle both the Section 301 and antidumping cases through negotiations. Trade law specified a strict date (outside the administration's control) for the rendering of the antidumping decisions, and this became the fixed endpoint to the talks. The SIA wanted two things from the negotiations: an end to "dumping" on a worldwide basis and "real" market access in Japan. Any agreement that just prevented dumping in the United States would be undesirable (given that the SIA could not make the antidumping petitions go away); this would not only make the United States a "high-price island" of semiconductors to the detriment of domestic user-industries, but (more directly in the SIA's interest) would harm the sales of U.S. firms in third markets as Japan shifted its sales elsewhere. The SIA also required not just better opportunities for sales in Japan, but the actual realization of sales ("the cash registers must ring," as it was put at the time) to be assessed by a quantitative appraisal of market access. USTR, the agency responsible for overseeing the negotiations, wanted any agreement that satisfied the SIA—including the ending of dumping in third markets, which it had no authority to negotiate. Japan (represented by the Ministry of International Trade and Industry, MITI) wanted an agreement with no specific promises.

Large preliminary antidumping findings and a material-injury decision by the USITC strengthened the bargaining position of U.S. negotiators: Japan had to settle the case to avoid the automatic and non-negotiable imposition of these duties, as well as possible 301 sanctions. In the end, Japan capitulated and largely acceded to most of the U.S. negotiators' (i.e. industry's) demands, although there was considerable ambiguity as to the exact obligations of Japan's government and an inexact timetable for achieving the objectives of the agreement.

Under the 1986 Semiconductor Trade Arrangement, Japan agreed to take actions that would end dumping in the United States. Based on Japanese production cost data, the Department of Commerce would determine company-specific price floors each quarter and provide this information to MITI for enforcement. The agreement stipulated that "the Government of Japan will take appropriate actions . . . to prevent exports at prices less than company-specific fair value." Despite the U.S. understanding that Japan was also obligated to prevent dumping in third country markets, the agreement makes no explicit statement of the Government of Japan taking "appropriate actions" to prevent dumping elsewhere. MITI later denied responsibility for preventing third country dumping, and the General Agreement on Tariffs and Trade (GATT) subsequently ruled that any monitoring of third-country exports was illegal.

How did U.S. negotiators handle the SIA's demand for specific targets for increased market access (i.e., sales) in Japan? Many agencies within the Reagan administration resisted specifying an exact import market share because it smacked of managed trade and raised questions of how Japan could implement such targets. The official text of the 1986 agreement simply states that "the Government of Japan will impress upon the Japanese producers and users of semiconductors the need to aggressively take advantage of increased market access opportunities in Japan for foreign-based firms which will improve their actual sales performance. Both Governments agree that the expected improvement in access should be gradual and steady over the period of this Arrangement." An infamous, secret side-letter to the final agreement, however, explicitly mentions a 20 market share target.[9]

Having made these commitments, Japan now faced the burden of making the agreement work. To prevent dumping, MITI did the only thing it knew how to do—reduce the quantity of semiconductors exported in an effort to raise export prices sufficiently. MITI essentially imposed an "antidumping VER"—a voluntary export restraint designed to meet a price target rather than a quantitative target, and therefore inherently more difficult to administer. MITI issued Supply and Demand Forecasts to provide targeted production levels and induce firms to trim output. These guidelines and regulations were at first ignored, and MITI's initial efforts to prevent dumping in third markets were not fully successful.

To monitor the market access provisions of the 1986 agreement, the SIA focused on the foreign share of the Japanese semiconductor market. As this share remained roughly constant at 8.5 percent through 1986, the SIA deemed this as evidence of Japan's noncompliance. Although this share rose to 9.0 percent in the first quarter of 1987, preparations had already begun for U.S. retaliation against Japan for failing to live up to the agreement.

By early 1987, MITI's export controls on sales to the United States succeeded in preventing "dumping," but the SIA renewed its complaints about dumping in third markets and about the lack of movement in its market share in Japan. Fearing a backlash on Capitol Hill, which around this time had been considering the Gephardt amendment, the Reagan administration gave Japan 60 days to demonstrate that it was enforcing the agreement. In March 1987, the Senate passed by 93-0 a non-binding resolution, introduced by Senator Pete Wilson (R-CA), calling on the administration to force compliance with the trade agreement. In one of the most dramatic events of post-war U.S. trade policy, President Reagan soon imposed 100 percent tariffs on $300 million worth of laptop computers, desktop computers, televisions, and power tools imported from Japan. According to administration calculations, $135 million of the retaliation was for the injury suffered by domestic firms from continued third country dumping, and $165 million for lack of progress in increasing the foreign market share.[10]

V. Towards the 1991 and 1996 Agreement Revisions

By the end of its first year of operation, the semiconductor agreement succeeded in ending Japanese "dumping" in the United States and, by and large, in third markets. Ironically, the agreement failed to assist U.S. DRAM producers because they had already abandoned that market for other more profitable types of semiconductors. Instead, Japanese exporters benefited from the production cutbacks, which were akin to cooperative industry behavior, raised the price of DRAMs abroad, and generated an enormous windfall for them.[11] Other beneficiaries included foreign producers not covered by the VER, particularly in South Korea where higher world-wide DRAM prices accelerated the entry of Samsung, Goldstar, and Hyundai.

Producer interests seeking protectionist policies sometimes face the countervailing force of downstream users of that particular good. Memory chips are an important input to the production of computers: semiconductors comprised 15 percent of the value of output in the electronic computing equipment industry in 1985. Computer manufacturers soon became the clear losers from the semiconductor agreement. DRAM prices, which usually fell sharply with time, shot up dramatically in 1988; the price of 256K DRAMs jumped from about $2.20 at the end of 1986 to $3.50 by the end of 1988. This price bubble proved so costly to users that it heralded the end of the SIA's monopoly position as USTR's adviser on U.S. semiconductor trade policy. Three major computer systems firms (IBM, Tandem, and Hewlett-Packard) invited others (such as AT&T, Apple Computer, Compaq Computer, Control Data, Cray Research, Digital Equipment, NCR, Prime Computer, Sun Microsystems, Tektronix, and Unisys) to help form the Computer Systems Policy Project (CSPP) in early 1989 to counter the SIA and oppose the agreement.[12]

As a result of this coalition of semiconductor consumers, trade negotiators at USTR no longer faced a single voice—the SIA's—on what should determine U.S. semiconductor trade policy. With the expiration of the accord on the horizon, USTR could not possibly negotiate a satisfactory agreement in the face of sharply conflicting domestic interests. Rather than mediate between the producers and users, USTR instructed the SIA and the CSPP to resolve their differences over trade policy themselves. Whereas the SIA wanted the status quo, the CSPP wanted to scrap the agreement, or at least the antidumping provision that kept U.S. semiconductor prices high. The CSPP was basically indifferent toward the market access provision, so long as sanctions for noncompliance did not impinge on its interests.

After lengthy negotiations, the SIA and the CSPP announced in October 1990 a joint proposal concerning the shape of a renegotiated agreement. They declared the antidumping provisions of the 1986 agreement a "success" and maintained that the Commerce Department should no longer collect costs or price data or issue foreign market values for DRAMs and EPROMs. They also agreed that "market access results should be measured by quantifiable indicators of progress" and that the 20 percent market share should be attained by the end of 1992, an extension of one year.

This compromise formed the basis for USTR's renegotiation of the agreement prior to its expiration in mid-1991. The new five year agreement emasculated the antidumping provisions and had the following market access provision:

> The Government of Japan recognizes that the U.S. semiconductor industry expects that the foreign market share will grow to more than 20 percent of the Japanese market by the end of 1992 and considers that this can be realized. The Government of Japan welcomes the realization of this expectation. The two governments agree that the above state-

ments constitute neither a guarantee, a ceiling, nor a floor on the foreign market share.

The comparative ease of the 1991 negotiations demonstrated how institutionalized the semiconductor agreement had become. Unlike the serious conflicts during the 1986 negotiations, both countries had grown accustomed to the arrangements by 1991. Cooperative interaction between the SIA and the EIAJ and their members had expanded significantly since 1986. The Deputy U.S. Trade Representative S. Linn Williams flatly stated that the accord was "a much more businesslike agreement than its predecessor." When asked what was different between the October joint SIA-CSPP proposals and the final agreement, Williams remarked, "I would characterize most of these differences as questions of technical matters, not policy."[13]

Thus, the CSPP succeeded in putting to rest the antidumping aspects of the earlier agreement. However, the issue briefly resurfaced in 1992-93 with South Korea the defendant. Micron filed an antidumping petition alleging less-than-fair-value imports of 1M DRAMs and higher from Korea. Faced with stiff antidumping duties, the Korean industry and government proposed in January 1993 a bilateral semiconductor trade agreement fashioned on the earlier one with Japan. But Micron strongly opposed suspension of the case, the Commerce Department had little authority to pursue the agreement, and USTR basically ignored the overture in the absence of any pressure from the SIA. The USITC split 3-3 on the final material injury determination, with the default being that a tie goes to the affirmative and duties were imposed, although the margins were low (less than one percent for Samsung, the largest producer).

The market access provision of the agreement lived on for several more years. Although there was some uncertainty about whether the United States would retaliate if foreign producers did not achieve 20 percent by the end of 1992, that mark was finally achieved in the fourth quarter of that year. The SIA (1990, p. 33) once maintained that "after a 20 percent level had been achieved, [the] foreign share would float to an appropriate level based on competitive merit and without further government targets . . . [the target was] a threshold from which market forces would then take over and operate." But even though the share continued to rise over the next four years, reaching 30 percent by 1996, and the ties between U.S. and Japanese firms proliferated, the SIA argued that the agreement should be renewed again that year.

In the meantime, Japan had strenuously resisted the Clinton administration's efforts to expand the use of import targets to other sectors and argue that the agreement should be allowed to lapse. The high foreign market share in Japan made questionable the necessity of another agreement. After negotiations in mid-1996, government involvement in the industry's trade came effectively to an end. Instead, the SIA and their Japanese counterparts formed a joint world council to resolve disputes and promote cooperation among producers.

VI. Lessons

Although there are many lessons to be drawn from U.S. semiconductor trade policy, I wish to highlight those that particularly relate to the topic of this volume.

Despite the constraints imposed by U.S. trade law on the types of remedies offered by government trade agencies, these agencies actually had considerable discretion as to what the policy toward the industry would be. USTR rejected the SIA's informal inquiries about filing a Section 301 petition in 1982, only to accept the petition in 1985. There was no marked change in Japanese policy between those years, just a change in the view of the Reagan administration about such market opening actions. The market share target was an unprecedented remedy offered by the government. The target put the United States in the position of possibly having to retaliate against Japan for non-compliance even if exchange rate movements (or other factors directly beyond MITI's control) worked against achieving the target. In attempting to limit Japanese dumping in third (i.e., non-U.S.) markets, the government also went way beyond U.S. antidumping law (and indeed violated the GATT) at the behest of the semiconductor industry. The extent to which government agencies accommodated the semiconductor industry's demands is remarkable. Both the antidumping and the market access issues also illustrate how trade policy can be driven by a coalition of a few vocal firms, or sometimes (as was the case in antidumping with Micron) just one firm.

But the case also reveals the potential influence of downstream user industries in offsetting trade remedies that are against their interest. When confronted with organized opposition to the agreement, USTR proved to be sensitive to the views of the downstream users. However, until those user interests were represented in the political arena, government agencies had no way of developing an independent conception of what sorts of policies would best serve the interests of the economy overall by accounting for such interests. Thus, in the 1986 negotiations, the bargaining stance taken by USTR was precisely the positions held by the SIA; in the 1991 negotiations, the stance was that taken by the SIA & CSPP. In the end, semiconductor policy reflected the views of those interest groups that were in play.

NOTES

[1] By concentrating on specific, quantitative "results" and "outcomes," the remedy provoked sharp debate: either it was heralded as a positive, concrete step toward gaining greater sales (and thereby opening) Japan's market, or scorned as a step toward cartelized "managed trade" and export protectionism via government-fixed market shares. For a more detailed discussion and critique of VIEs, see Irwin (1994).

[2] For a more detailed treatment of the issues in this paper, see Flamm (1996) and Irwin (1996).

[3] The industry has successfully lobbied for such policies. The National Cooperative Research Act of 1984 relaxed the antitrust treatment of joint R&D ventures and the Semiconductor Chip Protection Act of 1984 prohibited the unauthorized copying of chip designs. Starting in 1989 the government has also provided subsidies for Sematech, an industry R&D consortium. For an evaluation of Sematech, see Irwin and Klenow (1996).

[4] For an excellent introduction to the SIA's organization and purposes, see Mundo (1992).

[5] Many members of the SIA (such as Motorola, IBM, Texas Instruments, and Intel) maintain their own Washington offices to monitor policy developments of interest. These offices also work on SIA initiatives.

[6] Ong and Mar (1992) calculated how a sample of semiconductor workers laid off in 1985—a year in which half the work force was furloughed (either temporarily or permanently) and industry employment in northern California fell by 14 percent—were faring two years later based on data from California's unemployment insurance program. They found that workers reemployed by other semiconductor or high technology firms earned comparable wages to those rehired by their original semiconductor employer, suggesting the presence of sector-specific rather than industry- or firm-specific human capital. That labor was largely silent in the semiconductor trade dispute does not mean that its interests were neglected by politicians: labor's political action committee (the International Brotherhood of Electronic Workers Committee on Political Education) channeled $1.6 million to political candidates in 1985-86 and over $2.2 million in 1987-88, according to the Federal Election Commission.

[7] Four large merchant producers also formed political action committees with which to provide campaign contributions to national political candidates. The disbursements of these PACs appear to be related to the trade dispute with Japan: payments totaled $354,318 at the peak of the dispute in 1985-86, 40 percent higher than in 1983-84 and 17 percent higher than in 1987-88 after trade tensions had simmered down. Data from the Federal Election Commission.

[8] DRAMs are marked by well-defined generations that give rise to distinct product cycles. In 1970, the 1K random-access memory chip (capable of storing 1,024 bits of information) was introduced. This was followed by the 4K chip in 1973, 16K in 1976, 64K in 1979, 256K in 1982, 1M in 1985, 4M in 1989, and 16M in 1991.

[9] The language of the secret side letter is vague, however, reading simply that "the Government of Japan recognizes the U.S. semiconductor industry's expectation" that sales will rise to "slightly above 20 percent" in five years and that "the Government of Japan considers that this can be realized."

[10] The dumping sanctions were gradually eased for diplomatic reasons and as semiconductor prices firmed. The $165 million in market-access sanctions remained intact until the signing of the 1991 semiconductor accord.

[11] Flamm (1996) reports that profits on 1M DRAM sales for Japanese producers amounted to $1.2 billion in 1988 alone.

[12] Some firms in the CSPP were also members of the SIA, but the agenda of the SIA had been increasingly set by the merchant firms.

[13] Quoted in Irwin (1996).

REFERENCES

Flamm, Kenneth. 1966. *Mismanaged Trade: Strategic Policy and the Semiconductor Industry.* Washington, D.C.: The Brookings Institution.

Irwin, Douglas A. 1994. *Managed Trade: The Case Against Import Targets.* Washington, D.C.: The AEI Press.

Irwin, Douglas A. 1996. "Trade Politics and the Semiconductor Industry," in Anne O. Krueger (ed.), *The Political Economy of American Trade Policy.* Chicago: University of Chicago Press for the NBER.

Irwin, Douglas A., and Peter J. Klenow. 1996. "High Tech R&D Subsidies: Estimating the Effects of Sematech," *Journal of International Economics* 40:323-44.

Mundo, Philip A. 1992. *Interest Groups: Cases and Characteristics.* Chicago: Nelson-Hall.

Ong, Paul M., and Don Mar. 1992. "Post-Layoff Earnings Among Semiconductor Workers," *Industrial and Labor Relations Review* 45:366-79.

Semiconductor Industry Association. 1983. *The Effect of Government Targeting on World Semiconductor Competition.* Cupertino, CA: SIA.

Semiconductor Industry Association. 1990. *Four Years of Experience Under the U.S.-Japan Semiconductor Agreement: 'A Deal is a Deal'.* Cupertino, CA: SIA.

Yoffe, David B. 1988. "How an Industry Builds Political Advantage," *Harvard Business Review* 66:82-89.

CHAPTER 9

U.S. Trade Policy vis-à-vis the Aircraft Industry

Raymond J. Waldmann and Jay Culbert

I. Introduction

As one of the nation's top exporters, The Boeing Company is vitally concerned with the design and implementation of U.S. trade policies. Sales to international customers generate over half of Boeing's total commercial revenues. However, we face vigorous competition for these customers from government-supported competitors. In the past twelve years, two U.S. manufacturers, Lockheed and McDonnell Douglas, have seen their market share drop to the point where both have been forced to exit the civil aircraft business, in large measure because of the rise of government-supported foreign competitors. U.S. trade policies need to be responsive to the threat government-supported competition poses to the continued viability of the U.S. civil aircraft industry.

Airbus Industrie exemplifies this threat. Airbus serves as the central coordinating and administrative unit of a vast airframe manufacturing enterprise embracing some of Europe's largest aerospace firms: Société Nationale Industrielle Aérospatiale of France, Daimler-Benz Aerospace Airbus (DASA) of Germany (a unit of Daimler-Benz AG), British Aerospace plc of the UK, and Construcciones Aeronauticas SA (CASA) of Spain. Since 1970, the Airbus home governments have provided, in nominal terms, $13.5 billion in direct subsidies. When calculated at commercial rates of borrowing, this figure rises to $25.9 billion.[1] Government subsidies have allowed Airbus to develop a family of narrow-body and wide-body aircraft that competes with Boeing in practically every segment of the market and in every geographical region. Airbus has vowed to take 50% of the market for large civil aircraft by the year 2000. With demand for new aircraft expected to reach $1.1 trillion over the next 20 years, the stakes are vast.

The rise of Airbus has led to efforts to devise equitable, enforceable trade policies aimed at helping the U.S. maintain its leadership of the global aircraft industry. Boeing has been at the forefront of these efforts, beginning with the

GATT Agreement on Trade in Civil Aircraft,[2] commonly referred to as the Aircraft Code. Boeing also helped craft the 1992 U.S.- EC Bilateral[3] and the Subsidies Code during the Uruguay Round negotiations. These agreements, while falling short of expectations in some respects, nevertheless raised the visibility of the issues and provide a means of invoking U.S. government action when needed. U.S. industry was also instrumental in securing an agreement through the OECD on limiting official export financing. The Large Aircraft Sector Understanding, or LASU, helped reduce export financing as an element in sales campaigns and so leveled the playing field for U.S. manufacturers in their struggle with government-backed competitors.

II. The Aircraft Code

The concept of a GATT sectoral agreement in civil aircraft came from Boeing in 1975. William Allen, Boeing's Chairman Emeritus, wrote to Ambassador Dent, President Ford's Special Trade Representative: "all aerospace tariffs . . . and the non-tariff barriers to commercial jet transport sales should be eliminated where possible . . . I believe that the best way to achieve these results is through sectoral negotiations."[4]

Boeing argued for eliminating U.S. tariffs as a fair and reciprocal concession for agreements to bind European tariffs and eliminate non-tariff barriers (NTBs). The NTBs we felt warranted special attention were directed procurement and offset demands by foreign governments. Directed procurement involves airline purchases from a specific manufacturer that are mandated by the government. Offset demands, on the other hand, require as a condition of sale that the seller place work in the purchasing country to help defray, or offset, the purchase price of the aircraft. Boeing estimated that it had lost $1.2 billion in sales (through 1974) due to directed procurement demands from government-owned carriers,[5] and that while it had been able to withstand demands for offset, the company was under increasing pressure to provide it.

The threat posed by subsidies, while initially low, grew year by year as Airbus made inroads in the market. The fact that Airbus' first product, the A300, was subsidized was taken as a given and, if not condoned, considered water under the bridge. Boeing argued that, in the future, all product development costs should be reflected in the product price. But, because of the potential for retaliation, we advised against automatic countervailing duties.

Over the course of the next three years, Boeing worked through the Aerospace Industries Association and the Aerospace Industry Sector Advisory Committee (ISAC 24)[6] to promote the idea of a sectoral agreement. George Prill, Chairman of ISAC 24, was seconded from Lockheed to devote full time to pushing for a sectoral agreement that would not only eliminate tariffs but also include disciplines on subsidies and other NTBs.

The first draft of what became the GATT agreement was prepared by ISAC 24 on June 1, 1978. It was a distillation of the views of several European, Canadian, Japanese, and, of course, American companies. It called for the elimination of tariffs on aircraft and aircraft parts, government restraint in calls for directed procurement and offsets, and pricing based on the need "to obtain a reasonable return on investment."

Despite reservations about the idea of a sectoral agreement expressed by members of the U.S. delegation in Geneva, President Carter's Trade Representative, Bob Strauss, was more amenable. He was looking for a dramatic breakthrough which Carter could announce at the Bonn economic summit meeting in July 1978. At that meeting, the heads of state endorsed a statement which read in part:

> Agreement was reached on the objective of negotiating maximum freedom of world trade in commercial aircraft, engines, and parts and related equipment including the elimination of duties and, to the fullest extent possible, the reduction or elimination of trade restricting or distorting effects.[7]

Ambassador Strauss appointed a full-time aircraft negotiator, Dr. W. Stephen Piper, to begin government-to-government negotiations aimed at implementing this objective.

After a series of bilateral meetings in the fall of 1978, an agreement was reached which was initialed on April 12, 1979. The final agreement is not as clearly or as strongly worded as the original ISAC proposal. On the issue of government-directed procurement, for example, the original language which said that governments "shall refrain from directing or inducing airlines . . . to procure civil aircraft from any particular source" was softened to read: "shall not require airlines . . . nor exert unreasonable pressure on them, to procure civil aircraft from any particular source."[8]

The offset issue, meanwhile, encountered entrenched domestic opposition. Boeing and McDonnell Douglas wanted an outright ban on all offset demands, both civil and military; Airbus agreed. However, Northrup opposed any limitation on offset strategies, as did the U.S. Department of Defense (DoD). DoD had a series of offset memoranda of understanding (MOUs) with foreign governments that mandated offsets in civil aerospace in return for foreign military sales. The MOU with Australia, for example, required offsets in the civil sector to balance Australian purchases of U.S. military matériel. DoD therefore did not want a civil agreement interfering with its programs.

The compromise wording, based on a Boeing proposal, establishes the principle that purchases "should be made only on a competitive price, quality and delivery basis."[9] Governments reserved the right, however, to demand that firms in their jurisdiction be allowed to compete for sub-contracts associated with the purchase of civil aircraft; nothing was said about military offsets.

The strictures on government support, embodied in Article 6 of the Agreement, are somewhat ambiguous, reflecting the inability of the parties to agree on hard and fast rules in this area. The Agreement on Subsidies and Countervailing Measures, it states, applies to trade in civil aircraft, in particular the provisions stipulating that signatories shall "seek to avoid" injury or serious prejudice to another signatory through the use of any subsidy.[10] Pricing "should be based on a reasonable expectation of recoupment of all costs." The term "reasonable expectation" was understood to mean that companies will make an intellectually honest assessment of all direct and indirect costs and all recurring and non-recurring costs and then amortize the non-recurring costs over the number of units constituting the breakeven point. Government investment in basic aeronautical research and development is not considered a subsidy and therefore not subject to recoupment. Government funding which is program-specific, however, is subject to recoupment as part of the price of the end-product.

The Aircraft Code was, from Boeing's standpoint, a useful first step in that it covered most major issues (including the elimination of tariffs, our highest priority issue) even if it came short of meeting all our objectives. In order to build on what had been agreed, a Committee on Civil Aircraft was established to provide a forum for addressing issues affecting the operation of the Agreement. Boeing proposed the wording, set forth in Article 8.2, calling for further negotiations within three years, and periodically thereafter, aimed at broadening and improving the Agreement. In the event, negotiations did not begin in earnest until 1986 when the issue of subsidies to Airbus came to a head. It was an issue that would concentrate the minds of U.S. trade policy officials—and industry executives—for the next six years.

III. The 1992 U.S.–EC Bilateral

By the mid-1980s, the Aircraft Code had become a canon more honored in the breach than the observance. It was evident to U.S. observers that Europe was flaunting the provisions regarding sales inducements, political leverage, and government support.[11] In September 1985, the Trade Policy Review Group, an interagency committee chaired by USTR, singled out Airbus as a possible candidate for a Section 301 investigation and asked for Boeing's reaction. Boeing recommended that USTR convey to the European countries involved in Airbus the government's concern regarding the trade-distorting effects of subsidies. Bilateral negotiations were the preferred means of addressing the problem; failing that, a broad Section 301 case was not to be ruled out.

At the invitation of the Europeans, informal consultations began in Geneva in March 1986. A further round was held in June. Boeing, along with representatives from McDonnell Douglas and AIA, traveled to Geneva (the first of many trips) for the purpose of advising the U.S. negotiating team. U.S. industry's goals were to obtain greater disclosure of Airbus subsidies and finances, to end government inducements and political salesmanship in sales campaigns and, if possible, to tighten the conditions under which launch aid could be provided.

The outcome was mixed. The meetings achieved two Boeing objectives: greater transparency on finances and a reaffirmation of the need to avoid the use of inducements. The French provided the first public figures of their support for Airbus (FF 8.7 billion since 1969, of which 25% had been recouped), and the United Kingdom admitted to £250 million in support of the A320. The Germans demurred, saying that the numbers could be found in official budget documents.

While there was some satisfaction in reaching an agreement, however limited, that avoided a trade war, U.S. officials recognized that the major issue of government supports remained unresolved. The options the U.S. had to deal with the outstanding issues were to: (1) escalate the issue to the political level (i.e., Ambassador Yeutter/Secretary Baldridge); (2) initiate formal consultations under the GATT; (3) initiate unilateral action; (4) seek amendments to the Aircraft Code; or (5) do nothing.

Boeing favored escalating the discussions. Boeing CEO Frank Shrontz wrote to Treasury Secretary Baker, Secretary of State Shultz and White House Chief of Staff Regan asking them to support USTR and Commerce in raising the level of discussions. "Higher level talks will put the Europeans on notice regarding U.S. government insistence on compliance with GATT," he stated.[12] McDonnell Douglas CEO Sandy McDonnell also contacted several Cabinet members.

Subsequently, at a Cabinet-level meeting of the Economic Policy Council, it was agreed that USTR Yeutter should initiate high- level consultations with the Airbus governments to resolve outstanding issues. These consultations were held in February 1987 and were led by Deputy U.S. Trade Representative Mike Smith and Commerce Under Secretary Bruce Smart.

The talks ended in a stalemate. After reviewing the results of the Smith/Smart mission, the Economic Policy Council decided to launch an initiative in GATT to clarify the Aircraft Code. It also agreed to initiate a study of Airbus economics and to monitor closely the impending launch of the Airbus A330/A340 family of aircraft.

The GATT Aircraft Committee met several times beginning in March in an attempt to clarify the two most contentious articles, namely Articles 4 and 6. While there appeared to be an emerging consensus around the interpretation of Article 4 (on sales inducements), there was no meeting of the minds on the nature of obligations set forth in Article 6, regarding transparency and government support. "Our positions appear to be as far apart as when we began this exercise," a cable from the U.S. delegation in Geneva said.[13]

Meanwhile, Boeing (along with McDonnell Douglas) had been considering the merits of pursuing various trade actions against Airbus under U.S. trade laws: the countervailing duty statute; antidumping statute; and Section 301. The *threat* of using one or more of these measures was seen as important as taking the action itself, and a useful way to force a negotiated solution.

However, the European negotiators objected to this tactic and called on Ambassador Yeutter to seek a commitment from U.S. industry to refrain from taking any trade action. Yeutter responded that the only way to achieve this was through an agreement addressing U.S. industry's basic concerns. "A negotiated solution would be much preferable to the eruption of a trade conflict," Yeutter wrote to EC External Affairs Commissioner Willy De Clercq. "[B]ut I fear that such conflict is inevitable unless we move quickly."[14]

Yeutter and De Clercq met in London in October and agreed on a statement of "Joint Principles and Objectives" aimed at resolving the issues over which the Europeans had remained intransigent, namely, disciplines on new capital infusions, avoiding trade distortion, and improving transparency. The London Mandate, as it was called, helped guide negotiations through the tumultuous years that followed.

The exchange of draft texts, as well as verbal sparring, continued through much of 1988. When the new Bush Administration took office in 1989, the Airbus dossier figured prominently among USTR Carla Hills' priorities. Although it was not included in the list of Super 301 candidates announced in May (much to the chagrin of McDonnell Douglas), USTR asserted that Airbus would be "pursued actively." And it did not disappoint. When the German government announced a $2.3 billion program in exchange rate subsidies for the takeover of German Airbus partner Messerschmitt-Bölkow-Blohm by Daimler-Benz, USTR promptly filed a GATT case on the grounds that it was an illegal export subsidy.

While this case was making its way through the GATT process, further bilateral negotiations produced the so-called "elements of agreement," including: a ban on production subsidies; a (yet-to-be-specified) cap on development subsidies; a bailout clause, more precise identification of prohibited inducements; and disciplines on indirect supports. The U.S. made its final offer in December 1990 which provided for a 45% cap on government development support, to be reduced to 25% over two years; but even this attractive offer was rejected by the EC. The USTR promptly terminated the talks and took two actions to resolve the issue in the GATT: it requested a panel to rule on the German exchange rate subsidies case; and it initiated, with the concurrence of the Trade Policy Review Group, a broad case against all Airbus subsidies. U.S. industry was united in its support of the proposed measures.

This demonstration of U.S. resolve helped to elicit some flexibility on the EC's part and a willingness to negotiate a final agreement. They proposed a deadline of March 31, 1992. Another factor contributing to the EC's newfound desire to reach agreement was the ruling by the GATT against the EC in the German exchange rate subsidies case.

The U.S. and EC were able to reach a bilateral agreement by the proposed deadline. It bans production support, limits government support to 33% of total development costs, provides for government support to be repaid within 17 years, requires disclosure of loan terms and conditions, and limits indirect support (e.g., through government R&D). It also prohibits government inducements (such as landing rights, aid programs, government-supported airline financing, etc.) in sales campaigns and further controls offset requirements. While it does not eliminate foreign subsidies, the margin of subsidization has been reduced and the terms for repayment strengthened. Boeing CEO Frank Shrontz called it an "important milestone toward the resolution of this difficult issue." He further commented that "the controls in this agreement will reduce the substantial advantages government support has provided our European competitors."[15]

IV. Post-1992 Bilateral Negotiations

The issue did not end there, however. During the course of 1993, the GATT Aircraft Committee sought to "multilateralize" the bilateral to cover other signatories. In the process, the European Union (EU) attempted to undo the progress that had been achieved by trying to exclude aircraft from coverage under the Agreement on Subsidies and Countervailing Measures (the Subsidies Code), then under negotiation as part of the Uruguay Round.

Indeed, the EU attempted to link renegotiation of the Aircraft Code to the conclusion of the Uruguay Round itself. EU efforts were focused on making the Aircraft Committee the sole arbiter of subsidies rules for civil aircraft. U.S. industry believed, and continues to believe, that the proper venue for any further negotiations on subsidy issues concerning this industry is in the Committee on Subsidies and Countervailing Measures.

In the final hours of the Uruguay Round negotiations, U.S. Trade Representative Mickey Kantor and EU Commissioner Sir Leon Brittan struck a deal establishing the principle that the Subsidies Code applies to civil aircraft with three exceptions, embodied in footnotes to the subsidies agreement: the first excludes civil aircraft from the presumption of "serious prejudice" in cases where government subsidies exceed 5 percent of the cost of developing a new aircraft; the second exclusion protects a signatory (read: the European Union) from charges of serious prejudice in cases where royalty-based financing is not being fully repaid due to the level of actual sales falling below forecast sales; the third and final exclusion, a U.S. demand, exempts R&D for civil aircraft from the so-called "green light" provisions of the Subsidies Code, i.e., R&D subsidies for civil aircraft could be a violation of the Code.

U.S. industry's goal, the coverage of subsidies to the aircraft industry by the Subsidies Code, was thus achieved, with the exceptions outlined above. President Clinton, in a letter to Boeing CEO Frank Shrontz, wrote that "this was a major objective of the U.S. aerospace industry, including Boeing, whose foreign competitors have often benefited from such subsidies."[16]

The conclusion of the Uruguay Round left undisturbed the U.S. - EC bilateral. The bilateral is not a stand-alone agreement but, based on the 1979 Aircraft Code, establishes obligations in addition to the subsidies disciplines contained in the Subsidies Code and is complementary to it. This is what is known as the "belt and suspenders" approach. The two agreements provide the broadest coverage of all forms of government support to the civil aircraft industry.

V. Conclusion

Trade policy has been likened to doing acupuncture with a fork: there are bound to be unintended consequences, no matter how carefully defined the target. In the case of civil aircraft, minimizing those consequences involved extensive and painstaking negotiations. European intransigence over fundamental issues frequently caused negotiations to break down, but the prospect of a ruinous trade war always drove them back to the table. In the end, Europe and the U.S. agreed to compromise. The result has been a fragile truce, marked by mutual recrimination as the two sides accuse each other of bad faith in implementing the agreement.

From the beginning, Boeing's efforts to reach an agreement were informed by the threat subsidies posed to the continued viability of U.S. industry. This was not an idle threat. In the period since the dispute with Airbus began, two U.S. manufacturers have been forced to exit the civil aircraft industry. It would be tragic if that were to happen to a third. Continuous monitoring and enforcement of the relevant trade policies are needed to ensure that it doesn't.

NOTES

[1] *An Economic and Financial Review of Airbus Industrie*, by Gellman Research Associates, Inc., for the U.S. Department of Commerce, September 1990.

[2]General Agreement on Tariffs and Trade, MTN/W/38, 7 April 1979.

[3]Agreement Concerning the Application of the GATT Agreement on Trade in Civil Aircraft, 1 April, 1992.

[4]Letter dated February 24, 1975.

[5]A case in point was the requirement laid down by French Finance Minister, Jean-Pierre Fourcade, that Air France purchase A300 airplanes rather than U.S.-built airplanes. See *New York Times*, January 27, 1975.

[6]One of the 27 advisory committees established under the Trade Act of 1974.

[7]The Agreement on Trade in Civil Aircraft: A History and Commentary Prepared by the Aerospace Industry Sector Advisory Committee (ISAC 24), March 13, 1980.

[8]The Agreement on Trade in Civil Aircraft, Article 4.2.

[9]The Agreement on Trade in Civil Aircraft, Article 4.3.

[10]Agreement on Interpretation and Application of Articles VI, XVI and XXIII of the General Agreement on Tariffs and Trade, MTN/NTM/W/236, April 1979.

[11]Examples of the heavy-handed tactics employed by Airbus to win sales can be found in *The Japan Times* (April 21, 1982); *Time* (August 22, 1983); *Wall Street Journal* (March 20, 1984); and the *International Herald Tribune* (October 31, 1985).

[12]Letter dated December 3, 1996.

[13]"U.S. Delegation Statement at GATT Committee on Trade in Civil Aircraft," July 27, 1987.

[14]Letter dated August 24, 1987.

[15]Boeing Information Bulletin, July 7, 1992

[16]Letter dated January 31, 1994.

CHAPTER 10

The Role of Constituents in U.S. Policy Development Towards Trade in Financial Services

Harry L. Freeman

I. Introduction

This paper will principally address trade in financial services, with particular emphasis on negotiations in the GATT and subsequently in the World Trade organization (WTO). Particular reference will be made towards constituent interests and their role in policy development. To understand the present situation, as of mid-October, 1996, one must understand some of the origins of the subject, and its history to date.

The principal points made in this paper concern: (1) the first major "stirrings" for some international rules for trade in financial services; (2) repositioning of the issue from deregulation and classification of the subject in the "trade category"; (3) the major players in the late 1970s and 1980s and the change in players in the 1990s to date; (4) what happened in the final few days of the Uruguay Round in 1993; (5) what happened in the further period of negotiations in mid-1995; (6) the factors that will shape the result in the next scheduled WTO negotiations in late 1997; and (7) the author's prediction of precisely what will happen in those negotiations.

Partial List of Cast of Characters (titles at time of greatest involvement in key issues in this paper.)

Maurice Greenberg, CEO, American International Group (AIG)
Jim Robinson, CEO, American Express Company (Amex)-
John Reed, CEO, Citicorp
Bill Hawley, CITI, Director of International Relations
Ron Shelp, AIG, Director of Government Relations
Harry Freeman, Executive Vice President, Amex
Jeff Lang, Deputy USTR
Jeff Shafer, Undersecretary of the Treasury, International
Margaret Wigglesworth, Executive Director, Coalition of Service Industries

Joan Spero, Amex, Senior Vice President, International Corporate Affairs (now at State Department)

II. International Rules for Trade in Financial Services

The first serious push to include financial services in the GATT was made by the American International Group (AIG) during the Tokyo Round in the mid-to-late 1970s. AIG was having difficulties entering some of the Asian insurance markets and worked with the then USTR, Robert Strauss, to address their issues. Although "services" was too new an issue for the Tokyo Round, Strauss was successful in getting the term "services" within a new and broader definition of "trade" in the U.S. legislation implementing the Tokyo Round. This turned out to be significant in later years.

In 1978 the American Express Company (Amex) joined AIG in the effort to open services markets (with particular emphasis on financial services) by securing a place for services in any new multilateral trade talks. Amex, whose interests were broader than traditional "banking, securities and insurance," decided that it stood a better chance of securing liberalization if it sought to liberalize all services rather than just those of its own parochial interests. Inclusion of services in a traditional trade round took years of effort partly because many trade professionals thought services as a trade issue might crowd out concurrent tariff negotiations over goods.

Amex had a strong motive for leading the effort to liberalize trade in services. It was having serious market access problems, stemming from the fact that it was engaging in financial services activities as a non-bank in countries where, typically, a few very large banks dominated their domestic markets. Amex needed nondiscriminatory access to national telecommunications networks and payment systems, both of which were under the influence of Amex's foreign competitors. After examination of the challenge, Amex decided to devote substantial funds and staff to make an effort to get financial services into the GATT. It concluded that in order to get rules on financial services, all other services must be included.

This decision by Jim Robinson was probably the single most important decision in the history of this subject. He committed to provide substantial funds of an undeterminant nature to a crusade which might take a decade or two, provide the necessary staff, and spend significant amounts of his own time making speeches, lobbying, and forming close relationships with government officials around the world. His decision was also major in delegating most of the planning and execution of the program to one of his deputies, the author of this paper. My role was also staff hiring and that included such people as Joan Spero, David Ruth (now at State), Paula Collins (now at Kodak), Dick Moose (was at State), Bill Canis (at Amex), and involving others like Allen Sinai, economist, and Larry Summers as a consultant, now at Treasury. It paid off.

When the Uruguay Round negotiations actually started at the end of 1986, the outlook for a strong deal in any of the services areas, including financial services, was bleak at best. It went from bad to worse when the GATT model for such an agreement shifted from a "top down" to a "bottom up" approach. In a "top down" model, all areas are included in any agreement unless they are *explicitly excluded.* In a "bottom up," agreement, everything is excluded unless it is *explicitly included* in the agreement. The "bottom up" approach allowed countries to sign on to, or exclude themselves from, trade deals in each particular sector, rather than be forced to sign on to a broad deal or be excluded from the general provisions.

One overlooked factor that turned out to be a positive force working for the inclusion of services in the Uruguay Round was the sheer length of the Round. From 1986 to 1993 many persons unfamiliar with services became more comfortable with including services in trade negotiations. Services is now taken for granted as a subject for negotiation, just like goods, while such areas as "competition policy" are now regarded as "new."

During the Uruguay Round, services received steady support from the USTR and its professional staff. Pioneering work was done in the OECD by Geza Feketekuty. Dick Self, still at USTR, was a stalwart negotiator through the whole period. Warren Lavorel, the U.S. coordinator of Uruguay Round negotiations, and currently Deputy Director General of the WTO, was also a major player.

In the last weeks of the Uruguay Round negotiations there was a flurry of activity in all areas. It became obvious, however, that some areas, such as tourism and telecommunications, would make more progress than other areas such as professional services, basic telecommunications, and financial services. A last minute attempt was made to put together a deal to make some recordable progress in financial services. This attempt on December 15, 1993, in Geneva, which ultimately failed, was a forerunner of the problems of mid-1995. In 1993, at the close of the Uruguay Round negotiations, the United States wanted substantial liberalization commitments from both developed and developing countries in exchange for binding its completely open financial services market. This was not forthcoming in 1993, or in 1995. We hope it will occur in 1997.

III. Financial Services Negotiations Since Conclusion of the Uruguay Round

As just mentioned, in December, 1993, at the close of the Uruguay Round negotiations, the tentative commitments of other countries regarding financial services were deemed insufficient by the U.S. delegation, and a financial services deal appeared dead. At this point the U.S. Treasury representatives in Geneva consulted with representatives of the U.S. financial industry on a "last ditch" offer: a "two-tier" plan whereby the United States would bind its open market, but only to those who also had substantially or fully open markets.

Other countries could join when they wished. This proposal was roundly attacked by the Director General of GATT, the EU, other delegations, and the press as being "discriminatory" and violating the fundamental nondiscriminatory principle of the GATT (note that the EU asked for the same two tier approach in July, 1995, only one and one-half years later, and got it).

After the U.S. two-tier plan was rejected in December 1993, negotiations on financial services were scheduled to resume in mid-1995 with the expectation that the negotiating parties might then be willing to make improved and satisfactory commitments. The U.S. government and private sector lobbied throughout East Asia during 1994 and early 1995 seeking better commitments. The United States clearly stated its position going into the 1995 negotiations. For the United States to bind itself to MFN, it had to see a sufficient number of liberalizing commitments from both developed and developing countries. Secretary of the Treasury Rubin made this crystal clear in a statement to the Congress on June 8, 1995, just a week before intensive negotiations resumed in Geneva.

As the June 30, 1995 date approached, the commitments either tabled or promised did not meet the standards set by the U.S. negotiators. There were satisfactory promises from most of the developed countries. However, many of the developing countries' commitments did not meet minimal standards, particularly in the area of foreign ownership. The United States, disappointed at those poor commitments, then revised its own commitment. It filed one which had an element of reciprocity, namely, the United States intended to remain an open market as required by U.S. law, but reserved the right to limit or condition access to the U.S. market if the home country had significant restrictions. This change, if implemented, would have required a major, and unlikely, act of Congress, one of a series of points not reported by the press during the controversial days of June/July, 1995.

At this point, June 28, 1995, two days before the close of negotiations, the EU, led by Sir Leon Brittan, suggested a month's extension of the negotiations while it worked to secure better commitments. The United States favored and assisted the EU attempt (a fact not reported in the press), and the necessary consensus was obtained for a month's extension. Thereafter, the EU did two things: (1) made an effort to secure more favorable commitments from the developing countries, which failed; and (2) came to Washington, together with Japan, and asked the U.S. Treasury for letters stating that whatever the United States might do in limiting access to its market for foreign providers of financial services, it would not affect the EU and Japan. Thus, the EU and Japan accepted a two-tier system favoring the EU and Japan, the same plan that the U.S. Treasury had offered in December, 1993 (again, this event was not in the press accounts).

Regrettably, at least in this author's opinion, the U.S. Treasury did provide those letter assurances. Of course, the letters neither have the force of law, nor are enforceable in the WTO dispute settlement mechanisms, but they do represent political commitments by the U.S. Treasury which are unlikely to be ignored in the future. The two-tier approach which was rejected in 1993 was effectively established as a practical matter by 1995. Such a two-tier arrangement may reappear in the late 1997 negotiations.

By the end of July 1995, the EU came up with an interim agreement to maintain the status quo until November 1, 1997, with negotiations opening at that time and closing by the end of 1997. The United States signed, and is a party to, that interim agreement and took an MFN exemption, as did many of the countries signing the interim agreement (again, a fact not reported in the press).

The interim agreement was to go into effect June 30, 1997, if all necessary approvals by governments were in place. The EU found itself four member countries short, and thus could not sign by that date (again, try and find that in the press accounts). Various extensions of time have now been agreed and the key dates remain November 1, 1997, when countries can change or withdraw their commitments, and December 31,1997, by which time new commitments should be on file and negotiations completed.

It is worth repeating the U.S. role in the 1995 negotiations: it was supportive of the EU effort and the interim agreement it filed a commitment to this effect. The media continues to suggest the United States "walked out"; not so. The United States stated its position and filed its commitment on June 23, 1995, and declared that was its final position. The core problem, whatever critics of the United States might say, has been the same in 1993, 1995, and could again be the principal problem in 1997: most East and South Asian countries, as well as some key South American countries, are simply opposed to real liberalization in the financial services area.

IV. Where Do We Go from Here?

Writing in the autumn of 1996, on the eve of resumption of formal negotiations over financial services in the WTO, what then are the factors that are likely to come into play?

1. By and large the subject of financial services in the WTO is receiving increased attention in academic and "think tank" circles. This stems from: the lack of other negotiations for them to discuss; the controversial nature of prior negotiations over the subject; and the role of the negotiations in the development and prestige of the WTO.

2. Some influential trade experts argue that no progress can be made on individual subjects in general and financial services in particular, outside of a broad "round" where "trade-offs" can be made. However, those who call for another broad round to achieve "trade-offs" ignore the fact that financial services negotiations are handled by finance ministries which are not given to negotiating trade-offs in other areas. It may be that a financial services deal cannot be achieved in 1997; however, it might well be a non sequitur then to argue that a broad round is necessary to achieve meaningful financial services negotiations.

3. With respect to any progress toward the critical 1997 negotiations, the U.S. private sector, with the encouragement of the U.S. Treasury and together with elements of the European private sector, is now mounting a major effort to convince the Asian and South American countries to offer better commitments. Much of the effort will be targeted at customers of the banks who would benefit from the competition rather than the existing locally owned banks who prefer the status quo with less foreign competition.

4. Many of the Europeans prefer an "incremental" approach where a series of commitments to liberalize are spaced over a long period of years. The United States wants commitments to open markets fully, although it will accept reasonable phase-in periods from developing countries. The United States disfavors a formal incremental approach since it believes it would have to file, at the outset, a commitment to remain fully open in the first round of incremental negotiations, and thereby cease to have any leverage in securing subsequent improved commitments.

5. There is much sentiment that there must be a "successful" negotiation simply in order to maintain WTO prestige, even if in reality the deal is less than "successful" in terms of liberalization. Some forcefully argue that both the basic telecommunications negotiations scheduled for early 1997 and the financial services negotiations must have a successful outcome by the end of 1997. If not, the chances for other negotiations in both goods and services are greatly reduced. This argument is largely made outside of the industries directly concerned with the negotiations. The financial services industries in each country, and their respective finance ministries, do not place a powerful WTO at the very top of their priorities list, although they perceive the WTO as being important.

6. On the positive side, the world's financial services markets and providers of financial services are rapidly integrating. The world financial markets are constantly globalizing and countries will, over time, either open to foreign competition or find themselves isolated from efficient world capital markets. It may be that the markets themselves will achieve, over time, what negotiations cannot achieve. This suggests that the negotiations may become less important, and that liberalization will occur regardless of WTO negotiations.

7. Some fairly high level U.S.-EU cooperation will be necessary to have successful WTO negotiations.

8. Another variable is the identity of U.S. Government officials in the trade area in 1997. Even if President Clinton is reelected, major turnovers are common in second terms. Turnovers of people often mean new policies.

9. To have real success there has to be a major change in the attitude of many Asian, South American and other emerging market countries. They must view open markets not as a threat but as a profound economic opportunity. This is probably the most crucial factor in what happens in 1997.

10. Since there is little "give" in the United States or EU positions in respect of the more advanced developing countries in Asia and Latin America, the necessary attitude change may have to come from a desire to build the

power and prestige of the WTO, rather than any financial services market considerations per se. Or, some countries may go along in financial services to gain a "trade off" in another area. This might work, but increasingly "trade offs" are less likely as different ministries with their own political power bases become involved in WTO negotiations.

11. Another possibility is an interim deal with two or three tiers, as mentioned above, between the United States and Japan and the EU in one tier, and other countries signatory to the July 1995 interim agreement in another tier. This might be accompanied by a scheduled date for another round of negotiations, say, in 1998, or later, or as part of the overall services negotiations in 2000. This is the type of agreement that might emerge when all else fails at the end of 1997.

Conclusion: Pick #11 and you will most likely win. While we should make every effort, I do not think the ASEAN countries will change sufficiently to make sufficient concessions to please the United States and the EU. Financial integration will continue but that alone will not push the recalcitrant countries into the fold. A first and high tier with MFN among, say, the OECD countries, plus a few other countries, might be a reasonable plan. All others would be welcomed into that tier when they open their financial markets, but not before. This keeps some semblance of MFN among the first tier, but obviously violates it fundamentally below that tier. Of course, MFN may never have been meant to cover all trade in services negotiations.

Bet on it.

You and I bet wrong.

That is what happens when a whole year comes between the bet and the action. In fact a very substantive financial services agreement was achieved at WTO on the night of December 12-13, 1997. It was a major U.S. private sector deal.

But November-December 1996 to 1997 was virtually revolutionary in trade in financial services history. In 1986 the Coalition of Service Industries (CSI) was three years old and making little progress towards substantive talks on financial services. At that point, American Express Company caused the formation of a new wing of CSI, the Financial Services Group (FSG). Its purpose was to be a powerful lobbying group in solely the financial services area.

But very little was possible until 1993 and 1995 as described above. In the autumn of 1996 the leadership changed at CSI and FSG with a new top person coming in with energy and know-how. In one year the FSC quadrupled in size. It expanded its U.S. corporate membership from principally banks to banks, insurance companies, securities firms, financial information firms, asset management firms, as well as computer and information technology firms operating in the financial services industry. The following year, autumn of 1996 to autumn of 1997 was a year of intensive lobbying in the U.S. (with Treasury and USTR), Asian governments, and in Europe, seeking and finding private sector allies who, in turn, would press their own governments.

By mid year 1997 a Financial Leaders Group (FLG) was formed at the CEO level composed of both U.S. and European financial firms. In turn, this essentially forced the EU to listen to constituents from the financial industry as to what that industry wanted. This is not common in Europe, where CEOs usually refrain from a direct lobbying even with their own governments. This nut was cracked.

By September, 1997, three months before the final negotiations in Geneva, a very close working relationship had developed among the private sectors of the United States and Europe and working closely with the EU trade negotiators and the U.S. Treasury and USTR. There were meetings with all four groups to discuss strategy . . . occasions heretofore unheard of.

Meanwhile, the trade in services movement won a tremendous victory in spring, 1997, in obtaining the global telecommunications services agreement under WTO auspices. This deal was industry rather than government driven and moved the model of such a sectoral industry drive deal far forward. This meant that a sectoral negotiation of major consequence was doable in services. In turn, this gave further impetus to the United States—EU drive towards a financial services deal.

During the four months preceding the final financial services negotiation, there were monthly formal negotiating sessions at the WTO in Geneva. These were well attended by both the FSG and the FLG which enhanced the working relationship.

In very early December, 1997, the United States and EU negotiating teams, accompanied by the private sector teams, went to Geneva, optimistic that a financial services deal was obtainable. A nerve center operation was set up, with phones, faxes, copying machines, a secretariat, and a facility far better than most embassies in Geneva. The U.S. private sector delegation numbered over 40 persons. Day and night negotiations went on, with the U.S. Government frequently asking the FSG to meet with recalcitrant countries.

With fourteen hours to go before the negotiating deadline of midnight, December 12th, the EU negotiators cracked and demanded that the United States harvest what was then on the table and file an MFN commitment to keep U.S. markets open. With so many hours to go, the United States refused, choosing to pressure other governments for still better offers. They argued that trade agreements went down right to the wire. They were right. They got many improved offers with that brinksmanship strategy, and by 2 AM, December 13th, sufficient good offers were on the table for the United States to say "deal." Better two hours late than never.

The U.S. FSG returned a bunch of "happy campers" with the financial services deal of December, 1997. The offers on the table were far better than the 1995 exercise. The U.S. "walkout" in 1995, in retrospect, was a good move.

As the year 1997 closes, the *Washington Post* ran an editorial which endorsed the financial services deal as outstanding for all. It went on to a more basic point: in 1997 the United States had a "triple play" with the Information

Technology Agreement, the Telecommunications Services agreement, and the Financial Services agreement.

All three deals were in "high tech" areas where the United States was aggressive and competitive. All three agreements were sectoral and industry driven.

Does this mean that the future has no room for large traditional trade rounds? Perhaps, with three sectoral deals concluded in one year. The United States had little to "trade off" in all three deals. In financial services the threat of closing the U.S. market to foreigners were simply not credible. The U.S. argument that open financial markets were "good" for development of all countries was accepted. That philosophical war has been won.

The Uruguay Round Final Agreement calls for a new tr4ade in services across-the-board negotiation in the year 2000. No doubt the United States and others will push again for more market opening offers in financial services. If the countries that were more forthcoming in 1997 do well in their financial sectors, the U.S. bet is that the more recalcitrant countries will step up to the bar.

One year saw a complete change of momentum in the drive for more open financial markets. That change was due to the U.S. private sector being organized into a powerful lobbying machine, which, in turn, enlisted the EU private sector. They wrote a new textbook in constituent efforts, and they drove trade policy.

Sorry about the bet.

Comments on Conference Version of Papers

James A. Levinsohn

Recently, I was complaining to a colleague that I had not had time yet to read the papers I am discussing because some Departmental business arose unexpectedly. My colleague smiled and said this was fine because it meant my comments would not be prejudiced from having actually read anything. Well, it turns out, I really did read the papers. I am very glad that I did. They were each interesting and insightful.

In two cases, the autos and steel papers, the author's interest was beyond the merely academic and rather was professional. Mohatarem is chief economist of GM while Brooks is a VP of the LTV Corporation. I have come to realize that we academic economists can learn a tremendous amount from those in the industry, and their papers for this conference drives this point home. These gentlemen *really* know what they're talking about.

The storyline in the autos paper is that trade policy can have very unintended consequences. In the autos case, many of these are due to the direct foreign investment that arises as a response to protection. The idea is that if exporting to the United States means paying an import or export tariff, why not jump the tariff and just produce directly in the United States hence avoiding the tariff? One of the really neat ideas in Mohatarem's paper is that this process has the probably unintended effect of diminishing the impact of the protection. Indeed, over time, protection becomes less meaningful precisely because it was initially very meaningful—a new sort of built-in obsolesence. Many of the subtleties of this phenomenon have been explored in the academic literature by Jagdish Bhagwati, and the autos paper provides some very nice examples of these ideas.

The other related storyline is Mohatarem's observation that comparative advantage in today's world of foreign investment is company-specific. But, protection is typically country-specific. A message of the paper is that protection today just is not what it used to be. Given Mohatarem's observations and the tremendous international investment we see in the auto industry, I am left wondering whether protection in the auto industry is a thing of the past. Given Mohatarem's ingenuity and that of his counterparts at Ford and Chrysler, I suspect not. Although I am curious what is up their sleeves for the next cyclical downturn.

The message of the steel paper was hard to miss. In a polite, articulate, and persuasive manner, Brook basically says to the academic international economists, "Hey folks, wake up and smell the roses." Academic models and his real world day-to-day experiences just do not have a lot in common. This is an important message. I think Gene Grossman issued the appropriate "Mea Culpas" on behalf of our models in his comment on the Deardorff-Stern paper. Brook raises the appropriate tough questions and presents his case persuasively. In Dani Rodrik's defense, for his paper takes some pretty big hits, I think we need to remind ourselves that models are just that. They are by their very nature simplifications of a much more complex real world, and these simplifications are made to introduce rigor into the analysis. It is a tradeoff sometimes worth making.

I had a couple of questions after reading Brook's paper. The adverb "fairly" accompanies the verb "priced" with alarming frequency in the paper. In this regard, I sure wish I had a better grasp of what a fairly priced import really is. There is substantial discussion of "excess" foreign capacity. I sometimes wonder whether firms that use steel as an intermediate input as well as end-use consumers ought not, to use Paul Krugman's language, be writing a thank-you note to these foreign producers rather than trying to beat them up.

In the textiles and apparel paper, Scott nicely documents and explains why we should not lump apparel and textiles together when thinking about trade policy. He notes, for example, textile's qualified support for NAFTA, and apparel's firm opposition. He also suggests three reasons why apparel and textile's influence on trade policy has waned. These are declining democratic power in the South, the falling employment share in the industry, and the increasing influence of retailers. Each seems plausible enough to me, although the evidence offered is more along the lines of correlation rather than causation.

I found Scott's analysis of the impact of the NAFTA on the textile industry (not much of an impact) a little too simple. As he notes, a huge amount of big changes took place in Mexico after NAFTA, so it is hard really to discern what would have happened in NAFTA's absence. But that, it seems to me, is the appropriate thought experiment. It strikes me as a much more subtle question than the paper suggests.

Scott also raises the issue of labor rights abroad and how this is, in effect, a trade policy. I found his observations interesting and quite insightful. He notes that campaigns against sweatshop operators of firms like The Gap have the (probably intended) consequence of making protection more palatable. There are a lot of subtle issues here and, were this paper not so very brief, I think we all would have benefited from a more extensive discussion of these issues.[1] I think they are *especially* applicable to the textile/apparel industry.

NOTE

[1] Editors' note: see the discussion of human rights and labor standards in Chapter 12.

Comments on Conference Version of Papers

Gary R. Saxonhouse

The conference session in which I am involved contains six papers on "sectoral producing interests." The first three papers are about industries preoccupied with competition from imports while the second three papers that I am to comment on deal with industries whose main trade policy concerns are in overseas markets. Given this assignment, imagine my surprise on reading in the Deardorff-Stern paper (Chapter 2) that Dani Rodrik makes short shrift of this division by arguing that trade policies are universally biased against trade. Rodrik maintains that the same considerations that lead a government to protect an import-competing industry with a tariff should lead it to favor export industries with export subsidies, but in contrast to the widespread use of import protection, export promotion is rarely attempted. Judging from this morning's session, Rodrik's perspective is by no means unique. Baldwin (Chapter 3) also observes that "there does not appear to be any significant political constituencies lobbying for new export jobs, whereas there are well organized political groups who are very much concerned about the loss of domestic jobs due to increased imports resulting from reductions in tariffs and non-tariff barriers."

Rodrik and Baldwin seem to exclude the very trade policy activities by the aircraft, financial services and semiconductor industries that are so well documented in the papers by Waldmann and Culbert, Freeman, and Irwin. Each of these industries has for long periods of time captured the attention of the U.S. government trade-policy making apparatus. Waldmann and Culbert show how Boeing, in particular, was able to focus Cabinet-level interest on limiting foreign subsidies, protective tariffs and discriminatory government procurement policies on and off again for almost two decades. Freeman shows how American Express in seeking to gain non-discriminatory access to national telecommunications networks and payments, both of which were under the influence of its foreign competitors, built first an alliance with other financial services companies, and then a broader alliance with all companies with an interest in liberalizing trade in services of whatever kind, in an effort to change the U.S. government policy. Freeman argues that until this alliance had been organized and its influence applied to the policy-making process, the idea that the trade approach that had served to liberalize the international flow of goods in the post-war period could be applied to services was unknown.

In the last of this set of three industries studies and the only one not written by an industry insider, Irwin ably documents how the semiconductor industry's access to the Japanese market was significantly enhanced by the efforts of the U.S. government. In the 1986 negotiations with Japan, the bargaining position taken by the U.S. Trade Representative was precisely the position taken by the Semiconductor Industry Association. This trade group had effective veto over any agreement. In a testament to the semiconductor industry's political clout, Irwin concludes "few industries ever receive the sustained, high-level attention needed to bring about the negotiation of a government agreement on trade in just one sector."

In each of the three case studies noted, the U.S. government appears to be making strenuous efforts to gain foreign market access for the products of each of these industries. These efforts will bring rents to industry specific factors and will create new jobs. Can these findings be reconciled with the observations by Rodrik and Baldwin? Perhaps what is being observed in these industries is not export promotion at all. As the strategic trade literature makes clear, once oligopolistic competition is assumed in international markets, conventional distinctions between import protection and export promotion do break down. Perhaps the foreign market access activities undertaken on these industries' behalf by the U.S. government may have been more an effort to discourage further foreign entry into the U.S. market by denying foreign producers the sanctuary of protected home markets than a genuine effort to create new sales opportunities. As Irwin and others have shown elsewhere, it is theoretically possible that opening up export markets abroad with government help can lead to the creation of a global cartel with higher prices and smaller exports than might otherwise have been the case.

It is by no means clear that export promotion as import protection is the whole story or even the right story concerning U.S. policy for international trade in aircraft, financial services and semiconductors. Rodrik may see trade policy as anti-trade biased only because he does not fully allow for the Dixit-style coping mechanisms discussed by Deardorff-Stern in their paper. Deardorff-Stern are correct when they observe that "a subsidy to production is clearly a hand-out and the public understands that. Even when a subsidy is provided not by direct payment but by a tax break the public understands that as well." In contrast, if there is a subsidy element in the trade promotion activities the U.S. government undertakes on behalf of the aircraft, financial services and semiconductor industries, this might not be readily appreciated by even sophisticated observers. For example, the semiconductor agreements negotiated by the USTR with their market share targets very likely increased international trade even as they may have lowered overall production from what it otherwise would have been and implicitly subsidized the semiconductor industry by raising prices. This is an argument for graduate students in international trade and not for the evening radio or television business news, and from Dixit's perspective, a good example of a coping mechanism. In this fashion, when what are now the leading political economy models of international trade are interpreted from the transactions cost framework, they do give a rather better account of themselves than might be first imagined. Indeed, these three industry studies may confirm what these models suggest: export promotion is as common as import protection.

There are nonetheless still many relevant and important questions that remain unanswered. Quite apart from whether the successful experiences of these three export industries are at all typical of most other export industries, there is too little in these papers, particularly those by the two industry insiders, about how such industries achieve their influence in the U.S. trade policy making process. Irwin concludes that "the extent to which certain government agencies sought to accommodate the semiconductor industry's demands is . . . remarkable. . . . The Commerce Department and USTR proved incapable of any independent conception of what sorts of policies would best serve the interests of the economy overall." The lack of any firm understanding of how a situation such as this develops, is therefore a major stumbling block to the construction of really useful political economy models of international trade policy making.

Part IV

Other Constituent Interests

CHAPTER 11

Environmentalists and Trade Policymaking

Daniel C. Esty

I. Introduction

Until the 1990s, environmental groups played almost no role in trade policymaking. Their emergence on the trade scene has produced discomfort and even hostility. This reaction, while perhaps understandable, is misplaced. In the first part of this chapter, I discuss the objectives, activities, and effectiveness of environmental non-government organizations (NGOs[1]) in trade policymaking. In the second part, I move from a positivist analysis to a normative one, arguing that U.S. trade policymakers and the World Trade Organization (WTO) more generally should accept and even welcome environmental NGOs. More dramatically, I suggest that the future success of the international trading system depends in part on embracing non-government entities and developing formal roles for them. In particular, I conclude that an expanded trade policy role for environmental advocates would help to: (1) ensure that environmental externalities do not cause market failure in the international economic system and improve the quality of trade-related environmental decisionmaking by providing "competition" to governmental views; (2) provide the WTO with a better system of checks and balances reflecting the diversity of interests and views in the international policy domain; and (3) broaden the domestic coalition supporting liberalized trade, blunt environmentalist opposition to open markets, and enhance the WTO's legitimacy as part of the fabric of global governance.

II. Environmental NGOs and U.S. Trade Policymaking

Environmental NGOs have dramatically broadened their horizons in recent years (Bramble et al. 1992). The "sustainable development" paradigm developed by the Brundtland Commission in 1986 and advanced at the 1992 Rio Earth Summit has led many groups to focus on the interaction between economic forces and environmental results. In the late 1980s and early 1990s, a number of environmentalists targeted the role of the World Bank as an engine of environmental degradation—and possible environmental improvement (Rich 1994). The success of these efforts to build greater environmental sensitivity into the Bank's rules and procedures has driven the environmental community to look for other points of economic-environmental leverage and other institutions to "green." In this regard, environment-trade ties have taken on considerable prominence.

Two events—the North American Free Trade Agreement (NAFTA) and the 1991 GATT dispute settlement panel decision in the "tuna-dolphin" case[2]—brought the trade-environment linkage into sharp focus. The prospect of expanded U.S.-Mexico trade raised a number of environmental concerns including: (1) increased pollution spillovers along the U.S.-Mexico border; (2) downward "harmonization" of U.S. environmental standards to match less strict Mexican rules; (3) loss of U.S. regulatory "sovereignty" through NAFTA market access commitments; (4) competitiveness-driven pressure to relax U.S. environmental laws created by industries facing new competition from low-standard, low-cost Mexican facilities; and (5) the closed nature of the trade negotiations.

The tuna-dolphin case—in which a GATT dispute panel concluded that the U.S. ban on Mexican tuna imports, imposed because the fish were caught using nets that resulted in a large number of incidental dolphin deaths, violated GATT principles—seemed to suggest that when environment and trade goals clashed, the trade objectives would trump. This case, moreover, raised the specter of distant international trade bureaucrats overriding U.S. environmental laws. The results touched off a furor in the U.S. environmental community, offered many environmental advocates a not-very-reassuring first glimpse of the rules and procedures of the international trading system, and led to protests in the streets of Washington against GATTzilla.

"Trade and environment" issues now seem to lurk around every corner. Recent disputes include: the Venezuelan challenge to the reformulated gasoline requirements of the U.S. Clean Air Act; sanctions imposed on Taiwan for failing to control illicit trade in tiger bones and rhino horns; competitiveness questions arising from the prospect of tougher controls on greenhouse gas emissions; and U.S.–EU battles over beef hormones, pesticides in wine, and the U.S. Corporate Average Fuel Economy mileage requirements for cars. This diversity of issues is matched by an almost equally diverse set of environmental perspectives on trade. It is therefore impossible to distill any pure essence representing *the* environmentalist interest in trade policy.

Although no single or simple environmental perspective on trade exists, the handling of environmental issues in the course of the NAFTA debate offers a useful case study of environmental group activity in the trade domain. The NAFTA negotiations highlight a number of environmentalist objectives, provide a window into the internal debates and decision processes of the U.S. environmental community, and offer a basis for judging the effectiveness of environmental interests in shaping trade policymaking.

The environmental community in the United States (and to a lesser extent in Canada and Mexico) carefully tracked the progress of the NAFTA negotiations and debate at every stage.[3] But from the outset, there was no agreement among the various environmental NGOs about the stance that should be taken toward freer trade in general or NAFTA in particular. Some environmental advocates, particularly those that adhere to a "limits-to-growth" or "small is beautiful" paradigm, fought the proposal at every turn (Esty 1994c). These groups, such as Friends of the Earth, Public Citizen, and the Sierra Club, see trade leading to expanded industrial activity and thus resulting in more pollution and the unsustainable consumption of resources. Other activists, particularly those that believe in sustainable development, such as the Environmental Defense Fund and the National Wildlife Federation, view trade as potentially beneficial insofar as economic growth generates resources, some portion of which might be devoted to environmental protection. These groups ultimately supported the agreement in return for access to the negotiations and commitments to environmental provisions both in NAFTA and in an Environmental Side Agreement (NAAEC 1993, Audley 1997).

The varying objectives of the different parts of the environmental community led to a range of tactical responses to the NAFTA. The limits-to-growth crowd cast their lot with other die-hard opponents of the free trade agreement. They issued reports suggesting that dire public health and ecological consequences would result from freer U.S.–Mexico–Canada trade. They launched grassroots letter writing campaigns against the agreement. Some of the groups even sued the U.S. government for failing to prepare an Environmental Impact Statement (EIS) on the NAFTA, knowing full well that an EIS would delay the negotiations for years.[4]

The "pro-NAFTA" groups used their position to shape both the negotiation process and the substantive outcome. Their pressure—and willingness to work with the U.S. Trade Representative (USTR)—helped to ensure that environmental issues were a central NAFTA focus from the start to the finish. Both the Bush and Clinton Administrations took the environmental NGOs' NAFTA interest seriously (Esty 1994c). USTR officials met with environmental group leaders on a regular basis. Environmentalists were placed on the key USTR Public Advisory Committees. EPA officials were called before the Congress to testify alongside USTR on progress in meeting environmental goals within NAFTA and in environmental cooperation in parallel with the trade agreement. Congressional committees invited environmental group leaders to testify on the integration of environmental concerns into NAFTA. USTR, with the help of the EPA, produced a NAFTA Environmental Review, which offered a variety of thoughtful recommendations to the negotiators about how various public health and ecological concerns raised by the prospect of freer trade might be handled.

Special environmental provisions were written into NAFTA to ensure that the Parties to the Agreement would not lower their environmental standards or relax their enforcement of environmental rules to attract investors (NAFTA

Article 1114). Out of respect for the U.S. environmentalists' concern about downward harmonization of standards, no attempt was made to set common rules that would apply across the three NAFTA countries.[5] Other provisions made it clear that NAFTA would not override obligations established by major multilateral environmental agreements, notably the Montreal Protocol on ozone layer depletion, the Basel Convention on Waste Exports, and the CITES agreement on trafficking in endangered species.

The Environmental Side Agreement (NAAEC 1993) reinforces the NAFTA environmental commitment. It places (Articles 35-6) additional emphasis on the enforcement by each country of its own national environmental laws and establishes a provision by which any "persistent pattern of failure to effectively enforce" environmental regulations can be raised as an unfair trade practice.[6] It also sets up (Article 8.2) the trilateral North American Commission on Environmental Cooperation (CEC). The CEC's task is to institutionalize NAFTA-related trade-environment linkages. Specifically, it is called upon to: (1) facilitate cooperation between countries on environmental issues; (2) serve as a forum for regular ministerial-level meetings; (3) provide an independent secretariat to report regularly on significant public health or ecological issues confronting the NAFTA parties; (4) ensure that enforcement of environmental rules remains a priority in all three countries and produce an annual report on enforcement activities; (5) coordinate with trade officials in the United States, Canada, and Mexico on any issue requiring joint trade-environment attention; and (6) assure ample opportunities for public participation in the development and implementation of environmental laws and programs in the three NAFTA countries.

These results reveal some of the key trade policy goals of U.S. environmental activists. First, and perhaps foremost, they want open governmental processes, including access to information during actual negotiations. Second, they fear that economic forces, if not channeled appropriately, will run roughshod over environmental protection efforts. Thus, they want safeguards both within and alongside trade agreements to promote environmentally-sound economic development. It is worth nothing that the tools advanced by the environmental community in support of sustainable development tend to be crude (e.g., mandates and prohibitions), and there remains both ignorance of and skepticism about the potential for using market forces to achieve optimal controls on pollution. This analytic unsophistication is unfortunate because cost internalization represents the best hope for making trade liberalization and environmental protection mutually reinforcing.

The NAFTA outcome also demonstrates the considerable success of the pro-NAFTA environmental groups. They succeeded in putting environmental issues on the NAFTA agenda and holding them there. They opened up the negotiating process and became a major constituent group in trade policymaking. Deftly using their position as a "swing" constituency with influence over a key set of free-trade-oriented, environmentally-conscious Senators and Congressmen, the pro-NAFTA environmental advocates exercised considerable influence over the agreement itself and the institutional structure that will implement it. They got, in the words of former EPA Administrator William Reilly, the "greenest trade treaty ever" (*Business America*, October 19, 1992). To the extent that more could have been done—e.g., to promote harmonized pollution cost internalization efforts—the limited progress undoubtedly reflects the lack of focus on these issues by the environmental NGOs.

Given that many environmental groups opposed the NAFTA altogether, one could, of course, equally conclude that the environmental constituency failed to achieve its trade policy objectives. Indeed, the behavior of the environmental community is hard to fit into traditional models of the political economy of trade policy. From the positivist perspective, environmental NGOs pushed both for and against the NAFTA. Those that worked with the Bush and Clinton Administrations seem to have "won," and they achieved a good bit as noted above. The more difficult and perhaps more interesting issue is the normative question: Did environmentalist participation improve the NAFTA? Or, more broadly, what role *should* environmental groups play in trade policy development?

III. The Normative Question

Whether and how environmentalists should be allowed to participate in the work of the U.S. and international bodies that manage trade relations remains a matter of some contention. Although my discussion here focuses on the role of NGOs within U.S. policy apparatus and the WTO, the arguments apply with equal force in other trade contexts such as the European Union and APEC. They may also apply in the broader debate over the access of non-state actors to international organizations generally.

The Case Against NGOs

The case *against* a formal role for NGOs in the trade regime has several dimensions. First, environmental groups may act as "special interests." Whenever lobbying of a decisionmaking body is permitted, there exists a risk that certain interests will exert disproportionate influence. The potential for policy distortion has been studied exhaustively in general (Downs 1957, Olson 1965, Lowi 1969, Mayhew 1974, Buchanan and Tullock 1971) and in the trade context (Findlay and Wellisz 1982, Magee, Brock and Young 1989, Hillman 1989, Grossman and Helpman 1994, and Helpman 1995). According to some critics, the presence of NGOs within the walls of the Winder Building (USTR) on 17th Street in Washington or the WTO headquarters on Lake Geneva would lead to policy distortions and reduced social welfare.

A more refined version of the special-interest-domination fear focuses in particular on the vulnerability of the WTO to lobbying and the need to provide a forum where governments can go to "safely" (without public scrutiny or NGO oversight) cut deals that "sacrifice" inefficient industries that are hiding behind tariff barriers or other protectionist walls in favor of liberalized trade. Many trade officials note that opening markets is hard enough given the public choice problems inherent in trade policymaking (Nichols 1996, p. 319; Petersmann 1992). They fear that any role for environmental NGOs will heighten the lobbying investment of the contending parties and multiply the odds against achieving freer trade.

WTO staffers take especially seriously their role as defenders of the faith with regard to trade liberalization. They seek to fend off protectionists of every stripe no matter how loud the calls for "managed" trade or other actions to soften the pressures of the marketplace. They see vivid lessons in the experience of the 1930s when protectionist trade policies triggered retaliation around the world, resulting in economic chaos, the Great Depression, and World War II. The WTO Secretariat and many of the national representatives to the WTO view themselves as guardians of a critical yet fragile international commitment to collective action in support of open markets. Relaxing their vigilance in opposition to all interest group manipulation of the trading system they see as an invitation to disaster. The fact that some environmental groups are anti-free trade and others are in league with protectionists as a matter of political tactics gives some credence to these worries.

Fears of *undue* environmental group influence are, however, exaggerated in both the U.S. and WTO settings. Lobbyists by the dozen visit USTR every day, and special interests already inhabit the WTO as well. Adding a variety of environmental perspectives to USTR and the WTO internal debates would help to counteract the influence of (often protectionist) business interests and therefore reduce, not increase, the risk of special-interest-driven policies. Providing a more diverse set of interests with access to the trade policy process would furthermore allow the groups to monitor each other, exert countervailing pressures, and generally diminish the prospect of "capture" by any single interest group.

In addition, while some environmental groups are in bed with protectionists, many are not. Assuming, as free trade advocates tend to, that environmental NGOs will diminish free trade if they are given a greater trade policy role both misreads and overgeneralizes environmentalists' trade interest. The negative presumption about environmental NGOs overstates furthermore their zone of activity and influence, which is likely to be limited to the environmental links to trade rather than trade policy broadly.

A second major argument against an expanded NGO role at the international level derives from the belief that the WTO should be an inter*governmental* body. The trade policy process, according to this view, works best when governments can speak clearly to each other without a cacophony of other voices confusing the dialogue. As Nichols (1996, p. 317) suggests, "the spectacle of domestic constituencies opposing the positions of the governments that are supposed to represent those constituencies" can be distracting. Another strand of this argument recoils at NGOs getting two bites at the apple—one in the national debate over what position their government should take to the WTO and a second one at the WTO itself.

There are two rebuttals to these claims. First, giving NGOs a voice at the WTO, and, more importantly, the opportunity to observe WTO debates and dispute settlement proceedings does not preclude governments from discussing some issues behind closed doors. Just as the U.S. government conducts some of its business in public and some in private, the international trade regime could develop a procedure for both open- and closed-door meetings. Second, we live in a multi-dimensional civil society in which some interest groups are transnational in scope and their *raison d'etre* is to influence policy internationally. The Worldwide Fund for Nature, for example, derives its strength in no small part from its capacity to unite voices across many nations into a unified chorus. Furthermore, some political arguments are better carried out at the global level. International institutions which reflect the complex structure of modern life and provide for appropriate policy discussion and debate are likely to be more democratic and durable. The need for international-scale dialogue is made more pressing by the fact that not all countries provide adequate opportunities for interests to be heard in their domestic political processes.

A third set of concerns about the role environmental groups might play in the trade policy process and in the WTO in particular relates to the *representativeness* of NGOs. It may be difficult, so the argument goes, to ascertain how many people a particular group represents, and thus how much weight to give to its views. In addition, NGOs with ostensibly similar constituencies may cloud the policy process by presenting conflicting views. While the risk of confusion is real, it need not be crippling. Indeed, any issue worth debating will involve multiple viewpoints. At the national level, lobbying from many directions simultaneously occurs on almost all issues and is unremarkable in most policy contexts. And just as national officials learn over time which groups represent important perspectives, so too would the officials at the WTO. At the international level, the credibility and weight given to NGO positions would vary, as it does at the national level, with the political mobilization potential of the group and the quality of its past contributions to public debates. Some groups develop reputations for thoughtfulness and good analytic work while others are known for their misinformed and ill-considered positions.[7] While the accountability of non-government organizations is an important issue (Tarlock 1994), the need to preserve the value of one's reputation serves as a powerful mechanism of self-discipline on NGOs.

A fourth series of objections to an expanded NGO role in the trade regime centers on inequities that might be created or exacerbated by the particular mix of entities likely to take up the invitation to participate. Indeed, some environmental groups seem not to realize that if the policy development process is to be opened to them, business representatives must be accorded similar access. When faced with this prospect, many environmentalists become concerned that their voices will be drowned out by better-financed producer interests.

At the WTO, the risk of asymmetries of interest and action takes on an added dimension. Notably, Northern interests, whether environmental groups or business associations, may well have more resources to devote to WTO lobbying than Southern interests. Many developing countries object to a greater NGO role at the WTO for just this reason. They see the trade regime as already biased in favor of the North and fear even greater skewing of results if environmental groups, with overwhelmingly Northern perspectives, are allowed to shape WTO policies and decisions. Some countries also fear (although they do not admit it publicly) that NGOs at the WTO would be less polite than diplomats and will draw attention to environmental policy shortcomings, human rights violations, and other governmental failures.

The equity concerns can be addressed. At the national level, there is little risk that environmental interests will overpower business groups. If anything, the presence of NGOs within the USTR process will produce a better distribution of viewpoints and access. There are, moreover, numerous safeguards in place (such as disclosure and reporting rules and limitations on gifts to government employees) to ensure that any lobbying is done above board and that the influence exerted is not undue.

Internationally, much of the NGO participation in the trading system is likely to be "passive." Groups will observe what happens at the WTO and report back to their members. Where lobbying does occur, clear rules should be established to govern efforts to influence policy by environmental groups as well as business entities. Although WTO employees are bound by the conflict of interest provisions of the UN staff rules and Article 6 of the WTO Agreement, which provides general instructions about the international responsibilities of the WTO Secretariat, more strict limits should be placed on meals, gifts, and trips that the WTO staff can accept from those with interests in WTO decisions. Lobbying efforts should be made subject to disclosure requirements with WTO staff (and perhaps national representatives as well) required to file reports on who lobbied them on what issues.[8]

Concerns about North-South imbalances could be addressed in a variety of ways. Funds, from either the WTO or member governments, might be made available to support the participation of developing country NGOs. Moreover, the risk of Northern dominance is overstated. Environmental groups exist all over the world, and with modern communications, even the smallest and most distant groups can now be heard. Furthermore, the fact that the number of Southern NGOs is small is not in and of itself troubling. The views of those that do participate are likely to be given considerable weight because they will be seen as speaking for significant interests. The many competing voices from the North, moreover, will often present contradictory viewpoints and cancel each other out. In short, the idea of a monolithic environmental North confronting an underfunded South does not comport with reality.

The fear that governmental shortcomings will be exposed offers no substantive argument against NGOs whatsoever. Policy failures should be put under a spotlight whenever and wherever they occur. Nevertheless, the fear-of-exposure objection presents a very real political obstacle to enhanced NGO participation in the WTO.

A final set of criticisms leveled at expanded NGO participation in trade debates concerns the practical difficulties of credentialing NGOs and controlling their activities. At the national level, USTR has overcome this hurdle. Beginning with the early 1990s NAFTA debate, USTR opened its policy process to NGO participation. USTR has an environmental office with its own Assistant U.S. Trade Representative assigned to ensure that the lines of communication with the environmental community stay open. Special briefings focused on environmental issues are now held as a matter of course. EPA officials are included on USTR negotiating teams. A Trade and Environment Public Advisory Committee has been established. USTR releases most documents it generates or receives for public review and comment.

While not trivial, the administrative burden at the WTO should be similarly manageable. Despite the undeniable allure of the WTO, it seems unlikely that all that many NGOs would really be interested in its ongoing work. International environmental bodies and negotiations have included NGOs for some time and can therefore serve as models for NGO involvement. The Earth Summit, for example, successfully involved thousands of environmental advocates (Gardner 1993). In addition to the Earth Summit, there are many models to build upon in establishing workable modalities for NGOs in the WTO (Charnovitz 1996). The NAFTA Commission on Environmental Cooperation, the OECD's Business and Industry Advisory Committee,[9] and the U.S. Supreme Court all have established mechanisms for government-NGO information exchange.

The Case for NGOs

The growing literature on NGOs identifies a variety of roles that nongovernment entities play on the national and international stages. Depending on the circumstances, they may act as: (1) service providers, often as government subcontractors (Bebbington and Farrington 1993); (2) watchdogs or private enforcement agents (Wapner 1995; Cameron and Ramsey 1995; Sands 1995); (3) lobbyists (Zadek and Gatward 1996; Cameron and Ramsey 1995); (4) stakeholders (Shell 1995) or countervailing interests (Eikeland 1994); (5) agents of civil society enriching the public dialogue and representing interests not reflected in government viewpoints (Spiro 1995; Susskind 1994); (6) policy analysts or expert advisers to governments (Charnovitz 1996; Susskind 1994; Cameron and Ramsey 1995); (7) mobilizers of public opinion (Lindborg 1992; Clark 1995); (8) bridges between state and non-state actors connecting local and global politics (Princen and Finger 1994; Weiss and Gordenker 1996); (9) change agents offering new viewpoints (Susskind 1994; Nerfin 1986); and (10) consultants to industry (Eikeland 1994).

My purpose here is not, however, to catalogue *what* NGOs could do but rather to explore *why* they might be given an expanded role in trade policy development. There are three strands to this analysis, which might be called the economic, political theory, and political economy arguments for opening the trade regime more formally to environmental NGOs.

The Case from Economics

The economic case for an expanded NGO role derives from the risk that, absent a mechanism for internalizing environmental externalities, transboundary pollution spillovers will cause market failures that could undermine international economic efficiency and diminish the welfare gains from an open world trading system (Bhagwati and Srinivasan 1996, p. 167; Baumol and Oates 1988). The potential economic harm from pollution externalities is well established in theory. What seems to be disputed, or is the source of confusion, is the scope of transboundary environmental externalities in practice. Recent advances in environmental analysis have resulted in the discovery of a number of previously unrecognized large-scale pollution effects. These include, most notably, depletion of the ozone layer by chlorofluorocarbons (Kerr 1994) and possible climate change due to the accumulation of greenhouse gases in the atmosphere (IPCC 1995). Recent scientific work has also broadened the acknowledged geographic scale of a number of previously identified environmental problems. For example, scientists believe that the discovery of DDT, long banned in Canada and the United States, in the Great Lakes demonstrates that high level winds can transport airborne chemicals thousands of miles, in this case from Mexico (Rappaport 1985). Other recent studies have revealed significant transboundary spillovers of acid rain, heavy metals, and bioaccumulative toxics (Fitzgerald 1993; *New Scientist* March 16, 1996).

In addition to the potential for market failure from transboundary externalities, the "tragedy of the commons" poses additional risks to the international economic system. Absent a mechanism for achieving "collective action," individual nations and their industries have no incentive to manage common resources in a sustainable fashion (Cooper 1994). The rapid depletion of the world's fisheries provides an example of what can happen without policy coordination.

One need not expand the list of potential market failures to the more controversial claims about "economic" externalities and the risk of a regulatory race to the bottom (Esty 1996b; Revesz 1992), psychological externalities (Anderson 1992) and intergenerational equity (Brown Weiss 1989) to be convinced of the need for environmental policy coordination on a global scale. Of course, the first best policy alternative would be a stronger international environmental regime (Esty 1994a). Authoritative environmental analysis and decisionmaking by a Global Environmental Organization (GEO) could be incorporated by reference into the decisions of the WTO. But there is little prospect of a GEO being created in the near future. Thus the trading regime must manage the risk of trade-related environment market failures. Not to do so invites allocative inefficiency and reduced social welfare, not to mention environmental degradation.

One can, of course, accept the need for an environmental dimension to the international trading system without believing that environmental NGOs should have an expanded presence at USTR and the WTO. If one's focus is on NGOs that have narrow special interests—animal welfare groups, for instance—it is not difficult to conclude that on balance a greater role for environmental advocates would not result in better trade policymaking. Indeed, Earth Island Institute and the other groups that pushed for the now infamous ban on Mexican tuna imports view trade simply as a point of leverage. They single-mindedly pursue their environmental goals and do not care at all about any welfare loss inflicted by diminished trade.

But there are many other broader-minded groups whose participation in the policy process is likely to be constructive. Moreover, because environmental policymaking is fraught with uncertainty, it is extremely valuable to have a diversity of perspectives challenging the prevailing science, risk analysis, and policy conclusions. Multiple viewpoints allow triangulation on the "truth" and facilitate better valuation of environmental harms. Some analysts argue that it is the responsibility of governments to advance such competing policy perspectives. In fact, "regulatory competition" theory suggests that a world of decentralized governments competing in the policy domain will yield optimal results (Revesz 1992). But while policy competition should be encouraged, one cannot assume that the best "competitors" in the environmental policy "market" will be governments (Esty 1996b).

The American legal literature is, of course, rich in references to the benefits of states as "laboratories." But because so much of the difficulty in environmental policymaking derives from weak technical and scientific underpinnings and faulty causal assumptions, what is most needed for good policy is better analysis. This requires laboratory resources, carefully gathered data, skilled personnel, and a serious commitment to analytic rigor. Few U.S. state governments meet these requirements. Internationally, even fewer countries do serious environmental policy work, particularly across the full spectrum of public health and ecological issues. Relying on competing government analyses to sharpen the analytic content of USTR or WTO decisions at the intersection of trade and environmental policy thus makes no sense. NGOs are far better positioned to advance the debate and ensure that optimal (cost-internalizing), welfare-maximizing environmental policies are put in place.

Ultimately, trade policymaking without NGO perspectives resembles a monopolized market. With high barriers to entry, potential producers who might be able to offer goods (in this case, policy analysis and ideas) at a lower price or better quality are kept out of the market to the detriment of consumers and the efficiency of the system. Yet the internal coherence and success of the international trading system depends on finding optimal ways to address environmentally-derived threats of market failure. If for no other reason, trade policy debates should be opened to NGOs to ensure the presence of a wider range of intellectual competitors and constant reassessment of established thinking.

The Argument from Political Theory

The functions of government in modern life are evolving quickly. The public is being given a larger role in policymaking and a wider array of constituent interests are contributing to decision processes. Similarly, the view that states are or should be only actors on the international stage is changing. Within the United States, the belief that trade policymaking reflects "foreign affairs" and is thus uniquely the province of government has been largely abandoned. As Sylvia Ostry (1990) suggests: "No policy is as domestic as international trade policy." A wide range of constituent groups participate in U.S. trade policy development. Environmentalist contributions to the domestic trade policy process are recognized as valid, and even useful in ensuring that policy perspectives that might otherwise go unheard are folded in to the decision process.

At the WTO, change has come more slowly. Although the "liberal" critique of traditional "realist" international relations theory emphasizes that an important array of non-state actors exists (Hurrell and Kingsbury 1992) and that the actions of states are not solely determined by the individual wills of governments (Gordenker and Weiss 1996), many trade analysts see the international trading system as a government preserve. But as Shell (1996, p. 380) suggests, the "quiet days of trade adjudication and policymaking are gone." Trade liberalization through closed-door negotiations among diplomatic elites seems untenable as a means of achieving further policy progress. The result, Shell observes, will be a new "noisier" process of trade negotiation (p. 380).

The presence of NGOs in the trade policy process mirrors the emergence of an expanded global civil society. The presence of new, non-governmental voices promises to complicate negotiations, but it may also help to produce more sound and durable results. NGOs can help to mediate disputes between governments, provide new outlets for debate and policy development, and improve the representativeness of decision mechanisms by acting as a conduit for information flowing between everyday citizens and actors at the global level.

States are, furthermore, imperfect representatives of public opinion. When governments speak with one voice they inevitably neglect minority viewpoints within their jurisdiction. NGOs can ensure that views not reflected by national government can be heard in the course of the international policy development process. To the extent, furthermore, that individuals share a common policy vision across national boundaries, they can form global NGOs that might be more effective in bringing about change through international action than they would be in pursuing their objectives at the nation-state level. The transboundary nature of many ecological, public health, and animal welfare concerns makes this transnational representation especially valuable. Indeed, protection of the Brazilian rainforest, Pacific coral reefs, the ozone layer, and African elephants are seen by many to be issues for the global community and best addressed at a worldwide scale.

If the WTO were to allow broader public participation in its processes, it would be a better-informed, stronger, and more democratic organization. By creating a broader and richer "WTO politics," NGO participation in the international trading system would make the WTO more representative and better able to perform its responsibilities in the emerging system of global governance.

The Political Economy Argument

American environmentalists care a great deal about fair and open decision processes (Audley 1997). Being included in policy discussions matters to them. The efforts of both the Bush and Clinton Administrations to give NGOs a role in the NAFTA debate was an important reason that many influential environmental groups ultimately lined up in favor of freer Mexico-U.S.-Canada trade.

Similarly, an NGO-enriched WTO would be considered more democratic and legitimate. Participation in and understanding of the trade regime's decisionmaking is critical to the acceptance by environmental groups of the trading system's processes as fair and worthy of respect and, more importantly, to their support for further trade liberalization. Although the WTO has taken some steps toward procedural reform and greater "transparency," more remains to be done.[10] While the panel decisions of the WTO (and the GATT before it) have been subject to virulent attack, the U.S. Supreme Court, which has invalidated a much larger number of state environmental laws deemed inconsistent with the Commerce Clause, has never been similarly attacked for its "trade and environment" decisions. Clearly, the Supreme Court has much more institutional legitimacy than the WTO.

Respect for the Supreme Court's decisionmaking derives, in part, from the fact that arguments are heard in open court, briefs are made public, and decisions are published as soon as they are rendered. Any party that wishes to provide input to a case before the Court may do so in an *amicus curae* brief. The Supreme Court's environmental decisions are viewed as authoritative in part because the Court elicits technical information when cases require it. Submissions from NGOs are often part of the data pool on which the Court draws. Special "masters," including environmental experts, are brought in when particularly important technical questions underlie a decision.

Although new WTO provisions allow dispute panels to seek technical or scientific advice when environmental issues are at stake, no panel has availed itself of this opportunity. And the WTO has no provision for soliciting expert opinions from interested non-governmental bodies. A greater NGO role at the WTO would enrich the institution's deliberations, enhance the legitimacy of its dispute settlement process, and strengthen the institution as a whole.[11]

For WTO decisions to have legitimacy, they must be reached fairly and openly, be based on complete information, and consider the full array of interests at stake. NGOs can help to fulfill these requirements, and thus help to preserve the integrity of the international trading system. Rather than treating environmental groups as unwelcome special interests, the WTO should therefore open its doors and invite NGOs to contribute to the maintenance of the international economic system. Opening up the WTO's "formal" sessions to NGO observers would help to illuminate the decisionmaking process that undergirds the international trading system. Such transparency would help build public understanding of how the WTO operates. Further outreach might be undertaken through open meetings, to which any interested NGO would be invited, on all issues under debate within the WTO. In addition, the WTO should establish a formal advisory committee on environmental matters that would include representatives from business, labor, consumer, and environmental organizations (Esty 1996a).

Not only would broader NGO participation in the WTO improve the quality of its decisions and the legitimacy of its judgments, it would also expand support for trade liberalization more generally. If environmentalists felt that the WTO took their concerns seriously, there would be much less opposition to expanded free trade. In light of the role environmentalists play in the United States as a swing constituency in hard fought trade battles, ensuring that environmentalists do not systematically oppose efforts to promote freer trade should be a top priority for trade officials within the U.S. government and at the WTO.

IV. Conclusion

Trade and environmental policy are inescapably interwoven. This fact has been largely recognized in the U.S. domestic trade policymaking process. Elaborate structures have been developed to ensure that environmental voices are heard at USTR. But many participants in the trade policy process at the international level do not see or appreciate the environmental linkage. In the absence of a functioning global environmental regime, the WTO cannot avoid making decisions that have environmental policy implications. The question is how well these decisions will be made. The inclusion of environmental NGOs in WTO activities could help to achieve a proper integration of environmental considerations into the international trading system. The presence of NGOs would bring new information to bear and provide competition in the marketplace of ideas that is otherwise monopolized by a too-narrow set of government perspectives. Drawing NGOs into the international trading system would also strengthen the WTO as an institution and ensure that it reflects the growing diversity of international civil society. By embracing NGOs and providing opportunities for their observation of and participation in international trade policy development and dispute resolution processes, the WTO would enhance its own credibility, authoritativeness, and legitimacy—and broaden the constituency that supports trade liberalization.

NOTES

[1] This paper considers environmental NGOs to be any organization independent of government that works on public health, ecological or animal welfare issues. This domain includes: single issue organizations, such as Rhino Rescue, multiple issue organizations, such as World Wildlife Fund; and business entities such as the International Chamber of Commerce. The focus will, however, be on environmental groups since this subset of the NGO world is a new presence in trade debates; business groups have long played a role in trade policymaking (Charnovitz 1995).

[2] For more details on the origins of the trade-environment issue, the NAFTA environmental issues, and the tuna-dolphin case, see Esty (1994a).

[3] Esty (1994a, pp. 27-28) discusses the emergence of environmental NGOs on the trade scene. Note that the U.S.-Canada Free Trade Agreement was negotiated in the mid-1980s with little interest from either country's environmental community.

[4] The Circuit Court for the District of Columbia rejected the suggestion that the National Environmental Policy Act required an EIS for NAFTA in *Public Citizen v. U.S. Trade Representative* 5 F. 3d 549 (D.C. Cir. 1993). The Court concluded that submitting a trade agreement to the Congress is an act of the President and not subject to the EIS requirements of the National Environmental Policy Act.

[5] It is interesting to note that the environmental focus in the context of the European Union is on harmonization. Thus, it could be argued that the preoccupation of U.S. environmental groups with not having U.S. rules "watered down" resulted in a lost opportunity to improve standards across North America.

[6] Although the agreement permits "monetary enforcement assessments" (Articles 35-6), the range of intervening steps that must be followed before such penalties can be imposed makes it very unlikely that any "eco-duties" will ever be imposed (Esty 1994c).

[7] In fact, the quality of the information, arguments, and analysis that are presented will be the dominant determinant of NGO influence at the WTO where international bureaucrats are likely to be relatively immune to the importuning of lobbyists advancing self-interested positions no matter how significant the economic interests they represent.

[8] Currently, only panelists in GATT disputes are required to file disclosure forms.

[9] Expansion of the OECD process to include environmental groups is under review. In fact, the Declaration from the 1996 OECD Ministerial Meeting "warmly welcomed the proposal of international environmental non-governmental organizations for the establishment of an NGO environmental advisory committee to the OECD" and invited interested NGOs to submit a formal proposal for such a body.

[10] The WTO now publishes a variety of newsletters, has a home page on the Internet (www.unicc.org/wto), and has released summaries of the meetings of its Committee on Trade and Environment. In July 1996, the organization adopted new guidelines for the release of "restricted" materials. While these provisions are likely to mean faster public

access to some WTO materials, it is not clear whether they will actually make the work of the WTO truly transparent.

[11] Under the new WTO dispute procedures, in which the decision of a panel will automatically be adopted unless a negative consensus forms, the transparency and openness of the dispute settlement process will be even more important.

REFERENCES

Abbott, Fred M. 1992. "Trade and Democratic Values." *Minnesota Journal of Global Trade* 1: 9-34.

Anderson, Kym. 1992. "The Standard Welfare Economics of Policies Affecting Trade and the Environment" in Kym Anderson and Richard Blackhurst (eds.), *The Greening of World Trade Issues.* Ann Arbor: University of Michigan.

Audley, John. 1996. *Environmental Interests in Trade Policy: Institutional Reform and the North American Free Trade Agreement*, forthcoming.

Bhagwati, Jagdish and Srinivasan, T.N. 1996. "Trade and the Environment: Does Environmental Diversity Detract from the Case for Free Trade?" in Jagdish Bhagwati and Robert Hudec, (eds.), *Fair Trade and Harmonization: Prerequisites to Free Trade.* Cambridge, MA: MIT Press.

Baumol, William and Oates, Wallace. 1988. *The Theory of Environmental Policy* (2d ed.). New York: Cambridge University Press.

Bebbington, Anthony and Farrington, John. 1993. "Governments, NGOs and Agricultural Development: Perspectives on Changing Inter-Organizational Relationships" *Journal of Dev. Stud.* 29: 199.

Bodansky, Daniel. 1991. "Scientific Uncertainty and the Precautionary Principle," *Environment* (September) at 33.

Bramble, Barbara J. and Porter, Gareth. 1992. "Non-Governmental Organizations and the Making of U.S. International Environmental Policy" in Andrew Hurrell and Benedict Kingsbury (eds.), *The International Politics of the Environment.* New York: Oxford University Press.

Buchanan, James and Tullock, Gordon. 1971. *The Calculus of Consent.* Ann Arbor, MI: University of Michigan Press.

Cameron, James and Ramsay, Ross. 1995. *Participation by Non-Governmental Organizations in the World Trade Organization.* Global Environment and Trade Study No. 1.

Charnovitz, Steve. 1996. "Participation of Nongovernmental Organizations in the World Trade Organization." 17 *U. Pennsylvania Journal of International Economics L.* 331.

Charnovitz, Steve and Wickham, John. 1995. "Non-Governmental Organizations and the Original International Trade Regime." *Journal of World Trade* 29: 111.

Clark, A.M. 1995. "Non-Governmental Organizations and their Influence on International Society." *Journal. of International Affairs* 48: 504.

Clark, John. 1995. "The State, Popular Participation, and the Voluntary Sector." *World Development* 23: 593.

Conca, Ken. 1996. "Greening the UN: Environmental Organizations and the UN System" in Thomas Weiss and Leon Gordenker (eds.), *NGOs, the UN and Global Governance*, pp. 103-120. Boulder, CO: Lynne Rienner.

Cooper, Richard N. 1994. *Environment and Resource Policies for the World Economy.* Washington, DC: Brookings.

Downs, Anthony. 1957. *An Economic Theory of Democracy.* New York: Harper and Row.

Eikeland, Per Ove. 1994. "US Environmental NGOs: New Strategies for New Environmental Problems?" *Journal of Social, Political & Economic Studies* 19: 259.

Esty, Daniel C. 1996a. "Greening World Trade," in Jeffrey J. Schott, ed., *The World Trading System: Challenges Ahead.* Washington, DC: Institute for International Economics.

Esty, Daniel C. 1996b. "Revitalizing Environmental Federalism," *Univ. of Michigan Law Review* 94.

Esty, Daniel C. 1994a. *Greening the GATT: Trade, Environment, and the Future.* Washington, DC: Institute for International Economics.

Esty, Daniel C. 1994b. "The Case for a Global Environmental Organization," in Peter B. Kenen, (ed.), *Managing the World Economy.* Washington, DC: Institute for International Economics.

Esty, Daniel C. 1994c. "Making Trade and Environmental Policies Work Together: Lessons from NAFTA," *Aussenwirtschaft* (April).

Falk, Richard. 1994. "The Making of Global Citizenship." In B.V. Steenbergen (ed.), *The Condition of Citizenship*, pp. 127-140. Thousand Oaks, CA: Sage.

Findlay, R. and S. Wellisz. 1982. "Endogenous Tariffs, the Political Economy of Trade Restrictions, and Welfare," in Jagdish Bhagwati (ed.), *Import Competition and Response.* Chicago: University of Chicago Press.

Gardner, Richard N. 1992. *Negotiating Survival: Four Priorities After Rio.* New York: Council on Foreign Relations.

Ghils, Paul. 1992. "International Civil Society: International Non-Governmental Organizations in the International System." *International Social Science Journal* 44: 133, 417-31.

Grossman, Gene M. and Helpman, Elhanan. 1994. "Protection for Sale," *American Economic Review* 84: 833-850; reprinted in Alan V. Deardoff, James Levinsohn, and Robert M. Stern (eds.), *New Directions in Trade Theory.* Ann Arbor, MI: University of Michigan Press.

Haas, Peter, Keohane, Robert, and Levy, Marc (eds.). 1993. *Institutions for the Earth: Sources of Effective Environmental Protection.* Cambridge, MA: MIT Press.

Helpman, Elhanan. 1995. "Politics and Trade Policy." Discussion Paper No. 1269, Centre for Economic Policy Research, London (November).

Hillman, Arye L. 1989. *The Political Economy of Protection.* London: Harwood.

Hurrell, Andrew, and Kingsbury, Benedict (eds.). 1992. *The International Politics of the Environment.* New York: Oxford University Press.

Intergovernmental Panel on Climate Change (IPCC). 1995. *Second Scientific Assessment of Climate Change.* New York: World Meteorological Organization and United Nations Environment Programme.

Kerr, Richard A. 1994. "Antarctic Ozone Hole Fails to Recover," *Science* (14 Oct.) at 422.

Levy, Marc, Haas, Peter, and Keohane, Robert. 1993. "Improving the Effectiveness of Environmental Institutions" in P. Haas, R. Keohane, and M. Levy (eds.). *Institutions for the Earth: Sources for Effective Environmental Protection*, pp. 3-25. Cambridge, MA: MIT Press.

Lindborg, Nancy. 1992. "Nongovernmental Organizations: Their Past, Present, and Future Role in International Environmental Negotiations" in Lawrence Susskind et al. (eds.), *International Environmental Treaty Making.* Cambridge, MA: Program on Negotiation at Harvard Law School.

Magee, Stephen P., Brock, William A., and Young, Leslie. 1989. *Black Hole Tariffs and Endogenous Policy Formation.* Cambridge, MA: MIT Press.

Mayhew, David. 1974. *Congress: The Electoral Connection.* New Haven: Yale University Press.

Nichols, P.M. (1996). "Extension of Standing in the World Trade Organization Disputes to Nongovernmental Parties." 17 *University of Pennsylvania Journal of International Economics L.* 295.

North American Agreement on Environmental Cooperation (NAAEC). 1993. U.S.-Can.-Mex., 32 I.L.M. 1480.

Olson, Mancur. 1965. *The Logic of Collective Action: Public Goods and the Theory of Groups.* Cambridge, MA: Harvard University Press.

Ostry, Sylvia. 1990. *Governments and Corporations in a Shrinking World.* New York: Council on Foreign Relations.

Petersmann, Ernst-Ulrich. 1992. "Settlement of International and National Trade Dispute Through the GATT: The Case of Antidumping Law" in Ernst-Ulrich Petersmann and Gounther Jaenicke (eds.), *Adjudication of International Trade Disputes in International and National Economic Law.* Fribourg, Switzerland: University Press.

Princen, Thomas and Finger, Matthias. 1994. *Environmental NGOs in World Politics: Linking the Global and the Local.* New York: Routledge.

Rappaport, R.A. et al. 1985. "New DDT Inputs to North America—Atmospheric Deposition," 14 *Chemosphere* at 1167-73.

Revesz, Richard L. 1992. "Rehabilitating Interstate Competition: Rethinking the 'Race to the Bottom' Rationale for Federal Environmental Regulation" 17 *N.Y.U. L. Rev.* 1210.

Rhot-Arriaza, Naomi. 1992. "Precaution, Participation, and the 'Greening' of International Trade Law." 7 *Journal of Environmental Law and Litigation* 57.

Rich, Bruce. 1994. *Mortgaging the Earth: The World Bank, Environmental Impoverishment and the Crisis of Development.* Boston, MA: Beacon Press.

Sands, Phillippe J. 1995. *Principles of International Environmental Law.* New York: Manchester University Press.

Sands, Phillippe J. and Bedecarre, A.P. 1990. "Convention on International Trade in Endangered Species: The Role of Public Interest Non-Government Organizations in Ensuring the Effective Enforcement of the Ivory Trade Ban." *B.C. Environmental. Affairs Law Rev* 17: 799.

Shell, G. Richard. 1996. "The Trade Stakeholders Model and Participation by Nonstate Parties in the World Trade Organization." *University of Pennsylvania Journal of International Economic Law* 17: 359.

Spiro, P.J. 1994. "New Global Communities: Nongovernmental Organizations in International Decisionmaking Institutions." *The Washington Quarterly* 18: 45.

Stairs, Kevin and Taylor, Peter. "Non-Governmental Organizations and the Legal Protection of the Oceans: A Case Study" in Andrew Hurrell and Benedict Kingsbury (eds.) *The International Politics of the Environment* at 110-141. New York: Oxford University Press.

Streeten, P. 1993. "Markets and States: Against Minimalism." *World Development*, vol. 21 at 1281.

Susskind, Laurence E. 1994. *Environmental Diplomacy: Negotiating More Effective Global Agreements.* New York: Oxford University Press.

Tarlock, A. David. 1992. "Environmental Law: The Role of Non-Governmental Organizations in the Development of International Environmental Law." *Chi.-Kent L. Rev.*, vol. 68 at 61..

Wapner, Paul. 1995. "Politics Beyond the State: Environmental Activism and Civic World Politics." *World Politics*, vol. 47 at 311-40.

Weiss, Edith Brown. 1989. *In Fairness to Future Generations: International Law, Common Patrimony, and Intergenerational Equity.* Dobbs Ferry, New York: Transnational Publishers.

Weiss, Thomas G. and Gordenker, Leon. 1996. *NGOs, the UN, and Global Governance.* Boulder, CO: Lynne Rienner.

Wirth, David A. 1996. "Public Participation in International Processes: Environmental Case Studies at National and International Levels." *Colorado Journal of International Environmental Law and Policy* 7: 1.

World Trade Organization (WTO). 1996. *Guidelines for Arrangements on Relations with Non-Governmental Organizations.* In WT/L/162 (ed)., Decision Adopted by the General Council on 18 July 1996.

World Trade Organization (WTO). 1995. *Understanding on Rules and Procedures Governing the Settlement of Disputes.*

Zadek, Simon and Gatward, Murdoch. 1996. "Transforming the Transnational NGOs: Social Auditing or Bust?" in M. Edwards and D. Hulme (eds.), *Beyond the Magic Bullet: NGO Performance and Accountability in the Post Cold War World.* West Hartford, CT.: Kumarian Press.

Comments on Conference Version of Paper

Richard C. Porter

Nearly a year ago, I was asked to comment on a paper whose topic was to be "trade policy and the environment." I said yes. I made a mistake. If there is one thing worse than a lawyer commenting on an economist's paper, it must be an economist commenting on a lawyer's paper. But it is even worse than that. This paper barely mentions the making of environmental policy, about which I do know something, and talks at length about the administration of trade policy, about which I know embarrassingly little. But I am not at a loss how to proceed. Not at my age. Many years ago, a colleague-guru told me with respect to teaching: "teach what you know." I suspect the same holds true here. So I will talk about the environment as it relates to trade—and as it is often perceived to relate to trade.

Two connections stand out. One, trade between two countries imposes negative external costs upon one of them. For example, A's beef is not tested for some disease and tends to sicken B's citizens, or A's tankers are not double-hulled and tend to spill oil in B's harbors. These are classic Coasian confrontations.

Is there a role for the World Trade Organization (WTO) or some other international arbiter here? Of course, in that rights must be clearly defined, presumably by global agreement. But once rights are clearly delineated, if ever there was a situation where Coase was right, this is it—the governments should be able to negotiate a resolution. Is there a role for environmental nongovernmental organizations (NGOs) in all this at the WTO level? I don't see it—their place is at the national level, alerting their own governments to the perils of these environmental lapses by trading partners and urging their own governments to start proceedings to protect their own citizens.

And two, trade generates negative externalities at the global level. For example, A's use of DDT or harvesting of ivory extinguishes species that are valued by citizens throughout the planet; or A's use of CFCs or harvesting of rainforests damages the ozone layer and causes skin cancers in many other countries. We could list many other examples, but these four will suffice. Think about them for a moment.

In not one case is it really trade that causes the externality—it is really production or consumption, and it is of no importance whether any of the products end up being exported or imported to or from anywhere.

Trade sanctions here are a very second-best policy instrument. For first-best results, if Coasian negotiation were made impossible by the numbers of people involved, Pigovian taxes should be brought to bear; but those taxes should be on the production or consumption of the externality-generating activity in country A, not on its import into countries B, C, D, etc. However, it is not easy for countries B, C, and D to impose taxes on activities in country A. So it is tempting to apply trade taxes instead.

Where does the WTO come in? Consider the case where it is trade taxes or nothing. The role of the WTO, I guess, is to decide on the basis of previously decided and internationally accepted criteria, whether such trade taxes are better for world welfare than doing nothing at all. Provided the second-best trade taxes are not too remote from the primary target, they should cause a reduction in the offensive activity—the question is only whether the indirect costs are worth it, globally.

But the above assumes that the alternative is doing nothing at all. In fact we have alternatives to trade taxes that are not only better than doing nothing at all, they can come close to being a first-best approach to the externality. The alternative I am thinking of is not just neat "in theory"—we already have a case where it has worked and worked fairly well, especially when we consider that it was its first use: the Montreal Protocol.

At Montreal, the developed countries, in good Coasian style, collectively agreed among themselves to cease producing and using CFCs, and they induced developing countries to go along with this decision. The Montreal Protocol had two great virtues over trade taxes:

1. The Protocol attacked directly the externality-causing activity, the use (and leakage) of CFCs.

2. The Protocol concerned itself with fairness and equity. The developing countries, which did not cause the problem of overuse of CFCs and whose citizens will suffer disproportionately through more expensive refrigeration from the discontinuance of CFCs, were assisted in the transition by the richer industrialized countries, who are long refrigerated and can well afford the higher refrigeration costs. Trade taxes cannot offer carrots, only sticks.

What is the role of environmental NGOs in proceedings like the Montreal Protocol? They should deal with their own national governments and should urge strong negotiating positions on them. But why should they then be heard again at the negotiations themselves? Remember that the NGOs primarily represent the damaged parties—those citizens of the world who particularly value endangered species and who are particularly susceptible to skin cancer.

In short, it is hard for me to see, as Esty does, that "a formal WTO role for NGOs would help to . . . ensure that environmental externalities do not cause market failure in the international economic system and improve the quality of WTO environmental decisionmaking."

Am I saying that environmental NGOs are no good? Hardly. I sympathize with the goals of most, and I have belonged to many. They have achieved much in the United States at each of the federal, state, and local levels over the past thirty years. But I honestly do not see that they have any more role to play at the WTO than would pro-life and pro-choice groups.

CHAPTER 12

Trade and Human Rights

T. N. Srinivasan

I. Introduction

The use, or threat of use, of trade policy instruments to ensure that human rights are respected by governments of partner countries is not new. The most notable instance, of course, of multilateral trade sanctions to punish and eliminate the violation of human rights was against the South African government's apartheid policies. Clearly the collapse of the apartheid regime has been attributed by many to the opprobrium, if not the economic cost to South Africa, of the sanction.

Again, human rights advocates in the United States have lobbied, without success so far, against the renewal of Most Favored Nation (MFN) status to China. Ever since President Clinton issued an executive order in 1993 requiring that the Secretary of State shall not recommend renewal of MFN status unless certain human rights conditions are met, an annual battle between human rights groups and those, prominently business groups with significant stakes in trade with and investment in China, has raged over the renewal. The inefficacy of the ambiguous signals that a divided U.S. political scene sends to China is seen from the fact that, despite immense pressures not to do so, China recently charged and sentenced Wang Dan, a prominent student leader of the pro-democracy demonstrations in Tiananmen Square in Beijing in 1989, with the capital crime of conspiracy to overthrow the government, after holding him in prison for over six years. In his report on this event, Patrick Tyler of the *New York Times* writes:

> For the Clinton Administration, the prospect that the youthful Mr. Wang could receive a new and lengthy prison term presents a difficult foreign policy challenge. Earlier this year, Mr. Clinton privately signaled Beijing that if reelected, he would like to bring a permanent end to the campaign of sanctions and trade pressure that Washington has used to win improvements in human rights conditions here.
>
> To go forward with this plan, Mr. Clinton urged Beijing to show compassion to those who had been harassed or

> locked up for expressing political views.
>
> Now, in the midst of a Presidential campaign in which his foreign policy is under assault, Mr. Clinton will be under greater pressure to explain how his position toward Beijing has garnered any results and how the United States can influence the deteriorating conditions under which many intellectuals and political dissidents live in China.
>
> Most of the political prisoners on whose behalf Mr. Clinton has interceded with Chinese leaders are now back in prison or in permanent exile. (*New York Times*, October 13, 1996, p. 1)

But South Africa and China have not been the only cases that have drawn the attention of human rights groups. There is significant support in the United States for trade sanctions against Myanmar to punish human rights violations of the military dictatorship there. Interestingly, while the U.S. administration has suggested that by "constructively engaging" China economically through the grant of MFN status the cause of human rights there would be better served, not only has it opposed the same argument advanced by ASEAN countries against trade sanctions against Myanmar but in fact has "approved a ban on new American investment in Myanmar because of human-rights abuses by the Burmese Government" (*New York Times*, April 22, 1997, p. A1)! The facts that political and trade relations with China are far more consequential to U.S. foreign policy and business interests than those with Myanmar certainly played a role in the differing U.S. stance in the two cases.[1] Republicans and human rights groups in the United States have accused President Clinton of overlooking human rights violations in East Timor and poor labour standards in Indonesia in return for campaign contributions for the Democratic Party by a businessman of Indonesian origin (*Wall Street Journal*, October 16, 1996, p. A10).

The latest, and internationally controversial, issue relating to trade and human rights is that of labor standards.[2] It has surfaced in international fora including the World Trade Organization (WTO). I will focus exclusively on this issue in the rest of this paper since an analysis of it illustrates almost all of the difficult economic, moral, philosophical and political problems associated with using trade policy as an instrument for enforcing human rights. Indeed, the Council of Economic Advisers (CEA) to the President of the United States view "core" labor standards as representing "fundamental human and democratic rights in the work place, rights that should prevail in *all societies whatever their level of development*" (CEA, 1995, p. 250, emphasis added).

Thus a sweeping claim of universality and eternity is made for a particular set of "core" labor standards viz. "freedom of association, the right to organize and bargain collectively, freedom from forced labor, and a minimum age for the employment of children" (ibid, p. 250). Acceptance of such a claim will of course imply, for example, that any diversity in the content and scope of core standards among countries according to stage of development would be illegitimate. As such, one has to examine the validity of the claim and I do so in Section II. Section III is devoted to moral and philosophical arguments, such as the humanitarian concern that citizens of one country may have about what they deem "poor" conditions of work or "exploitation" of children by parents or employers. It will be argued that although such concerns are legitimate, their alleviation requires solutions that do not include the use of trade sanctions. Section IV analyzes the economic arguments, pro and con, for the use of trade policy instruments and briefly reviews the empirical evidence on the effects of diverse labor standards on export performance and inflow of foreign direct investment. Section V discusses the role of multilateral institutions in improving labor standards and concludes the paper.

II. Universality and Eternity of Human Rights and of Core Labor Standards

According to a recent report from the Organization for Cooperation and Economic Development (OECD), starting from several international treaties early in this century on the elimination of slavery, a body of international law on human rights, including certain basic workers' rights, has evolved. This body of law

> considers human rights as universal, transcending all political, economic, social and cultural situations. They are characterized as such because they involve the fundamental liberty, dignity and respect of the individual. Moreover, freedom of association, prohibition of forced labor, elimination of child labor exploitation and the principle of non-discrimination are well established elements of the human rights international jurisprudence; in fact these workers' rights are an inseparable part of human rights (OECD, p. 27).

The World Social Summit of the United Nations held in Copenhagen "reinforced international consensus on fundamental human and workers' rights. In Commitment 3 of the Declaration from this summit, nations affirm their adhesion to certain workers' rights, which are identical to the core labor standards selected in this study" (ibid, p. 27).

The International Labour Organization (ILO), founded in 1919 as part of the implementation of the Treaty of Versailles[3],

> over the past 75 years . . . has adopted a series of conventions which set international labor standards. Through ratification, these conventions create binding obligations for member states. The conventions cover a wide range of issues in the world of work, including basic human rights such as

> freedom of association, the right to organize and bargain collectively, freedom from forced labor, freedom from discrimination in employment, and severe restrictions on the use of child labor (Maier, p. 12).

Nine ILO conventions are particularly relevant from the perspective of labor standards. These relate to freedom of association such as the right to organize (No. 87), and collective bargaining (No. 98), forced labor (no. 29) and its abolition (No. 105), non-discrimination in employment and occupation (No. 111) and in remuneration (No. 100), employment policy (No. 122), minimum age of employment (No. 138) and tripartite (i.e. workers, employers and government) consultation (No. 144).

Although the CEA, as noted in the introduction, views several of the subjects of these conventions as representing "fundamental human and democratic rights in the work place," ironically the United States has ratified only two of the nine conventions just cited: those on abolition of forced labor and on tripartite consultation (World Bank (1995), table A4). Indeed, the record of U.S. ratification of ILO conventions is even more disappointing. Charnovitz (1995, p. 178) reports that

> The United States has become a party to only 12 ILO conventions, including 5 in recent years. This is the worst record of any major industrial nation. . . . This disinclination to ratify ILO conventions stems mainly from two concerns. First, because U.S. treaties are the "supreme law of the land," ratifying an ILO convention could supersede federal and state labor laws if provisions of the convention can be enforced in domestic courts. Second, many Americans are reluctant to have U.S. policy reviewed by an international organization. As a consequence, the United States has not ratified the core ILO conventions on freedom of association and the right to organize, nor has it ratified any of the child labor conventions.

Interestingly, OECD countries other than the United States have ratified most of the nine conventions. At the same time, the conventions on freedom of association and forced labor and non-discrimination have been ratified by all but a handful of countries who are members of the ILO. Although President Carter signed a convention on Women's Rights in 1980, the U.S. Senate is yet to ratify it (*New York Times*, December 11, 1996, p. A7).[4] Compliance, however, is another matter, though (and this is important) it is subject to periodic monitoring and review once a convention is ratified.

Ever since its creation, the United Nations (UN) has been concerned with human rights. Article 55 of the UN charter requires that countries should, inter alia, promote respect for human rights and basic liberties for all, without distinction of race, gender language or religion, not only as an end in itself, but also as a necessary condition for maintenance of peaceful relations between countries. The Universal Declaration of Human Rights of 1948 adopted by the UN General Assembly without dissent gives an even more detailed description of human rights. These include

> civil and political rights (the right to life, liberty, freedom from torture, freedom of opinion and expression, freedom from slavery and servitude, right to peaceful assembly and association) and economic, social and cultural rights (right to join and form trade unions, right to work, right to equal pay for equal work, right to education). Again, the right to decent living standards is regarded as one important element (OECD, 1996, p. 27).

The Declaration did not require ratification. It took nearly 20 years to transform the principles of the Declaration into treaty provisions establishing legal obligations on the part of each ratifying state. At the end of 1966, two covenants, one dealing with civil and political rights, the other with economic, social and cultural rights, and an optional protocol were adopted by the General Assembly. Another 10 years elapsed before the required minimum number of states ratified the two covenants and the optional protocol. As of this year, a total of 132 states (including the United States) have ratified the covenant on civil and political rights, 133 the covenant on economic, social and cultural rights and 87 the optional protocol. The United States has signed, but not ratified, the covenant on economic, social and cultural rights and is not a signatory of the optional protocol.[5] An even larger number of states (168) has ratified the UN convention on the Rights of the Child adopted in 1989. Clearly the obligations of the Charter are binding on members of the U.N.

Besides international agreements, conventions and covenants, the constitutions of some countries require their government to promote human rights. For example, the Constitution of India has a chapter entitled Directive Principles of State Policy which enjoins the state to strive to secure "a social order in which justice—social, economic and political—shall inform all the institutions of national life" and "to minimize inequality in income, status, facilities and opportunities, amongst individuals and groups." Further, the state is required to ensure "that the ownership and control of the material resources of the community are so distributed as best to subscribe to the common good; that the operation of the economic system does not result in the concentration of wealth and means of production to the common detriment" (Basu, 1983). The constitution also protects the rights to work, to education, and to public assistance in case of unemployment, disability, or sickness.

This review leads to two conclusions. First, except for a notable few, almost all states have signed and ratified a set of covenants that recognize an immense and overwhelming array of civil, political, economic, social and cultural rights that go beyond the so-called 'core' labor standards. All of these are universal rights, *not* just the few selected for trade sanctions by the proponents of the Social Clause, whether at the OECD or by the CEA in Washington. That selectivity must be explained and has to do, in all likelihood, with competitive pressures rather than human rights (Bhagwati, 1995)). Second, almost none of the many rights are satisfied in reality including in OECD countries: for example, discrimination on the basis of race and sex still exists even in the United States. This suggests that, at best, the rights recognized are universal aspirations, perhaps to be attained at some unspecified and distant future, though cynics might view them as empty rhetoric. Be that as it may, it is worth reiterating that the claim of universality and eternity, for a subset of rights covering the so-called 'core' labor standards, is overblown.

In conclusion, let me cite one final comment by Heribert Maier, the Deputy Director General of the ILO, on the question of "core" labor standards: "the ILO has not yet reached a political consensus of its ILO constituents to identify clearly a core group of convention or minimum standards" (Maier, 1994, p. 13).

III. Concern in High Income Countries About Labor Standards in Developing Countries

A concern about poor labor standards in general, and child labor in particular, has been expressed by various groups in high income countries. Groups in the United States such as "Save the Children" have raised funds to help poor children in less developed countries. It would indeed be wrong to dismiss such concerns out of hand since they could arise from *altruism*, e.g. the welfare of workers and children in poor countries could be an argument in the utility functions of at least some individuals and groups in rich countries, so that their utility increases if the welfare of workers and children in poor countries increases. On the other hand, such concerns could also arise from purely *selfish* motives: the fear of erosion of one's high standards through a "race-to-the-bottom" in the global economy, where "low" labor standards anywhere threaten the sustainability of "high" labor standards everywhere. Thus low labor standards in one country are perceived as negative externalities imposed on high standard countries by low standard countries.

Altruistic citizens of rich countries have, in principle, many ways of more efficiently and effectively expressing their concerns than through lobbying for imposing trade sanctions on countries with poor labor standards in the expectation that such sanctions would be effective in inducing the governments of such countries to institute policies for raising labor standards. First of all, it is conceivable that a country threatened with trade sanctions for failure to raise its labor standards might not respond by raising them but instead choose to forego gains from trade. Second, instead of relying on the *indirect means* through linkage which depends on the desired response by the developing country for its success, the citizens of the developed countries could adopt a more effective *direct means* of pressuring *their own governments* to lift any restrictions on immigration of workers from countries with poor labor standards. If they choose to migrate, such workers would enjoy higher labor standards prevailing in the country of immigration. Indeed there is support for lifting such restrictions on moral-philosophical grounds as in the writings of John Rawls (1993a). He views freedom of movement and freedom of choice of occupation as essential primary goods equivalent to other basic rights and liberties, the entitlement to which is not open to political debate and allocation through the political process. While Rawls was writing about these freedoms in the context of constitutional essentials of a just society, implicit in the very expression of humanitarian concerns about others must be a view of the whole human race as one society. As such, a natural extension of Rawls' ideas would treat freedom of movement of humans across artificial political boundaries as a basic human right.[6]

Even if lifting immigration restrictions is deemed infeasible politically, still citizens of rich countries could make income transfers to the workers in poor countries. With higher incomes, it is reasonable to presume that the *supply* price (broadly defined to include labor standard) of their labor would rise and to restore labor market equilibrium, labor standards would have to rise. Indeed a test of the depth of their humanitarian concern is the price that citizens are willing to pay for translating the concern into an actual increase in welfare of workers in poor countries. Willingness to make needed income transfers is a demonstration of the willingness to pay the price.

Turning now to child labor, excepting the abusive ones, most parents will weigh welfare of their children significantly in making choices for them. And in making those choices, given their resources and opportunities, such parents could reasonably be expected to take into account the cost of putting their children to work in terms of their health and education relative to the income they bring in. As such, if some parents choose to put their children to work, it reflects more than anything else the limitations of their resources and opportunities, viz. their poverty. Once again, citizens of developed countries concerned with the welfare of such working children among the poor in developing countries could influence the choices of parents away from putting their children to work altogether or at least reduce the amount of work done by their children through income transfers to parents. Such transfers relax their resource constraints.

The fear of a "race-to-the-bottom" arises from the expectation that faced with competition from low cost (*because* of their low labor standards) developing countries, producers in countries with high labor standards would lobby for lowering labor standards are home by threatening to move production to lower labor standard countries. Those who harbor such fears have the option of not buying such imported products so that domestic producers will no longer face import competition.

By not buying products of a firm or a country that does not observe what consumers view as acceptable labor standards, they can send a clear and effective signal to that firm or country to force it to choose between observing standards and retain the market or lose the market altogether.[7] If it chooses to retain the market by observing acceptable labor standards, to the extent the cost of the import goes up because of such observance, both the exporting country and the buyers of imports share the cost of improving labor standards. If it chooses to forego the market, then while workers in the exporting industry do not gain welfare through higher standards, there is a penalty to the firm in the form of lost exports. If the citizens of the developed countries are interested only in raising the welfare of the workers and not in penalizing the exporting firm, they will have to compensate the firm or make income transfer to workers. The basic point is that there is a real cost to raising labor standards, and that has to be incurred if the intended raise is to come about.

It should also be pointed out that the standard characterization of a "race-to-the-bottom" as a classic Prisoner's Dilemma game can be questioned. For example, consider a game of strategy between two countries with respect to their choice of labor standards. It has a conventional pay-off matrix reflecting the real incomes yielded (in brackets) when different labor standards are set at levels "low" and "high" by the two countries, Home and Foreign.

There are thus four possible combinations of home and foreign labor standards. The pay-offs associated with each combination (with the first (resp. second) component being the pay-off of the Home (resp. foreign) countries are given by the following pay-off matrix:

		Foreign Strategy	
		Low	High
Home	Low	(-2,-2)	(2,-3)
Strategy	High	(-3, 2)	(1, 1)

It is easily seen that each country has a *dominant* strategy, viz. to set a low standard, because by doing so it maximizes its pay-off whether the other country chooses to set a high or low standard. Yet, compared to this *individually*-rational dominant-strategy Nash equilibrium with both countries setting low standards, the *collectively* rational strategy of each setting a high standard will yield a *higher* pay-off for *both.*[8]

Of course competition need not necessarily lead to such a "prisoners' dilemma" type of Nash equilibrium. For example, if the pay-off matrix is as follows,

		Foreign Strategy	
		Low	High
Home	Low	(-4,-4)	(2,-3)
Strategy	High	(-3, 2)	(1, 1)

then (Low, High) and (High, Low) are both (pure strategy) Nash equilibria. In each of these one jurisdiction sets a low standard while the other sets a high standard.

In both cases above, the Nash equilibrium is characterized by a "race to the bottom" in the sense that at least one country sets a low standard. But this need not be so, as consideration of the following pay-off matrix shows. Thus, consider:

		Foreign Strategy	
		Low	High
Home	Low	(-2,-2)	(2,-3)
Strategy	High	(-3, 2)	(3, 3)

It is readily seen that we have a unique Nash equilibrium where each country sets a high standard.

Of course, these are arbitrarily-constructed pay-off matrices and we need to ground them in underlying models of economies to see whether such outcomes are sensible within them. However, they are adequate to demonstrate that a destructive "race-to-the bottom" is not inevitable in the competition to set labor standards.

To sum up, the fact that citizens in rich countries could be, and often are, genuinely concerned about poor working conditions, and the use of child labor in poor countries does not necessarily imply that such concerns can be addressed only through the use of trade policy instrument.

IV. Economics of Labor Standards

There is an extensive and growing literature on the economics (theoretical and empirical) of labor standards (see Brown et al. (1997) and references therein). Stern (1997) has critically surveyed this literature. Other useful surveys are by Anderson (1996) and Maskus (1996). Instead of going over the ground covered by them, I will confine myself here, first, to reproducing the argument that I have made elsewhere (Srinivasan (1996)) that diversity in labor standards among countries is not only legitimate but also does not detract from the case for free trade. In other words, such diversity, like diversity in tastes, technology or factor endowments, is a source for gainful trade based on comparative advantage. Second, I will offer a critique of two recent contributions (Rodrik (1996) and Krueger (1997)). Krueger's contribution is particularly relevant from the perspective of political economy.

Legitimate Diversity of Labor Standards

In modeling diversity of labor standards, I follow Brown et al. (1996) in postulating that standards divert resources from production and they also affect welfare, as an argument of consumers' utility function in addition to the amounts consumed of various goods.

Consider first a small-open economy producing and consuming two goods. Let Q_i and C_i denote respectively the production and consumption of good i (i=1,2). Let S denote the level of *economy-wide* labor standards. Let

$U[C_1, C_2, S]$ be the strictly concave Samuelson social utility function with $U_j > 0$, where U_j denotes the partial derivative U with respect to its jth argument. Let $Q_1 = F(Q_2, S; \overline{K}, \overline{L})$ denote the production possibility frontier denoting the efficient combination of Q_1, Q_2 that could be produced, given the level S of labor standard and inelastically supplied endowments of $\overline{K}$, $\overline{L}$ of capital and labor respectively. F is concave in Q_2 and S with $F \geq 0$, $F_1 < 0$, $F_2 < 0$, $F_3 > 0$, $F_4 > 0$, where F_j is the partial derivative of F with respect to its jth argument. In effect, the labor standard is treated as if it is a good produced and consumed within the country, i.e. a non-traded good. With good 1 as the numeraire let the world price of good 2 be p. Under balanced trade, the economy's choice of C_1, C_2, Q_1, Q_2 and S is determined by maximizing

$$U[C_1, C_2, S] \qquad (1)$$

subject to

$$C_1 + pC_2 = Q_1 + pQ_2 \qquad (2)$$

$$Q_1 = F[Q_2, S; \overline{K}, \overline{L}] \qquad (3)$$

$$C_i \geq 0, \geq Q_2\ 0; S \geq 0 \qquad (4)$$

Substituting (2) and (3) in (1) the problem reduces to maximizing $U[F + p(Q_2 - C_2), C_2, S]$ with respect to Q_2, C_2 and S. Assuming an interior maximum, the first-order conditions yield

$$U_2/U_1 = p \qquad (5)$$

$$F_1 = -p \qquad (6)$$

$$U_3/U_1 = -F_2 \qquad (7)$$

The interpretation of (5)-(7) is straightforward. Equation (5) states that the marginal rate of substitution in consumption of good 2 for 1 viz. U_2/U_1 equals its world price p. Equation (6) states that the marginal rate of transformation of good 2 into good 1 viz. $-F_1$ equals its world price p. Thus (5) and (6) together imply that both consumers and producers should face world prices were the optimum to be implemented as a competitive equilibrium. *Thus free trade is the optimal policy.* Equation (7) states that the *marginal rate of substitution* (MRS) of labor standard for good 1 in *consumption* viz. U_3/U_1 should equal the *marginal rate of transformation* (MRT) of labor standard and good 1 in production, that is, the cost of labor standard in terms of foregone output of good 1 in production viz. $-F_2$.

Since the *exogenous* variables of the problem are the terms-of-trade p and the factor endowments $\overline{K}$, $\overline{L}$ the optimal values of the *endogenous* variables Q_i, C_i and S will be functions of them. In a world of small open economies, in a free trade equilibrium, while p is the same for all countries, even if tastes and technology (i.e., the utility and production functions) respectively are the same, the endowment $\overline{K}$, $\overline{L}$ will in general differ. As such the optimal values of endogenous variables, particularly the level of labor standards would differ across countries. Under plausible assumptions on U and F it can be shown that a richer country, i.e., one with a greater endowment of one or both factors, will choose a higher standard. Clearly there is nothing illegitimate or unfair about such diversity.

In the above discussion the determination of p through global market clearance was left implicit. To make it explicit and to explore other aspects of labor standards, it is useful to set up the problem as one of choosing Pareto Optimal (across countries) levels of output, consumption and labor standards.

Let (C_i^j, Q_i^j, S^j) denote respectively the consumption of good i, production of good i (i=1,2), and labor standard in country j (j = 1,...N). Under appropriate assumptions on utility functions and production functions, any Pareto Optimum can be characterized as the solution to the maximization of a positively weighted sum of individual country utilities,

$$\sum_{j=1}^{N} \alpha^j U^j(C_i^j,\ S^j) \qquad (8)$$

subject to

$$\sum_j C_i^j = \sum_j Q_i^j \quad i = 1,2 \qquad (9)$$

$$Q_1^j = F^j(Q_2^j,\ S^j;\ \overline{K}^j,\ \overline{L}^j) \quad j = 1,2,\ldots N \qquad (10)$$

$$C_i^j \geq 0,\ Q_i^j \geq 0,\ S^j \geq 0 \quad i = 1,2;\ j = 1,2,\ldots N \qquad (11)$$

Equation (9) represents global market clearance for good i and it replaces the balance of trade equation (2) of the small-country problem.

Assuming that the non-negativity constraints (11) do not bind, the first-order conditions for the optimal choice of C_i^j, Q_i^j and S^j are:

$$\alpha^j \frac{\partial U^j}{\partial C_i^j} = \lambda_i \quad j = 1,\ldots N;\ i = 1,2 \qquad (12)$$

$$\alpha^j \frac{\partial U^j}{\partial S^j} = -\mu^j \frac{\partial F^j}{\partial S^j} \quad j = 1,\ldots N \qquad (13)$$

$$\lambda_1 = \mu^j \quad j = 1,\ldots N \qquad (14)$$

$$\lambda_2 = -\mu^j \frac{\partial F^j}{\partial Q_2^j} \quad j = 1,\ldots N \qquad (15)$$

In (12)-(15), λ_i is the Lagrangean multiplier associated with constraint (9), which ensures that there is no excess supply or demand for good i in the world. m^j is the Lagrangean multiplier associated with the production transformation constraint (10) for country j. Taking (12) and (15) together, one gets:

$$\frac{\partial U^j}{\partial C_2^j} \Big/ \frac{\partial U^j}{\partial C_1^j} = \frac{\lambda_2}{\lambda_1} = -\frac{\partial F^j}{\partial Q_2^j} \qquad (16)$$

Thus the MRS is consumption of good 2 for good 1, viz. ($\frac{\partial U^j}{\partial C_2^j} \Big/ \frac{\partial U^j}{\partial C_1^j}$) is the same in all countries j, with the common value being λ_2/λ_1. Also the MRT of good 2 for good 1 in production, i.e., $-\frac{\partial F^j}{\partial Q_2^j}$ is the same in all countries j and its common value is also λ_2/λ_1. This in turn means that if the chosen Pareto Optimum (i.e., the one corresponding to a particular set of a^j) is implemented as a competitive equilibrium, then consumers and producers in all countries will have to face the same relative price of good 2 in terms of good 1. *In other words, a Pareto Optimum implemented as a competitive equilibrium will be characterized by free trade.*

It is seen from (12)-(14) that the MRS of labor standard for good 1 in country j, viz. $\frac{\partial U^j}{\partial S^j} \Big/ \frac{\partial U^j}{\partial C_1^j}$ equals the MRT of labor standards for good 1 in production in country j, viz. $-\frac{\partial F^j}{\partial S^j}$. However this common value of MRS and MRT can differ across countries. Once again such diversity is legitimate.

In the above analysis there was no requirement that each country's trade be balanced, only that globally there was no excess supply or demand for each commodity. Thus, given an *arbitrary choice* of a^j if the corresponding Pareto Optimum were to be implemented as a Pareto Optimum, the world market clearing relative price of good 2 in terms of good 1 will obviously be λ_2/λ_1. However, there is nothing to ensure that at these prices the value of the optimal consumption bundle of country j, i.e., $C_1^j + \frac{\lambda_2}{\lambda_1}C_2^j$ equals the value of its optimal production bundle, i.e., $Q_1^j + \frac{\lambda_2}{\lambda_1}Q_2^j$ (i = 1,2). However, global clearance of the world market for each of the two goods ensures that for the world as a whole the value of its consumption equals value of production. In other words, while trade need not be balanced for any country, for the world as a whole it is balanced. Thus to implement any *arbitrary* Pareto Optimum transfers to each country (equaling the excess of the value of its consumption bundle over the value of its production bundle) will in general be required. Of course some countries will *receive* and others *make* positive transfers. Because world trade is balanced, such transfers added over all the countries is zero. Thus making such transfers is feasible. However, following Negishi (1960) it can be shown that a set of positive a^j will in general exist such that the associated Pareto Optimum could be implemented without intercountry transfers. That is to say, a Pareto Optimum can be shown to exist which can be implemented as a competitive equilibrium at which the trade of each country is balanced. Let such a Pareto Optimum be denoted as No-Transfer Pareto Optimum or NTPO. For simplicity let us assume that NTPO is unique.

Clearly the analysis does not suggest that at such an NTPO the associated labor standard S^j is the same in all countries. Such diversity is legitimate: after all the situation being characterized is a Pareto Optimum and it does not call for intercountry transfers. What if the vector $(S^1, \ldots S^N)$ is deemed unsatisfactory in the sense that the standards in some country or countries are below some minimum acceptable level $\bar{S}$?

Suppose for concreteness, let $S^j < \bar{S}$ for $j = 1,2,\ldots M$ $(M < N)$. Leaving aside the questions as to how the minimum $\bar{S}$ is set and if there is a consensus on $\bar{S}$, how such a consensus came about, one could proceed as follows.[9] Suppose among the set of Pareto Optima (i.e. the set obtained as a^j are varied) there is a non-empty subset the elements of which satisfy $S^j \geq \bar{S}$ for all j. Then by definition any element of this subset will obviously meet the minimum standard criterion. However two points are noteworthy. First, by assumption NTPO is not an element of the subset. As such intercountry transfers would be necessary were any member of the subset is to be implemented as a competitive equilibrium. Second, if there is more than one element in the subset, different elements will differ with respect to the distribution of welfare as well as transfers among countries. However, there is no way to choose among elements of this subset since the only requirement was that the minimal standard $\bar{S}$ be met. In a sense this is nice since additional criteria about the distribution of welfare and transfer could be brought to bear in making a choice. Be that as it may, *the important point is that as long as there exists a non-empty set of Pareto Optima meeting the minimal standards, it is feasible to meet such standards with income transfers but without departing from free trade. As such there is no need for a social clause or to put it another way the only rationale for a social clause has to be the odious one of protection of import competing industries.*

What if there is no Pareto Optimum satisfying $S^j \geq \bar{S}$ for all j? *Suppose that the minimum $\bar{S}$ is the result of an international consensus as is the case with ILO conventions.* Then it is natural to look for Restricted Pareto Optima, i.e. Pareto Optima subject to the additional restriction

$$-S^j \leq -\bar{S} \tag{17}$$

It can be seen that once (17) is added to (9)-(11), the only first-order condition that is altered is (13) which replaced by

$$\alpha^j \frac{\partial U^j}{\partial S^j} = -\mu^j \frac{\partial F^j}{\partial S^j} - \upsilon^j \quad j=1,2,\ldots N \tag{18}$$

where u^i is the Langrangean multiplier associated with constraint (17). Taking (12), (14) and (18) together it follows that

$$\frac{\partial U^j}{\partial S^j} \Big/ \frac{\partial U^j}{\partial C^1_j} = -\frac{\partial F^j}{\partial S^j} - \frac{\upsilon^j}{\lambda_1} \tag{19}$$

Thus from (19) it is seen that now there is a wedge between MRS in consumption of good 1 labor standard, viz. $\frac{\partial U^j}{\partial S^j} \Big/ \frac{\partial U^j}{\partial C^j_1}$ and MRT in production, viz. $-\frac{\partial F^j}{\partial S^j}$, the wedge being $-\frac{\upsilon^j}{\lambda_1}$. Now $\lambda_1 > 0$ and $\upsilon^j \geq 0$ (the reason being reducing $\bar{S}$ cannot reduce global welfare). As such (19) implies that the shadow consumer relative price of labor standard in terms of good 1, namely the MRS is lower than its shadow producer price, namely the MRT. Thus, in effect a consumer subsidy inducing demand for higher labor standards relative to goods or equivalently a producer tax that induces a lower supply of goods relative to standards is needed to sustain the optimum. *However, since the other first order conditions are unchanged, it is the case that restricted Pareto Optima are characterized by free trade.* Thus *international income transfers* (depending on a^j) and a *domestic tax or subsidy* to induce the appropriate level of standards are needed to sustain a Pareto Optimum. Indeed one could view the *international assistance* and *domestic compliance* measures associated with implementing ILO conventions as precisely the right approach.

The analysis thus far shows that diversity in labor standards or the implementation of a common minimal standards do not call for deviation from free trade as long as Pareto Optimality is the objective and there is willingness not only to make income transfers between countries as necessary but, to the extent standards in one country directly affects the welfare of another, such externalities are internalized in each country. What if this situation of "first best" does not obtain? In answering this question it is useful to distinguish between departures from first best in a closed economy from those in an open economy. Obviously the possible use of trade policy to improve labor standards arises only in an open economy.

In a closed economy, labor standards could be sub-optimally low because of possible market failures. For example, if improving the safety of the work environment involves some initial investment that will pay off in terms of improved future worker productivity, if capital markets are not efficient, the employer may not be able to obtain the resources for such investment. Suffice it to say that departures from first best arising from domestic market failures do not raise new issues in the context of labor standards. And policies that address the failure at its source (the capital market in the above example) are the appropriate interventions. Even if there are no market failures, so that the prevailing labor standards are consistent with a domestic Pareto Optimum, still the real income distribution associated with the laissez-faire Pareto Optimum may be deemed unsatisfactory. In particular, the labor standards (along with factor and commodity prices) are also a reflection of the real income distribution. Changing the income distribution through policy will also change the equilibrium labor standards. Once again there is nothing peculiar to labor standards in this and, as seen in the international context earlier, non-distortionary lump-sum income (or wealth) redistribution policy is the first best to move the income distribution (and consequently the equilibrium labor standards in the right direction). If the first-best policy is infeasible, then other policies (such as, for example, commodity or factor taxes or subsidies) could in principle be used to achieve a better income distribution and labor standards albeit at the cost of a dead weight loss. In general, which taxes and what levels are to be used in achieving the desired change in labor standards while minimizing the dead-weight loss will vary across economies.

One of the core labor standards promoted by the ILO is the freedom of workers to form labor unions and presumably engage in collective bargaining. Such rights are rarely absolute: some workers (e.g., in public administration) are denied these rights by law in many countries. Whether such freedoms should be deemed a fundamental human right on par with other primary goods in the Rawlsian sense is arguable. In any case, for an overwhelming majority of poor workers in developing countries whose dominant mode of employment is self-employment in rural agricultural activities or in the urban informal sector, unionization has little relevance. Even where relevant and where the freedom to form unions has been exercised to a significant extent, namely in the organized manufacturing and public sectors in poor countries, labor unions have been seen promoting the interests of a small section of the labor force at the expense of many.

Of course, whether or not unions promote general welfare there is no rationale for their suppression. But it should be recognized, first, that unionized labor often constitutes a small labor aristocracy in poor countries. Besides, even in rich countries, members of some unions have little voice in decision making within the union, not to mention the association of organized crime with the leadership of a few. Second, and more important, promoting labor standards that cannot be sustained in equilibrium at the particular stage of development of a country could be very expensive in terms of foregone growth. Depending on whether such standards vary across industries and the time phasing of their introduction, wage and profit rates, as well as employment in different industries as well as in the aggregate would be affected differently. As the analysis of Brown et al. (1996) shows, the effects will depend on the technology and the characteristics of labor standards and no general answer can be given.

Turning now to open economies, it is clear that in the absence of a first-best non-trade related policy, trade policies could be used to change equilibrium labor standards. This can be seen simply in the case of trade in a two-country world, where one of the countries is "small" in that it behaves as if it has no influence on its terms of trade. As we saw earlier, a "small" open economy's optimal choice of its labor standard depends on its factor endowment and terms of trade. By exercising its own trade policy instrument, say tariffs or quotas, the large country can influence the terms of trade faced by the small country and thereby affect its choice of labor standards. If the small country's labor standard influences the welfare of the citizens of the large country (because of their humanitarian concerns), then the terms-of-trade effect of its choice of tariffs has two effects on welfare of the large country. The first is the usual direct welfare effect of changes in terms-of-trade and the second is the indirect welfare effect arising from induced changes in small country's labor standard. To the extent a tariff shifts the terms-of-trade in favor of the large country, the first effect is positive. But the second effect could be negative since the adverse shift in terms of trade of the small country might induce a reduction in its labor standard. Depending on the balance between the two effects, it is possible that by choosing its welfare maximizing tariff, the large country could induce the small country to improve its labor standards relative to free trade.[10] But it could also deteriorate the standards if the balance between the two effects were different. The upshot is that if first-best policy instruments are unavailable, trade policy instruments could, though not necessarily would, help in raising labor standards in poor countries. However, welfare of such countries need not rise.

Rodrik (1996) and Krueger (1997) on Labor Standards

Rodrik (1996) draws an analytical distinction between two arguments, which he claims "are often mixed-up" (p. 5), for the use of trade policy instruments for enforcing particular labor standards. The first is "that trade is a channel through which labor standards are arbitraged across countries towards the lowest level, requiring the use of trade policy to prevent a "race to the bottom" (p. 5). The second is "that trade (and trade sanctions in particular) should be used to enforce internationally agreed standards such as ILO conventions, or to simply get trade partners to improve their labor standards" (p. 5). The distinction arises from the intended effect of trade policy. In the first case, the primary intention is to prevent trade with poor countries eroding domestic labor standards, and not so much to change the labor standards in the poor countries themselves. On the other hand, in the second case, the primary goal is to enforce different, presumably higher, labor standards in poor countries than those prevailing in them through the threat of denial of access to markets of developed countries.

The "race to the bottom" referred to in the first argument is not that between governments in setting their mandatory labor standards. As argued in Section III, a non-cooperative game between governments in setting labor standards need not necessarily result in a "race to the bottom." What Rodrik has in mind is competition among producers in different countries. As generations of students have been taught, trade in goods is a substitute (and under appropriate situations, a perfect substitute) for trade in non-traded factors of production, including labor. Indeed, the ancient pauper labor argument was in fact based on wage compeition. Rodrik's "race to the bottom" argument for the use of trade policy in enforcing on labor standards is the same old pauper labor argument, now couched in terms of competition in labor standards. But there is little empirical evidence for the actual use of labor standards as a competitive tool. The available evidence summarized in OECD (1996) suggests the core labor standards do not play a significant role in comparative costs and export performance. In any case, the conventional answer to the pauper labor argument in the context of trade between rich North and poor South, as Rodrik himself points out, is "While unskilled labor may lose, the North is richer as a whole, and if governments in the North wished to do so they could compensate the losers and still come out ahead" (p. 8).

Thus in the absence of market failures[11] and any constraints on the ability of Northern governments to compensate potential losers from competition in trade with the South, comparative advantage, even if it reflects in part differences in prevailing labor standards, is legitimate and so are gains from trade based on it. Thus, there is no case for trade restrictions. Clearly, if such advantage is gained by flouting universal moral norms, it is obviously illegitimate. For example, any cost advantage in products produced by prisoners could be universally deemed illegitimate. Indeed, it is for this reason that GATT-WTO allows countries to place otherwise disallowed quantitative restrictions on trade in such products. China has been accused of exporting such products.

If universal moral norms are indeed the foundations of the case against unfettered trade in products made by prisoners, then what should one make of the activities of UNICOR, a corporation wholly owned by the Federal Government of the United States, run by the Bureau of Prisons in the United States?[12] It operates 100 factories, sells over 150 products including "prescription glasses, safety eyewear, linens, monogrammed towels, executive office furniture, bedroom sets, gloves, brooms and brushes of all kinds, even targets for target practice. They also make cables and electronic component parts for Army tanks, jet fighters and the Patriot missile." Its gross sales in 1995 were around $500 million, of which wages paid to prisoners was about $35 million! According to Mr. Schwlab, Assistant Director of Corporate Management of UNICOR, prisoners are "not covered by Fair Labor Standards Act, minimum wage laws. They don't get retirement benefits, unemployment compensation, etc. They're workers, but they're not employees." Besides publicly owned UNICOR, private industry has been attracted and allowed to operate within prisons, and as the owner of one such private company agreed, it was a fantastic deal all the way around and he liked "the financial advantages of a prison business, namely, getting to hire the cream of the crop from a pool of cheap prison labor, not to mention the use of . . . brand new air-conditioned factory space, rent free." The cost advantage of UNICOR and any private business operating with prison labor should be obvious. Yet, as the narrator of the story put it, without realizing the absurdity of the economic reasoning involved,

> Back in 1934, when Congress created UNICOR, it restricted its sales to one and only one customer, the federal government. The reason: to prevent UNICOR's cheap prison labor from undercutting private industry in the commercial marketplace. But Congress also armed UNICOR with one big advantage: It gets first crack at the government's business, even at the expense of private companies competing for the same work.

Clearly, any sale to government by UNICOR displaces what another producer, *domestic* or *foreign*, would have made! It is irrelevant that UNICOR is not allowed to export or sell to the domestic private sector. Yet those in the United States and the OECD, who accuse less developed countries with lower labor standards than their own as engaging in social dumping, fail to see that the operation of UNICOR has the same effect!

Instead of relying on universal norms to question the legitimacy of *all* trade in particular products, Rodrik (1996, p. 9) builds his case on the arguments that "Nations do have collective preferences over what kinds of production technologies are admissible ("fair" or "legitimate") and "All governments take into account consideration of fairness and legitimacy in their regulations governing which technologies are admissible and with are not. The concern over labor standards is just another manifestation of this principle" (Rodrik (1996), p. 32).[13] He then appeals to the self-evident proposition that having an opportunity to exchange what one produces with one's resources for what one consumes through trade is equivalent to adding another technology to the domestic production technology for transforming one's resources for final consumption. As such, "free trade with a low-standard country would be no different than importing workers abroad and allowing them to work under the same poor conditions" (p. 11). If a country proscribes "sweat shops" at home, it should be allowed to reject free trade and importation of goods produced in "sweat shops" abroad.

Leaving aside the fact that there are numerous sweatshops in the United States itself and that the Department of Labor has confessed its inability to finance even moderately adequate enforcement of laws against their operation, Rodrik's argument does not carry weight if it is used to deny market access to foreign goods manufactured with domestically "unacceptable" procedures. First, government regulations operate not only with respect to labor standards, but also a whole host of other factors that influence cost of production, such as, for example, building codes, zoning laws etc. The Rodrik principle applied to these implies that, if a country prohibits certain types of structures (such as, for example, buildings that exceed a specified height) or the use of certain types of building materials within its territory, then free trade with, and importing the same product from, a country which does not have such regulations is no different than producing the same product at home in a structure that does not meet the regulations. Thus any and all regulations that affect the cost of production of any product at home, in principle could induce home producers to call for restrictions on imports of the same product. A moment's reflection is enough to convince oneself that this opens the door for attempts to offset comparative advantage of foreign producers by depicting it as arising from differences in regulations relative to those prevailing at home.[14]

The second argument for the use of trade sanctions to enforce particular labor standards of advanced nations in poor countries is unpersuasive. As argued in Sections II and III, first of all, in no sense can one attribute universality and eternity to those standards. Second, even if humanitarian concerns about the welfare of workers in poor countries were behind the desire to enforce higher standards on them, more efficient instruments than trade sanctions are available to enforce them. In any case, as Rodrik himself points out, in a related context, the reason why advanced nations do not "condone a substantially lower set of working conditions for migrant workers (temporary or otherwise) . . . have less to do with humanitarian concerns for foreigners than with ensuring labor standards for *domestic* workers do not erode" (Rodrik 1996, p. 11). One is therefore led to conclude that conventional protectionist pauper-labor type argument, rather than lofty humanitarianism, that is behind the clamor for the use of trade policy instruments to enforce particular labor standards in poor countries. As such, succumbing to the clamor would amount to using inefficient distortionary trade restrictions, rather than non-distortionary domestic policies in rich countries, for redistributing gains from trade, thereby imposing avoidable welfare losses on poor countries.

Krueger (1997) analyzes some political economy aspects of linkage between trade policies and labor standards. He finds from his linear probability regressions that members of U.S. Congress representing districts with relatively many unskilled workers, who are most likely to compete with child labor, are less likely to support a ban on imports made with child labor. He concludes from this finding that lobbying in industrialized countries for linking market access of developing countries to their observance of labor standards does not necessarily represent disguised protectionism. But, by the same token, it is not necessarily a refutation of the claim that it does. First of all, if a representative did not choose to cosponsor the Child Labor Deterrence Act of 1995, it does not imply his or her lack of support for the legislation, although, to be fair, cosponsoring could be construed as indicating stronger support. Second, since the proportion of eligible voters who actually vote differs across population groups and the less educated and unskilled are less likely to vote, their interests might weigh less heavily in the decision of the representative to cosponsor or not.[15] Third, and most important, even if one accepts Krueger's econometric analysis as valid, as Krueger himself notes, his regressions suggest that those who support international labor standards are more likely to support protectionist policies more generally and that representatives from districts that have a higher rate of unionization are more likely to be cosponsors.[16]

A number of empirical studies on various aspects of competitiveness in world markets, flow of foreign direct investment and labor standards are available. Serious data and econometric problems plague many of them. Most are based on multiple regressions usually estimated by ordinary least squares (OLS). Few of the regressions estimated are derived from any well-specified theoretical framework: the explanatory variables are often chosen based more on their plausibility than on theory. Proxies used, as for example by Rodrik (1996), for labor standards obtaining in a country (e.g., total number of ILO conventions ratified), statutory hours of work, etc.) are subject to significant measurement errors. Not all explanatory variables can be deemed truly exogenous. For example, whether to satisfy an ILO convention or not is a matter of choice. As is well known, if explanatory variables are either subject to measurement errors or endogenous or both, the OLS estimates of regression parameters will be inconsistent.

Stern (1997) and OECD (1996) summarize the results from many of the empirical studies. The conclusions of OECD (1996) are worth excerpting:

> *On core labor standards and export performance:*
>
> Within these limitations, empirical findings confirm the analytical results that core labor standards do not play a significant role in shaping trade performance. The view which argues that low-standards countries will enjoy gains in export market shares to the detriment of high-standards countries appears to lack solid empirical support. . . . Moreover, the main result that emerges form a cross-country analysis of comparative advantage is that patterns of specialisation are mainly governed by the relative abundance of factors of production and technology differences. . . . These findings also imply that any fear on the part of developing countries that better core standards would negatively affect either their economic performance or their competitive position in world markets has no economic rationale. (p. 38)
>
> *On core labor standards and trade liberalization:*
>
> The empirical results presented for the sample of 44 countries do not provide unambiguous support for one pattern of sequencing over the other as to whether trade liberalisation or freer association rights come first. Rather, the clearest and most reliable finding is in favour of a mutually supportive relationship between successfully sustained trade reforms and improvements in association and bargaining rights. (p. 43)
>
> *On core labor standards and FDI:*
>
> Empirical evidence on the direct relationship between FDI and core labor standards is scarce and remains open to different interpretations. . . . According to reports by MNEs from OECD countries, core labor standards are not considered a factor in assessing investment opportunities in a potential host country. (p. 50)

On trade, employment and wages:

> Typically, analysts find that the impact of trade on employment and wage relativities has been significant in specific sectors. They also find that the measurable negative impact arising through increased import penetration is highest in sectors that employ relatively large numbers of low-skilled workers. Almost all studies find that the impact of trade on employment is small relative to changes in employment overall. (p. 51)

In sum, economic theory and empirical evidence confirm that the case for linking trade with observance of core labor standards is far from persuasive.

V. Multilateral Institutions and Labor Standards

The deceptively appealing notion that lower labor standards in a country relative to its trading partners confer on it an *unfair* competitive advantage was already present in the charter of the International Trade Organization (ITO) negotiated by participant countries at Havana in 1948. Charnovitz (1987, pp. 566-67), in his historical review of labor standards in the world trading regime, notes that Article 7 of the ITO stated that "The members recognize that unfair labor conditions, particularly in the production for export, create difficulties in international trade, and accordingly, each member shall take whatever action may be appropriate and feasible to eliminate such conditions within its territory." The ITO did not come into being primarily because the United States did not ratify its charter. However, the General Agreement on Tariffs (GATT) consisting of tariff reductions and general clauses consisting of a set of rules and obligations which had been negotiated earlier and intended to operate under the umbrella of the ITO, came to be applied through its Protocol of Provisional Application. Except for allowing countries to prohibit trade in goods made with prison labor, the articles of GATT did not deal with labor standards. Various administrations in the United States, Democrat and Republican, have proposed the inclusion of a labor standards article in the GATT, unsuccessfully as it turned out, during several rounds of multilateral trade negotiations. Similar proposals have been made by political parties in national parliaments in several European countries and also in the European Parliament.

The latest proposal is for the formal inclusion of a "social" clause in the mandate of the WTO that would allow restrictions to be placed on imports of products originating in countries not complying with a specified set of minimum standards. Such a proposal in itself is not a surprise except in its timing, namely that it was raised *after* the painful and lengthy negotiations of the Uruguay Round had been completed, almost holding the negotiated agreement hostage. The agreement was signed, but not without an understanding that the topic of labor standards could be discussed by the preparatory committee for the WTO. Of course, the facts that the demand has been raised repeatedly and an understanding to discuss it has been arrived at do not necessarily make it legitimate. Indeed, as was argued in Section III, if ethical considerations were the only factor behind this recent interest in labor standards, there would be no reason for demanding a social clause.

The late Jan Tinbergen, Nobel Laureate in economics, pointed out that in general there must be at least as many instruments of policy as there are objectives and that in achieving any objective that policy instrument which has the most direct impact on that objective is most likely, though not always, to do so at the least social cost. His principle applies as well to the creation of agencies that set the rules governing international economic transactions and the specification of their mandates. Thus the GATT and the United Nations Conference on Trade and Development were created as agencies specializing in issues relating to international trade; the World Bank and the International Monetary Fund were designed to deal respectively with financing long-term development and short-term stabilization. The Universal Postal Union covered postal and other matters of international communication. The Berne and Paris conventions addressed some aspects of intellectual property rights. The International Labour Organization (ILO) deals with labor issues. Clearly such specialization makes eminent sense. Loading one specialized agency with matters that fall within the purview of another, such as including a social clause in the mandate of the WTO rather than leaving labor standards within the purview of the ILO while ensuring consistency of actions of both through mutual consultation where appropriate, is not conducive to addressing them efficiently. Yet, ostensibly because of their presumed relatedness to trade, intellectual property rights and investment measures were included in the Uruguay Round (UR) of multilateral trade negotiations and have become part of the WTO. A committee on Trade and Environment has been constituted in the WTO as envisaged under the UR agreement.

It is becoming clear that the issues of labor standards, environment and employment "will be the big three issues, as will the integration of developing countries into the trading system" at the first Ministerial Meeting in December 1996 of WTO (R. Ruggiero, Director-General of WTO, in an interview, *International Herald Tribune*, July 29, 1996). Even though Australia, Japan and ASEAN nations have already expressed their opposition to the discussion of issues which are not specifically related to trade, such as corruption and social clauses, the Secretary of State of the United States, Mr. Warren Christopher, has gone on record at the July 1996 meeting of ASEAN that the relationship between trade and labor standards would be one of Washington's priorities besides the issue of illicit payments (i.e., corruption) at the Singapore meeting.

It is clear that the issue of labor standards will continue to be brought up in the WTO, particularly by the United States, as it was several times in the past in GATT. But the facts that support for labor standards in developed countries rests in part on genuine moral grounds of the concern of their citizens with the welfare of children in developing countries and that the belief that "unfair" labor conditions, particularly in the production of export, create difficulties in international trade is long standing, do not mean that protectionism is not currently the driving force behind the demand for a "social" clause in the charter of the WTO.

First of all, this demand is being pushed with great vigor by major developed countries at the present time when imports from developing countries are penetrating their markets to an increasing extent. Second, there is a curious asymmetry in the contents of the proposed clause: they focus almost exclusively on those labor standards which are presumed to be "low" in developing countries and not on those equally plausible ones which are absent in many, but not all, developed countries (Bhagwati, 1995). The asymmetry would be unlikely, if the driving force behind the social clause was some universal moral concern with labor standards. For example, along with the workers' right to unionize and bargain collectively, one might also include the right to be represented in the management of firms, if not a right to a share in the firm's profits. To take another example, it is argued that many developing countries do not enforce their own laws such as those relating to compulsory schooling or to labor standards. By the same token many developed countries do not enforce their own laws on drug use as effectively as their resources would allow. Should the resources devoted to law enforcement, given the resource and information constraints, and the difficult choices facing governments as to the allocation of these resources among alternative targets, become matters for *international* negotiations? Can developing countries tell the outgoing U.S. Labor Secretary, Robert Reich, when he laments the lack of funds to bring monitoring of sweatshops up to snuff, that the United States must find the resources or face WTO suspension of market access for exports of goods that are produced in sweatshops?

The timing of the demand for and contents of the proposed clause as well as the concern only with enforcement of a particular set of laws, viz., those relating to labor standards, all point to only one conclusion: that protectionist interests have captured the drive for labor standards.[17] It is extremely essential that developing countries together with Australia, Japan and other like-minded industrialized countries take a firm stand at the Singapore Ministerial Meeting against the inclusion of a discussion of labor standards in the agenda.[18]

Of course, excluding labor standards from the ambit of WTO does not mean the issue is neither important nor relevant for international fora. There is already an international forum for discussing it viz., the ILO. The main reason why the issue is being pushed in the WTO, rather than the ILO, is that while the ILO has no enforcement mechanism for its conventions other than persuasion and technical assistance, in the WTO there is the possibility of the use of trade sanctions as a means of enforcement. Since trade measures are not necessarily the best instruments of enforcement, a far better alternative than including a social clause in the WTO is to seek other ways of ensuring that members of the ILO comply with conventions on labor standards that they sign and ratify. Clearly, with substantial overlap in the membership of the two organizations, even without a social clause in the WTO, if such a future ILO compliance mechanism fails, the members of the ILO in their dual capacity as members of WTO as well, could decide to use trade measures if necessary.

Finally, there is the danger that if the issue of labor standards is not discussed in an appropriate multilateral forum such as the ILO, it will be taken up in other contexts such as bilateral, plurilateral and regional trade agreements.[19] For example, as part of the price to get congressional approval in the United States of the North American Free Trade agreement, Mexico and Canada had to agree to side agreements on labor and environmental standards. Since the start of the Uruguay Round, there was a disturbing and unfortunate increase in the number of discriminatory regional trade agreements concluded, as well as proposed. Contrary to the expectation of some, the successful conclusion of the Round did not stop this trend—on the contrary, there is some evidence of acceleration. Many developing countries are already members or eager to become members of such agreements. This eagerness might lead them to accept side agreements on labor standards that are not necessarily in their interest.

NOTES

I thank Steve Charnovitz, Phil Levy, my discussant Robert Pahre, and the conference participants for their comments. Jagdish Bhagwati's detailed and valuable comments on an earlier draft helped me in clarifying the analytics as well as the political economy of labor standards. Dani Rodrik and Alan Krueger were generous enough to read and respond to my criticisms of their work on labor standards. Of course, neither they, nor any of the others who commented on the paper, are necessarily in agreement with all the views expressed here. Research support of Ford Foundation under Grant 950-1341 to the Economic Growth Center, Yale University is greatly appreciated.

[1] Of course, it should be no surprise that domestic politics, foreign policy, and trade policy interact. As early as a quarter century ago, Richard Cooper (1972) recognized the linkage, at least of the last two, by entitling his article "Trade Policy is Foreign Policy" and publishing it in *Foreign Policy*! The most recent instance is the intense pressure put on Mexico to agree not to sell their tomatoes in the United States (with which it has a Free Trade Agreement) at a price lower than 20.68 cents a pound. David Sanger (*New York Times*, October 12, 1996) quotes a senior official of the Clinton Administration: "This was Mexico's moment to pay back for the bailout" (p. 1) presumably referring to the U.S. decision to lend Mexico $12.5 billion following the peso crisis of December 1994. He quotes another official as saying "The math was pretty simple, Florida has 25 electoral votes, and Mexico doesn't." (p. 9)

[2] Lal (1981, Chapter 3) offers a trenchant critique of human rights arguments in favor of minimum labor standards.

[3] Some of the conventions adopted by the ILO over the years reflect the tenor of the times: a faith in the need for the state to play a very active role in the economy and its ability to fulfill the assigned role efficiently and effectively. Such a faith would seem misplaced in the light of experience.

[4] Negotiating and signing a treaty or convention by a representative of the U.S. executive are the initial steps, and its ratification by the U.S. Senate is the final step in its becoming legally binding on the U.S. government.

[5] I thank Bruce Russet for enlightening me on the history of human rights in the United Nations.

[6] By accepting existing political boundaries, Rawls himself does not make such an extension in his essay on "Law of Peoples" (Rawls 1993b) and is criticized for this failure by Ackerman (1994). In his earlier work, Ackerman (1971, pp. 89-95, 256-57)) argued that while there may be some grounds for restriction on immigration in real-world states, not only such restrictions should be exercised with great care, given the ease with which they may be abused, but also, such restrictions must be accompanied by a massive increase in foreign aid.

[7] It might appear that consumers must have the information needed to distinguish the non-observing firms from observing ones to engage in such behavior. However market forces might themselves generate such information as long as the consumers refuse to buy that product (or *all* products from a country) if they suspect *some* firms (or some *products* from that country) are being produced under unacceptable conditions. In such a case, producers (or countries) who maintain acceptable standards will have an incentive to invest in signalling (in a credible way) to the consumers that they in fact do so and thus distinguish themselves from those that do not.

Michiel Keyzer, in a private conversation, raised a troubling aspect of consumer boycott. Of course boycott of products produced under working conditions that consumers deem unacceptable would seem appropriate. But how should one view boycott of products because they have been produced by particular groups in other countries that consumers in one country deem unacceptable for reasons of racial, ethnic or other prejudices?

[8] Aficionados of common-knowledge repeated game theory will point out that the collectively rational outcome could be sustained as an equilibrium through a suitable punishment strategy for deviation as long as both participants do not discount the future too heavily. Despite the fascination of political scientists for repeated Prisoners' Dilemma games, their relevance for real-life politics is dubious.

[9] Indeed with each country's labor standards entering only its production and utility functions, i.e., with no international spillover effects on other country's production or utility functions, it is hard to rationalize a common minimum standard $\bar{S}$. The case of spillover effects is considered below.

[10] With spillover externalities, a laissez-faire free trade equilibrium is not Pareto Optimal. However with a one-way spillover effect, i.e., labor standards of the small country affect the welfare of the large country and not vice versa, with the unilateral exercise of market power by the large country, even though labor standards of the small country improve over its free trade value, welfare of the small country need not.

[11] It is not very difficult to construct theoretical examples of failures in the labor market and of the possibility of multiple equilibria, where the imposition of labor standards could alleviate the market failure or move the economy to a Pareto superior equilib-

rium. But the issue is not one of theory but of its wide empirical relevance. Establishing the existence of a significant externality *empirically* in a convincing and econometrically sound fashion is more difficult and hence rare, than assertions of such existence. Also, it is not enough to show that mandating of labor standards would address the failure in labor markets. It has to be shown that there are no other more cost-effective means of addressing such failures. If everything else fails, a resourceful economist can always think up an uninternalized "externality" and the resultant market failure!

[12] The description of the activities of UNICOR and the quotations in this paragraph are taken from the transcript of the programme "60 Minutes" broadcast by CBS on October 20, 1996. [Transcript prepared by Burrelle's Information Services, Box 7, Livingstone, N.J.]

[13] Rodrik rationalizes collective preferences over technologies with the argument that individuals "May have preferences not only over outcomes (their "consumption bundles") but over the processes through which these outcomes are generated" (Rodrik 1996, p. 32). For example, an individual may prefer a shirt produced by a worker above the age of 18 to that produced by one below 18. Whether such a preference should be viewed as arising from an altruistic concern over the welfare of children below the age of 18 is arguable. Rodrik refers to Sen (1995) in this context. Sen's discussion of processes or procedures critically examines the distinction between consequentialist and deontological reasoning founded on procedural fairness. Whether procedural fairness is in effect consequentialist because the fairness of a procedure "rests squarely on previous evaluation of its consequences" (Dasgupta 1993, p. 31) or it is not, so that "pure procedural justice obtains when there is no independent criterion for the right result: instead there is a correct or fair procedure such that the procedure has been followed" (Rawls 1972, p. 86), it is hard to see how either view is of any relevance to Rodrik's characterization of individual preferences.

[14] Distinguishing products by the processes by which they are produced can easily lead to the imposition of trade restrictions that are prima facie non-discriminatory but de facto discriminatory. I cannot resist quoting from Haberler's (1936, p. 339) classic work to illustrate this possibility:

"Another reason for the increasing complication of tariff schedules is the effort to evade the Most Favoured National Clause. To this end, the specialisation of tariff items is sometimes carried so far that a slight difference of quality, if it is found only in goods coming from a certain country or countries, is listed as a separate item. In this way it is possible, if desired, to reduce the duty on goods coming from one country without also reducing it--under the provisions of the Most Favoured Nation Clause--upon similar goods from other countries. The example of this always quoted is a provision in the German tariff, dating from 1902 and still valid, which is clearly meant to apply to Switzerland and Austria, relating to 'brown or dappled cows reared at a level of at least 300 metres above the sea and passing at least one month in every summer at a height of at least 800 metres'."

[15] Whether or not Krueger's econometric estimates are biased for these reasons depends on the theoretical framework underlying the estimating equation. For example, consider a two-stage decision making by a representative. At the first stage the representative decides whether he would vote for any legislation that might come up mandating international labor standards. If he decides he would not vote, there is no second stage. If he

decides that he would vote, then there is a second stage decision whether he would be proactive and cosponsor such legislation or not. Under some specifications of explanatory variables and distribution of error terms for each decision, a bias could arise in the estimates.

Also under certain circumstances even politicians who ignore worker's interests might still vote for import restriction. For example, consider a specific factors model in which the capital in industries competing with imports of products from countries with low labor standards is specific to those industries and suppose a proportion (but not all) of the unskilled labor force is employed in those industries as well. Intensification of import competition in these industries will affect the interests of owners of specific factors adversely, while its effect on the welfare of unskilled labor is ambiguous. Suppose it is adverse. Then even politicians who ignore interests of labor would support import restriction in this case since it protects the interests capital specific to these industries.

[16] It is argued by some that it is extremely unlikely that union members stand to gain from a ban on imports of goods made with child labor because almost all union members do not compete with child labor. However, there is a slippery-slope argument on the other side. If the unions did not take a stand on one labor issue, viz. ban on imports of goods made with child labor, albeit one in which their members may not have a direct interest, their credibility and clout could be weakened on other issues in which their members have a direct interest.

[17] Robert Pahre, in his comment that follows, presents an example of a complete information game in which, but for the support of protectionists, the threat of trade sanctions is not credible. With such support and hence credibility of the threat, the country being threatened capitulates and improves its human rights record without the threatening country having to impose the sanctions. While this example highlights the role of credibility, the fact that credibility is achieved with the support of protectionists is incidental and not essential. The essential point is that credibility, however achieved, serves to ensure that the threatened country capitulates without sanctions having to be imposed.

[18] It is extremely heartening to note that at the Singapore meeting, the ministers, in their draft declaration, have wisely decided to "renew their commitment to core labor standards but say the International Labour Organisation is the competent body to set these standards. They affirm support for the ILO's work, reject the use of labor standards for protectionist purposes and say the comparative advantage of low-wage countries 'must in no way be put in question'" (*Financial Times*, December 13, 1996, p. 8).

[19] I should also mention here some unilateral actions. GATT allows developed countries to offer preferential access to their markets to developing countries under the Generalized System of Preferences (GSP). The United States and EU have conditioned the grant of such preferences to the observance by developing countries of particular labor standards that the United States and European Union (EU) deem important. I should add, however, that whether or not its grant is conditional, GSP is the analogue of "crumbs from the rich man's table" which the developing countries should do well without.

REFERENCES

Ackerman, B. 1994. "Political Liberalisms," *The Journal of Philosophy* 91:364-86.

Ackerman, B. 1971. *Social Justice in the Liberal State.* Cambridge: Harvard University Press.

Anderson, Kym. 1996. "Environmental and Labor Standards: What Role for the World Trade Organization?," paper presented at the Conference on Institutional Aspects of the World Trade Organization's Effectiveness, Stanford University, September 26-28.

Basu, D.C. 1983. *Introduction to the Constitution of India*, 10th edition. New Delhi: Prentice Hall.

Bhagwati, J. 1995. "Trade Liberalisation and 'Fair Trade' Demands," *The World Economy* 18: 745-59.

Brown, Drusilla, Alan Deardorff and Robert Stern. 1996. "International Labor Standards and Trade: A Theoretical Analysis," in Jagdish Bhagwati and Robert Hudec (eds.), *Harmonization and Fair Trade*, Volume 1. Cambridge: MIT Press.

Council of Economic Advisers (CEA). 1995. *Economic Report of the President.* Washington, D.C.: Council of Economic Advisers.

Charnovitz, Steve. 1995. "Promoting Higher Labor Standards," *The Washington Quarterly* 18: 167-90.

Cooper, Richard. 1972. "Trade Policy is Foreign Policy," *Foreign Policy*, No. 9:18-36.

Dasgupta, Partha. 1993. *An Inquiry into Well-Being and Destitution.* Oxford: Clarendon Press.

Haberler, Gottfried V. 1936. *Theory of International Trade.* Glasgow: William Hodge & Company, Limited.

Krueger, Alan. 1997. "Labor Standards and International Trade," *Annual Bank Conference on Development Economics, 1996.* Washington, D.C.: World Bank.

Lal, Deepak. 1981. *Resurrection of the Pauper-labour Argument*, Thames Essay No. 28. London: Trade Policy Research Centre.

Maier, Heribert. 1994. "The Perspective of the International Labor Organization," *International Labor Standards and Global Economic Integration: Proceedings of a Symposium.* Washington, D.C.: Bureau of International Labor Affairs, U.S. Department of Labor.

Negishi, T. 1960. "Welfare Economics and the Existence of an Equilibrium of a Competitive Economy," *Metroeconomica*, 12:92-97.

OECD. 1996. *Trade, Employment and Labor Standards, A Study of Core Workers' Rights and International Trade.* Paris: Organization for Economic Cooperation and Development.

Rawls, John. 1993a. *Political Liberalism.* New York: Columbia University Press.

Rawls, John. 1993b. "Law of Peoples" in S. Shuto and S. Hurley (eds.), *On Human Rights.* New York: Basic Books.

Rawls, John. 1972. *A Theory of Justice.* Oxford: Oxford University Press.

Rodrik, Dani. 1996. "Labor Standards in International Trade: Do They Matter and What Do We Do About Them?" in Robert Lawrence, Dani Rodrik, and John Whalley, *Emerging Agenda for Global Trade: High Stakes for Developing Countries.* Washington, D.C.: Overseas Development Council.

Sen, Amartya K. 1995. "Rationality and Social Choice," *American Economic Review* 85:1-25.

Srinivasan, T.N. 1996. "International Trade and Labour Standards, in Pitou van Dijck and Gerrit Faber (eds.), *Challenges to the New World Trade Organization.* Amsterdam: Kluwer Law International.

Stern, Robert. 1997. "Issues of Trade and International Labor Standards in the WTO System," in *The Emerging WTO System and Perspectives from East Asia*, Joint U.S.-Korea Academioc Studies, Vol. 7. Washington, D.C.: Korea Economic Institute of America.

World Bank. 1995. *World Development Report.* New York: Oxford University Press.

Comments on Conference Version of Paper

Robert Pahre

Labor Standards, Trade Sanctions, and the Hijacking Hypothesis

I. Introduction

Srinivasan has given us an ambitious and thought-provoking paper on "Trade and Human Rights." In it, he first examines whether the international community shares a moral consensus on labor standards. After this, he develops a normative model of labor standards and trade, followed by a discussion of some issues relating to the political economy of labor standards and trade policy.[1]

Because the core of his argument is normative, Srinivasan gives political economy problems only secondary attention. However, the political economy of trade sanctions provides an important motivation for Srinivasan's normative analysis and cannot be ignored. He worries that normative justifications for sanctions might be "hijacked" by protectionists who are driven not by national welfare considerations but by economic self interest. In contrast, a political economy perspective raises the possibility that some sanctions are more easily hijacked than others, and this may change the normative analysis. Such political economy concerns are the primary focus of my comments.

To examine both the normative and political economy problems, it is helpful to recognize two different kinds of trade intervention in the labor standards area. The first of these are "compensatory" labor standards, by which a government uses tariffs as permanent compensation for "unfair" standards abroad. A parallel from outside the labor standards issue is the antidumping/countervailing duty (AD/CVD) provisions of U.S. trade law. In contemporary political rhetoric, compensatory sanctions help prevent a "race-to-the-bottom" by which high-standards countries are forced to lower their standards to compete with low-standards imports.

The other kind of intervention is "coercive," designed to achieve its goals by the *threat* of trade sanctions. A good parallel from elsewhere in United States trade policy is the Section 301 provision that seeks to open "unfairly" closed foreign markets by the threat of retaliatory tariffs. The central issue concerning coercive sanctions is not their economic implications when imposed; indeed, when a state applies coercive sanctions it has failed its purpose (at least temporarily). Instead, the major problem is the credibility of the threat.[2] If the threat succeeds in changing the target's behavior, then this policy is costless and effective—making this policy preferable to any of those that Srinivasan criticizes.

II. The Universality of Labor Standards

Srinivasan argues that the international community generally lacks any agreement about which labor standards represent fundamental rights worth protecting. He is undoubtedly right for most labor standards. However, such an argument fails to consider the possibility that our definition of which constitutes a "right" generally changes over time. To take an obvious example, most of the world saw slavery as morally permissible through the nineteenth century. Some currently-contested rights that Srinivasan discusses will doubtless end up being a part of some future moral consensus, while others will not. It would be unwise to dismiss any claim of a fundamental right merely because it does not enjoy a present consensus behind it.[3]

As further evidence for the lack of a moral consensus, Srinivasan makes much of the fact that the United States has not signed many International Labor Organization (ILO) conventions on labor rights. However, this may be irrelevant for the problem of a moral consensus. International conventions can play an important focal role even if they are never ratified; a good example is the SALT II treaty limiting strategic weapons, which the Reagan administration observed although it refused to submit it for ratification. Similarly, the United States observes many ILO conventions, such as those on freedom of association, the right to organize, and child labor, among others.[4]

These questions of a moral consensus are especially important for Srinivasan's political economy. He fears that protectionists will hijack any poorly-defined right, who will then cloak their self-interest in the altruistic rhetoric of fundamental rights.

Hijacking aside, having a moral consensus might also affect the credibility of coercive sanctions. When, as in the case of South African *apartheid*, the international community shares a moral consensus, sanctions are more likely to change the target's behavior. Uncertainty about whether there exists a moral consensus also plays an important role in the political economy of sanctions, since it affects players' beliefs about the votes to be gained from human rights activists.

Evaluating these problems requires closer attention to the political economy of sanctions. In particular, we need to know under what conditions protectionists will choose to make a labor standards claim when other claims (such as AD/CVD) may be available. We also need to know under what circumstances the political decision makers will find these moral claims persuasive. I will address some of these questions below.

III. The Welfare Analysis of Labor Standards

Having explored the lack of a moral consensus on labor standards we observe, Srinivasan then turns to examine whether trade policy is the best policy tool available for addressing altruistic concerns about foreign labor standards. Answering these questions is the analytic meat of his paper, which focuses solely on what I have labeled compensatory sanctions.

Srinivasan makes a strong argument that immigration policy and international transfers are better policy instruments than trade policy in an undistorted general equilibrium setting. His claims here are compelling. These policy mechanisms also avoid the risk that political demands for sanctions will be hijacked by protectionists, an issue I discuss in detail in the next section.

One recurring question in the literature has been why observed labor standards vary across countries, and whether differences reflect "unfair" competition for high-standards countries. To answer this question, Srinivasan also shows that we can think of labor standards as endogenous. When we do so, we should expect diverse standards across countries depending on their factor endowments. This finding nicely undercuts the claim that foreign competitiveness is *caused* by low labor standards, since Srinivasan can show how competitiveness might be correlated with low standards without any causal mechanism connecting the two. He also proves that we can have endogenous labor standards equilibria with free trade. Even if an international organization sets some minimum standards that all countries must meet, an equilibrium characterized by free trade will generally exist, though it may also require international transfers.

A natural way to extend Srinivasan's analysis here would be to consider the possibility that different sectors could have different levels of labor standards, even within the same country. In the United States, for instance, many laws on working hours and conditions do not apply to the agricultural sector. A Srinivasan-type model might find a social welfare justification for these differences, though a political economy model would probably present a more natural explanation.

Despite the analytic force of his argument, Srinivasan does not address several important implementation problems. For instance, those workers whose rights are being violated are likely to be the persons who would find it most difficult to meet the cost of international migration. International transfers are also problematic, since they must be carried out by governments for whom national security or political economy concerns will generally dominate social welfare considerations. As a result, such transfers will likely not be directed in the socially optimal way that Srinivasan assumes.[5] These political economy concerns also affect the political rationality of sanctions, to which I now turn.

IV. The "Hijacking Hypothesis"

As I have mentioned above, Srinivasan is concerned throughout the paper that protectionists might hijack altruistically-motivated attempts at sanctions in the labor standards area. He argues that the lack of moral consensus on labor standards makes this issue particularly amenable to hijacking. Moreover, the main regime in this area, the ILO, lacks enforcement mechanisms. This lack of alternatives makes the World Trade Organization (WTO) and its mechanisms for possible trade sanctions attractive to those whose true goal is protectionist.

This hijacking hypothesis does a lot of work in the paper. Srinivasan sometimes rejects plausible arguments about trade policy as a second-best tool because he fears that even potentially valid tools are subject to hijacking. Similarly, Srinivasan dismisses Rodrik's (1996) argument that governments frequently regulate technologies of production, because Srinivasan fears that such claims are too open to hijacking.

Because of its role in the paper, an empirical evaluation of this hypothesis would be useful. Srinivasan's chapter presents some circumstantial evidence for the hijacking hypothesis. For instance, he notes that the demands for a "social clause" in the WTO were raised only after the Uruguay round negotiations were completed. As a result, these demands had the potential to hold the entire agreement hostage. This was presumably the purpose in raising them. These demands are also selective in a suspect way, focusing on those standards that are "low" in developing countries but "high" in developed countries. As this suggests, these demands often entail substantial hypocrisy, in that many labor rights are not fully observed in OECD countries.

Reasonable as all that sounds, some recent empirical work should make us skeptical of Srinivasan's claims. In a quantitative study of congressional voting on a labor standards issue, Krueger (1997) shows that members of Congress representing unskilled workers are less likely to support a ban on imports of goods made with child labor. This finding suggests that a desire to protect American workers against cheap foreign labor did not motivate the legislation. Rodrik (1996) also presents quantitative evidence that the political economy of the race-to-the-bottom logic only weakly explains trade patterns; it explains foreign investment patterns not at all.[6]

In short, evidence for the hijacking hypothesis is mostly lacking. This finding is probably more surprising than it should be. From the rent-seeker perspective, labor standards are a poor tool for redistributing income. The hijacking hypothesis assumes not only that direct transfers to rent-seekers are unavailable, but that openly protective tariffs are also less attractive than tariffs disguised as compensatory sanctions. As a result, hijacking probably plays only a minor role in the incidence of compensatory sanctions.

The Political Economy of Hijacking

Hijacking is more important for coercive sanctions. This is especially true when we move beyond the protectionist's point of view to examine the policy maker's decision calculus. To do this, I will look at the case of coercive sanctions, ultimately pointing toward a costly signaling game in which players are uncertain about the domestic political calculus in the sanctioning country. Once we understand the policy-maker's decision calculus, we will also better understand what might make sanctions attractive to rent-seekers. Surprisingly, the analysis will also show how being hijacked by protectionists can even be attractive to human rights activists.

To analyze the problem, assume that some political economy tariff equilibrium exists. When a labor standards issue appears on the political agenda, the policy maker faces a situation similar to that outlined in table 12.1. Because we start at an equilibrium, any move toward protection will gain fewer votes from protectionists than it will lose among consumers and exporting firms. However, if the potential sanction also addresses a human rights issue, the policy-maker will gain votes from human rights activists.

In such a case, threatening sanctions will be politically credible only if human rights issues are at stake. Because the threat is credible, the target will back down rather than suffer the imposition of sanctions.[7] With complete information, we will never observe sanctions, yet coercion in the face of potential sanctions will be common.

Several points are worth noting. First, the hijacking hypothesis is correct in cases such as table 12.1: protectionists may frame issues so that human rights activists will also be mobilized. However, the size of the human rights lobby determines whether hijacking is attractive. If the human rights lobby is small, the protectionists cannot hijack many votes. When this happens, protectionists will use other means to obtain protection, such as bringing an AD/CVD case. On the other hand, if the human rights lobby is sufficiently large, the lobby may itself prefer the first-best instruments such as international transfers that Srinivasan's

TABLE 12.1. How Hijacking Helps: A Numerical Example

Political calculus in United States, if it imposes sanction against a recalcitrant target:

70,000 votes lost from consumers, etc.
50,000 votes gained from protectionists
30,000 votes gained from human rights activists

Political calculus in target, if United States imposes sanctions:

20,000 votes lost among exporters

Complete information, using a trade policy instrument

1. The United States makes a threat
2. The target believes the threat
3. The target ends human rights violations
4. The United States does not impose sanctions

Complete information, using non-trade policy costing 70,000 votes (free immigration?)

1. The United States does not make a threat
2. The target continues human rights violations
3. The United States does not impose sanctions

normative analysis recommends.[8] In this case, human rights lobbyists will see no need to include protectionists in their coalition. Here, too, protectionists will not hijack the human rights lobby and must use other means to obtain protection.

Second, the government will be better off if labor standards issues are couched in protectionist terms. Policy makers can artificially strengthen a policy of coercive sanctions by bringing protectionists into the coalition. Because successful threats are costless (with complete information), they are a cheaper instrument than the first-best instruments that Srinivasan recommends.

For similar reasons, human rights activists can gain from having their issue hijacked. Table 12.1 also illustrates the case when the human rights lobby chooses a first-best instrument such as free immigration. When the lobby falls into the mid-sized range illustrated in the figure, the activists alone are not sufficiently powerful to make free immigration politically rational. Having protectionists hijack a trade sanction threat makes a human rights policy politically feasible.

The Hijacking Hypothesis with Uncertainty

The situation is somewhat different with incomplete information. For simplicity, I will suppose that the only source of incomplete information is the strength of the human rights lobby. This is a good way to analyze Srinivasan's claim that the lack of a moral consensus makes the labor standards issue subject to hijacking by protectionist interests. This lack of consensus makes it uncertain how many human rights voters will mobilize in a given case.

Being uncertain of the domestic political costs and benefits of sanctions poses a problem for the government, just as uncertainty about domestic political costs affects the likelihood of war (see Bueno de Mesquita and Lalman 1992; Fearon 1997; Papayoanou 1997). These models of war suggest that an analogous model of coercive sanctions with domestic political costs would yield the following kinds of results. First, the credibility of a threat should monotonically increase in the strength of a protectionist lobby. In other words, sufficiently strong protectionists can hijack sanctions in a way that improves the credibility of the policy maker's threat. Second, the credibility of a threat should also monotonically increase in the political strength of human rights activists. This means that for a sufficiently strong human rights lobby, hijacking is irrelevant; policy makers will choose another instrument instead. Both results are intuitively reasonable, and follow the logic of the complete information case.

Another likely result is more surprising. In such signaling models, those actors who gain from making threats are more likely to use costly instruments to signal their resolve, and to distinguish themselves from those unwilling to use costly threats. As a result, it may be true that using "worse" economic policies, such as those with larger deadweight losses, should increase the credibility of the threat. Only governments with a large human rights lobby will use such bad policies as a threat, so the choice of this instrument signals the existence of a strong domestic lobby.

This analysis provides a possible positive theory of why states choose the second-best policies that Srinivasan criticizes on normative grounds. If these threats succeed in forcing the target to change its policy, then again the policy is both costless and effective. Credibly threatening bad policies can effectively improve foreign countries' observation of labor standards. This a feature of coercive sanctions that challenges some of Srinivasan's analysis of compensatory sanctions.

Similar reasoning suggests that constraining governments to "small" threats or to "first-best" policy tools reduces the credibility of threats. In such cases, a highly committed government cannot make a sufficiently costly threat to distinguish itself from bluffers. This is apparently a common problem, as many targets believe that threatened sanctions are really bluffs. Having an international regime that restricts sanctions in this way may lead to more frequent incredible threats; international rules that allow these sanctions will, in contrast, enable governments to separate themselves into credible and incredible threateners. While this would not reduce the incidence of threatened sanctions, it should make the actual imposition of sanctions less likely by making the threats more credible.

Having considered the problem for policy makers, we can now return to the problem faced by would-be hijackers. When the domestic polity lacks a moral consensus on labor standards, it is unclear how many human rights activists might be mobilized behind a particular coercive sanction. From the protectionist standpoint, this situation poses the choice between a venue in which the support for protectionism is certain or a venue in which human rights activists may provide an uncertain level of support. To some degree, the choice of venue will rest on protectionists' risk-aversion and the riskiness of other possible uses of a protectionist lobby's energy (see Austen-Smith 1981 for a general analysis of uncertainty in rent-seeking). Risk-averse protectionists will probably avoid issue areas lacking a moral consensus, since they are uncertain how many human rights activists will support a given claim. This uncertainty also makes such claims unattractive to risk-averse policy-makers, who will prefer to be certain of the political support they can obtain from human rights activists.

In short, the hijacking hypothesis is not as clear-cut as Srinivasan would have it. As a result, the hypothesis poses an attractive problem for future research in this area. Other areas of international economics have seen a progression from such normative theories to an explicitly political economy approach (see Deardorff and Stern above). This would also be fruitful direction for the literature on labor standards as well.

NOTES

[1]Srinivasan chooses to examine labor standards because he believes that they are a good proxy for human rights problems in general. This is probably too ambitious a claim. Labor standards, and perhaps many other rights, affect the production functions of an economy in a way similar to his model. At the same time, many other human rights do not affect

production functions. It is not clear to me that freedom of speech or voting rights have any direct effects on production functions.

[2]Agreeing to refrain from sanctions presents a similar but not identical problem. Schelling's (1960) classic analysis of compellence and deterrence provides a good starting point for thinking about these issues.

[3]In any case, there is a lot of agreement on many standards: slave labor, prison labor, and sweatshops are three examples. These standards may not be observed, but their violation gives rise to a claim by those whose rights are violated.

[4]Politics aside, there are serious constitutional issues that make ratification of international conventions different in the United States than in many other countries. Of course, these constitutional issues may be "hijacked" by protectionists, in which case my comments later in this paper apply.

[5]Another way for altruists to influence foreign labor standards is a consumer boycott, though this requires that someone supply the public good of information about labor standards violators.

[6]Srinivasan offers several criticisms of both authors' claims, which are subject to any number of measurement problems, but he never offers any evidence of his own in support of the hijacking hypothesis. For the time being, then, Krueger's and Rodrik's studies present the best systematic evidence that we have.

[7]I have constructed the political calculus in the target so as to obtain this result, but presumably the sanctioner will choose a sanction large enough to make the target back down.

[8]Alternatively, the sanctioner may impose sanctions that are politically popular but which will not change the target's behavior. American sanctions against Cuba are a good example.

REFERENCES

Austen-Smith, David. 1981. "Voluntary Pressure Groups," *Economica* 48:143-153.

Bueno de Mesquita, Bruce and David Lalman. 1992. *War and Reason: Domestic and International Imperatives*. New Haven: Yale University Press.

Fearon, James D. 1997. "Signaling Foreign Policy Interests: Tying Hands Versus Sinking Costs," *Journal of Conflict Resolution* 41:68-90.

Krueger, Alan. 1997. "Labor Standards and International Trade," *Annual World Bank Conference on Development Economics 1996*. Washington, D.C.: World Bank.

Papayoanou, Paul A. 1997. "Intraalliance Bargaining and U.S. Bosnia Policy," *Journal of Conflict Resolution* 41:91-116.

Rodrik, Dani. 1996. "Labor Standards in International Trade: Do They Matter and What Do We Do About Them?" in Robert Lawrence, Dani Rodrik, and John Whalley, *Emerging Agenda for Global Trade: High Stakes for Developing Countries*. Washington, D.C.: Overseas Development Council.

Schelling, Thomas C. 1960. *The Strategy of Conflict*. Cambridge: Harvard University Press.

CHAPTER 13

Trade Law and Trade Policy: The Advocate's Perspective

Richard O. Cunningham

I. Introduction

In most of the literature on trade policy, the principal focus is on major trade matters—import relief cases in particular, but also market access cases and various types of bilateral and multilateral negotiations. Typically, the author will characterize the outcome of each such matter as a trade policy decision and will, in effect, see an administration's "trade policy" as being revealed by those determinations. In general, since most commentators have what they conceive to be a free-trade perspective, the basic thrust of the author's inquiry will be to determine the extent to which the decisions in such cases or matters result in trade restrictions and why such derogations from free trade occur. In that type of analysis, many commentators come to the conclusion that the major explanation for U.S. decisions to restrict trade flows is the political influence of such industries as steel, textiles and semiconductors.

From the perspective of the international trade law practitioner, the world is very different. In the import relief area, the vast majority of U.S. restrictions on trade flows have nothing whatsoever to do with the political influence of the petitioning U.S. industry. Rather, import restrictions flow in a largely nondiscretionary manner from a long-established U.S. (and multilateral) trade policy that defines price discrimination, sales below cost and subsidization as unfair practices against which import restrictions are the appropriate remedy. Only in a few of the nondiscretionary cases, and in the even fewer cases that arise under discretionary import relief statutes, is the political might of the petitioning industry at all relevant. And even in those cases, domestic political pressure by the petitioning industry is rarely the decisive factor.

Similarly, in cases involving market access, protection of intellectual property rights and other issues dealing with conditions in foreign markets, the U.S. industry's political force is necessarily a factor of secondary importance. From the trade lawyer's perspective, such matters involve an extremely complex interplay of forces and strategies—necessarily complex because of one fundamental fact: unlike cases of import relief, the United States cannot unilaterally dictate the outcome of cases involving practices encountered in foreign markets. Where U.S. import restrictions are imposed in such cases, it is this factor—not simply the political influence of the domestic industry—that is likely to be the major cause.

The trade lawyer, one must remember, is an advocate and does not purport to be a policymaker. The advocacy task is to achieve for the client a specific economic objective. Among those objectives are:

- The protection of a U.S. industry from the effects of unfair—dumped, subsidized or intellectual property infringing—imports.
- Obtaining temporary shelter from import competition in order to enable a U.S. industry to regain competitiveness by cost reduction, introduction of new products and the like.
- Elimination or reduction of foreign government subsidies.
- Removal or reduction of a foreign government's barriers to imports (and, under the new World Trade Organization agreements, barriers to investment).
- Obtaining improved protection of a U.S. firm's intellectual property rights in a foreign country.

It will be noted that the foregoing list of objectives does not include, contrary to what one would expect from reading much of the academic and political literature, such goals as limiting imports' role in a U.S. market or gaining for U.S. firms a greater market share in a foreign country. This is because neither trade law nor trade policy recognizes those objectives except in very rare, aberrational cases. Rather, both trade law and trade policy—today and at least since the author began international trade law practice in 1969—operate under a sort of Universal Principle that trade flows should not be artificially restricted or distorted. Thus almost all types of trade cases have as their gravamen the elimination of or counteraction against a practice defined as unfair under U.S. and/or international law.

In summary, the perspective of the trade lawyer focuses on the legal gravamen and legal/political/diplomatic strategies of trade issues. For this author, at least, that perspective leads to conclusions quite different from those of an economist or political scientist, whose analysis focuses on and draws conclusions from the outcome of the case.

This paper will explore three categories of trade cases from the perspective of the trade lawyer/advocate.

- nondiscretionary import relief proceedings under the antidumping and countervailing duty laws,[1]
- discretionary import relief cases under the escape clause, the market disruption statute and the national security amendment, and
- discretionary cases involving unfair practices in markets outside the United States.

In each category, specific examples will be analyzed to illustrate the dynamics of decision-making in each type of case.

II. Nondiscretionary Import Relief Cases

It is important to understand at the outset that the historic function of the U.S. antidumping[2] and countervailing duty laws[3] was not to redress or prevent injury to U.S. producers. Rather, both laws were originally enacted to counteract a specific type of unfair practice, *regardless of whether or not injury was caused to a U.S. industry* by the dumped or subsidized imports. Until 1979, countervailing duties could be imposed without any determination of injury to the petitioning U.S. industry.[4] And while the Antidumping Act of 1921 required a determination of injury, the law's legislative history demonstrates that this requirement was intended only to weed out cases in which the imports were inconsequential.[5]

The absence of injury requirements in the original antidumping and countervailing duty laws illustrates a fundamental, but often ignored, underpinning of U.S. trade law and policy. Certain practices are viewed as being unfair, and thus justifying measures to offset the unfairness, simply because they are wrong. The unfairness does not, in this view, depend on adverse effects on U.S. producers. Rather, the practice in question is seen as inherently distortive of the competitive position of the foreign exporter vis-à-vis the U. S. industry.[6] Although the international trading community has forced application of a material injury standard in both the U.S. countervailing duty and antidumping laws, the underlying objective of offsetting unfairness rather than preventing injury remains clear in the fact that the amount of duty assessed is measured by the amount of dumping or subsidy, not by the amount necessary to eliminate injurious effect.

It is thus true, in a sense, that decisions under these laws represent implementation of a "trade policy." That policy, however, does not grow out of the cases. Rather, the policy is inherent in the concept underlying the statutes. To criticize implementation of these laws as "protectionist" or "contrary to free trade" is therefore to take issue with the underlying proposition—a proposition that underlies the GATT/WTO Agreements on these issues as well as U.S. law—that dumping and subsidies are unfair practices that should be offset by duties equal to the per-unit amount of the dumping or subsidization.

To the extent that individual case decisions turn on interpretations—by the Department of Commerce or the International Trade Commission—of particular issues under these statutes, it may be argued either that such an interpretation constitutes an exercise of trade policy or that the overall trend of such interpretations evidences a more or less "protectionist" policy. In assessing such arguments, the following points should be considered:

First, the vast majority of antidumping and countervailing duty cases are brought by industries that could not conceivably bring significant political pressure to bear on the outcome of a proceeding. While cases involving steel products, semi-conductors and automobiles get the headlines, the typical petitioners are manufacturers of such products as canned clams[7] or birch three-ply doorskins.[8] To view decisions in these cases as politically motivated or as exercises in Administration trade policy is simply silly. These—the great majority of cases—are simply decided one way or the other on the statutory merits.

Second, the International Trade Commission was created to be a non-political independent commission, precisely for the purpose of avoiding any danger that its determinations would become subservient to the policies of the incumbent Administration. To this end, the law requires that no more than three of the six Commissioners be a member of one of the two major political parties.[9] Thus, to the extent that the Commission may in some periods be seen as more protectionist than in other periods, this reflects the economic and legal views of the majority of Commissioners, not any policy dictates of the incumbent Administration. An Administration that desired either more or less protectionist decisions by the Commission could achieve this only to the extent that it could appoint new and more (or less) protectionist Commissioners.[10]

Third, there exists in the Department of Commerce a Congressionally-intended predisposition to "vigorous enforcement" of the antidumping and countervailing duty laws. Indeed, the administration of the two statutes was transferred from the Treasury Department to the Commerce Department in the Trade Agreements Act of 1979 primarily because Congress viewed Treasury's administration of the law as insufficiently responsive to legitimate needs of U.S. industries for action against dumping and subsidies. That history, coupled with continued Congressional oversight and an institutional self-identification of the Department as spokesman within the Administration for the interests of American business, combine to give the Department's International Trade Administration some degree of bias toward tough enforcement. This "toughness" is particularly evident in three areas:

- *Procedural Toughness.* Commerce Department investigations, especially under the antidumping law, require the accused foreign exporter to respond within quite short time limits to massively detailed questionnaires. Many foreign respondents, especially smaller companies, find it difficult or impossible to provide such a mass of information on a timely basis, especially with Commerce often taking the position that financial and cost data must be furnished on a basis that differs from the company's normal business accounting. When the response is not complete or found to be inaccurate or in improper form, the Department often bases its determination on the "facts available," normally obtained in substantial part from the petitioner and thus yielding draconian dumping margins.[11]
- *Burden of Proof.* As a general matter, an antidumping investigation is just that: an investigation, not an adversary proceeding, with no "burden of proof" on any party. In one important area, however, the Department explicitly places the burden of proof on the foreign exporter. In many investigations, comparison of the raw prices of the U.S. and home market sales (each worked back to the point of shipment) would yield a significant "dumping margin," but the exporter argues

that "adjustments" to those prices should be made for differences in quantities, merchandise specifications, level of trade, selling expenses, credit terms, etc. On all such "adjustment" issues, which are often the difference between winning and losing for the foreign exporter, Commerce places the burden of proof on the party claiming the adjustment (almost always the foreign respondent) to establish the adjustment to the Department's satisfaction.

- *Appeal Tactics.* One of the Department's great tactical advantages is its ability to wear out in the court process any respondent (or petitioner, in fairness) that has the temerity to challenge an antidumping or countervailing duty determination in an appeal. Such appeals rarely result in the first instance in a decisive reversal of the Department's determination. Rather, a remand to the Department will result in a partial (but not complete) change in the Department's computations or even in an essentially unchanged determination with an altered rationale.[12] Then, if the appellant continues to litigate and achieves a dispositive resolution by the Court of International Trade, the Department will normally appeal to the Court of Appeals for the Federal Circuit and, pending disposition of that appeal, refuse to honor the order of the Court of International Trade on the ground that the appellate process has not reached a final judgment. This process can be, and often is, strung out for many years. All the while, the appellant must continue to put up cash deposits for the dumping on countervail margins found in the very decision it is contesting on appeal. Most foreign companies give up the ghost before reaching the final judgment that they may have a very real chance of winning.

The sense of all of the foregoing is that decisions under the antidumping and countervailing duty laws, while reflecting a general, continuing policy of tough enforcement, do not constitute trade policy decisions as to individual cases and are not in general the product of political influence by the petitioning U.S. industry. There are, however, exceptions—cases resolved by a trade policy decision (or something very like it) and influenced in that decision by political and/or diplomatic forces. Such exceptions occur primarily in two circumstances, as follows.

Novel Issues

With some frequency in countervailing duty proceedings and occasionally in antidumping cases, the Department will find that the case turns in whole or in part on an issue as to which there is no clearly dispositive precedent. In most such cases, the Department will resolve such issues by the normal processes of statutory and precedential reasoning, augmented by economic analysis. However, where a determined and politically adept U.S. industry (or respondent government) is involved in such a case, the Department may come to view the issue as a policy judgment. Such cases become interesting indeed. Two countervailing duty examples—privatization and natural resource pricing—will illustrate this phenomenon.

The effect of privatization on the continued countervailability of prior capital subsidies has in recent years become an issue of paramount importance because of its centrality in the 1992-93 steel cases. The subsidies in several of those cases consisted of very large amounts of government funding given (or provided on non-commercial terms) in the 1970s and 1980s to government-owned companies that were incurring large operating losses year after year. The Department found those capital infusions to be countervailable subsidies. Rather than countervailing the infusions entirely in the year of receipt, the Department reasoned that the subsidies conferred benefits over subsequent years and determined that the subsidies should be allocated over a period determined by the useful life of the recipient's depreciable assets (15 years in the case of steel producers). However, the Department also had to consider the fact that some of the subsidy-recipient companies were later privatized in whole or in part after receipt of the subsidies but before the end of the period of countervailability. The privatized entities argued that, since their new owners had paid full market value for all of their assets—including whatever portion represented the remaining benefits of the earlier capital subsidies—the operations after privatization derived no benefit from those past subsidies and should not be countervailed.

Initially, the Department accepted the privatized respondents' argument, ruling in the first preliminary determination that a purchaser of a division of a subsidized company did not benefit from the seller company's past subsidies where the purchaser paid market value for that division.[13] The domestic steel industry, however, launched a major campaign to reverse that preliminary determination, augmenting their arguments to Commerce with efforts in Congress to amend the statute. While the Congressional initiative produced only an ambiguous statutory amendment,[14] the industry won a complete victory on this issue in Commerce's final determinations.

- In the case involving sale of a subsidized company's division, Commerce determined (essentially without explanation) that where a productive unit of a subsidized company is sold, a portion of the seller company's subsidies "travel with the productive unit to its new home" even if market value is paid by the purchasing company.[15]
- With respect to the full privatization of a subsidized government-owned company, the Department determined initially that such privatization—whether or not for market value—did not affect continued countervailability of the past subsidies.[16] In reaching this conclusion, it reasoned that continuation (or not) of subsidy benefits was not the issue. Indeed, the Department opined that it is irrelevant whether a subsidy confers a benefit on the recipient's production, either at the time of receipt or in later years.[17] Later, under pressure from an adverse but somewhat ambiguous GATT panel decision, the

Department modified its determination by establishing a formula purporting to determine that some portion of the price paid in privatization constituted partial "repayment" of the past subsidies.

The Department's privatization decisions are now on appeal. The initial Court of International Trade determination reversed Commerce's "subsidies travel with a productive unit to its new home" decision,[18] but that decision was in turn reversed by the Federal Circuit Court of Appeals.[19] In the most recent remand determination, however, Commerce has concluded that the Courts' rulings require a determination of no countervailability against the purchaser where a subsidized company sells one of its divisions.[20] The cases involving full privatization have also been appealed. In an initial, somewhat opaque decision, the Court of International Trade appears to have concluded that full privatization for market value through a sale of assets eliminates subsidization, but that a share sale privatization does not affect continued countervailability.[21] Both Commerce and the respondent exporters have appealed to the Federal Circuit. Thus, while the decision-making process on these issues has clearly been altered by the domestic industry's pressure to raise the issue to the level of a policy determination, the ultimate outcome is not yet clear.

The continuing battle over imports of softwood lumber from Canada provides another example of how, in a politically charged case, the U.S. industry can raise an issue of statutory interpretation to the level of policy decision-making and bring political pressure to bear on that policy issue. In a dispute that has raged since the early 1980s, U.S. lumber producers have contended that imports of softwood lumber from Canada are subsidized by two Canadian government programs:

- the Government of Canada's log export restrictions, which increased domestic supply of logs and thus reduced the lumber companies' price paid for logs, and
- the price charged by the various Canadian provinces for "stumpage" (i.e., the right to harvest timber) on government-owned land. These "stumpage fees" were claimed to be "below market value", primarily on the ground that they were substantially lower than the stumpage fees charged by the U.S. government.[22]

These arguments raised novel issues for the Department and in some instances were inconsistent with prior U.S. interpretations. For example, the United States had in the early 1980s refused to characterize Argentina's export restrictions on soybeans as a subsidy to the production of soybean oil and meal. And as to the stumpage fee issue, there was no precedent for finding a price, even a very low price, to constitute a countervailable subsidy if that price was generally available to purchasers of the item (i.e., stumpage rights).

Moreover, the Canadian respondents advanced an economic argument to the effect that neither of these programs should be countervailed, even if they benefited the Canadian lumber industry by reducing its cost of raw material. According to this argument, the market for softwood lumber is entirely demand-driven, to the point that both prices and the level of output are entirely determined by demand factors. Thus, so the argument goes, the subsidies had no effect on the market and should not be countervailed.

Initially, the domestic lumber industry prosecuted these issues in a more or less straightforward countervailing duty proceeding. Although the International Trade Commission reached an affirmative preliminary injury determination,[23] the Department of Commerce concluded that the provincial stumpage fee programs were not countervailable, and that other subsidies were *de minimis.*[24]

After this defeat, U.S. producers embarked on a major effort to politicize the issues and raise them to a level of policy decisionmaking. A Coalition for Fair Lumber Imports was organized and embarked on an aggressive lobbying and litigating campaign:

- In a new countervailing duty investigation in 1986, the Coalition succeeded in obtaining a reversal of the earlier Commerce Department ruling, in a determination that found the stumpage fees to be below "market value" and announced a preliminary duty estimate at 15 percent.[25]
- The 1986 case was settled before the final determinations by a U.S.-Canada Memorandum of Understanding (MOU). The MOU provided that Canada would impose a 15 percent temporary surcharge on softwood lumber exports to the United States. That MOU remained in effect for over four years, during which period the surcharge was removed on 80 percent of Canadian exports as several of the provinces increased their stumpage fees. Then, in September 1991, the Government of Canada announced that it would in 30 days terminate the MOU.
- The United States reaction was dramatic and political. It not only self-initiated a new countervailing duty case,[26] it also acted under Section 301 of the Trade Act of 1974[27] to require immediate posting of bonds for estimated countervailing duties.[28] In July, 1992, the Commerce Department imposed countervailing duties of 6.51 percent (2.91% for stumpage fee subsidies and 3.60% for log export restrictions).[29]
- The Canadian side responded by taking these issues to international adjudication. It obtained a GATT panel ruling that required the United states to refund $12 million to the Canadian exporters on the ground that the use of Section 301 to accelerate the bonding requirement was improper. In addition, a series of binational panel decisions under the U.S.-Canada Free Trade Agreement overturned both the Commerce Department's subsidy determination and the International Trade Commission's finding of material injury.
- The Coalition then launched a two-pronged effort to invalidate the binational panel process. It persuaded the U.S. Government to bring

an Extraordinary Challenge, contending that the Canadian panelists had conflicts of interest. That challenge was rejected. Simultaneously, the U.S. producers filed a lawsuit challenging the constitutionality of the entire binational panel process. That suit was eventually withdrawn.

- Meanwhile, the Coalition was working politically and internationally to change the law in their favor. They obtained, in the legislation approving the North American Free Trade Agreement, language forbidding Commerce to consider the effect of a subsidy on the recipient's prices or output. And in the Uruguay Round's new Agreement on Subsidies and Countervailing Measures and in the U.S. Uruguay Round Agreements Act, they obtained more favorable language on the issue of general availability.

In 1996, the softwood lumber dispute again became the subject of a U.S.-Canada negotiated resolution. It can be argued that the U.S. industry here, as in the steel privatization issue, was able by political pressure to change the interpretation of the law to suit its needs and—ultimately—to obtain at least a substantial portion of the import protection it sought.

What is striking to this author, however, is how difficult it was, how fraught with uncertainty, for these politically powerful U.S. industries to achieve their desired legal interpretations, even where the issues were novel and where immense political pressure was applied. In steel, for example, it is still not clear that the U.S. industry's interpretation will ultimately prevail. What these cases show is that there is in nondiscretionary import relief cases a sufficiently strong rule of law that political efforts to achieve protectionist legal interpretations are by no means guaranteed success.

It should also be noted that a policy decision to alter an interpretation of law in a nondiscretionary import relief case does not always come from the protectionist side. In the early 1980s, an antidumping case was brought against imports of fresh winter vegetables from Mexico. The then-Administration (specifically, the State Department and certain parts of the White House) were concerned at the effect the case might have on U.S.-Mexico relations, especially since a "mechanical" application of the antidumping law would result in significant duties. At that time, the law required that the price of each individual sale in the United States be compared with a weighted average price of home market sales.[30] Since vegetable prices fluctuate widely during each *day*, such a comparison would inevitably find many of the U.S. sales priced below the weighted average price of contemporaneous home market sales. Motivated by a desire to avoid what was perceived as an economically irrational restriction on a major Mexican export category, the White House dispatched economists from the Council of Economic Advisers to help Commerce devise a more sophisticated price comparison methodology that would avoid such an "irrational" result.[31]

Settlement of Cases

The other situation in which a policy decision can supplant a litigated result in nondiscretionary import relief proceedings is the settlement of such cases. The settlements in which such policy decisions are made are usually those to which the statutory settlement device (a "suspension agreement")[32] is inapplicable or impractical, yet where there is a political or diplomatic imperative to resolve the case in a manner other than imposition of duties. In such cases, a negotiated resolution may be reached, in connection with which the U.S. Government will persuade the U.S. industry to withdraw the petition.[33]

The dynamics of these non-statutory settlements is such that, in almost all cases, the impetus for settlement comes from the foreign exporters or governments, not from the petitioning U.S. industry. Typically, these settlements occur after the Department of Commerce has reached a preliminary determination that is intolerable to a foreign government or group of foreign governments—or to the U.S. Government—for any one or more of several reasons:

- The duties to be imposed are prohibitive.
- The duties cover some exporters or countries, but not others, creating disparate impacts intolerable to the government of the foreign country or group of countries.
- The foreign country in question is one against which such severe import restrictions would be inimical to U.S. diplomatic or geopolitical policies.
- The United States and the foreign government in question prefer a negotiated solution to one imposed unilaterally by the United States.

Where such an impetus for settlement comes from the respondent side of the case (or from U.S. Government reluctance to impose duties), a quantitative or price-floor arrangement may be negotiated. This agreement, however, will have to be approved by the petitioning U.S. industry, since it must agree to withdraw its petition. Such agreement may be forthcoming in response to some combination of the following considerations:

- The agreement, although reducing the degree of import restriction on some foreign exporters, provides broader coverage (i.e., more products, more exporters and/or more countries).
- There is no longer uncertainty as to whether Commerce might be more lenient in its final determination or as to whether the International Trade Commission might reach a negative injury determination.
- Promises of non-trade benefits to domestic producers (e.g., tax, pension or regulatory benefits).
- Direct White House persuasion of industry CEOs.

The 1986 and 1996 settlements of the Canadian softwood lumber cases illustrate different ways in which non-statutory settlements can be reached. The 1986 MOU was sought by the Government of Canada as an alternative to Commerce's preliminary determination of 15 percent countervailing duties (and the possibility that duties could be higher in the final determination). To the Canadian side, the MOU allowed the revenues to accrue to the Canadian Government through the 15% export surcharge, rather than to the U.S. Government through duties. Moreover, the MOU enabled the Canadian side to reduce and eventually eliminate the surcharge on the bulk of softwood lumber exports as several provinces raised their stumpage fees.

The 1996 U.S.-Canada agreement came about under a different U.S. threat. In this instance, a countervailing duty case had not yet been initiated, but there was a clear threat of such initiation if no agreement was reached. Moreover, the threat was made credible by recent changes in U.S. law that the U.S. side would eliminate the major defenses on which the Canadians had relied in past cases. This produced a preliminary agreement under which the Province of British Columbia (the largest source of exports to the United States) would impose an export tax on shipments to the United States that exceed specified annual quantities, and the Province of Quebec would increase its stumpage fees. This preliminary agreement was later replaced by a tariff-rate quota intended to reduce Canadian imports from their then-prevailing annual level of 16.2 billion board feet. Under the agreement, imports exceeding 14.7 billion board feet per year are subject to a Canadian export tax, the amount of which increases at certain quantity levels. For its part, the U.S. side made two commitments. First, no trade cases would be initiated, and second, a petition filed by the U.S. industry would be dismissed as long as the agreement remains in effect and is not breached by the Canadian side.

The 1978 steel Trigger Price Mechanism exemplifies the motivation that may exist for both the petitioning U.S. industry and some foreign governments to avoid a result in which some exporters are subjected to prohibitive antidumping duties, while other exporters have no or low duties. For the petitioners, especially in cases involving commodity products, the concern is that the foreign exporters not subject to duties will simply replace the volume of low-price imports that had previously been sold by the firms now excluded from the U.S. market. On the other hand, the prospect that some European Community exporters would be excluded from the U.S. market while others would remain free to sell created intolerable political pressures within the Community, at a time when the European Commission was implementing a steel industry restructuring program requiring delicate balances among the industries of the various Member States. This mutual interest in avoiding a scattershot incidence of U.S. import restrictions produced a system in which most major steel exporting nations (except Canada) agreed to require that their exporters sell to the United States at delivered prices no lower than certain "trigger prices." These trigger prices were computed on the basis of Japanese cost of production plus delivery costs to the major U.S. markets. The theory was that the Japanese producers had the lowest costs of any world steel industry, so that any steel entering the United States below the trigger prices could be assumed to be sold at less than fair value and would therefore be investigated under the antidumping law.

The overall import-limiting effect of the trigger price mechanism was undoubtedly less than would have resulted from the imposition of antidumping duties. The lesser degree of restriction, however, was preferable from the U.S. industry's standpoint to leaving some major foreign producers unrestricted. And uniformity of restrictions was absolutely essential to the European Community.

A final example—the series of suspension agreements in the antidumping investigations of uranium from Russia and several other Newly Independent States—shows that other U.S. policy interests can bring about settlements intended to ameliorate the impact of antidumping or countervailing duties on one or more foreign countries. With respect to the uranium cases, senior Administration policymakers were concerned that limits on imports from Russia, Kazakhstan, Kyrgystan, Tajikistan, Uzbekistan and the Ukraine were inconsistent with the goal of assisting those countries in their transition to capitalism. There was also concern that the Russian antidumping proceeding might interfere with ongoing negotiations for the disposition of highly enriched uranium derived from the dismantling of Russia's nuclear weapons. These concerns were heightened when the Commerce Department's preliminary determinations found commercially preclusive antidumping margins with respect to all six countries—115.82 percent in the case of Russian uranium imports.[34]

Fortunately for the Administration, the statutory provisions for suspension agreements in nonmarket economy antidumping cases provide greater latitude to negotiate suspension agreements and thus reach a settlement that does not require the consent of the petitioning U.S. industry. Unlike other antidumping proceedings, NME cases may be settled on the basis of quantitative export restrictions, among other devices, provided that the agreement eliminates import-caused price suppression and prevents imports from undercutting the prices charged by U.S. producers.

Negotiations between the United States and the respondent county governments initially resulted in suspension agreements that limited the quantity of uranium imports to amounts keyed to the level of U.S. uranium prices.[35] However, these agreements failed in their purpose of permitting the respondent countries to continue exporting to the United States, because U.S. uranium prices never rose to the lowest of the levels that would trigger an import quantity allowance.

What followed next might be characterized as "Rube Goldberg writes a suspension agreement." A new "amendment" to the Russian agreement[36] permitted certain annual quota amounts to be imported,[37] but only pursuant to what the agreement characterizes as a "matched sale." In a "matched sale," a quantity of Russian uranium must be sold with an equal quantity of newly-mined U.S. uranium, with the total quantity sold to the purchaser for a single price. Since that price for the overall transaction is composed half of low-priced Russian uranium and half of higher-priced U.S. uranium, U. S. producers in effect actually benefit in higher profits and arguably in ability to obtain increased sales volume[38] from use of the Russian uranium to reduce the overall transaction price. Astonishingly, the new suspension agreement seems to be working fairly smoothly.

III. Discretionary Import Relief Cases

The fundamental point to understand about all three of the U.S. laws providing for discretionary Presidential decisions to restrict imports—the Escape Clause (§ 201),[39] the National Security Amendment (§232)[40] and the Market Disruption Law (§ 406)[41]—is that every administration has regarded them as rarely-used derogations from the principle of "free but fair" trade. These laws, especially the Escape Clause, are the pressure valves of trade policy, not the policy itself. From the standpoint of the trade lawyer/advocate, the goal in invoking these laws is to develop a strategy that persuades the Administration that this case is one of the rare circumstances in which this derogation from normal trade policy is warranted. In a few cases, the political power of the petitioning industry may be a major component of such persuasion. More frequently, however, the cases do not turn on raw political power.

Each of these statutes deals with imports that are fairly traded, and there is no suggestion that they provide a remedy against foreign unfair practices.[42] The Escape Clause authorizes, pursuant to WTO/GATT rules, a temporary restriction of imports where a U.S. industry has suffered or is threatened with "serious" injury, where increasing imports are the greatest cause of that serious injury, and where the U.S. industry will be able to use the period of relief to "adjust"—i.e., to regain competitiveness by reducing costs, introducing new products, etc. The National Security Amendment, also sanctioned under GATT/WTO rules, permits imposition of import restrictions where necessary for national security reasons. Finally, the Market Disruption Law is probably not WTO-consistent, but is applicable only to imports from certain countries that are not WTO members. It imposes duties or quantitative limits on imports from a "communist" country that cause or threaten "market disruption."

The Escape Clause

Of the three discretionary import relief statutes, the Escape Clause is by far the most important, but its use is relatively rare. Moreover, the success rate under this statute is far below 50 percent. And while a few cases involving politically powerful industries—steel and automobiles come to mind[43]—attract most of the attention, the majority of escape clause cases are brought by small industries and, if won, are won by political/merits strategies very different from the juggernaut political influence suggested by the academic literature. Two examples—the Harley-Davidson heavyweight motorcycles case and the 1984 steel and copper cases—suggest the complexities and uncertainties of escape clause advocacy.

Heavyweight Motorcycles

The "industry" that brought this case[44] certainly did not have awesome political power. It consisted entirely of Harley-Davidson Motor Company and its two plants in Milwaukee, Wisconsin and York, Pennsylvania. Nevertheless, Harley succeeded in obtaining unusually forceful escape clause relief—additional duties of 45 percent ad valorem, phased down over a five year period—and used it to "adjust" so successfully that the company asked the government to lift the duties after less than three years of the scheduled five year period. The Harley strategy is not only the classic Escape Clause success story; it also demonstrates that obtaining relief under the statute does not necessarily turn on raw political power.

With no possibility of generating massive political pressure for import relief, Harley-Davidson developed a strategy in which its smallness, when used in conjunction with its strong case on the statutory merits, became an asset rather than a liability. Harley certainly had a compelling case of serious injury caused by imports. Japanese brands had increased their market share to a point of clear commercial dominance. They had done so by low pricing and by marketing tactics targeted directly at Harley-Davidson, closely copying not only its product designs, but even its advertising campaigns. The U.S. company's financial position had deteriorated to such a point that its chief banker told the International Trade Commission that he intended to "pull the plug on Harley's loans" if import relief was denied.

More important, however, was Harley-Davidson's ability to demonstrate that it not only had plans for a program of competitive adjustment, but was relatively far along in implementing that program. New and more advanced motorcycle models had already been put on the market. Introduction of new manufacturing and management techniques—many, ironically, derived from Japanese practices—had already significantly reduced both costs and manufacturing defects. Such facts are critical in persuading any Administration that a temporary period of relief will not be "wasted," with the industry asking at the end of the period for yet more import restrictions.

The case on the merits, then, was the easy part for Harley-Davidson. The more difficult task was to devise an effective policy/political strategy. That strategy had three major elements. First, the company took maximum advantage of what might justifiably be called its "mystique." Harley was, after all, the last surviving American motorcycle manufacturer. Moreover, the company had an image that few other companies could match. From Marlon Brando in "The Wild One" to Peter Fonda in "Easy Rider", Harley-Davidson projected an image of independence, freedom and Americanism. To portray that image as now threatened by imports was politically potent indeed. Second, timing was critical. Although the Escape Clause does not focus on imports from a specific country, the fact of the matter was that almost all heavyweight motorcycle imports were Japanese. Bringing the case in a period of widespread public concern about U.S.-Japan trade (the bilateral deficit, the machine tool controversy, etc.) increased prospects for success. Third, Harley turned its smallness, and the smallness of the amount of motorcycle trade, into an asset. In any trade controversy (and during this period, especially any matter involving Japan), there is division within the Administration between those who are concerned about the fate of the U.S. industry and those who oppose import relief either on the ground: (a) of concern about the inflationary effect of import restrictions or (b) of unwillingness to take protectionist action against a country whose diplomatic or geopolitical ties to the United States are seen as important. The latter consideration always looms large in cases against Japanese practices or imports. The motorcycle case, Harley argued, was one in which the small volume of trade in motorcycles made those concerns immaterial. No action limiting motorcycle imports could conceivably have an inflationary impact. More importantly, here was a case in which the economic effect on Japan of a temporary import restriction would be minute, creating no strain on the overall bilateral relationship.

Putting these three themes together with the strong case on the merits presented a uniquely appealing argument for relief. This was a company and product of high public visibility. Saving Harley-Davidson—a company whose strong adjustment program made it clear that Harley *could* be saved—would be of substantial political benefit. Moreover, the Administration could demonstrate that it could "get tough with Japan" where a clear case was made for the need to do so. And all this could be accomplished with respect to a trade issue on which import restrictions would do no serious harm to Japan or to U.S. inflation.

One final tactical issue should be mentioned. As in most such cases, the foreign side (once it saw that the tide was running against it) proposed an effort to negotiate a compromise—in this case, Japanese financial assistance for Harley-Davidson. Within any Administration, there are those to whom such a compromise is appealing. Harley made the decision to enter such negotiations, expecting that the Japanese offers would not be attractive. They were right. As Harley's chairman put it, "They offered us the sleeves off their vests." The patent inadequacy of the Japanese proposals made wholly untenable the positions of those in the Administration who opposed relief. In the end, this was the final element that ensured that the duties recommended by the International Trade Commission would be ordered by the President.

The Harley-Davidson case, in the view of this author, illustrates the way in which the Escape clause is supposed to work. The presence of a clear prospect of successful adjustment constituted the proper justification for temporary protectionism. And relief was not granted in response to political pressure.

Steel and Copper

A very different picture of the Escape Clause in action was seen in the summer of 1984. In that election year, the Reagan Administration had to decide on not one but two Escape Clause cases. Two major industries—steel[45] and copper[46]—had both won International Trade Commission recommendation for import restrictions. Neither industry presented the strong prospect of successful adjustment that Harley-Davidson had shown. Moreover, these cases involved very large import volumes, and thus restriction of imports would raise significant issues as to inflation and U.S. relations with numerous foreign countries. In short, both cases posed difficult issues politically as well as on the merits. In two major respects, however, the cases were significantly different:

First, relief in the copper case was vigorously opposed by a group of major copper consuming industries, led by the electrical equipment companies. Steel consumers, with the exception of a few companies, made no effort to oppose import restrictions. Second, the steel industry represented a far more potent political force, especially in the 1984 election year, than did the copper industry. In part, this was true because the steel industry's nationwide employment substantially exceeded that of the copper industry. More important, however, was the location of steel industry employment in major electoral states, some of which were states as to which the election outcome was not yet clear. The copper industry, in contrast, was concentrated in less populous Western states with less electoral votes—states which were seen by the Republican Administration as "safe" in the upcoming election.

These differences were reflected in the differing strategies of the two petitioning industries. The steel industry, utilizing a powerful Congressional Steel Caucus, conducted an essentially political campaign. The copper producers, lacking such political resources, sought to negotiate a compromise with the opposing consumer industries, in part by proposing that the Administration seek an international commodity agreement instead of imposing import restrictions.

The two cases reached very different results, despite the fact that the Administration—in "a great day for free trade," as Trade Representative Bill Brock described it—officially rejected both International Trade Commission recommendations. Copper got little or nothing. All the President gave them was an agreement to organize a multilateral discussion group to "address" problems in the copper market. Steel, on the other hand, got a system of global quantitative restrictions. The President ordered the U.S. Trade Representative to press all steel producing nations to enter into Voluntary Restraint Arrangements, placing a volume cap on their steel exports to the United States. In short, steel won a huge victory and copper got almost nothing.

The observation of this author is that very large industries can sometimes obtain Escape Clause relief through sheer political muscle. There are, however, few examples of such success because few industries have such political strength. At the other extreme, a small industry, where import restrictions would not affect a large volume of trade, may be able to obtain relief if it has a strong case on the merits (especially on the issue of adjustment) and develops an effective strategy. The industries that will have greatest difficulty under this statute are those large enough that import restrictions will affect a substantial amount of trade, but not large enough to have truly exceptional political clout. Overall, Escape Clause relief will continue to be an infrequent phenomenon and an exception to prevailing trade policy, not the policy itself.

The National Security Amendment

This statute deserves little discussion. It has been implemented only twice: once as to oil imports in a decision based on energy policy rather than trade policy, and once for machine tools. All Administrations avoid § 232, wary of setting a precedent that might attract additional petitions. With the end of the Cold War, it is now even less likely that this statute will be revived in the foreseeable future.

The Market Disruption Law

This is, one hopes, a soon-to-be-obsolete statute. It authorizes the President to impose restrictions on imports from a "communist" country found by the International Trade Commission to be causing "market disruption." The term "market disruption" is defined as material injury to a domestic industry caused or threatened by a rapid increase in imports.

The great problem with this statute is that the statutory criteria are almost invariably overwhelmed by politics and/or ideology. The clearest example is the most important case under the statute, involving ammonia imported from the U.S.S.R. the case challenged imports arising from Occidental Petroleum's 20 year, $20 billion fertilizer countertrade agreement. That agreement, ironically had been negotiated with the blessing and encouragement of the Nixon Administration, whose Secretary of Commerce dubbed it "the flagship of detente." Soon after imports under the agreement began, however, they were met by a Section 406 petition. Then the fun began. In late 1979 a 3-2 affirmative determination by the Commission[47] was followed by a highly public, fiercely contested battle in the Presidential decision phase of the case. In December, President Carter issued a strongly worded rejection of import restrictions, stating that there was no evidence whatever of market disruption. Only a few weeks later, the President reversed himself. Citing "changed economic circumstances," President Carter not only self-initiated a new Section 406 investigation; he took the extraordinary step of ordering emergency import restrictions pending the outcome of the new investigation. Cynical observers may be forgiven for suspecting that the "changed economic circumstances" had something to do with the fact that Russian troops had marched into Afghanistan.

The case had one more surprise twist, however, This time, it was the turn of the International Trade Commission to reverse itself, issuing a 3-2 *negative* determination[48] that ended the case! The author was counsel to the importer (Occidental) in that proceeding, but claims of a brilliant defense presentation must be tempered by a realization that the make-up of the Commission had changed between the first and second investigations. A hawkish Commissioner's term had expired and his free-trade-oriented replacement cast the deciding vote that ended this bizarre trade "policy" spectacle.

Section 406 . . . R.I.P. (We hope.)

IV. Initiatives Against Unfair Trade Practices Encountered in Foreign Markets

The trend that *should* emerge in trade policy matters over the next decade is an increasing shift in focus toward initiatives aimed at unfair practices—subsidies, barriers to market access or to investment, failure to protect intellectual property rights, etc.—encountered by U.S. companies in foreign markets. Certainly a principal thrust of United States efforts in the recent Uruguay Round of Multilateral Trade Negotiations was to create both more effective rules against such unfair practices and a more effective WTO enforcement mechanism to make those rules work. The premise of that negotiating strategy—a valid premise, in this author's view—is that, as more and more U.S. industries see their markets as global markets, they will increasingly need a level playing field in markets outside the United States. To achieve this, companies will increasingly seek U.S. Government action—WTO proceedings, Section 301[49] cases, bilateral and multilateral negotiations—to ensure fair treatment for U.S. exports and investments.

Whether that trend in trade policy advocacy will in fact emerge is, however, by no means certain. Initiatives against foreign unfair practices present a number of serious difficulties not encountered in import relief cases. First and foremost, the U.S. Government cannot unilaterally resolve a case involving foreign market unfair practices as it can in a domestic import relief proceeding. If the foreign government is intransigent, it is of course possible for the United States to retaliate. However, such retaliation rarely benefits the U.S. industry that complained of the foreign unfair practice. Only in the unusual case in which the foreign country in question has substantial exports to the United States of the same product will retaliatory U.S. import restrictions benefit the U.S. industry that complained of the unfair practice in the foreign market. In most cases, therefore, the petitioning U.S. industry has lost if the case ends in U.S. retaliatory measures instead of elimination of the unfair foreign market practice.

Second, there is the "many-headed Hydra" problem. A foreign government truly determined to protect a domestic market has a multiplicity of access-denying practices at its disposal. Thus an initial effort by U.S. negotiators may succeed in ending a WTO-illegal quota or import licensing scheme, only to see it replaced by an equally preclusive discriminatory standard. Then, when the standards problem is resolved, the foreign government tolerates or even encourages concerted refusals by industrial customers to buy from foreign suppliers. In short, just as new heads appeared on the Hydra as quickly as the old heads were chopped off, so new access barriers are constantly created each time one of the old ones is negotiated away. It is the perception of this phenomenon that sometimes lends U.S. trade negotiators to seek guarantees from the foreign government (especially Japan) of increased market share for U.S. sellers.

Third, the efficacy of both unilateral and multilateral remedies for foreign market unfair practices remains uncertain in the eyes of most U.S. companies. In major part, this uncertainty stems from the discretionary nature of the U.S. Government's process for asserting these issues. These are not, after all, remedies to which petitioners have a right, even if they prove their case on the merits beyond question. Rather, the extent to which and the method by which the U.S. company's claim will be asserted depends on policy and tactical judgments made by U.S. government officials. For example, the petitioner may desire that its foreign market practice issue be pressed as a bilateral initiative backed up by the threat of retaliation under Section 301, only to see the U.S. Trade Representative insist instead that the issue be taken to WTO dispute resolution, as is now happening with Eastman Kodak's petition against practices that limit foreign participation in the Japanese film market.

Finally, there is an as-yet unresolved issue as to the extent to which U.S. obligations under the new WTO agreements prevent this country from taking unilateral action under Section 301 against foreign market unfair practices. While senior U.S. officials stated repeatedly during ratification of the Uruguay Round Agreements that the United States would retain the right to take unilateral action under Section 301, it seems clear that action in the form of trade restrictions would subject the United States to WTO-authorized trade retaliation. That having been said, the view of this author is that unilateral action against foreign market unfair practices remains a viable option

- as to trade restrictions, where the United States is willing to accept WTO-authorized retaliation,
- as to trade restrictions in response to a foreign practice that violates a trade agreement between the United States and the offending foreign government, and
- as to action other than trade restrictions.

The last point is particularly important. There exist numerous actions that can be taken in response to foreign market unfair practices that would not be trade restrictions in the sense that they would subject the United States to WTO-authorized retaliation. Such actions include suspension or denial of various U. S. Government patents, approvals (FDA, for example), licenses (e.g., FCC), etc. The offending country's eligibility for U.S. benefits—foreign aid, Export-Import Bank financing, Overseas Private Investment Corporation Guarantees or duty-free treatment under the Generalized System of Preferences—could also be withdrawn or limited.

It should be emphasized that there are significant success stories in U.S. companies' use of Section 301 and/or the GATT/WTO processes against unfair practices in foreign markets:

- The U.S. aluminum industry used the threat of a Section 301 proceeding to reduce market access barriers in Japan.
- Boeing brought a successful GATT case that ended Germany's exchange rate guarantee export subsidy, and then used the filing of a broader WTO attack on Airbus subsidies as leverage to negotiate with the European Community a bilateral agreement reducing the amount of subsidies provided to Airbus.
- The corn refining industry has repeatedly used GATT challenges (and threats of challenges) to prevent the European Community from imposing restrictions on imports of corn gluten feed.
- U.S. telecommunications equipment manufacturers worked successfully with the U.S. Government to open up procurement by Nippon Telephone & Telegraph to foreign suppliers.
- And the United States has successfully pressured numerous countries to accord protection to intellectual property rights.

The list of successes could be extended significantly. The point is that effective action can be taken against unfair practices in foreign markets, provided that a strategy is crafted that approaches the problem as a policy issue, not simply a litigation. In devising such an approach, certain considerations are particularly important. First, the petitioning company or industry must develop the facts necessary to demonstrate the existence and effect of the foreign unfair practice. Although Section 301 contains references to an "investigation", neither USTR nor any other government agency in fact conducts—or has the resources to conduct—any meaningful investigation. Second, consideration must be given to how the issue in question can be raised in a manner consistent with the Administration's trade policy and the current state of relations with the foreign government in question. This entails an assessment of the likely reaction of the foreign government to presentation of the issue, and of the best ways to gain support of the major U.S. Government agencies that will be involved in the requisite policy decisions. Third, alternative means of putting leverage on the foreign government must be assessed. These include a WTO proceeding or threat thereof, various forms of U.S. unilateral action, prospects for linking the problem to other current issues between the United States and the foreign country, and visible demonstrations of the domestic political importance of the issue. Finally, a negotiating strategy must be crafted. This must include full analysis of the various potential resolutions of the issue and assessment of the most effective ways of choreographing the negotiating process.

Admittedly, this is a far more complex and uncertain process than, say, the litigation of a nondiscretionary import relief case. It remains to be seen whether many U.S. companies and industries—especially those made up of small to medium sized firms—will see Section 301, WTO dispute resolution or government-to-government negotiating initiatives as attractive or even feasible approaches to unfair practices encountered in foreign markets.

V. Summary and Conclusion

This paper has sought to present a view of trade issues "from the bottom up"—that is, from the perspective of the trade lawyer/advocate and her or his client, rather than from the academic point of view that characterizes much of the literature. From this perspective, dichotomies between "free trade" and "protectionism" seem almost irrelevant.

In import relief proceedings under non-discretionary statutes – principally the antidumping and countervailing duty laws – political or diplomatic pressure plays little role, except in the settlement of such cases and in the relatively few instances in which a major issue in the proceeding is sufficiently novel that the administering authority has interpretive discretion that may be subject to political or diplomatic influence. Even in such cases, however, it has proven to be extremely difficult even for large and powerful U.S. industries to affect the outcome by political pressure.

Discretionary import relief proceedings are, of course, more overtly political. However, two important points must be remembered. First, these laws are rarely used – the vast bulk of import relief proceedings are brought under the non-discretionary laws. Second, the "batting average" of petitioning industries under the Escape Clause and the other discretionary statutes is very low. Even the most politically powerful industries fail more often than not to obtain the protection they seek, because every U.S. Administration has a built-in bias against taking actions that can be condemned as "projectionist."

Finally, there is an open question as to the role political pressure will play in proceedings seeking elimination of foreign practices that restrict U.S. exporters' access to overseas markets. As yet, relatively few U.S. industries are invoking Section 301 and the new WTO dispute settlement procedures to address such market access issues. When and if such proceedings become more frequent, the fact that negotiated resolutions are the optimal result from the U.S. petitioner's standpoint means that success will depend on a complex interplay between legal advocacy and political/diplomatic strategy.

In summary, the trade law practitioner does not, as the academic literature would lead one to belief, focus primarily or even in substantial part on the politics of a trade issue. The issues more relevant to the practitioner are those of finding the right mechanism – sometimes in litigation, sometimes in policy advocacy, often in negotiation, only rarely in the application of raw political power – to resolve real-world problems.

NOTES

[1] The other principal category of nondiscretionary import relief proceedings, cases under Section 337 involving imports that infringe U.S. firms' intellectual property rights, is not discussed herein.

[2] 19 U.S.C. § 1673 (1994).

[3] 19 U.S.C. § 1303 (1994).

[4] 46 Stat. 687 (1930).

[5] See analysis by Commissioner Bruce Clubb of the legislative history of the injury provision, to the effect that it was intended to make clear that "the Secretary of the Treasury [was] to investigate only those cases where a domestic industry complained" and thus the injury "amendment was made in order to relieve the Customs Service of the necessity of examining every importation for possible violation of the statute." *Cast Iron Soil Pipe from Poland*, Inv. No. AA 1921-50 (TC Pub. 124, 1967).

[6] The U.S. attitude toward dumping and subsidies is, in this regard, not unlike the GATT and WTO view of such practices as export subsidies and discriminatory standards, which are condemned regardless of whether they are shown to cause adverse effects.

[7] *Canned Clams from Canada*, Inv. No. 731-TA-17 (USITC Pub. 1060, 1980).

[8] *Birch Three-Ply Doorskins from Japan*, Inv. No. 751-TA-6 (USITC Pub. 1271, 1982).

[9] 19 U.S.C. § 1330(a).

[10] The author does, however, hold the view that the Commission is subject to some degree of continuing pressure from the Congress. This pressure flows from the Congress's power to fund the operations of the Commission and, to a lesser extent, from the possibility that Congress may change the law to "correct" Commission interpretations to which it objects. The author's judgment is that the effect of this continuing Congressional pressure is to make the Commission's decisions marginally more protectionist, especially in high-visibility cases.

[11] The Department, aware of criticism for excessively harsh use of "facts available," is now revising its approach in this procedural area. 61 Fed. Reg. 7379 (Feb. 27, 1996). To be codified as 61 Fed. Reg. § 351.308.

[12] In one recent opinion, a Court of International Trade Judge severely chastised the Department for such tactics. *British Steel plc v. United States*, Slip Op. 96-130 (Ct. Intl. Trade, Aug. 13, 1996) at p. 29, n. 14.

[13] *Certain Hot-Rolled Lead & Bismuth Carbon Steel Products from the United Kingdom*, 57 Fed. Reg. 42974 (Sept. 17, 1992) (preliminary countervailing duty determination).

[14] 19 U.S.C. § 1677(5)(F).

[15] *Certain Hot-Rolled Lead & Bismuth Carbon Steel Products from the United Kingdom*, 58 Fed. Reg. 6237 (Jan. 27, 1993) (final countervailing duty determination).

[16] *Certain Steel Products from Austria*, 58 Fed. Reg. 37062, 37259-65 (July 9, 1993) (final countervailing duty determination).

[17] *Id.* at 37260.

[18] *Inland Steel Bar Co. v. United States*, 858 F. Supp. 179 (Ct. Intl. Trade 1994).

[19] *Inland Steel Bar Co. v. United States*, 86 F.3d 1174 (Fed. Cir. 1996).

[20] *Remand Determination on Certain Hot-Rolled Lead & Bismuth Carbon Steel Products from the United Kingdom Pursuant to Inland Steel Bar Co. v. United States*, slip op. 96-134 (Ct. Intl. Trade Aug. 13, 1996) (Sept. 13, 1996).

[21] *British Steel plc v. United States*, 879 F. Supp. (Ct. Intl. Trade 1995), *appeal docketed*, Nos. 96-1401-06 (Fed. Cir. June 21, 1996).

[22] Later in the dispute, the argument was altered to contend that the various provinces provided stumpage at below-cost prices or below-value prices.

[23] USITC Pub. 1320 (1982).

[24] 48 Fed. Reg. 24159 (1983) (final countervailing duty determination).

[25] 51 Fed. Reg. 37453 (1986) (preliminary countervailing duty determination).

[26] 56 Fed. Reg. 56055 (1991).

[27] As amended by the Trade Agreements Act of 1979 and the Omnibus Trade and Competitiveness act of 1988.

[28] Normally, potential liability for duties does not arise until Commerce issues a preliminary determination.

[29] 57 Fed. Reg. 30955 (1992) (countervailing duty order).

[30] This was changed in the Uruguay Round Agreements Act. The normal comparison now is between a weighted average of prices in sales to the U.S. and a home market weighted average price.

[31] Price comparisons were made through a "matched pairs analysis", by "fitting an ordinary least squares regression line through the price pairs." Certain Fresh Winter Vegetables from Mexico, 44 Fed. Reg. 63588, 63590-92 (Nov. 5, 1990) (preliminary antidumping determination). It is perhaps instructive to contrast this result with the handling of a similar case in 1996—an election year in which Florida was a contested state—where the resolution was a settlement establishing minimum prices for imports of Mexican tomatoes. Notice of Postponement of Preliminary Antidumping Duty Determination: Fresh Tomatoes from Mexico, 61 Fed. Reg. 53702 (Oct. 15, 1996).

[32] The types of suspension agreements permitted in antidumping cases are narrowly defined and rarely found to be practicable. 19 U.S.C. § 1673c(b). In countervailing cases, however, where quantitative export restraints are a permissible form of suspension agreement, this form of settlement is more frequently—though still rarely—used. 19 U.S.C. § 1671c(b)(1).

[33] 19 U.S.C. § 1673c(a). If an order has already been entered, the U.S. industry would provide to the Department an expression of no further interest in the enforcement of the order.

[34] 57 Fed. Reg. 23, 380 (1982) (preliminary antidumping determination).

[35] See, e.g., *Uranium from Russia*, 57 Fed. Reg. 49,235 (1992) (antidumping suspension agreement). Separate provision was made, and later modified, for importation from Russia of the uranium extracted from dismantled nuclear weapons.

[36] 59 Fed. Re. 15,373 (1994) (amendment to antidumping suspension agreement).

[37] The amounts agreed by the United States, in a negotiating session elevated to the level of the U.S. Vice President, were the amounts desired by the Russian side.

[38] The "matched sale" concept is based on the premise—disputed by U.S. uranium producers—that the U.S. industry's cost of production is higher than the prevailing market price level. Thus the "matched sale" allows U.S. producers to make sales they otherwise could not profitably make, by using the low Russian price to achieve an overall transaction price at the prevailing market level while receiving an above-cost price for the U.S.-produced component of the sale.

[39] Section 201 of the Trade Act of 1974 (19 U.S.C. § 2251).

[40] Section 232 of the Trade Expansion Act of 1962 (19 U.S.C. § 1862).

[41] Section 406 of the Trade Act of 1974 (19 U.S.C. § 2436).

[42] Despite the legal irrelevance of any "unfairness" argument, however, it is not unusual for a petitioner to add political coloration to its case by claiming that the imports are in some way "unfair."

[43] Ironically, although both industries obtained relief after their escape clause cases—steel is discussed below—both industries lost on the merits. In the automobile case the International Trade Commission reached a negative determination. And President Reagan rejected the Commission's recommendation for import restrictions on steel products. The fact that both cases led to the *ultra vires* negotiation of voluntary restraint arrangements (surely one of trade law's great euphemisms!) suggest that relief obtained by political force tends to come outside of and in spite of trade law, not through trade law.

[44] *Heavyweight Motorcycles*, Inv. No. TA-201-44, USITC Pub. No. 1110 (1980).

[45] *Carbon and Certain Alloy Steel Products*, Inv. No. TA-201-51, USITC Pub. No. 1553 (1984).

[46] *Unwrought Copper*, Inv. No. TA-201-52, USITC Pub. No. 1549 (1984).

[47] *Anhydrous Ammonia from the U.S.S.R.*, Inv. No. TA-406-5, USITC Pub. No. 1006 (1979).

[48] *Anhydrous Ammonia from the U.S.S.R.*, Inv. No. TA-406-6, USITC Pub. No. 1051 (1980).

[49] Section 301 of the Trade Act of 1974 (19 U.S.C. § 2411).

Comments on Conference Version of Paper

John D. Greenwald

I. Introduction

After years of opposing Dick Cunningham in the context of trade law litigation, the temptation is to take issue with any and all assertions he makes. Here, the problem in doing so is that Cunningham's thesis is right. For the most part, U.S. trade law follows the law of the General Agreement on Tariffs and Trade (GATT)[1] and in most cases, a constituent's political influence has little or no bearing on the outcome of a trade law case. Even in the handful of cases that do become politicized, the size, geographical reach, and resources of the domestic industry involved are less important than the way in which a case is articulated and the effectiveness of the opposition. There are, as Cunningham suggests, exceptions to this rule but even in the exceptional cases, the political influence of a party has more bearing on the means by which a particular case is resolved than on the basic decision of whether or not trade action is taken. Because political muscle will rarely, if ever, turn a bad case into a "winner," a trade lawyer invites trouble if she premises her representation on the client's ability to exert political pressure.

Basic agreement with Cunningham's conclusions does not, however, mean that there is nothing to add to the analysis. To the contrary, I think that Cunningham's paper can be usefully expanded in four areas:

First, there is room for elaboration on the degree to which the foreign interests in a dispute can exert "political" influence on the U.S. government. The tendency is to think about pressure by "constituent interests" in the context of activity by U.S. industry. In fact, foreign governments often actively, and occasionally effectively, represent their constituent interests in trade litigation. For example, I think the evidence indicates that departures from the straightforward application of U.S. trade law (e.g., steel VRAs, the U.S./Japan Semiconductor Arrangement, the Uranium "suspension agreement") are, more often than not, an effort to accommodate the foreign interests involved in the case.

Second, there could have been a closer examination of the influence of bureaucratic or agency interest on decision-making. The ideological predisposition of individual decision-makers matters enormously; so too do issues of bureaucratic convenience.

Third, a complete analysis of the representation of constituent interests on trade law questions must include an examination of the process and forces that shape the provisions of U.S. trade law. The substantive and procedural provisions of trade law statutes and regulations dictate the outcome of most trade law cases. The statutes and regulations are amended periodically to address perceived problems. The process of amendment allows constituencies considerable opportunity to lobby the Administration and the Congress; it is much more responsive to the political influence of a constituency than is case-specific decision-making.

Fourth, the importance of Cunningham's observations might have been highlighted if more attention had been paid to the central role of trade law in U.S. trade policy.

These brief comments on Cunningham's paper address, in reverse order, each of these four points. They conclude with a case study designed to (1) illustrate the difficulty a domestic industry encounters in pressing for trade relief outside of a trade law context, and (2) explain why trade laws that seem so foreign to so many economists make sense in the world of businessmen, lawyers and government officials.

II. U.S. Trade Policy Is, Increasingly, a Creature of U.S. Trade Law

There was a time when large U.S. industries (e.g., textiles, autos) could effectively address their import problems outside the context of a trade law case. That period probably ended with the voluntary restraint agreement (VRA) on Japanese auto exports negotiated in 1981. Since then, almost all industry-specific trade initiatives have been the direct or indirect consequence of petitions for relief under U.S. trade law or the threat of a petition (e.g., the steel VRAs, the U.S./Japan semiconductor arrangement, the U.S./Canada understanding on softwood lumber). This change reflects the policy triumph of a rule of trade law based on the provisions of the GATT (although the use of Section 301 to impose or threaten to impose sanctions against imports after a unilateral determination that a foreign country engaged in "unfair" trade practices had been a clear exception to the general rule of GATT-consistency). The gains of the rule of law advocates have recently been expanded to include Section 301 and consolidated in the package of Uruguay Round trade agreements, particularly the new agreement on international trade dispute settlement.

A trade policy based on the rule of trade law fits well with U.S. tradition. We have an established national preference for regulation by means of a transparent decision-making process in which all competing parties are given an opportunity to defend their interests at the administrative level and appeal an unfavorable result to the Courts. In fact, our methods of international trade regulation are so transparent that the U.S. government probably would not have the means to address trade problems in ways that fall outside effective GATT scrutiny (such as Japan's reliance on "administrative guidance") even if it wanted to. It is also questionable whether the United States still has the political wherewithal to persuade foreign governments to negotiate "voluntary" export restraint agreements (à la autos) or special GATT regimes (à la textiles). In other words, reliance on trade law cases as the vehicle for resolving sector-specific problems may be the only real option left for U.S. industry. For the time being, the new World Trade Organization (WTO) dispute settlement procedures will strengthen the emphasis on a trade policy built on trade law (although over the longer term, a string of major WTO losses could erode U.S. support for a predisposition to resolve trade problems through GATT-consistent legal actions).

It might seem counterintuitive, but the Congress accepts and may actually welcome the prominence given to trade law in U.S. trade policy. The rhetoric of various members of the House and Senate and, from time to time, the majority of both might lead an observer of U.S. politics to conclude otherwise, but it is important to distinguish between Congressional bark and Congressional bite. The Congress often sounds hawkish on trade issues, put in practice tends to defer to Administration policy.[2]

There are at least two reasons for this. First, a majority in Congress subscribes to the view that an open international trading system based on GATT rules is, on balance, a good thing. Second, the availability of trade law remedies offers a useful means of responding to constituent pressures for protection. The evidence shows that, as a body, the Congress is generally unwilling to force "GATT-illegal" measures on the Administration. To illustrate, the efforts of the textile industry to pursue legislated quotas was destined for failure (i.e., they would always fall a few votes short of support needed to override the President's veto) and even legislation that appears to require action that cannot be reconciled with the GATT rules (e.g., Section 301, Iran-Libya) actually leaves the Executive Branch with sufficient flexibility to avoid such action. More importantly, each of the major trade liberalization initiatives since 1978 (e.g., the Uruguay Round, the Tokyo Round, NAFTA) was approved by the Congress without any serious derogations from the obligations accepted by the U.S. negotiators.[3]

The combination of a strong executive branch commitment to a rule of trade law and the utility of the trade laws as a response to pressure on the Congress for legislated solutions means that trade measures are now very difficult to achieve no matter what the political strength of the interested domestic industry unless the measures flow from a credible trade law case.

III. The Process of Shaping U.S. Trade Law Is Political in Nature, but Is Subject to Clear Constraints

U.S. trade law is developed through the following dynamic: (1) the Executive Branch, seeking to strengthen the international trading system and further specific U.S. interests through international trade negotiations, asks Congress to delegate to it negotiating authority; (2) the Congress, believing that the policy instincts of the Executive Branch are directionally sound, but that the United States must vigorously enforce its GATT rights (including its right to act against "unfair imports") adds to the trade bill provisions that "toughen" U.S. trade law; (3) the Executive Branch negotiates a package of trade agreements and seeks the necessary implementing legislation, (4) the Congress enacts the implementing legislation with trade law amendments that allow domestic interests to take advantage of new U.S. rights or that toughen trade laws in ways that are not proscribed by the new agreements.[4] The entire process is overtly political. In it, large industries with resources to hire effective advocates can do well.

However, there are clear limits on what a domestic industry can hope to accomplish through lobbying. The central free trade/fair trade thrust of the GATT system and of U.S. trade policy is unassailable. The Administration will not accept anything that forces significant GATT-illegal action on it or, in many cases, that makes a radical change to U.S. trade laws.[5] The Congress (and probably the Administration as well) will not accept anything that seriously compromises the ability of the United States to provide relief from "unfair" or "injurious" imports. To illustrate:

- Although the Uruguay Round Agreements provide for binding dispute settlement, the Uruguay Round implementing act preserves the President's authority to impose unilateral sanctions against "unfair" foreign practices if he decides such sanctions are warranted. However, preserving authority to act unilaterally is a far cry from requiring it. Over the near term, the probability of unilateral retaliation in the post-Uruguay Round world against an "unfair" foreign trade practice of another WTO member on trade that is subject to WTO discipline is close to zero.[6]
- The United States agreed to a modest liberalization of its antidumping regime in the Uruguay Round Antidumping Code. The implementing legislation limited the liberalization as narrowly as possible and included pro-petitioner amendments on points not addressed in the negotiations. At the same time, a change to the U.S. antidumping statute that would have made the U.S. law far more potent a weapon for domestic industry—i.e., a statutory amendment that would have required foreign producers to adjust their U.S. prices rather than absorb the dumping duties—was defeated by determined Administration opposition.

The industries that understand the limits on what can be accomplished and work closely with the Administration and Congress within those limits can have a real impact on the outcome of both trade negotiations and the shape of the implementing legislation. Industry groups that participated in the Uruguay Round exercise in this spirit (e.g., steel, semiconductors, the Intellectual Prop erty Committee) did relatively well. Industry groups that opposed the Uruguay Round (e.g., some textile producers) or held out for radical change (e.g., a group of industries that wanted radical pro-petitioner changes to the anti-dumping law; a group of importing companies that sought major liberalization of U.S. antidumping law) fared poorly. The lesson is that the size and strength of a constituency is almost irrelevant if the constituency seeks a result that falls outside either the Administration's or the Congress' concept of what is acceptable.

IV. Bureaucratic and Agency Interest Have a Major Impact on Trade Decision-Making Under U.S. Trade Law

In order to effectively represent a client in a trade law proceeding, a lawyer must understand the biases of the decision-maker, the concerns of bureaucracy, and the policy objectives of the top level agency officials.

- Many ITC Commissioners have strong views on the merits of the antidumping law. In close cases, those that do not like the law will vote in the negative unless the petitioner can present a persuasive case that appeals to their idiosyncracies. In the early 1990s, this meant an argument based on a particular econometric model of what would have happened "but for" the dumping. Further, the Commission as a whole is uncomfortable with an uninterrupted string of negative or affirmative injury decisions in antidumping, countervailing duty or escape clause cases. Thus, a weak case for the domestic industry has a distinctly better chance of an affirmative decision if it follows four or five negative decisions.[7]
- An industry can effectively use the influence of a particular Congressman or Senator if, because of personal relationship or position, that Senator or Congressman is important to the agency. Senator Packwood's interest in the softwood lumber cases was clearly a factor in agency decision-making at both the ITC (where one of the Commissioners relied on Packwood's support for her nomination) and the Commerce Department (where, as Chairman of the Senate Finance Committee, he was listened to).
- There is a clear free-trade bias at most agencies (the Commerce Department and the ITC are exceptions), but this can be overcome if the domestic industry pitches its case in a way that strikes the right chord. For example, one of the reasons for USTR's interest in Kodak's Section 301 case was the emphasis in Kodak's complaint on the relationship between competition policy and trade; the issue was becoming "hot" when Kodak filed. For the same reason, a "high-tech" industry has a better shot at a favorable government reaction than a low-tech or "sunset" industry. The Commerce Department's high level interest in Cray Research's antidumping complaint against supercomputers

from Japan is much more a function of the importance of supercomputers than of Cray's political influence.

- There are cases that, while strong on the merits, are simply unwinnable because they would create an unmanageable problem for the agency. In 1983/1984, the textile industry charged that China's use of multiple exchange rates operated as an export subsidy. On the merits, there was little doubt that China used its exchange rate system to promote certain exports and limit certain imports. However, the textile industry brought its countervailing duty case against China knowing that the Administration would never challenge the Chinese with a finding of subsidization and, instead, accepted an offer to tighten import regulation through the MFA in exchange for withdrawal of the case. A year later, the steel industry filed a similar case against Poland and Czechoslovakia, pursued the case to term, and lost when Commerce ruled that countervailable subsidies cannot exist in non-market economy countries. The fact was that the Commerce Department was never prepared to complicate relations with the Communist world by taking an aggressive posture on their subsidies.

On a more general level, bureaucratic interest has a major influence on decisions under U.S. trade law. The bureaucratic tendency to follow the path of least resistance, i.e., established policy, is often close to irresistible. In routine antidumping or countervailing duty cases, it is all but impossible to persuade the Commerce Department to depart from what it considers established practice, even if the case presents a fact pattern that is distinct from prior cases. In an important way, therefore, the bureaucracy acts as a protector of the status quo and as a defender against sharp change of any sort, whether pro-domestic industry or pro-foreign producer. This comes at a price. It is rare to find administrators that are creative in the application of U.S. trade law; at the same time, the influence of the bureaucracy has helped to ensure a remarkable stability in U.S. trade policy over the past fifty years; change has come in relatively small increments.

V. Foreign Governments Often Bring Effective Political Pressure on Decision-Makers in U.S. Trade Law Cases

The materials that accompanied the description of this Conference seemed to take for granted the idea that the constituent influence that shapes U.S. government decision-making on questions of trade policy is, overwhelmingly, the influence that is brought to bear by domestic interests. As trade policy has become more closely linked to trade law, this is no longer the case. With very few exceptions, a domestic industry looking for either import relief or the removal of a barrier to their exports must present a credible trade law case to engage the U.S. government. At that point, and depending on the merits of the case, a foreign government or foreign industry may press for a settlement in order to avoid the normal consequences of the law.

This sequence of events has characterized the major bilateral or multilateral agreements on sector-specific trade. The steel voluntary restraint arrangements negotiated in the early 1980s were directly attributable to European concern over the consequences for the EU industry of the series of antidumping and countervailing duty petitions and an escape clause action filed by U.S. industry. To be sure, the U.S. industry welcomed the VRAs because they offered more comprehensive protection than would have been otherwise available, but the domestic industry's leverage was the cases, *not* political influence. There was no EU pressure to resurrect the VRAs in the 1990s when the steel industry filed a new round of cases because the EU Commission and several EU producers were prepared to live with the results (although if the French industry had not benefitted from a "no injury" finding by the ITC on hot and cold rolled sheet, the EU position might have been very different). Thus, notwithstanding the U.S. industry's interest in a new set of VRAs, the cases went to term.

Similarly, the U.S./Japan semiconductor arrangement was the product of antidumping cases on DRAMs and EPROMs and a Section 301 case on Japanese barriers to market entry. The antidumping cases produced very high dumping margins that prompted Japanese industry interest in settlement. For its part, the Japanese government wanted to settle the cases to remove a major bilateral problem at a time when its surplus in bilateral trade with the U.S. was soaring. Again, the U.S. industry took advantage of the leverage created by its trade law initiatives, but the political pressure for settlement came from the Japanese side.

The same process occurred in two other proceedings, i.e., *Softwood Lumber from Canada* and *Uranium from the Former Republics of the USSR*, although in both cases the pressure for settlement was as much a function of U.S. government interest as foreign government pressure. In *Softwood Lumber* (which, in my view, was one of the most politically-driven decisions ever) the Department of Commerce was *not* entirely comfortable with its decision and welcomed settlement as a means of avoiding an appeal. In *Uranium*, the Administration had a national security interest in the outcome (the Department of Energy had agreed to purchase for recycling vast quantities of warhead material from Russia and other Republics) as well as a general interest in easing Russia's transition to a market economy. Indeed, it seems as if the settlement of the Uranium case was in spite of the domestic industry's views on the matter. The latest case to attract editorial (if not public) outrage over manipulation of the antidumping law is *Tomatoes From Mexico*. A recent *Washington Post* editorial deplored the settlement, contending that it was a product of pre-election jockeying for Florida votes.[8] In fact, the Mexican industry (although *not* the Mexican government) pressed hard for settlement. The Commerce Department, which had been embarrassed by negative publicity, was only too happy to close its investigation with a suspension agreement.

Like the Tomato case, most of the arrangements described above attracted considerable attention and probably fueled the notion that important trade policy decisions involve a U.S. government bow to the political influence of powerful domestic interests. The facts show otherwise; provisions of U.S. trade law and the GATT allow U.S. industry to attack foreign producer practices. The probable outcome of the cases leads foreign governments or foreign industries to protect their interests by pressing for settlement. The domestic industry often has considerable leverage over the terms of the settlement, but, to repeat, that leverage stems from its position as a petitioner.

VI. Case Study—Supercomputers from Japan

Another recent trade law/trade policy case that has drawn the fire of the establishment press is Cray's antidumping case against *Vector Supercomputers from Japan*. The case revolves around a decision by the University Corporation for Atmospheric Research (UCAR) to negotiate a final purchase of a very large supercomputer system produced by Japan's NEC and Cray's opposition to the UCAR purchase. The UCAR purchase was to be funded by NSF. Congressman Obey of Wisconsin added to NSF's appropriation bill a provision that would not permit payment of the salary of any federal official involved in the procurement of a dumped Japanese supercomputer. Although the provision was accepted by the House, Senate (and Administration) concerns over its GATT-legality, killed it. By mid-June, it was clear that Cray's only recourse was to file an antidumping petition on supercomputers from Japan.

The antidumping case was filed at the end of July. Cray has, with solid supporting evidence, alleged a dumping margin of over 400 percent and has cleared its first legal hurdle—i.e., an ITC preliminary injury determination. The case is now before the Department of Commerce, where NEC has said it will refuse to participate in the investigation. There are also reports that given the possibility of very steep antidumping duties, UCAR will cancel the supply contract.

The case has attracted attention because it involved the first purchase of a Japanese supercomputer funded by the federal government at a time when the United States had been pressing Japan to open its government procurement market to Cray. The press perception, fostered by an aggressive public relations campaign by NEC, seems to be that Cray's use of the antidumping law is cynical and that the Department of Commerce, which, in response to an NSF inquiry before Cray filed its petition, had said its own analysis indicated dumping, has "prejudged" the merits. I have not heard any economist express views on the matter, but knowing the distaste which the profession regards the antidumping statute, it would greatly surprise me if they were favorable.

To a businessman, a lawyer or a government official, however, it is easy to conclude that Cray not only did the right thing but had no other option. Supercomputing has important national security applications. The prospect that U.S. market prices would drop to a point where the sole remaining U.S. producer of vector supercomputers (i.e., the supercomputing architecture best suited to a number of key applications) would, over the short term, be forced to cut sharply R&D expenditures and, over the longer term, would face a challenge to its viability as a commercial enterprise, is a very serious issue for the U.S. defense and intelligence community. Yet that was precisely the situation facing Cray.

The world-wide market for vector supercomputers is in the $800 million range. It costs about $200 million to develop a new generation of supercomputer and each generation has about a four-year shelf-life. Four companies are in the vector supercomputer market—Cray and three very large, diversified Japanese companies, NEC, Hitachi and Fujitsu. Two of the Japanese companies, NEC and Fujitsu, have announced aggressive plans to expand their respective shares of the world supercomputer market. Given the economics of the business, i.e., the very heavy R&D burden and limited demand, one or more of the four producers cannot operate profitably even under normal market conditions. If pricing relative to costs ever drops to the level of the NEC bid to UCAR, each of the four will lose large sums. NEC, Hitachi and Fujitsu have the resources and the apparent willingness to lose money in the vector supercomputer market.[9] Cray does not. In its view, the long-term issue posed by Japanese producer dumping is, ultimately, one of survival.

Over the past three years, Cray has seen its share of the world vector supercomputer market shrink. There is little it can do about below cost pricing in Europe or the difficulty it has encountered in Japan's public sector procurements. Thus, although Cray still depends on overseas sales for a large portion of its business, the recent erosion of its position in overseas markets means that its position in the United States has become that much more important. The choice to defend its U.S. market position and U.S. market prices against Japanese producer dumping was, therefore, its only real option.

From a government perspective, there was no reason to quarrel with Cray's decision to invoke U.S. antidumping law. Cray's action was no different from the action of hundreds of past petitioners in the United States and other WTO signatories; antidumping investigations are part of the GATT system and have been ever since the GATT first entered into force. Indeed, given the national security significance of vector supercomputer production capability, Cray's decision to invoke the antidumping law meant that the Administration did not have to worry about alternative measures.

The Administration could have taken a different tack; it could have pressured Cray to downsize and rely solely on national security demand. This would, no doubt, have been very unattractive to Cray. Moreover, it would have entailed risks that the antidumping action avoided. Participation in the commercial market exposes Cray to competition, spurs technological developments and creates pressure to control costs. At the same time, commercial market sales in the United States and overseas absorb the very heavy fixed costs (R&D and manufacturing) associated with vector supercomputer production. Thus, both Cray and its national security customers benefit greatly by Cray's successes in the commercial market. The prospect of reducing Cray to a national security contractor has to raise concerns about its cost structure as well as its ability to remain at the leading edge of supercomputer technology. The antidumping solution, which simply insists on "normal value" pricing by Japanese producers in the U.S. market, avoids both problems. In short, whatever quarrels the economic profession may have with the antidumping law, it offers an attractive solution to the sort of problem created by very aggressive below cost pricing by Japanese supercomputer producers.

NOTES

These comments are not heavily footnoted. Most of the cases cited are reasonably well known; most of the observations regarding the reasons for the outcome of the cases are based on personal involvement in the case or conversations with other lawyers that were involved. The opinions expressed, while informed by experience, are opinions.

[1] Until 1994, the Administration's willingness to exercise its Section 301 retaliation authority without prior GATT approval was a significant departure from GATT rules. The Uruguay Round agreement on dispute settlement and the revisions to Section 301 in the U.S. implementing legislation have effectively closed the gap between the requirements of the GATT and U.S. trade law. More recently, the Iran-Libya Sanctions Act along with the Helms-Curton legislation on sanctions against Cuba are being challenged in the WTO, but they are more foreign policy/national security legislation than trade legislation.

[2] This is not always the case. As a result of the GATT panel decision on U.S. gasoline taxes, the United States is already faced with a question of how to deal with an adverse ruling that requires a change in non-trade legislation. It is not at all clear that the Congress is willing to amend U.S. law to bring it into conformity with the GATT panel decision.

[3] The Congress has, however, refused to implement an agreement on shipping subsidization.

[4] This was the sequence of events that produced the Trade Act of 1974, the Trade Agreements Act of 1979 and the Uruguay Round Agreements Act.

[5] While not "radical" in nature, the transfer of authority to administer antidumping and countervailing duty law from Treasury to Commerce at the end of 1980 did have a major impact on the outcomes of cases. So too did the introduction of time limits on investigations.

[6] Over the longer term, a string of significant WTO panel decisions that are adverse to the United States could regenerate a willingness to act unilaterally. The critics that contend that the U.S. has effectively surrendered sovereignty over trade policy by agreeing to the WTO dispute settlement rules have more to their argument than is generally credited. While the United States maintains the ability to act without regard to the GATT rules, a serious concern about the "GATT-legality" of a proposed measure within the bureaucracy will likely be enough to kill the initiative.

[7] A recent affirmative ITC determination on *Polyvinyl Alcohol from China, Japan and Taiwan*, ITC Pub. 2960 (May 1996) falls into this category.

[8] *The Washington Post*, "A Rotten Tomato Deal," Friday, October, 27, 1996, p. A-24.

[9] I suspect that the reasons for this trace back to the *relative* indifference of Japanese shareholders and financial markets to profit maximization. Japanese corporate law provides for effective control of the company when a stockholder or group of stockholders acquire 33 percent of voting shares. In many cases, Keiretsu affiliates or financial institutions that have a business relationship with a manufacturer control over 33 percent of the voting stock of the manufacturer. In addition, financial markets in Japan are still heavily regulated.

CHAPTER 14

Trade Policy and the Media—Part I

Joe H. Stroud

I chose nearly four decades ago to be a journalist, rather than to continue with graduate school and become a history teacher, because I wanted to be a generalist. Have I ever been a generalist! I do care about trade and the making of trade policy, but I must say it's hard work to do an intellectually respectable job of keeping up with it, translating it into understandable terms and yet not clouding important issues of public policy.

To understand what we do, and to understand what we have to do, let me share one bit of perspective. One of my favorite correspondents—a federal judge who is a frustrated newspaper editor—once sent me a tearsheet of an editorial on a Supreme Court decision with a message scrawled across the top. The message said, "You have greatly oversimplified this issue." I couldn't resist writing back to him the following letter: "Dear Judge Cohn: It is the business of journalists to oversimplify what lawyers and judges overcomplicate." To some extent that describes our role as it relates to even important issues of public policy. We are inherently oversimplifiers, who are trying to describe complex matters in ways that are readily understandable. When I meet for dinner once a month or so with Bob Stern and his colleagues to hear discussions of trade issues, that's what I'm struggling to do. I need to keep trying to understand the seemingly arcane issues of trade policy in the hope that I can translate them for myself, my staff and the public.

My concern about interpreting trade issues arises in part from my graduate studies. I've also had enough economics to carry with me an abiding conviction that the more or less rational allocation of resources, goods and services is essential to the efficient functioning of human society. That has led me to the belief that a relatively open trading system is important to our society and to international relations. That's been reinforced through a good bit of travel, and particularly from seeing what closed trading systems did to societies such as Argentina and South Africa, and through exposure to the Detroit business community, which necessarily operates in world markets but sometimes still carries with it the attitudes of people who operated under the protection of a cartel during many of their formative years. Detroit has sometimes been a tough place to write about trade policy, because of the abiding conviction of many in our principal industry that trade was in fact the source of much of the present danger to "our way of life." It's easier now, after the NAFTA and GATT fights, to talk about the advantages of maintaining a relatively open trading system, but it still isn't easy.

As we struggle to translate trade issues into terms that connect with the every day lives of our readers, it seems to me there are at least three issues that pose difficulties for us and probably help to explain some of our deficiencies:

1. *How do we evaluate supposed expert opinion in an area such as trade policy, and how do we make sure it is reflected in our reporting and opinion writing and in more or less unexpurgated form on op-ed pages?* Media people themselves have a major responsibility to find ways to reach out to academicians for information and insight. But if you care about the connection between academic research and analysis and policy, you had better spend some time thinking about how you do some informal teaching and advocacy with people in the media. We in our business get assaulted daily by self-interested promoters of one policy perspective or another, much of it slickly disguised as disinterested. There are a number of think tanks that crank out propaganda at an incredible rate. While we need to know how to discount the undeserving and self-serving, it's important that you do enough missionary work that you don't leave us totally disconnected from theory and analysis within the university. I've long been grateful to Bob Stern for thinking I might be able to absorb something from an esoteric discussion of the behavior of exchange rates. You may be casting your pearls before swine, but it is a necessary and important process.

2. *In a time when the means of communication are becoming more and more fragmented, how do we provide any serious continuity of coverage of trade issues when many editors are panicked into becoming more like their more fragmented competitors?* In preparing these remarks, I was asked to reflect a little on the interaction of print media with other means of communication. That is in many respects the central problem of our times in the media business. We're dealing with a public that has heard, or thinks it has heard, everything before. The cacophony of voices produces a herd instinct and a susceptibility to propaganda that I find quite daunting for anyone who is at all concerned about public policy.

I find myself often at a loss as to how to avoid lowest-common-denominator thinking as a result of this pressure. I don't want to throw up my hands at providing some serious treatment of trade issues, but you do need to understand how the competitive climate tends to dumb down the discussion. Unfortunately, as the competition intensifies, the market fragments even more and the scramble for audience share intensifies, you may well find that what passes for general-audience news coverage will afford less coverage of trade issues and that more and more coverage is relegated to specialty publications. I think that could be a real problem in the future.

If I were spending my time thinking primarily about how to see that the public has enough information and hears enough debate to make good decisions about trade issues, I would worry about the evolution of the media in this country. And while you have to get what you can into specialty publications or the op-ed pages of East Coast newspapers, I would worry a great deal about being swept away by the propaganda of interest groups or the passions of the moment. The rise of the Buchanan candidacy during the Republican primaries suggests to me that there's a vacuum on trade issues and that there are demagogues ready to fill it. The responsible way the Republican Party rejected the claims of protectionism, at the same, offers some basis for hope that the public may be more sophisticated than we think on this issue. The obligation of academics to lead the discussion, though, seems to me to be quite strong.

3. *I would urge you to give some thought to how you can do some periodic missionary work among the press on trade issues.* The need is more intense of course when we're dealing immediately with a question such as NAFTA or GATT, but I would urge you to think of ways in which you can help to educate the media at other times. That includes being willing to write op-ed pieces on trade issues or other economic matters. The University of Michigan has had several people who've been particularly alert to the possibilities of that kind of personal attempt to provide a connection between academic theory and public debates at the street level. Marina Whitman and Paul McCracken certainly are good examples of academicians who have been conscious of the need to write for a general audience on occasion.

I wonder if you might not also try to put together on occasion some short courses for interested media—an afternoon and evening perhaps. I must say my own view of the issue of most-favored-nation status for China was changed in part by dinner-table conversations and papers at Bob Stern's occasional dinners. Much of the press will be tough to reach and hard to interest, but I think it's worth continuing the effort.

You don't have to pursue an ideological agenda to do the educational job. Tom Bray at the *Detroit News* and I don't agree on much, but we mostly tend to come out at the same place on trade policy. We start from different premises, but wind up concluding pretty much the same thing—that Michigan is a manufacturing state, must be an exporting state and that relatively liberal trade works best as a way of allocating resources and benefiting consumers.

I hope this bit of perspective is helpful. The point at which debate about issues such as trade often breaks down is in the popular press. In the absence of informed debate and factual data, the arguments of interest groups and the fears of people will take over. When that happens, it may not matter how many Saturday afternoons you spend talking to the choir about trade policy. As hard as it is, you have to keep trying to share broadly the clash of ideas and theory and the economic arguments that help to shape trade policy.

Trade Policy and the Media—Part II

Jutta Hennig

I. Introduction

This paper seeks to contrast the view of how trade policy is formulated and implemented as reflected in major daily and weekly publications with the insights I have gained on the same subject by reporting for the newsletter *Inside U.S. Trade* (IUST). Any comments I make are my own, not those of the publication.

IUST is a publication sold to policy makers in the U.S. and foreign governments, as well as U.S. and foreign constituents that seek to influence their decisions. It is also a source of interest for academics, who sometimes use its information for their studies or analyses.

I am presenting these remarks from the perspective of a journalist who has covered trade policy in Washington, D.C., for twelve years, including the negotiation and congressional approval of the Uruguay Round agreements and the North American Free Trade Agreement.

I will limit my remarks to the trade policy coverage of such papers as *The Washington Post*, *The New York Times*, *The Financial Times*, and *The Wall Street Journal*. Journalists for these papers face a big hurdle in their presentation of trade and economic stories that no reporter for a more specialized publication ever faces: they must present the information in a way that is relevant to the every day lives of their readers, who in turn are bombarded with information from competing sources.

As my fellow panelist, Joe Stroud of the Detroit Free Press, pointed out, this competitive climate tends to "dumb down" the presentation of issues, and may ultimately lead to less and less coverage of trade issues in the general press. In contrast, readers of *Inside U.S. Trade* already have an intense interest in the trade policy area, which means articles do not have to pass such a high hurdle.

This paper will not touch on the obvious differences in the coverage of trade policy that arise from this high threshold for deciding which article has a sufficient general appeal to run. Similarly, I take it as a given that daily newspapers cannot go into the details of an issue as much as *Inside U.S. Trade* does. Both these factors increasingly have led reporters for general newspapers to buy specialty publications as a way of following trade developments until they reach the "general audience" threshold necessary to publish a story.

Instead, my remarks will focus on three more substantive points: first, they will cover how daily papers tend to see trade policy decisions in a rigid framework defined by the opposite poles of "free trade" and "protectionism," and how that is not borne out in "real life." A related second point will highlight how the daily papers often do not capture the process of making policy very clearly, particularly the complicated interplay between constituent groups and government officials. Thirdly, I will point out how reporters fail to understand crucial details of an issue, which leads them to miss the story or not present the "whole picture." Government officials can effectively use this failure to portray vital details as "mere technical issues" that are not relevant to the overall story.

II. Free Trade vs. Protectionism Framework

In daily publications, trade stories are often presented as an epic battle between free trade and protectionism, with the assumption that free trade is good and intellectually superior to protectionism. That framework may be designed to counteract the view in one segment of the public that trade is the reason for many economic and social ills in the United States.

In reporting for IUST, I have found that this view of trade policy as a simple dichotomy tends to sacrifice the complexity of the issues, and makes the false assumption that trade decisions are reached in isolation instead of being weighed against many other factors that may or may not be related to a given issue. In reality, governments consider many factors inside and outside the trade arena when making trade policy decisions. From my perspective, trade policy making is less an epic battle between two opposing philosophies than it is a mixed picture of tradeoffs.

Sometimes, reporters' preoccupation with this framework gets in the way of reporting the facts of a story, as reporters hold forth on whether a given U.S. decision represents a departure from the free trade obligations of the World Trade Organization (WTO). The WTO financial services negotiations are a case in point. Much of the coverage at the end of the negotiations in 1995 seemed to focus on the European Union's allegations that the U.S. was undermining the multilateral trading system by taking a Most Favored Nation (MFN) exemption on the deal because it did not provide sufficient access in markets critical to the United States. That, the press reported, was creating a two-tier discriminatory system of world trade, a fact disputed by U.S. officials. What was lost in the charges and countercharges over whether the U.S. commitment to multilateral trade was waning was the reporting legwork that would have revealed that the EU, its public statements notwithstanding, and Japan accepted such a two-tier system as long as it protected them. Officials from both governments received written assurances from the U.S. Treasury

Department that any future measure the United States might take to limit access of foreign financial services providers would not affect firms from Japan and the EU. As Harry Freeman pointed out in his contribution to this conference in Chapter 10 above, few general papers covered the story. You can read it in the July 28, 1995 edition of *Inside U.S. Trade*.

The free trade vs. protectionism framework does not take into account the other factors that are brought to bear on trade policy decisions in the interagency process. These sometimes relate to a larger economic issue, such as the fear of destabilizing the currency of a given country, or to foreign policy or national security interests. In general, the latter two factors often take priority over trade issues. There are many examples that illustrate how outside factors influence trade decisions ranging from the national security arguments that Defense Secretary Cap Weinberger used to ward off serious U.S. trade actions against Japan in the Reagan Administration to the refusal of the Clinton Administration to take on Japan in a fight over access to the insurance market. Clinton Administration officials let that fight drag on for fear of making the bilateral trade deficit an issue in the 1996 Presidential elections.

In the Reagan Administration, U.S. semiconductor firms stepped up their fight for access to the Japanese market and against the sale of low priced chips in the U.S. market. To hear former Commerce Undersecretary Paul Freedenberg tell it, Weinberger was able to block U.S. trade sanctions against Japan by arguing the country's strategic importance. Freedenberg says that the Department of Defense (DOD) only signed off on the controversial U.S.-Japan semiconductor agreement in 1986 because two of its major suppliers made it clear that failure to get the deal would ultimately eliminate them as U.S. suppliers to the DOD.

The fact that national security factors can play a major role in trade decisions is as true after the demise of the Soviet Union as it was at the height of the Cold War—notwithstanding the claims by senior officials in the Clinton Administration that economic decisions are now being made on their own merits.

The next time this assertion will be put to the test is in the decisions regarding China's accession to the WTO. I am convinced that the economic concessions China is required to make will more likely be defined by the National Security Council than by the Clinton Administration's trade team.

In the insurance fight, the presidential election prevented an escalation of threats despite the fact that Japan missed several U.S. deadlines to resolve the dispute. The Office of the U.S. Trade Representative (USTR) never directly threatened Japan with retaliation because USTR did not want to risk a conflict with Japan at a time when senior officials claimed that the Administration had pursued a successful policy with Japan in its first term. Retaliation threats against Japan would have contradicted the claims that the Clinton Administration had already opened the Japanese market to U.S. goods and services exports.

A similarly mixed picture arises when looking at constituents for whom the labels of "free trader" or "protectionist" also do not seem to fit. Companies and constituent groups may well advocate positions in line with free trade principles on one issue and seek import protection on another. Or they may take a trade-restricting stance under the guise of free trade—as the U.S. textile and apparel industry did in the NAFTA. The National Pasta Association is a case in point—at the same time the group was wrapping itself in the mantle of free trade in order to oppose curbs on durum wheat imports from Canada in 1994, it was using trade remedy law to block imports of cheaper pasta from Italy and other countries. Durum is the main ingredient in pasta. Similarly, at the same time the U.S. aerospace industry wants to curb foreign subsidies, particularly those paid by four European governments to the Airbus consortium, it fights tenaciously not to focus international scrutiny on the indirect subsidies it receives from Defense Department contracts.

This mixed picture of the constituents makes sense if one recognizes that free trade advocates in business have couched their own parochial quest for profit in terms consistent with the free trade philosophy. In that sense they have become "special interest" free traders—a clear illustration that the term "special interests" has a broader application than its current usage of largely describing organized labor.

One of the reasons groups couch their own parochial interests in terms of defending free trade is that it plays well in the mainstream media. If an industry gets tagged as "protectionist," it risks losing both public sympathy and government support. Therefore, no industry ever favors blocking imports simply because it robs them of profits and costs jobs—they simply want a "level playing field" with foreign competitors that they deem to play by "unfair" rules.

III. General Interest Publications Fail to Accurately Capture the Role of Constituents

General interest publications often do not accurately capture the ways in which constituent groups influence decisions of the U.S. government. Some dailies, particularly those with a European base, seem to hold the view that every U.S. government trade decision that does not reflect textbook free-trade principles is a direct payoff to a protectionist constituent group. I think reality is more complicated than that for the reasons laid out above, even if one cannot deny that powerful companies or business groups are often effective in convincing the government to do their bidding.

One such incident that has been heavily covered by the general interest press is the fight waged by Chiquita Brands International against the European Union's banana import restrictions. These curbs limit Latin American banana sales to the EU to ensure a market for bananas from former colonies of member states. The limits on Latin American bananas are administered in a way that makes it hard for Chiquita to export from Latin America under conditions that it would find most profitable. Chiquita's owner, Charles Lindner, who has been identified as a major donor to both the Republican and Democratic parties by the public interest group Common Cause, pushed U.S. officials at the highest levels to fight against the EU import quotas. The banana fight became a top priority of the Clinton Administration backed by key members of Congress from both parties even though the United States grows very few bananas and is not an exporter.

General interest papers were probably attracted to the story because it constituted a particularly outrageous example of constituent pressure. The U.S. produces few bananas, and does not export any. And still, then Senate Majority Leader Robert Dole (R-KS) and then U.S. Trade Representative Mickey Kantor pushed the issue to the top of the U.S.-EU agenda.

From my view, the way constituents influence the process is generally not as blatant and more complicated than the Chiquita case. Frequently, it is much less direct and involves more hurdles, particularly if executive branch officials initially rebuff a demand by a given group or company. That leads business groups to have members of Congress raise the issue with the Administration in a hearing or in letters demanding that the executive branch explain its position and change it. If that route of political pressure does not achieve the desired result, an effective constituent group may skillfully wield the threat of a trade remedy case or another legal challenge, as the Coalition for Fair Lumber Imports did in a dispute over Canadian exports to the United States. The group withdrew a constitutional challenge against the NAFTA dispute settlement process in exchange for a promise to negotiate a trade deal with Canada that put a quota on Canadian exports. In some situations, the government may decide that the political fallout from a trade remedy case would be more damaging than negotiating a bilateral solution with a given country.

The most effective constituent groups are those whose goals are most closely tied to either the political or economic goals of the sitting Administration. In the Clinton Administration, these industries include telecommunications, computers, semiconductors, intellectual property holders and financial services providers. They are generally highly competitive abroad and/or are located in key electoral states, like California. In addition, a group may be effective because it has strong congressional connections that are too powerful for the Administration to ignore and is well positioned to use the trade remedy laws. This description could be applied to the steel, lumber and agriculture industries. Other industries may be able to successfully press an issue even if an Administration would love to ignore them, but can't quite afford to do so for political reasons. This includes the U.S. textile industry, which lost out in the Uruguay Round, but was paid off in the NAFTA negotiations. The NAFTA textile and apparel provisions include restrictions to ensure that only regional producers can benefit from the new free trade area.

In addition, it is important to be able to present a well documented and researched case to the government, especially in this time of tight budgets. The more U.S. government resources are stretched, the more vital it is for an industry group to do its own research because government officials simply do not have the time and resources to devote to it.

But these observations on who is an effective constituent can be turned on their head when politically adept constituents with clout run up to unsurpassable hurdles, and small companies may get their day with policymakers. A powerful firm like the Eastman Kodak Co., which charges that the Japanese market is closed to imports of colored film and photographic paper, is a case in point. Kodak convinced the U.S. government to get the issue on the agenda, but no connection to U.S. government officials and no amount of money spent in publicizing and researching the case convinced Japan to negotiate a bilateral solution. Kodak had to settle for a U.S. complaint in the WTO, which was not its desired outcome. The case has proved to be significantly more costly and complicated than bilateral negotiations. Kodak may have also been the victim of bad timing—the dispute came to a head at a time when the Administration had decided to make up with Japan.

In some cases, smaller companies and associations can be catapulted into being players in the trade policy arena. Take the congressional approval of the NAFTA, and to a lesser extent the approval of the Uruguay Round. Any industry group located in a congressional district with an undecided member could exert influence, and obtain at least the promise of government action to fix its respective trade problem. This is how the Iowa-based Maytag Corporation obtained language in the implementing bill designed to ensure that it could use the NAFTA safeguard provisions in the event of Mexican import surges.

IV. Failure to Understand the Details Leads Reporters to Miss the Story

In my third point, I want to emphasize how the failure to understand the details of an issue can lead reporters to miss the story. This observation does not relate to the failure of articles in daily papers to include many details. Rather, it relates to failure of understanding an issue as much as possible and then pulling that knowledge together into a big picture story appropriate for their readership.

Daily reporters, particularly those working for wire services, frequently pronounce their disdain for the details of a trade issue by insisting that they are arcane and unimportant. They seem convinced that dealing with these details will detract from the big picture. What they fail to understand is that the opposite is true—understanding the details is vital to writing an accurate big picture story.

The most recent example is the coverage of the first ministerial of the World Trade Organization in December 1996. In Singapore, Acting U.S. Trade Representative Charlene Barshefsky announced that the Clinton Administration had achieved its primary goal and struck an agreement to cut tariffs for information technology products by the year 2000. Barshefsky announced that the United States and its trading partners had reached an

Information Technology Agreement (ITA)—provided they could work out in 1997 the "technical" details of the timing of tariff cuts and the participation of a sufficient number of countries. She made that announcement after she and her EU counterpart, Commissioner Leon Brittan, failed to agree on when the EU would eliminate its tariffs on semiconductors, and that the U.S. would eliminate tariffs on its import sensitive items.

Most newspapers and major wire services published articles from Singapore proclaiming the conclusion of the ITA, even though countries issued a proclamation that committed them only to making "good faith efforts" to negotiate the agreement in 1997. This was because they accepted Barshefsky's explanation that the timing of tariff cuts is a very technical issue without realizing that these decisions are usually made by senior policymakers because of the sensitivities involved. In the NAFTA, negotiators could fairly easily agree on the elimination of tariffs in principle, but often senior officials had to make the political decisions of how quickly tariffs should be cut on specific products. To claim that an ITA had been reached and only the "technical" question of timing remained was a deliberately misleading posture adopted by Barshefsky and others to make the Singapore ministerial look like a big success. They perceived that as necessary to convey the impression that the WTO is a dynamic organization.

Top officials understand that this lack of detailed knowledge on trade issues is the real Achilles heel of most daily and wire reporters. A reporter who lacks this knowledge and is nonetheless determined to appear knowledgeable to his editors and readers is easy prey for politicians like Barshefsky and Kantor. This is exacerbated if reporters only rely on their access to top politicians and fail to cultivate other sources who can provide a reality check on what top Administration officials are feeding them. In contrast, it is not easy to "spin" a reporter who is intimately familiar with the details of an issue, and has a wide range of sources throughout the government, industry and foreign governments to use for a story. Therefore, journalists in the general press have to put more energy into pursuing a story and understanding its details. Access to senior officials is not a substitute for hard work—by relying on these sources to the exclusion of others, journalists become only their messengers instead of telling the story like it is.

NOTE

I would like to thank Edward Alden of the *Vancouver* (British Columbia) *Sun*, who formerly was my colleague at *Inside U.S. Trade*, for his very helpful insights in preparing this paper.

CHAPTER 15

Constituent Representation: Exploring the Context of the Key Policy Questions, Some Preliminary Observations

John H. Jackson

I. Introduction

This conference is in many ways an intriguing juxtaposition of the analytical techniques of economists and political scientists, and some particularly interesting observations of practitioners who have been confronted with specific circumstances of their tasks. I would like to try to present a tentative view of a somewhat broader perspective for this material, and suggest some aspects of a framework.

I will first introduce some of the dimensions and different roadways of the landscape of our subject concerning constituent representation (CR), followed, second, by a statement of the "big question" for this conference, namely the question of how many and varied CR activities fit into some of the models suggested as aids to understanding. Third and final, I would like to offer a suggestion (obviously not the only one possible) about where some of this analysis may lead us, and in doing that I will bring to bear my particular expertise as a legal scholar and suggest that a critical part of our subject is the role of institutions or "constitutions" and how they contribute to, or inhibit pursuit of some of the goals of constituent representation that many of us would feel are appropriate.

II. The Landscape

The question of constituent representation, or what is sometimes called "lobbying," and which I prefer to call "policy advocacy," is not only a many faceted subject, but one which can lead in a number of different directions.

It seems logical that we first try to consider some criteria for evaluating the role of constituent representation and its varied forms. I believe that an undercurrent of the diverse interventions in this conference is that at least some kinds of constituent representation can enhance welfare and good government. Governmental resources to do all of the research necessary to fully comprehend the potential impact of policy determination are usually too limited to provide an adequate understanding of many policy issues. Constituent representatives or policy advocacy can provide an enormously useful and sometimes vital amount of information and arguments, which the policy makers should consider.

An analogy can be made to litigation before courts. In many forms of litigation, particularly in the United States and a number of other countries, advocates are encouraged to present a variety of views, often but not always opposing views, so that the courts will better understand how to make the best possible decision. To some extent the same model could be considered for legislative or executive branch activities that involve policy decisions. However, it is also understood in another undercurrent of this conference, that certain types of constituent representation, policy advocacy, or "lobbying," may influence policy makers to make decisions that are against the best interests of the nation, or a nation's welfare. This is the problem of "special interest" advocacy, which can distort the decision making processes. Thus, for example, certain kinds of campaign contributions can influence "wrong decisions."

Another step we can then take for a framework for analysis is to inventory and explore the number of different types of constituent representation and the "landscape" on which they act.

First, we can note that there are a number of different types of decision makers who are the target of constituent representation. A very quick inventory could include the following:

- The Congress (Parliament), both at the federal level and sub-federal (state) level.
- The Executive Branch and its various sub-divisions, many of which must formulate policies, either in the broader sense, or in the interstitial sense to carry out policies mandated by higher level authorities or the Congress.
- The Judiciary and Courts at many different levels: these also are governmental institutions, and litigation performs a form of constituent representation.
- Administrative agencies, not only those which are subordinate to the President or Chief Executive, but also those which have a quasi-independent role under mandates of the Congress.
- The public and public opinion as a necessary component (particularly in a democracy) of policy making.
- Institutions which assist in forming public opinion, such as the public media (press, radio, television).
- Various specialized groups of researchers and teachers, such as professors in universities.

In addition, we can note a number of different kinds of *techniques* which constituent representation follows. An inventory would include at least the following:

- "Lobbying" in the traditional sense of influencing Congress persons through direct percussion; oral, written, hearings, etc.
- Contributions to elected officials' campaign funds.
- Legal (court and administrative hearings) representation and litigation in specific cases.
- Studies and advocacy by a wide variety of non-government organizations.
- Academic studies and representations.
- Press studies and reports.
- Public relations campaigns.

It can be noted that many of these various techniques are becoming "internationalized," in the sense that the constituent representatives now find that they must pursue their advocacy on a broader landscape than that contained within national borders. This might mean advocacy at international organizations or advocacy encouraging action by a national government entity, which action has international implications beyond its own borders.

The trend in the world today clearly is towards a greater integration and interdependence of activities, especially economic activities. Thus an important question that is posed is how the world and the various governmental entities within it, can effectively and appropriately govern international economic behavior which crosses borders. This involves a number of different players from different levels of government, and it also involves the vital question of distribution of power: at what level should power to make certain kinds of policy determinations be placed.

It should also be noted that governmental institutions themselves become "constituent representatives," in that they represent the particular groups of constituents to which a particular governmental entity would respond, in fora that are not controlled by those particular government entities. Thus a nation state may pursue its representation and policy advocacy at an international organization or an international tribunal (such as the World Court, or a dispute settlement body in the new WTO). Likewise, representatives of the Congress may bring litigation in the courts of the United States, or pursue Executive Branch decisions of certain types by advocacy with executive officials.

There is a footnote to all of this; the attempt by the national government, particularly in the United States, to regulate and control the processes of constituent representation and policy advocacy can be noted. Thus, campaign contribution regulation, as well as the Foreign Agents Registration Act, are examples. One of the questions that will begin to loom much larger than at present, will be what types of such regulation will be necessary at the *international* level, rather than just the nation state level.

III. The Models and Case Histories

The second major question that I will address is how the various specific activities and anecdotal cases that we have struggled with during the conference fit some of the ingenious and intriguing models that have been put forward for our consideration as ways to better understand what is going on. In my view, what these models should try to test is whether a certain form of constituent representation, targeted at one or more of the entities suggested in my brief inventory above, would on balance generally contribute to the welfare of the world or a nation, or not. In some cases, this is a question of "efficiency," but it also may be a question of "justice and equity," such as distribution of economic resources. Then we need to appraise how the specific "case histories" fit the models, if they do.

In that context I could mention three rather specific constituent representation activities which could merit further study in depth, to try to answer some of the questions posed above.

Case Number 1: The special interest and business group constituent representation and policy advocacy relating to the international and national antidumping and countervailing duty rules is very interesting. It can be noted that the antidumping law in particular has been a cause for great controversy. Almost all academic economists, many practitioners (as well as a number of the legal academics), and relatively powerful newspapers have criticized the current antidumping laws. For example, *The Wall Street Journal*, *The New York Times*, *The Financial Times* of London, and the *Journal of Commerce* (New York), have all taken editorial positions sharply critical of anti-dumping laws.

On the other hand, other advocates have pursued efforts in the court, with administrative officials, and with attempts to influence legislative activity, to support and promote anti-dumping laws. Some groups have sought to obtain changes in the statutes of the United States, which would make it more likely that the outcome they are pursuing (allegedly with the objective of limiting competition from foreign products so as to enhance the profitability of the interest being represented), would be more likely to be achieved by administrative and judicial action carrying out the statutes.

In addition, there has been considerable constituent representation and policy advocacy at the international level, trying to influence the outcome of treaty negotiations, knowing that treaty language will in turn find its way into national statutes which then of course may bind the domestic legal institutions, including courts.

A particular example of ingenious policy advocacy of this type has been the activities of the U.S. steel industry over the past two or three decades, actively pursuing treaty negotiation results in the Tokyo Round and obtaining language in the treaty text regarding antidumping that was particularly interesting and useful to the steel industry, which then later filed domestic cases in the United States based on the U.S. statutory implementation of those agreements.

Case Number 2: The activity of policy advocates in the Uruguay Round, to achieve an extraordinarily important treaty text regarding the protection of intellectual property is also very interesting. Without going into detail, I might just observe that in many cases the policy advocacy was very effective and arguably beneficial, urging national governments (sometimes through the use of multinational private groups with similar interests) to develop a discipline for intellectual property that in some cases existed more or less in prior treaties, but had never been adequately enforced. One thing that was missing in all of this policy advocacy, however, was any rethinking or reconsideration of some of the basic goals of intellectual property protection. For example, it was not questioned that there might be some situations where intellectual property protection should be more narrowly constrained so as to enhance developments of new ideas and techniques in the world and thus enhancing world welfare.

Case Number 3: The environmentalist, and particularly non-government organizations with environmental objectives, have been extraordinarily active and often very effective. In pursuing their goals of better environmental protection in the world, these groups have worked toward treaty language developments, as well as litigation, national legislation and pressures on executive administrative actions. Once again, a very interesting case study could be undertaken to explore the degree to which this policy advocacy was welfare enhancing or inhibiting.

IV. Institutions

My third and last topic is the question of where the analysis might lead us. My suggestion is that at least one of the directions in which the analysis might lead us is to give more attention to the broad question of "institutions." Particularly in the economic literature of the last decade, including that authored by some Nobel Prize winners, there has been increasing attention to the role of institutions (mostly governmental institutions, both international and national) in carrying out and channeling policy decisionmaking which is responsive to at least some constituent representation and policy advocacy, which we have been exploring.

The "constitutions" of organizations such as the World Trade Organization (WTO) have an extraordinarily profound and vital influence on the shape of policy implementation, as well as policy development. It is in the context of these institutions generally that the more constituent representation will occur. Thus, considerable attention should be directed toward these institutions and "constitutions" to ascertain whether they have the procedures and specific rules which can help shape and channel the processes of policy advocacy so as to maximize the possibility that such advocacy will in fact result in decision making which enhances world welfare, instead of diminishing it. For example one of the vital questions in this regard is the degree to which the public, or at least non-government organizations (NGOs) will have better access to the policy decision making processes of organizations such as the WTO.

V. Conclusion

I conclude by simply noting that the elements which I have outlined above pose an enormous agenda for future work, research, analytical attention, and in some cases experimentation with a variety of different kinds of practices. The organizers of this conference are to be congratulated for having brought together this relatively unique set of papers and presentations, that can give us at least some information and ideas to further approach these perplexing issues.

CHAPTER 16

U.S. Trade and Trade Policy: Challenges for the New Administration

Marina v.N. Whitman

I. Introduction

However spotty its overall record may appear to trade-policy purists, the first Clinton administration presided over the completion and ratification of two major trade-liberalizing agreements: the Uruguay Round of multilateral negotiations which established the World Trade Organization (WTO) and the North American Free Trade Agreement (NAFTA). The second Clinton Administration confronts a triple-threat of challenges in the trade-policy arena. It faces delivering on a number of trade-related commitments that were suppressed by the political exigencies of the election campaign. It needs to deal with issues related to the implementation of the Uruguay Round, the legitimatization of the WTO's new dispute-settlement procedures, and the appropriate range of "new business" for the organization to tackle in the future. Finally, the new administration must take account of the need to conduct domestic economic policy so as to minimize protectionist pressures, if it is to avoid backsliding and enhance the possibility of making further progress in liberalizing international economic transactions.

II. Regional Issues: Latin America and Asia

High on the list of unfulfilled commitments is the expansion of NAFTA. The bipartisan "hemispheric vision" articulated by President Bush and endorsed by a newly-elected President Clinton, included the expectation that Latin American countries whose economic policies made them appropriate candidates would be admitted to NAFTA membership on a case-by-case basis. But Chile, by general agreement an "A" candidate for admission, has been waiting for several years without any indication of progress on the American side. Meanwhile the Latin nations, impatient with American inaction, have been going ahead on their own. At last count, various combinations of nations in Central and South America and the Caribbean had formed five different and sometimes overlapping regional free trade areas or customs unions. In 1996, Canada went ahead and formed its own free trade area with Chile, which already was part of such an arrangement with Mexico, leaving the United States as the odd man out.

The impact of prolonged paralysis on the part of the United States as regards NAFTA expansion could reach well beyond trade issues to undermine this nation's leadership in the Western Hemisphere. But the administration's ability to act faces a formidable political barrier at home: the need to renew the so-called "fast track" authorization to negotiate trade agreements, under which the Congress commits itself to vote "up or down," without amendment, any trade agreement agreed to by the President and brought to it for ratification. The difficulties the President encountered in securing ratification of the Uruguay Round and the NAFTA, the fact that these agreements became the focal point of Pat Buchanan's brief but intense presidential campaign, and that the NAFTA has not so far delivered on some of the more extravagant promises made by its supporters all suggest that obtaining fast-track renewal from Congress would be an uphill battle at best.

There is a more fundamental issue at stake as well. It was one thing for the Congress to delegate authority to the President to negotiate agreements regarding border barriers such as tariffs and quotas. In the future, however, trade negotiations are likely to include such issues as competition policy, investment, intellectual property protection, and environmental and labor regulations—all matters of domestic policy regarding which the Congress is unlikely to be willing to delegate authority to the executive branch. The fact that a Democratic President would be requesting such authorization from a Republican Congress only increases the difficulty of the challenge.

A number of significant issues are also on the administration's platter as regards its trade relationships with Asia. The President apparently made some headway at APEC and the WTO Ministerial Meeting in Singapore in late 1996, obtaining agreement on a carefully-worded commitment by the membership to support a phased liberalization of high-technology trade. But at the heart of our trade relations with this fast-growing region are those relations with its two economic giants, Japan and China. And these relations have, over the course of several administrations, been marred by variability, *ad hoc*ery, and the absence of clearly-defined goals. We have tended to define the intensity of our concern in terms of the state of the other nation's trade balance, regarding an expansion of its bilateral or overall trade surplus as a sin and its reduction as a virtue, rather than focusing on the underlying issue: be it the closedness of certain Japanese markets to foreigners or the absence of intellectual property protection in China.

Even more fundamentally, our trade-related policies need to be integrated into a consistent view of our overall foreign policy goals vis-à-vis this critical region. The administration needs to decide how its differences with Japan on trade issues should be handled in light of its views regarding the role Japan should play in supporting our security concerns in Asia. It needs to decide also to what extent, if at all, our trade interactions with China, including our attitude toward Chinese membership in the WTO, should be linked to China's behavior with respect to such non-trade issues as human rights or nuclear proliferation. Trade policy is an increasingly important aspect of foreign policy in the post- Cold War era, but it is not the whole thing, and the various aspects should be linked in a consistent and mutually supportive way.

III. The WTO: Implementation, Credibility and Scope

Having presided successfully over the creation of the WTO, the administration now needs to make closure on several fronts. As regards issues of implementation, American leadership is critical in delivering concrete results from sectoral negotiations on high-technology trade, telecommunications and financial services, for example, and in insuring that commitments made under the agreements on liberalization of textiles and agriculture are in fact carried out.

The signals sent by American behavior will also do much to determine the credibility, and therefore the usefulness, of the WTO's new dispute-settlement mechanism. So far, those signals have been somewhat mixed. On the one hand, the United States has shown some confidence in the new system by bringing some 20 cases (of the roughly 60 currently pending) to the organization for adjudication. On the other hand, the aggressive unilateralism displayed in the extraterritorial reach of the Helms-Burton legislation, imposing what is effectively a secondary boycott on certain foreign companies doing business in Cuba, has led our trading partners to question the good faith of our commitment to the multilateral dispute-settlement process.

Finally, the administration must establish a coherent US view on the appropriate scope of issues to be encompassed by the WTO, and therefore subject to the possibility of trade sanctions for non-compliance. Should such issues as competition policy, labor standards and environmental standards fall within the purview of the WTO or not? The Bush administration took a stand against the inclusion of the latter two issues; the Clinton administration reversed that position, but insistence on their inclusion will almost certainly complicate the task of eliciting renewed fast-track authority form the Congress.

There is no question that the reduction of border barriers to trade and the global integration of economic activity have made differences among national policies in the areas cited above an increasingly important source of trade friction and of distortions in international patterns of economic activity. But to try to bring them all within the jurisdiction of the WTO risks overloading the fledgling organization and increasing the suspicion and hostility of many developing nations, who see such efforts as a form of disguised protection on the part of the industrialized countries. Nor are trade sanctions necessarily the best, or even a desirable, way to bring about some degree of policy harmonization in these areas. The provision of financial and/or technical assistance to developing countries and the establishment of voluntary monitoring and labeling schemes to discourage undesirable practices are two possible alternative approaches.

IV. Domestic Policies to Support Trade Liberalization

Perhaps the most fundamental challenge facing the Clinton Administration in the trade arena does not fall under the rubric of trade policy at all. That is the need to implement domestic policy measures that help to minimize pressures for protection and thus to preserve and expand momentum for trade liberalization. Such measures fall under three broad headings: macroeconomic policies that avoid misaligned exchange rates; policies to facilitate labor-market transitions and reduce earnings inequality; and policies to stimulate the sustainable growth rate of the American economy.

Ironically, in light of Milton Friedman's assertion a quarter of a century ago, that one of the major benefits of a flexible exchange rate is that it makes the case for free trade clear and simple, one of the major factors producing pressures for trade protection is misaligned exchange rates. Such misalignments can overpower the effects of tariff reduction but can also severely affect the competitiveness of domestic firms and industries involved in international trade. This points to the importance of avoiding a mix of monetary and fiscal policies that produces such a situation. The excessively expansionary fiscal stance of the Reagan Administration during the early 1980s, for example, exerted upward pressure on the interest rate which led in turn to a severely overvalued dollar and forced a president who believed strongly in free markets to grant more import relief than any of his predecessors in more than half a century.

The major requirement for avoiding an inappropriate monetary-fiscal mix in domestic macroeconomic policy is to free up fiscal policy so that it can once again be used as a tool for macroeconomic stabilization. Indeed, over the long run, only a change in the savings-investment balance in the United States can alter the size of U.S. trade deficit in goods and services with the rest of the world. And, since no one knows how to raise the low savings habits of American citizens, a reduction in the government's budget deficit is essential. Beyond that, a revival of the moribund macroeconomic coordination process among the Group of Seven leading industrialized nations could be helpful, but only if the participants bear in mind that trade balances are primarily homegrown and should not become a source of trade friction or an excuse for restrictive trade measures.

Even when the exchange rate is in accord with economic fundamentals, the intertwined processes of trade and foreign investment are bound to create winners and losers by affecting the distribution of income in the domestic economy. Contrary to widespread belief, trade does not increase unemployment or hold back overall earnings growth. In fact, there is evidence that expanded trade, rather than destroying good jobs, creates them; exporting firms pay better and experience faster growth of both wages and employment than non-exporters. Nor does trade appear to be a major cause of the increase in earnings inequality. But trade certainly does affect jobs and wages in particular industries and communities, and empirical studies suggest that a major function of trade protection is to ameliorate, or perhaps delay, the costs of trade-related adjustments in labor markets.

These relationships suggest strongly that domestic policies that reduce friction and enhance employability security in labor markets, as well as policies directed toward reducing the growing inequality in earnings between skilled and unskilled workers, are key to holding protectionist pressures at bay. Most such measures fall into two broad categories. One is education and training to enhance the work-related skills people will need to insure their employability. The second is the ability to carry pension rights and health insurance along when changing employers or moving in and out of the workforce. In addition to these changes, modifications of the unemployment insurance system, to extend coverage to part-time and temporary workers and to integrate benefits with effective reemployment services, would better adapt the system to the realities of the American work environment of the 1990s.

Better education and work-related training are also key factors in reducing skill-related earnings inequality. But such programs are long-range propositions at best, and their effectiveness will vary widely among individuals. Some form of wage subsidy would have a more immediate impact on the earnings and employability of low-skill and therefore low-wage workers, suggesting that reforming the existing Earned Income Tax Credit (EITC) makes more sense than scrapping it as some members of Congress have pushed for. Finally, voluntary measures to promote international labor standards could help neutralize concern about the impact of global competition on the economic position of low-skill workers.

The most effective way of easing adjustment to structural change is economic growth, and high unemployment or a low growth rate have been found to be a major factor in trade protection. Policies directed toward accelerating the economy's aggregate growth rate by reversing the still-unexplained slowdown in productivity growth since 1973 represent the best hope for a sustained increase in the compensation of American workers and a corresponding reduction in protectionist pressures. There are no sure-fire prescriptions for bringing this about, but changes in the tax structure and in patterns of government spending to encourage savings and investment, a reduction in the federal budget deficit, preservation of an open trade environment, regulatory reform, and government support for basic research and development and for diffusion of new technologies are all promising candidates.

V. Conclusion

President Clinton initially came into office promising an intensified focus on the domestic economy and the elevation of commercial diplomacy—described as "restoring America's competitiveness"—to a higher priority in the conduct of foreign policy. He embarks on a second term confronted with the reality that trade policy, foreign policy and domestic economic policy are inextricably intertwined. From that reality, two challenges emerge: to embed trade policy in an integrated framework for U.S. foreign policy and to implement domestic economic policies consistent with maintaining support for continued progress on the liberalization of economic transactions that cross international boundaries.

CHAPTER 17

Trade and the 105th Congress: Overview

Bruce Wilson

I. Introduction

Trade will continue to be an active topic in the 105th Congress. However, with passage of the Omnibus Trade Act of 1988, NAFTA in 1993, and the Uruguay Round implementing legislation in 1994, the basic structure of U.S. law is well established for the foreseeable future. It is unlikely that there will be serious efforts in the 105th Congress to pass comprehensive trade legislation to alter fundamentally this basic structure. Rather, legislative initiatives in trade will be directed at specific issues and coalitions will form across party lines both in favor of, and in opposition to, such initiatives.

At the time of writing (January 1997), the Clinton Administration had not yet stated what its trade legislation goals will be for the 105th Congress. We can expect some of the trade legislative initiatives to be similar to those unsuccessfully pursued in the 104th Congress. Possibilities include: renewal of fast track; CBI parity; revision of Jackson-Vanik dealing with conditional MFN for China and others; and implementation of the OECD Shipbuilding Agreement. In addition, the 105th Congress will have to address expiring trade law provisions, most notably, renewal of GSP, which expires on May 31, 1997, and renewal of Trade Adjustment Assistance, which expires on September 30, 1998. Bipartisan initiatives that have Member interest include the Subsaharan Trade and Investment Act. Certain Democratic Members may push trade initiatives they introduced in the last several Congresses—Mr. Gephardt's China and Japan bills; Mr. Frank's Child Labor Deterrence Act; Ms. Kaptur's NAFTA Accountability Act; and Mr. Spratt's Textile and Apparel Competitiveness Act. These Democratic proposals would be largely controversial for both the Administration and most Republicans.

In the oversight area, the Ways and Means Committee, which is the Committee in the House of Representatives primarily responsible for international trade matters, will likely review the results of the Singapore Trade Ministerial, developments in APEC, developments in the Transatlantic Trade Dialogue, developments on a Free Trade Agreement for the Americas, implementation of NAFTA (the Administration must submit its 3-year assessment of NAFTA by July 1, 1997), and the enforcement of U.S. trade agreements.

Of all the trade legislation that might come before Congress next year at the request of the Administration, the most politically sensitive are likely to be any bills on fast track and China. These two topics are addressed in further detail below.

II. Trade Legislation in the 104th Congress

Trade was not a major item on the agenda of the 104th Congress. There were only two pieces of trade legislation that had to be passed because they were time sensitive—GSP and implementing legislation for the OECD Shipbuilding Agreement. While the Republican Congress did succeed in getting GSP renewed through May 31, 1997, as part of the minimum wage bill, it failed to enact the OECD Shipbuilding Agreement Act. That bill did pass the House with a series of agreement-inconsistent amendments but died in the Senate because of a division in the shipbuilding industry over the desirability of the legislation.

The 104th Congress also enacted legislation extending permanent MFN to Bulgaria, Romania, and Cambodia; a law to extend the U.S./Israeli Free Trade Agreement to the West Bank and Gaza Strip; and a miscellaneous and technical trade bill. The 104th also passed several secondary country sanctions bills ostensibly aimed at our enemies (Cuba, Iran, Libya) but which have instead created major trade frictions with our allies.

III. Politics of Trade in the 105th Congress

Individual trade initiatives aimed at additional trade liberalization, either through new trade agreements or otherwise, face uncertain prospects in the 105th Congress. In the House, about one-third of all House Members will be either Freshmen or Sophomores without well-established trade positions. As for the 286 returning Members who voted on NAFTA and GATT in the 103rd Congress, they tend to be less pro-trade as a group than was the full House in the 103rd. For example, the 105th will have more Members who voted against NAFTA than who voted for it (143-140). This is due in large part to a disproportionate shrinkage of the pro-trade segment of the Democratic caucus. In this regard, only 28 percent of returning Democrats who voted on NAFTA in 1993 voted yes (as opposed to 40 percent of the Democratic caucus when the vote was cast). Moreover, only 58 percent of returning Democrats who voted for GATT in 1993 voted yes (as opposed to 66 percent at the time of the vote). By contrast, the percentage of returning Republicans who voted for NAFTA and GATT has held pretty constant (75 percent for NAFTA, 68 percent for GATT). Clearly, the Administration's success in enacting pro-trade legislation in the 105th will depend in no small measure in how much support they can get from the first and second termers on both sides of the aisle.

In the Senate, there also appears to have been erosion in the ranks of the pro-trade forces. For example, in 1993 the Senate passed NAFTA by a vote of 61-38. Of the 85 Senators in the 105th Congress who voted on NAFTA in the 103rd Congress (either as Senators or as House Members), 47 voted in favor of NAFTA and 38 voted against it. This means that all of the slippage in the vote count on NAFTA occurred entirely on the pro-NAFTA side. This does not augur particularly well for potentially controversial trade legislation, such as renewal of fast track, which will undoubtedly require 60 votes in the Senate to overcome possible filibuster attempts. Moreover, in recent years the Senate has lost its pro-trade leaders on both sides of the aisle who have led the way on trade legislation over the last decade. This includes Senators Dole and Packwood on the Republican side, and Senators Bentsen and Bradley on the Democratic side. Their successors as leaders in the Senate in the pro-trade legislative battles in the years ahead have yet to emerge; moreover, it is difficult to even imagine who they might be at this point.

IV. Fast Track

Prospects for fast track in the 105th Congress are not promising. Even though House Republicans have recently indicated a willingness to be more flexible on labor and environment issues, it is unclear they are willing to go far enough to satisfy Democratic and Administration concerns. In addition, the Administration will have a difficult time making a compelling case on why it needs fast track at this time, since no ma]or trade agreements other than Chile are likely to be concluded in the next five years. Fast track renewal will be necessary at some point in the future, but it is questionable whether the Clinton Administration will be willing to expend precious political capital on a skeptical Congress or accept likely objectionable "riders" or conditions when it will not even be around to conclude the next major trade agreements, such as the Free Trade Agreement for the Americas around the year 2005.

Even if the Administration succeeds in moving a fast track bill through the House, they will face an even bigger challenge in the Senate. A number of Senators, particularly newer ones, appear less willing to relinquish their legislative prerogatives to a fast track mechanism than has been the case in the past. Moreover, as noted above, the Senate has lost the pro-trade leaders who have moved major trade bills through the Senate in the last decade (notably Dole, Packwood, Bentsen, Bradley). One possible successor on the Democratic side is Senator Moynihan, who worked hard on behalf of GATT while Chairman of the Finance Committee; however, he strongly opposed NAFTA and is skeptical of bilateral free trade agreements with developing countries. On the Republican side, Senator Grassley, who currently chairs the Senate Subcommittee on International Trade, is an ardent free trader. However, as representative of the largely agricultural state of Iowa, his focus has been primarily limited in the past to agricultural trade issues.

However, assuming the Administration decides to proceed on fast track, there is a belief among Republican trade staff in both the House and Senate that the only window of opportunity for accomplishing something on fast track is early in the next Congress. If it is not done early, it will recede on the agenda as Congress moves to other more pressing business.

V. China

China is arguably the biggest trade issue that will face the United States over the next decade. After years of stalemate on negotiating Chinese accession to the WTO, there have been recent indications by both the Administration and the Chinese that each is willing to approach this negotiation on a more flexible and pragmatic basis. Some within the Administration are likely to argue that we should subordinate China's WTO accession to U.S. geopolitical and national security interests. However, Ambassador Barshefskky continues to insist that Chinese WTO accession be on "commercially reasonable terms."

If the Administration and the Chinese agree on terms of Chinese accession to the WTO, the Administration will likely ask the Congress to remove China from Jackson-Vanik and grant China permanent MFN. This undoubtedly will be highly controversial, even more so if the Administration does not come back with a strong commercial deal with the Chinese.

Until Chinese WTO accession is clearly resolved one way or the other, Congress will continue to go through its annual debate on renewal of MFN for China under Jackson-Vanik. A number of Republicans, led by Congressman Bereuter and encouraged by major U.S. exporting companies who do business with China, may try to move legislation granting China permanent MFN regardless of what happens on China's WTO accession. This effort may not get very far, particularly since the Administration is not likely to support this legislation while it is still negotiating with China on WTO accession.

Contributors and Conference Participants

REPRESENTATION OF CONSTITUENT INTERESTS IN THE DESIGN AND IMPLEMENTATION OF U.S. TRADE POLICIES

UNIVERSITY OF MICHIGAN, ANN ARBOR NOVEMBER 8-9, 1996

Conference Organizers

Alan V. Deardorff
Department of Economics and
School of Public Policy
University of Michigan
Ann Arbor, MI

Robert M. Stern
Department of Economics and
School of Public Policy
University of Michigan
Ann Arbor, MI

Contributors and Conference Participants

Robert E. Baldwin
Department of Economics
University of Wisconsin
Madison, WI

Jagdish Bhagwati
Department of Economics
Columbia University
New York, NY

Douglas Brook
LTV Corporation
Washington, DC

Richard Cunningham
Steptoe and Johnson
Washington, DC

Kenneth W. Dam
University of Chicago Law School
Chicago, IL

Timothy Deal
U.S. Council on International
Business
Washington, DC

I. M. Destler
Center for International
and Security Studies
School of Public Affairs
University of Maryland
College Park, MD

Angela Paolini Ellard
Trade Subcommittee
Committee on Ways and Means
U.S. House of Representatives
Washington, DC

Dan Esty
School of Forestry and Environmental Studies
Yale University
New Haven, CT

Simon Evenett
School of Business Administration
University of Michigan
Ann Arbor, MI

Geza Feketekuty
Monterey Institute of International Studies
Center for Trade and Commercial Diplomacy
Monterey, CA

Harry Freeman
Chevy Chase, MD

John D. Greenwald
Wilmer, Cutler & Pickering
Washington, DC

Joseph A. Greenwald
Washington, DC

Gene Grossman
Woodrow Wilson School
Princeton University
Princeton, NJ

Richard L. Hall
Department of Political Science
and School of Public Policy
University of Michigan
Ann Arbor, MI

Jutta Hennig
Inside U.S. Trade
Arlington, VA

David Hummels
Graduate School of Business
University of Chicago
Chicago, IL

Douglas Irwin
Department of Economics
Dartmouth College
Hanover, NH

John E. Jackson
Department of Political Science
University of Michigan
Ann Arbor, MI

John H. Jackson
Georgetown University Law Center
Washington, DC

Thea Lee
AFL/CIO
Washington, DC

James A. Levinsohn
Department of Economics
University of Michigan
Ann Arbor, MI

Mustafa Mohatarem
General Motors Corporation
Detroit, MI

Robert D. Pahre
Department of Political Science and School of Public Policy
University of Michigan
Ann Arbor, MI

Richard C. Porter
Department of Economics
University of Michigan
Ann Arbor, MI

Edward Sarpolus
EPIC/MRA
Lansing, MI

Gary R. Saxonhouse
Department of Economics
University of Michigan
Ann Arbor, MI

Robert E. Scott
Economic Policy Institute
Washington, DC

Pamela J. Smith
Department of Economics
University of Delaware
Newark, DE

T. N. Srinivasan
Department of Economics
Yale University
New Haven, CT

Joe Stroud
Detroit Free Press
Detroit, MI

John Sweetland
Winsford Corporation
Los Angeles, CA

Raymond Waldmann/Jay Culbert
Boeing Company
Seattle, WA
Robin Walker-Lee
General Motors Corporation
Detroit, MI

Marina v.N. Whitman
School of Public Policy
University of Michigan
Ann Arbor, MI

Bruce Wilson
U.S. House Ways and Means Committee
Washington, DC

Bernard M. Wolf
Schulich School of Business
York University
North York, Ontario, Canada

STUDIES IN INTERNATIONAL TRADE POLICY

Studies in International Trade Policy includes works dealing with the theory, empirical analysis, political, economic, legal relations, and evaluations of international trade policies and institutions.

General Editor: Robert M. Stern

John H. Jackson and Edwin Vermulst, Editors. *Antidumping Law and Practice: A Comparative Study*

John Whalley, Editor. *Developing Countries and the Global Trading System.* Volumes 1 and 2

John Whalley, Coordinator. *The Uruguay Round and Beyond: The Final Report from the Ford Foundation Project on Developing Countries and the Global Trading System*

John S. Odell and Thomas D. Willett, Editors. *International Trade Policies: Gains from Exchange between Economics and Political Science*

Ulrich Kohli. *Technology, Duality, and Foreign Trade: The GNP Function Approach to Modeling Imports and Exports*

Stephen V. Marks and Keith E. Maskus, Editors. *The Economics and Politics of World Sugar Policies*

J. Michael Finger, Editor. *Antidumping: How It Works and Who Gets Hurt*

Horst Herberg and Ngo Van Long, Editors. *Trade, Welfare, and Economic Policies: Essays in Honor of Murray C. Kemp*

David Schwartzman. *The Japanese Television Cartel: A Study Based on* Matsushita v. Zenith

Alan V. Deardorff and Robert M. Stern, Editors. *Analytical Perspectives and Negotiating Issues in the Global Trading System*

Edwin Vermulst, Paul Waer, and Jacques Bourgeois, Editors. *Rules of Origin in International Trade: A Comparative Study*

Alan V. Deardorff and Robert M. Stern, Editors. *The Stolper-Samuelson Theorem: A Golden Jubilee*

Kent Albert Jones. *Export Restraint and the New Protectionism: The Political Economy of Discriminatory Trade Restrictions*

Alan V. Deardorff, James A. Levinsohn, and Robert M. Stern, Editors. *New Directions in Trade Theory*

Robert Baldwin, Tain-Jy Chen, and Douglas Nelson. *Political Economy of U.S.–Taiwan Trade*

Bernard M. Hoekman and Petros C. Mavroidis, Editors. *Law and Policy in Public Purchasing: The WTO Agreement on Government Procurement*

Danny M. Leipziger, Editor. *Lessons from East Asia*

Tamin Bayoumi. *Financial Integration and Real Activity*

Harry P. Bowen, Abraham Hollander, and Jean-Marie Viaene. *Applied International Trade Analysis*